COX + MEAD ed: A sociology of medical practice

D1364441

Contents

Foreword

Those of us who are old enough will recall the feeling of optimism which prevailed in the late 1940s. We believed that the great human potential unleashed during the war would be deployed to eliminate or reduce poverty, squalor, idleness, ignorance and disease—Beveridge's five giants—and create the conditions in which men could live happily and productively together.

As far as the reduction of diseases then prevalent was concerned, the optimism seemed justified. Despite shortages, and thanks to the full employment of their fathers, children born during the war years were demonstrably better nourished than earlier generations and consequently more able to resist infections. There seemed every reason to believe that given the continuation of full employment, the widespread dissemination of health information to mothers, and the purchasing power placed in their hands in the form of family allowances, the amount and severity of childhood illnesses would continue to diminish. Moreover, the discovery of anti-biotics in the 1930s followed by their mass production in the 1940s made it possible to envisage a time when the infectious diseases of childhood and early adult life would no longer take the major toll of human life or account for most morbidity. The successful production of a diphtheria vaccine suggested that it was merely a matter of time before that killing disease was eliminated altogether, and research workers were confident that other serious diseases such as tuberculosis, poliomyelitis, measles and whooping cough could be similarly prevented. Advances in clinical medicine and surgery were also being made which suggested that in the foreseeable future they would be able to repair much of the damage caused by accidents or organic malfunctioning.

Furthermore, we foresaw a time when no one would be deterred from obtaining preventive services or seeking medical advice or treatment through an inability to pay for them, and when services would be distributed throughout the country in such a way that all those who needed them had reasonable access to them. The National Health Service was seen as the vehicle by which these ends could be secured.

The optimists of the 1940s were right in many of their predictions. The toll of life in childhood and early adult life from infectious diseases has since been dramatically reduced. Physicians and surgeons, backed by research scientists in the laboratory, have been able to cure some hitherto incurable diseases, modify their course or prevent their occurrence. Most children are well nourished and better able to resist infections. The air we breathe in our cities and towns is less likely than it was to poison us with noxious substances.

Nevertheless, looking back on the last quarter century, we cannot see it as an unqualified success story. Indeed, the successes themselves are now seen as contributing to the present pattern of disease, to have created new hazards to health and to have had other unforeseen consequences. For example, while the infectious diseases of childhood no longer constitute the threat they once did, the prevalence of degenerative diseases of middle and old age has not diminished, and since more people survive to advanced ages they dominate the health scene. Medical advances have also helped the severely handicapped to survive into adulthood with the consequence that the community is faced with the need to cope with their prolonged dependency. Again, some of the powerful drugs which, when they first appeared, seemed to have an almost magical effect and were hailed as nostrums, are now known to have addictive properties or other deleterious side effects.

Moreover, medicine is now being called upon to deal with problems which were once considered moral rather than medical issues—for example, alcoholism, drug addiction, crime, marital disharmony, behaviour disorders and fertility control—as well as with the unwelcome fruits of technological and social change—for example, the toll of morbidity from road accidents, smoking and obesity.

For all these reasons, and because the level of expectations has risen and that of acceptance of pain or discomfort fallen, there has been no diminution in the pressure of demand on the health services. Moreover studies such as that of Professor Butterfield and his colleagues in Bermondsey have made us more aware than ever before of the still submerged part of the iceberg of disease, that is of needs for medical care which are known to exist but are not brought to the attention of the health services.

A feature of all the diseases which now make or ought to make demands on health services is that they are not amenable to the kind of medical intervention which until recently brought about such signal successes in the fight against infectious and deficiency diseases. Social and psychological as well as physiological factors are inextricably implicated in their causation, and their successful treatment depends on understanding them and taking social action as much as it does on sound diagnosis and systemic, clinical treatment of their underlying pathology.

In short all those engaged in the delivery of health services at the present time have to deal daily with problems which call into question the adequacy of their basic knowledge and the appropriateness of their established practices. This is not to say that the present and continuing concern to push back the frontiers of knowledge in the biological field and to disseminate such knowledge to doctors and nurses in training and in practice is wrong or cannot achieve much. It is to suggest, however, that the contributions made to human welfare by advances in human biology are likely to be limited unless they are matched by an equal understanding of the human behaviour which helps to create morbidity and to determine how health services are used. It is for this reason that the health professions need to consider, more seriously than they so far have, the contribution which the social or behavioural sciences can make to their work.

Sociology is one such discipline. Indeed, the Royal Commission on Medical Education reporting in 1968 recommended that all medical students should learn its elements in order to become aware 'of why patients and families behave as they do in situations of illness; of the social and cultural factors which influence patients' expectations and responses; of the problems for doctor, patient and family in the management of illness and handicap in the community; of the social, ethnic, occupational and psychological forces which can hinder prevention and treatment; and of the difficulties of communication, and other problems which arise from established expectations about the way a person in a defined situation will behave, particularly in hospital'.*

The Commission further suggested that the teaching of sociology could demonstrate to the student the cultural relativity of his own environment and values and enable him to acquire objective methods of observing and analysing human behaviour in relevant medical care settings.

One of the major difficulties of implementing these recommendations in medical schools, or indeed in the training of nurses and other health workers in Britain, has been the relative inaccessibility of relevant sociological British-based studies of illness behaviour or medical care institutions. Such studies are seldom published in the journals or books which appear on the shelves of medical or nursing libraries. By bringing together a number of papers which exemplify various sociological approaches to problems in the health field and introducing them with some general comments on the varied perspectives which sociologists bring to their work, Caroline Cox and Adrianne Mead have sought in part to remedy this deficiency. They have at least provided teachers and students with a number of readings which should stimulate discussion and further exploration of the concepts employed.

I hope that this collection of papers will encourage professional workers in the health and welfare services to extend their knowledge of the work currently being undertaken by sociologists in their fields. It is not of course suggested that sociology has the answer to all the unsolved problems which

* Report of the Royal Commission on Medical Education, April, 1968, HMSO, Cmnd. 3569. (The Todd Report.)

doctors and nurses confront. It is claimed, however, that a sociological perspective can throw light on some of the dark corners. Looking at familiar tasks or underlying traditional assumptions from such a perspective may be an uncomfortable exercise: it may suggest that some cherished attitudes, beliefs and modes of conduct need to be re-examined if not changed. The invitation is a challenging one. I hope it will also be an exciting and rewarding one.

MARGOT JEFFERYS
Bedford College, London
November 1972

Introduction

We anticipate that many of our readers may be new to the discipline of sociology and therefore our introduction has two specific aims: firstly, to provide a general framework within which the selected readings can be located; secondly, to introduce the reader to some of the basic sociological approaches and concepts contained in the readings and to show how these relate to a wider body of sociological knowledge.*

Although our selection focuses primarily on the medical and nursing professions and their patients, we hope the issues discussed will be of interest to many others who are concerned with contemporary health and welfare problems.

THE STRUCTURE OF THE BOOK

The book is divided into four sections: i. the sociology of illness and illness behaviour; ii. the sociology of the healing professions; iii. the sociology of health service organizations; iv. the sociology of doctor/patient relationships. The papers in the first section are concerned with what is called 'illness' in different social situations and with variations in the ways people who perceive themselves to be ill respond to this experience. The second section considers some of the social factors which influence those engaged in dealing with illness—the 'healers' and the 'carers'—and aspects of their training. The third section contains papers which consider the formal organizational setting in which present-day health practice takes place. The final section includes papers which look at the interface between the providers and the consumers of medical care.

Within the confines of one book we can do no more than illustrate some of the current themes in the sociology of medicine. Selection is always invidious and many articles which we would have liked to include have had to be omitted. We have chosen a greater proportion of British articles than has been the case, to our knowledge, in other selections, but we have also included certain 'classics' from other countries as we believe the book would have been impoverished without them, and as they provide

* For accounts of the various perspectives within the discipline of sociology, the non-sociologist reader is referred to the suggestions for further reading at the end of this introduction.

1

an important comparative element. The division of the articles into four sections is to some extent arbitrary, the content of many papers being equally relevant to other sections.

THE SOCIOLOGY OF ILLNESS AND ILLNESS BEHAVIOUR

Doctors and nurses are aware that individuals can exhibit a wide variety of reactions to identical pathology. Sometimes the variations are attributed to physiological differences: for example, different patients have been shown to have varying pain thresholds and an individual's own particular threshold may itself change over time. However, physiological differences do not fully explain the varying ways in which human beings respond to painful stimuli, and sociological studies have shown that differing attitudes and behaviour can in part be attributed to a patient's culture.

The term 'culture' in sociology refers to a body of learned values, beliefs and behavioural expectations which individuals derive from those with whom they interact. Prevailing beliefs and knowledge influence the ways in which a patient perceives his illness, the relative significance he attributes to the physical signs, and his attempts to explain their meaning in a coherent way.[1] Social anthropologists have shown that there are both similarities and differences in the ways in which people in different societies respond to particular physical signs. It is possible to attribute some of these differences to varying levels of scientific knowledge, associated with stages of technological development. For example, the apparent tolerance of certain preventable diseases by some groups of people in less developed countries may be due to sheer ignorance of the potential advantages of scientific medicine, and hence the acceptance of certain pathological conditions as normal. But knowledge in itself may not be the only differentiating factor. Culturally rooted beliefs and ideologies about the cause and course of disease also influence the ways in which different illness states and actions are perceived. Certain patterns of behaviour which would be defined in our society as pathological and deviant may be considered as benign and normal in other cultures. For example, hallucinations are usually considered as a sign of mental illness in our society, but in other cultures may be esteemed as a 'gift of the spirit'. Even within our own society, the context in which a form of behaviour occurs may determine whether it is evaluated as sane and normal, or mad and bizarre. As R. D. Laing says: 'Someone is gibbering away on his knees, talking to someone who is not there. Yes, he is praying. If one does not accord him the social intelligibility of his behaviour, he can only be seen as mad.'[2] The significant factor lies in the difference in 'social meaning' given to the same behaviour.

Not only do people perceive and react to physical symptoms and types of behaviour in different ways, but their culture will also influence the way in which they respond to therapies and preventive measures. If within the world-view provided by his culture an individual is unable to see a rational and logical reason for a treatment or prophylactic procedure, he will tend to disregard it in favour of traditional remedies and practices which he finds more comprehensible. One such example is given by Wellin who describes how a hygiene worker and a visiting physician were able to persuade only eleven out of over two hundred women in a Peruvian village to boil contaminated water. The reasons for the deep-seated resistance were complex. They included a lack of understanding of the principles underlying the procedure, but there was also a suspicion in the village that the health workers were agents of an élite who had exploited the poorer families.[3] Much interest has been generated by the differences between folk and scientific medicine and the implications of this distinction for health education programmes. It should also be remembered that even in so-called science-based cultures, a great deal of non-scientific thinking about the causes and remedies of illness persists, and health problems may be taken to a whole range of non-medical practitioners.[4]

A vivid example of the way in which beliefs may affect receptivity to modern health practices came to light in a recent study of West Indian women living in Britain. Some of the Jamaican women believed that there is a passage leading directly from the vagina to the mouth and consequently that any device inserted in the vagina or uterus was in danger of moving up through the body to the mouth, where it could finally choke them. An awareness of such 'body fantasies' is important in understanding attitudes to birth control methods and willingness to accept contraceptive devices.[5] This example illustrates the relationship between patterns of belief and health practice, although it must be emphasized that not all members of a particular social group, in this case West Indian women, will necessarily adhere to these beliefs.

While marked differences in the perception and meaning of illness and health exist between societies, subtle variations may also exist within a society. Any large society, or nation, can only be conceived as a homogeneous entity at the most general level of analysis, for every large society is constituted of a number of sub-groups, each with some norms, values and beliefs of their own. These groups are often referred to as 'sub-cultures'. Such sub-cultures in a country like Britain are generally based on possession of a common characteristic which has social significance attached to it, and include, for example, socio-economic, ethnic and religious groups. These may also act as 'reference groups' for individuals—that is, they serve as a frame of reference for self-evaluation and attitude formation.

Many empirical studies have described substantial sub-cultural variations in response to both physical and mental signs and symptoms. One such investigation by Zborowski, in the USA, described how Italian, Jewish and

'Old American' patients reacted to pain in very different ways. While the Italian and Jewish patients responded to their symptoms in an overtly similar way—they were very emotional, highly sensitive and had a tendency to exaggerate—their *attitudes* to pain were very different. The Italians focused on the immediacy of the pain and were primarily concerned with obtaining quick relief, while the Jewish patients were more preoccupied with the long-term effects of the illness of which the pain was symptomatic, particularly those effects which would be detrimental to their occupational and familial roles. The 'Old American' patients behaved in a more controlled manner and were less emotional in their response, but their attitudes and concerns were similar to those of the Jewish patients.[6]

Zola (p. 24) points out that there may be little direct relationship between the doctor's view of the seriousness of the disease and the patient's decision to seek aid. He concludes, from his empirical findings, that socially conditioned selective processes may operate to determine what is brought for medical attention. In his study, he held the diagnosed disorder constant and contrasted the ways in which Italian and Irish patients presented their symptoms. He maintains that we cannot understand illness behaviour unless we relate it to the patients' cultural background, and in particular to the ways in which they have learnt to cope with stressful events in their respective social environments.

The previous two studies have illustrated ethnic sub-cultural variations in illness behaviour. Another significant factor may be the socio-economic status (social class) which an individual has. Varied responses to physical ailments by people from different social classes were observed in a now classical study in the USA by E. L. Koos. Definitions of illness, use of medical facilities, and attitudes to public health were found to differ significantly for the three social classes studied.[7] Of course it is difficult to estimate the precise influence of the economic variable—the cost of medical care in the USA. A recent research study in Canada has attempted to measure health service utilization by social class before and after introduction of a public medical care insurance scheme.[8] In Britain, some studies have shown differential utilization of health services by social class but as yet the factors which underlie such differentiation have not been adequately elucidated.[9] In an early paper, Jefferys speculated on the causes of observed differences in the pattern of health service utilization by different social class groups.[10] More recent research has attempted to assess to what extent socially disadvantaged groups have been able to secure equality of access to medical care in the face of comparable needs.[11] Unfortunately the truth is that there are few reliable studies to indicate how far social class membership affects responses to illness or the threat of illness. One British study which investigated attitudes to cervical smears did indicate that with regard to cancer prevention in women there existed patterns of beliefs and behavioural propensities which could be described as 'class attitudes'.[12] Variations in the perception of illness and response to it by people in different social classes are not merely of academic interest but are relevant to questions of social policy and the efficacy of the welfare state in providing health and social services according to need.[13]

The notion of varying health perspectives has been used to try to understand some of the reasons for differential use of the health services. For example, it has been suggested that the middle and working classes hold different attitudes to health care, especially with respect to preventive health measures. Studies in the United States have shown that the working classes' greater commitment to and understanding of folk medicine poses problems when they are confronted by the scientific medicine practised by the medical profession.[14] Milio (page 49) discusses the implications of these attitudinal variations for the provision and utilization of medical care, with particular reference to maternity services. She found that middle-class women were more likely to follow the 'ideal' prenatal regime suggested by their medical practitioners, these practices being based on value assumptions held by the dominant middle-class culture. Working-class women found it more difficult to follow this regime because the suggested activities often failed to take into account the values and social organization of the working-class culture. A crucial differentiating factor appears to be the extent to which people hold a 'present' or 'future' time orientation; the middle-class women were more likely to hold a future orientation which involved thinking ahead and planning for possible contingencies.

The evidence from studies such as these must be used with caution. They show that in aggregate middle and working classes may have different 'health perspectives', but this does not mean every individual member of each group adheres to a particular perspective. Knowledge of an individual's social position is thus likely to improve prediction of his attitudes and behavioural responses to illness and the health care services; it is a sensitizing tool in the hands of health workers but needs to be used with an awareness of the limitations associated with any kind of statistical inference.

Epidemiological studies have considerably advanced our knowledge of the demographic and social distribution of many diseases, and some studies have established, by inference, which social and behavioural factors are implicated in the occurrence of certain illnesses. For example, Doll and Hill, using a longitudinal prospective design, were able to establish beyond reasonable doubt that smoking was a more common characteristic of doctors who died of carcinoma of the lung and certain other diseases within a given time-span, than of doctors who survived.[15] Many epidemiological studies use social science concepts to explain the relationship between biological and behavioural variables. To take a specific illustration: epidemiologists have established a statistical relationship between certain demographic variables—age, socio-economic status and sex—and the occurrence of coronary heart disease. Two major factors which have been considered as being causally implicated are diet and stress, and social scientists have been particularly interested in the mechanisms by which the latter may operate.[16] The influence of 'stress' as a socio-psychological phenomenon has been investigated in some depth by Hinkle and his associates, who emphasize the complexity of the relationships involved.[17] In this paper, they advocate further research into different types of social mobility, using more sensitive multifactorial analyses which could incorporate a wider range of significant social and psychological variables than those previously employed.

'Social mobility' is the term used by sociologists to describe an individual's movement between various social strata. In some societies such movement is severely restricted, as for example in the Hindu caste system, which formally inhibits a person from moving out of the caste into which he is born. Similarly, social mobility in societies of the feudal type, although possible in certain circumstances, is comparatively rare. In industrial societies changes in the occupational structure are endemic and engender some inevitable social mobility but it can be postulated that individuals who are socially mobile pay a price in psychological terms, and that this strain may have clinical manifestations. For example, they may lose contact with their original friends and associates and find that they are not accepted by the new group of people with whom they are trying to identify. They may consequently suffer acute problems of loneliness and crises of personal identity.[18]

The concepts of 'identity' and 'self-image' are widely used in sociology, and the processes whereby they are created have been a primary focus of a school of theorists known as 'interactionists'. The development of identity is seen as an integral part of the process of socialization, by which a 'raw' human infant becomes transformed into a social being who has internalized certain beliefs, values and behavioural expectations from those people who have been emotionally significant to him. As he moves into contact with a wider sphere of acquaintances he may change his beliefs, behaviour and self-image. Studies focusing on social and symbolic interaction have demonstrated the crucial importance, for both children and adults, of the perceptions, evaluations and expectations of 'significant others'. Becker (page 62) discusses the subtle processes by which the individual's self is created and sustained during the early socialization experience. He describes some problems in social understanding and verbal communication which certain children and young people may encounter; if these arouse negative evaluations and hinder the development of social relationships, the experience may be so cumulatively traumatic to their self-image that the situation becomes schizophrenogenic.

In the paper by Rose (page 74) the interactionist approach is utilized to help our understanding of social-psychological factors in both the aetiology and the treatment of neurosis. While he does not deny the significance of biological factors, he takes into account the dynamic and compounding effects of biological, psychological and sociological variables on human behaviour, so postulating a multi-causal rather than a mono-causal approach to the aetiology of some mental illnesses.

THE SOCIOLOGY OF THE HEALING PROFESSIONS

Using the concept of socialization, sociological studies of medical education have attempted to explain how the medical student is initiated into the medical profession. The explicit aim (manifest function) of the educational process is to impart a body of medical knowledge and related expertise; an implicit objective (latent function) involves teaching him how to feel and behave as a doctor, a process which is achieved by inculcating a set of 'appropriate' beliefs and values.

Studies of medical education in Britain have been largely descriptive, many of them trying to identify which intellectual, social or personality traits are the best predictors of performance in the medical school. Other studies, notably those undertaken in the USA, have perceived the medical school as a social system which operates in a complex manner to prepare the student for acceptance into the medical profession.[19] Of the many studies, only two will be mentioned here. These were undertaken by social scientists from Columbia University and Chicago University respectively; although both were interested in the socialization process, they adopted somewhat different perspectives and methodologies. The earlier study by Columbia University consisted of a series of separate studies which focused on the student's developing 'self-image as a physician', his attitudes to the doctor/patient relationship, the profession and the community.[20] The later study by Chicago University of one medical school also studied the socialization process but concentrated on the medical student's sub-jective awareness of 'becoming' a doctor, and in particular the part played by the student sub-culture in allowing students to come to terms with the 'disparities between aspiration and reality' involved in the education process.[21] Although there were similarities in the findings of the two studies, they differed in their interpretations of the status of the student vis à vis the medical faculty: the Columbia study showed the student as an already accepted colleague of the medical faculty—a 'student-physician' —who is guided as rapidly as possible towards full partnership in the profession; the Chicago study saw the student as a 'boy in white', in an overtly subordinate position separated from the faculty by a high social barrier, and forced to undergo a difficult trial by ordeal before being allowed to enter the profession.

The study by Fox (page 87) from the Columbia study investigates one sensitive area of medical training, the way in which medical students are helped by the medical culture to cope with the inevitable uncertainty associated with medical diagnosis and treatment. Another study, which emphasizes the sequential nature of socialization, but which is concerned with nursing education, stresses the importance of comprehending the existential process of becoming a nurse from the point of view of the 'actor' in the situation.[22] Davis (page 116) describes how these subjective changes are experienced by the student nurses and how their self-images and orientations to nursing change as they move progressively from lay to professional status.

Unfortunately, there is a paucity of studies which relate performance of the student in the medical school to the style of his subsequent practice as a physician. A few studies which have tried to relate performance in medical school to practice performance have limited themselves to very narrow 'process' criteria. For example, in one American study general practitioners were ranked according to whether, in reaching a diagnosis, they undertook certain procedures such as taking a full clinical history, performing a thorough physical examination and using appropriate laboratory tests. But the 'affective' functions of the primary care physician, for example his ability to use his sympathy for the patient to build up confidence, were not taken into account in this study which judged general practitioners on criteria approved by specialists who had little interest in psycho-social factors in therapy.[23]

There have been few sociological studies of general practice in Britain, despite the fact that the majority of illness episodes which are brought to a doctor are seen by the primary care physician. It has been estimated that only about 10% of cases—albeit the most serious—are referred to the hospital-based specialist. In Britain, Cartwright used a questionnaire survey to ascertain patients' attitudes to and expectations from their general practitioners. She also analysed the general practitioners' attitudes to their patients, and looked at the different types of practice organization and variations in care provided. With regard to the general practitioners' attitudes to their work situation she found, on the positive side, that 46% of them mentioned personal contact with their patients as a most important aspect of job satisfaction, while on the negative side, a third of the respondents complained about the frustrations engendered by unnecessary consultations for trivial complaints.[24]

Another analytical study was undertaken by Mechanic (page 132) who distinguished various 'value orientations' among British general practitioners and related these to their medical practices. He began by assuming that doctors would hold either a 'scientific' or a 'social' orientation to their work. In practice he found that they could more realistically be divided into four sub-groups: 'technicians' who had a scientific but not a social orientation, 'counsellors' who had a social but not a scientific orientation, 'moderns' who had both and 'withdrawers' who had neither. Younger doctors were more likely to be 'technicians' and older doctors 'counsellors'.

Yet another approach to the sociology of general practice is contained in the paper by Jefferys (page 145) which analyses the changing status of general practitioners in contemporary society, and considers how far the proposals made by the Royal Commission on Medical Education for a speciality of general practice are likely to be achieved, given the play of social forces which determine the prestige and status of occupations.[25]

Gill (page 155) shows how the institution of medicine is related to the state. Concentrating on a particular period in recent medical history—the creation of the National Health Service—he discusses the conflicts of interests which have affected the structure and subsequent functioning of health services.

The role of doctors in society has been analysed from various standpoints, using different conceptual frameworks or 'models'. One such approach is associated with the name of Talcott Parsons and is generally called the structural-functionalist approach. Parsons sees the institution of medicine as an essentially benign and integrative force with the medical profession fulfilling an uncontentious function in alleviating the burden of sickness and disease in society.[26] In short, this approach emphasizes the welfare functions of medicine. A contrasting approach associated particularly with Eliot Freidson's work focuses on the power and autonomy of the profession, analysing the mechanisms whereby doctors as an occupational group have been able to attain a monopolistic situation in which they have the state's sanction to control their own procedures, to set their own standards, to define illness, to exclude potentially conflicting groups from operating within the jurisdictional sphere of medicine, and to determine how other occupational groups within the health service system (e.g. nurses) shall function.[27] In simple terms, one viewpoint emphasizes the role of medicine as a servant of society, while the other sees it as a master exercising social control through its professional dominance. The approaches provide conflicting explanations of the same phenomenon, and as such are stimulating and thought-provoking. Those interested must decide for themselves which offers the most satisfactory explanation of the empirical data.

Zola (page 170) traces the spread of the medical profession's influence into the sphere of societal values. For example, he cites the increasing range of 'anti-social' and 'deviant' behaviours which are now categorized as mental illness and which have come within the orbit of medical care and therapy. He asks whether, in a society consisting of a plurality of social groups with varying and possibly opposing ideologies, the medical profession, a minority group, can legitimately impose its own values on the rest of society. A recent book by Kittrie raises similar fundamental questions, suggesting that the use of medical diagnosis and treatment for an increasing range of deviant behaviours may have more serious implications for the individuals concerned than the more punitive measures which they are replacing.[28]

THE SOCIOLOGY OF HEALTH SERVICE ORGANIZATIONS

The feeling that the medical profession may hold attitudes and values which are representative of only a minority sector of society is in part derived from empirical evidence which shows that physicians in most western societies are mainly drawn from a narrow stratum of the population. Tudor Hart (page 189) points to the fact that medical students in Britain are almost exclusively drawn from the Registrar General's social classes 1 and 2 (that is, mainly the business and professional classes) while the majority of their patients are likely to come from social classes 3-5 (composed mainly of manual workers). Furthermore, he demonstrates how the provision of the health services, especially in the primary care sector, is very unevenly distributed throughout the country. In the final analysis he concludes that 'the availability of good medical care tends to vary inversely with the need for it in the population served'.

Variation in definitions of need and the relationship of these to the provision of services is a central theme in the paper by Blaxter (page 207). Using evidence from her own research, she calls attention to variations in the administrative, medical and social definitions of handicap and the consequent influence these have on the quantity and quality of care provided by the health and welfare services.

When analysing health service organization, a distinction must be drawn between community and domiciliary care such as that provided by general practitioners and local authority health services on the one hand, and care provided in out-patient departments and residential institutions. Institutions can themselves be categorized according to the functions they perform. The general hospital today is seen as the place where patients requiring surgery or complicated medical diagnosis and therapy should be admitted, usually for short periods of intensive and specialized treatment. Since the elderly often have chronic disabilities which make speedy treatment and discharge difficult, hospitals are often reluctant to admit them to their general wards. Consequently, they are frequently admitted to special geriatric wards, or to hospitals designated for this purpose, which are situated in buildings which used to be poor law 'infirmaries' housing aged 'paupers', leaving much to be desired as residential environments. There is also a legacy of large psychiatric hospitals, often in isolated places, which used to be devoted to the custodial care of those deemed to be incurable; these now house most of the patients with long-term psychiatric illness. The general hospital on the other hand is now considered an appropriate place to treat, on an in-patient or an out-patient basis, patients referred for shorter psychiatric treatment. These changes reflect wider changes in the views of those charged with helping the mentally ill. Mental illness is now seen as 'an illness like any other' rather than a distinct affliction which presents a danger to society as well as to the sufferer.

Traditionally in the USA and now more frequently in Britain, the long-term residential institution caring predominantly for those with chronic disabilities has been a favourite area of study for social scientists.[29, 30] This may be partly due to the fact that both patients and staff constitute a 'captive' population for the researcher. Studies of mental hospitals in the USA undertaken in the 1940s and 1950s viewed these institutions as small societies with cultures of their own. These studies utilized methodologies and techniques of observation which had been found useful by anthropologists when studying 'primitive', small-scale societies. The researchers often used the technique of 'participant observation', entering the hospital in the role of staff or patient.[31] These studies were particularly concerned with what was interpreted as the dehumanizing influence of mental hospitals, and alleged that the pre-eminence of the custodial functions had a brutalizing effect on the inmates. Considerable attention was also paid to the divergence and conflict between staff and patient sub-cultures. Subsequent trends in psychiatric treatment have undoubtedly been influenced by the interpretations and suggestions for change generated by these studies (combined, of course, with important advances in chemotherapy, neurosurgery and other forms of physical treatment such as ECT).

The 'human relations' approach, which emphasized the therapeutic advantages of a more democratic structure within the psychiatric hospital, also emerged from these analyses. In their wake, attempts have been made to democratize the social structure of many hospitals by reducing barriers between staff and patients and between the staff themselves, and to make the culture of the hospital itself a therapeutic agent.[32]

Studies of general hospitals have viewed them as social systems, as complex organizations, and as small societies.[33] While numerous valuable studies have been undertaken in America and elsewhere, it is sometimes difficult to apply these analyses to the British situation because of national differences in the organization of medical care, and particularly the place of the hospital within these systems.[34] Much of the research concentrates on the formal organizational structure of hospitals, especially the locus of power and the nature of the decision-making process.[35] Less work has been

done on the outcome of hospital care, although one series of British studies
looked at the inter and intra-professional relationships between staff and
related these to the effectiveness of patient care and speed of recovery.[36]

The study by Cassee (page 224) takes up this theme and explores it
further, showing how tensions felt by the nursing staff can be detrimental
to patient care. He suggests ways in which these tensions might be relieved
by adopting a more open communication network between staff members
and between staff and patients.

A central concept in many of these hospital studies has been that of
'bureaucracy' developed by Max Weber. He delineated an 'ideal type', or
model, of a bureaucratic organization seeing it as a rational and efficient
system, with a hierarchical authority structure, a division of labour derived
from specialized competence and a system of formal rules not dependent
on personal relationships.[37] While this model of bureaucracy has been
often used in studying large-scale industrial organizations, hospitals do not
appear to conform closely to it, but tend rather to exhibit certain deviant
features. This discrepancy is in part attributed to the fact that hospitals
contain more than one authority structure: for example, the medical,
nursing and administrative staffs each have their own hierarchies.[38] Another problem with the pure bureaucratic model is that professional staff
in the hospital are subject to both bureaucratic and professional demands,
which may at times conflict with each other.[39] Davies, in a recent paper
which discusses the consultant's role in hospital, emphasizes that there is
a need to look not only at the way in which bureaucratic organizations
influence the professions, but also to consider how professional groups
may influence organizations.[40]

Most studies of hospitals have viewed the organization from the management or staff side, while the patients are usually seen as playing a passive
role. Few writers have paid attention to the influence patients may exert
on the organization, or considered it significant to study the creation and
dynamics of a patient culture. Goffman is an exception: his analysis of
the mental hospital seen as a 'total institution' provides insights into the
part played by the inmates. He sees an inmates' culture as distinct from
the staff culture in terms of attitudes and values, and suggests that this
counter-culture is highly significant to the patients and should not be
neglected in attempts to understand the processes at work in total institutions.[41] In his analysis, Goffman also uses the concept of 'career', by
which he means the sequential process whereby an individual moves from
one stage in his illness to another. He depicts how the patient is subjected
to contingencies at each stage, which he must learn to negotiate. His paper
included in this book (page 235) describes an early stage: the admission
of the patient to the hospital, and the type of identity crisis which this
experience may provoke. The notion of 'stages' has also been used to

describe the social processes operating in the development, treatment and recovery of patients from physical illness.[42]

The social contingencies associated with a particular aspect of medical care are the theme of a paper by Strauss and Glaser (page 247). They discuss the social relationships surrounding the dying patient in hospital and show how his degree of awareness of impending death may affect the care he is given in the terminal stages of his illness.

THE SOCIOLOGY OF THE DOCTOR/PATIENT RELATIONSHIP

Much of the sociologists' interest in medicine is derived from the fact that the practice of medicine is essentially based on a social encounter—the meeting of the practitioner with the patient in a face to face social situation. Such encounters can often be understood better if the concepts of 'role' and 'role-playing' are used. A role can be described as a set of norms and behavioural expectations which apply to an incumbent of a particular social position or status. Role-playing can be seen as the dynamic aspect of status, for when a person puts the rights and duties which constitute that status into effect, he is performing the role: thus, if 'patient' is the social status of the individual, the 'sick role' is the part he is meant to play. A great deal of sociological research has been directed towards the nature of the sick role, a concept which has been elaborated in detail by Parsons.[43] He suggested that the sick role differs from many other customary social roles in that it is a contingent and temporary role, usually only entered for negative reasons due to the breakdown of health. Although it is generally a temporary role, assumed reluctantly, like other roles it has important prescriptions attached to it in the form of certain rights and obligations.

Parsons starts from the assumption that illness is usually unwelcome and dysfunctional as it hinders a person from fulfilling his normal social obligations. Society is prepared to exempt a person who is ill from his usual responsibilities and to allow him sympathy, on the condition that he fulfils two major obligations attached to the sick role: he must behave in a manner conducive to recovery, or so as to minimize the effect of his illness; and he must seek competent professional assistance. Parsons alleges that non-compliance with these role requirements elicits social disapproval, charges of malingering and possibly the use of formal or informal sanctions against the patient.

Parsons has also provided a model of the medical professional role, in terms of four major attributes. Firstly, it is 'functionally specific'—this means that as a specialist in health and disease, a doctor is expected to apply his knowledge and skills to problems of illness and the promotion of health and to restrict his professional concerns to these areas. Secondly, Parsons asserts that it is 'affectively neutral', meaning that the physician is expected to be objective and emotionally detached in the interaction with his patient. There is however a subtle balance required in this aspect of the role, as the doctor is also expected to have concern for the patient and to be sympathetic. The third role attribute is denoted as 'collectivity-orientated', in contrast to 'self-orientated', by which Parsons means that the doctor is obliged to treat his patient according to the health requirements and expectations of the community rather than according to the doctor's own interests and needs. The fourth characteristic of the role is that it is 'universalistic' in that the physician is subject to the universal rules of the profession and not to the requirements of a unique, personal relationship with the patient.

These models of doctor and patient roles as depicted by Parsons can be seen as complementary, for if both partners conform to them a reciprocal relationship would be established. Moreover, there is an implication that the partnership is a consensual one, both physician and patient being in agreement both about the means and about the outcome. However, this view of the doctor/patient relationship is not universally accepted by sociologists, and Parsons's models or 'ideal types' have frequently been challenged. Bloor and Horobin (page 271) provide such a critique. They believe that, far from being a reciprocal, unequivocal relationship, there are sources of conflict which are intrinsic to the interaction between doctor and patient. For example, prior to consultation, doctors wish their patients to exercise initiative and knowledge with regard to medical matters, in order to minimize unnecessary claims on their time. However, once a patient has sought medical advice, doctors tend to demand an abrogation by their patients of any critical faculty and to encourage complete, unquestioning dependence on their judgement. In other words, in contrast to the consensus model of Parsons which views the doctor/patient relationship as relatively stable and predictable, they regard many interactions as problematic and precarious.

Paradoxically, criticisms of the Parsonian model serve to illustrate the contribution he has made to our understanding of the sick role. Parsons's models must be viewed as heuristic devices, rather than as descriptions of an empirical reality; as such they provide ideal types or yardsticks for measuring deviations and variations. The literature is rich in studies which have attempted to describe and explain deviations from Parsons's norms. These variations are often attributed to the age, sex, ethnic or other demographic characteristics of the patient.[44] Other studies have suggested that Parsons's sick role applies to acute, but not to chronic or long-term illness, and that the model needs expanding or refining still further.[45, 46]

Like Bloor and Horobin, Freidson (page 285) stresses certain tensions in the doctor/patient relationship. He indicates how the relationship can be clarified if we take into account the differing perspectives of the partners, which can be partly attributed to the fact that doctor and patient come from different worlds—those of the professional and the layman—which possess divergent values and beliefs. While both may agree on the goal of the relationship, the recovery of the patient, they may disagree as to the means whereby this is best achieved: the practitioner will apply the general rules and categories learned during his professional training, while the patient, who is very personally involved in what happens, tries to judge and control what is happening to him, using whatever information he as a lay person may possess. Freidson concludes by suggesting that there are various ways in which inherent conflicts may be forestalled, but there are problematic aspects in each of these.

The concept of the sick role is perhaps best understood within the wider framework of role theory, which in practice is not so much a theory as a set of propositions or sensitizing concepts. Among role theorists, some see the individual as if he were an actor, with a number of roles or parts to play, each having a script, or prescription for appropriate behaviour. Some roles, such as those associated with age and sex, are biologically constrained, but even these are socially determined to some extent, and the role expectations may vary markedly between cultures or even within one culture over time. Clearly, however, there may be variations in the ways in which particular roles may be defined and played by different actors. Another perspective in role theory is concerned with the extent to which roles may be created or negotiated by the role incumbents. For example, one study of staff in psychiatric hospitals demonstrated the wide variations in the ways in which their occupational roles were performed. Thus, although the hospital laid down certain role prescriptions for specific occupations, the role incumbents defined their roles in widely divergent ways, according to the extent to which they saw their role as primarily custodial or thera-peutic.[47]

While role theory is useful in clarifying the dynamics of interpersonal relationships, it is also important to look at roles within their social context and to take into account the influence of extraneous social and other variables. This brings us back to the content of the first section: the influence of culture and sub-culture on the behaviour and expectations of individuals. One important way by which culture is mediated is through language. Even within one culture, different speech systems, or modes of verbal expression, may be used by various sub-groups.[48] For example, as already mentioned, most doctors differ in socio-economic status and sub-cultural background from the majority of their patients. Not only are they likely to have different verbal styles and ways of expressing themselves, but they will also possess a whole medical vocabulary which is unfamiliar to their patients.[49] Our concluding paper by Boyle (page 299) describes an empirical study which highlights these differences in the knowledge and use of medical terms, and indicates some of the problems in communication which may ensue.

CONCLUSION

The reader will have observed from this introduction that sociology consists of a number of different perspectives, rather than a body of unified theory. Among the major variations, one can point to three crucial divergences in approach.

Firstly, there is the 'macrosociological/microsociological' continuum. At one end of this continuum there are sociologists, such as those in the marxist school, and some of the structural functionalists, who focus primarily on the characteristics of a particular social system, for example the nature and distribution of power; having established these aspects of the social structure, they may then discuss their implications for the individuals concerned. Alternatively, at the other end of the continuum, there are sociologists, among them the interactionists, who take the study of interpersonal relationships as their starting point.

Secondly, there is a distinction between 'objective' and 'subjective' approaches. Those sociologists who are more interested in objective data would be more likely to concentrate on quantifiable material such as the statistics of mortality and morbidity used in epidemiology, while the subjectivists are more concerned with the social meanings given by people to particular events, situations and experiences.

Thirdly, there is a contrast between 'conflict' and 'consensus' orientations. The conflict theorists argue that an element of conflict is endemic to many types of social structure and relationships, and that an understanding of this is a theoretical prerequisite. Conversely, the consensus theorists, while recognizing the existence of conflict, assert that the interesting phenomenon which requires explanation is the creation and maintenance of some degree of consensus, without which social life would be impossible.

Clearly, the different premises and assumptions underlying the various perspectives are associated with different approaches to the subjects being studied and different methods of investigation. For example, the structural and objective approaches are likely to use relatively 'hard' data, such as statistical analyses, while the schools in the subjectivist tradition, being more concerned with beliefs, attitudes and meanings, may use more personal information. This may be gained either by interviews or by participation by the researchers in the social group being studied. These alternative approaches are not mutually exclusive; indeed, they may complement each other.

We hope that this book, despite its limitations, may by illustrating some of the ways in which the sociological imagination can be used, stimulate new insights into the significance of social factors and social meanings in the aetiology, experience and treatment of illness. Moreover, we hope that we have shown how an increasing awareness of the processes associated with medical and nursing training and informed sensitivity to the problems inherent in organizations such as hospitals, may help health personnel to function more effectively, and thus to provide a higher quality of care for their patients.

This in the last analysis is the ultimate justification for the attempt to relate sociological perspectives to medical practice, for as Froude claimed: 'The knowledge which a man can use is the only real knowledge, the only knowledge which has life and growth in it, and converts itself into practical power. The rest hangs like dust about the brain, or dries like raindrops off the stone.'

REFERENCES

1. For further discussion, see: L. Saunders, *Cultural Differences and Medical Care*, Russell Sage Foundation (New York 1954); S. H. King, *Perceptions of Illness and Medical Practice*, Russell Sage Foundation (New York 1962); R. M. Coe, 'Systems of Medical Beliefs and Practices', in *Sociology of Medicine*, McGraw-Hill (New York 1970).
2. R. D. Laing, *The Politics of Experience*, Penguin (London 1967).
3. E. Wellin, 'Water Boiling in a Peruvian Town', in B. Paul (ed.), *Health, Culture and Community*, Russell Sage Foundation (New York 1955).
4. See B. Cobb, 'Why do people detour to Quacks?', *The Psychiatric Bulletin*, 3, 1954, pp. 66-9; W. E. Wardwell, 'Limited, Marginal and Quasi-Practitioners', in H. E. Freeman *et al.* (eds.), *Handbook of Medical Sociology*, 2nd edition, Prentice-Hall (Englewood Cliffs, NJ, 1972).
5. S. Kitzinger, 'Body Fantasies', *New Society*, 21 (no. 510), 1972, pp. 12-13.
6. M. Zborowski, 'Cultural Components in Responses to Pain', *Journal Social Issues*, 8 (1952), pp. 16-30.
7. E. Koos, *The Health of Regionville: What People Thought and Did About It*, Columbia University Press (New York 1954).
8. R. G. Beck, 'Economic Class and Access to Physicians' Services under Public Medical Care Insurance', *International Journal of Health Services Research*, 1973, 3, pp. 341-55.
9. For a general discussion of this topic, see: O. W. Anderson and R. M. Andersen, 'Patterns of Use of Health Services', in Freeman *et al.* (eds.), *Medical Sociology*, 1972, *op. cit.*
10. M. Jefferys, 'Social Class and Health Promotion: Some Obstacles in Britain', *Health Education Journal*, 15 (no. 2), 1957, pp. 109-17.
11. See, e.g.: T. Arie, 'Class and Disease', *New Society*, 7 (no. 174), 1966, pp. 8-12; M. Rein, 'Social Class and the Health Service', *New Society*, 14 (no. 373), 1969, pp. 807-10; M. R. Alderson, 'Social Class and the Health Service', *Medical Officer*, 124 (no. 3), 1970, pp. 50-2.
12. J. Wakefield, *Cancer and Public Education*, Pitman Medical Publications (London 1963); J. Wakefield and C. D. Sansom, 'Profile of a Population of Women Who Have Undergone Cervical Smear Examination', *Medical Officer*, 116, 1966, pp. 145-6.
13. For a discussion of the American context of this problem, see: A. L. Strauss,

'Medical Organization, Medical Care and Lower Income Groups', *Social Science and Medicine*, 3, 1969, pp. 143-77. For a more general discussion of the relationship between health and poverty, see: J. Kosa *et al.* (eds.), *Poverty and Health: a Sociological Analysis*, Harvard University Press (Boston, Mass., 1969).

14. E. A. Suchman, 'Health Orientation and Medical Care', *American Journal of Public Health*, 56 (no. 1), 1966, pp. 97-105.

15. R. Doll and A. Bradford Hill, 'Mortality in Relation to Smoking: Ten Years' Observations of British Doctors', *British Medical Journal*, 1964, pp. 1399-1410, 1460-7.

16. For an interesting example of how sociological insights can throw light on the part played by cultural factors in the aetiology of disease, see: Y. Scott Masumoto, 'Social Stress and Coronary Heart Disease', in H. P. Dreitzl (ed.), *The Social Organization of Health*, Macmillan (New York 1971).

17. E. W. Lehman, J. Schulman and L. E. Hinkle, 'Coronary Deaths and Organizational Mobility', *Archives of Environmental Health*, 15, 1967, pp. 455-61.

18. E.g.: R. J. Kleiner and S. Parker, 'Goal Striving, Social Status and Mental Disorder', *American Sociological Review*, 28 (no. 2), 1963, pp. 189-203.

19. For a further discussion of medical education, see H. S. Becker *et al.*, 'Medical Education' in H. E. Freeman *et al.* (eds.), *Medical Sociology*, 1972, *op. cit.*; S. W. Bloom, 'The Medical School as a Social System', *The Milbank Memorial Fund Quarterly*, 49 (no. 2), April 1971, part 2.

20. R. K. Merton *et al.* (eds), *The Student Physician*, Harvard University Press (Cambridge, Mass., 1957).

21. H. S. Becker *et al.*, *Boys in White: Student Culture in Medical School*, University of Chicago Press (Chicago 1961).

22. V. L. Olesen and E. W. Whittaker, *The Silent Dialogue: a Study in the Social Psychology of Professional Socialization*, Jossey-Bass (San Francisco 1968).

23. O. L. Peterson *et al.*, 'An Analytical Study of North Carolina General Practice 1953-4', *Journal of Medical Education*, 31 (Part II), December 1956.

24. A. Cartwright, *Patients and their Doctors*, Routledge & Kegan Paul (London 1967).

25. *Report of the Royal Commission on Medical Education* (Todd Report), HMSO, April 1968, Cmnd. 3569.

26. T. Parsons, 'Social Structure and Dynamic Process: the Case of Modern Medical Practice', in *The Social System*, The Free Press (New York 1951).

27. See, e.g.: E. Friedson, *Profession of Medicine: a Study of the Sociology of Applied Knowledge*, Dodd, Mead (New York 1970); E. Friedson, *Professional Dominance: the Social Structure of Medical Care*, Atherton Press (New York 1970); and also T. Johnson, *Professions and Power*, Macmillan (London 1972).

28. N. N. Kittrie, *The Right to Be Different: Deviance and Enforced Therapy*, John Hopkins Press (Baltimore and London 1971).

29. For a comprehensive review of the sociology of mental hospitals, particularly the American studies, see: C. Perrow, 'Hospitals, Technology, Structure and Goals', in J. C. March (ed.), *Handbook of Organizations*, Rand McNally (Chicago 1965).

30. See for example such British studies as: P. Townsend, *The Last Refuge*, Routledge & Kegan Paul (London 1962); P. Morris, *Put Away: A Sociological Study of Institutions for the Mentally Retarded*, Routledge & Kegan Paul (London 1969); M. Meacher, *Taken for a Ride: Special Residential Homes for Confused Old People: A Study of Separation in Social Policy*, Longman (London 1972).

31. Examples of such studies are: A. H. Stanton and M. S. Schwartz, *The Mental Hospital*, Basic Books (New York 1954); W. Caudill, *The Psychiatric Hospital as a Small Society*, Harvard University Press (Cambridge, Mass., 1954); J. A. Roth, *Timetables: Structuring the Passage of Time in Hospital Treatment and Other Careers*, Bobbs-Merrill (Indianapolis 1963).

32. An evaluation of one British experiment is to be found in R. N. Rapoport *et al.*, *Community as Doctor*, Tavistock Publications (London 1959).

33. For further discussion of the sociology of the hospital, see: C. Perrow, 'Hospitals', in March (ed.), *Organizations*, 1965, *op. cit.*; E. Friedson, *The Hospital in Modern Society*, The Free Press (New York 1963); S. H. Croog and D. F. Ver Steeg, 'The Hospital as a Social System', in H. E. Freeman *et al.* (eds.), *Medical Sociology*, 1972, *op. cit.*; R. M. Coe, 'Health Institutions: the Hospital' (Part III), in R. M. Coe, *Medicine*, 1970, *op. cit.*

34. W. A. Glaser, *Social Settings and Medical Organization: A Cross-National Study of the Hospital*, Atherton Press (New York 1970).

35. For a discussion of organizational structures and relationships within British hospitals, see: M. W. Susser and W. Watson, 'Medicine and Bureaucracy', in *Sociology and Medicine*, Oxford University Press (London 1971).

36. R. W. Revans, *Standards of Morale: Cause and Effect in Hospitals*, Oxford University Press (London 1964). Published for the Nuffield Provincial Hospitals Trust.

37. M. Weber, *Essays in Sociology*, Oxford University Press (New York 1946), pp. 196-204; M. Weber, *The Theory of Social and Economic Organization*, The Free Press (Glencoe, Ill., 1947), pp. 329-36.

38. See, e.g.: H. L. Smith, 'Two Lines of Authority: the Hospitals' Dilemma', *Modern Hospital*, 84, 1955, pp. 59-64; M. O. Mauksch, 'It Defies All Logic—but a Hospital does Function', *Modern Hospital*, 95, 160, pp. 67-70.

39. See, e.g.: M. E. W. Goss, 'Patterns of Bureaucracy among Hospital Staff Physicians', in E. Friedson (ed.), *Hospital*, 1963, *op. cit.*

40. C. Davies, 'Professionals in Organizations: Some Preliminary Observations on Hospital Consultants', *The Sociological Review*, 20, 1972, pp. 553-67.

41. E. Goffman, *Asylums: Essays on the Social Situation of Mental Patients and Other Inmates*, Doubleday-Anchor (New York 1961).

42. E. A. Suchman, 'Stages of Illness and Medical Care', *Journal of Health and Human Behaviour*, 6, 1965, pp. 114-28.

43. T. Parsons, *The Social System*, *op. cit.*

44. For example, see: S. V. Kasl and S. Cobb, 'Health Behaviour, Illness Behaviour and Sick-role Behaviour', *Archives of Environmental Health*, 12, 1966, pp. 246-66, 531-41; R. J. Ossenberg, 'The Experience of Deviance in the Patient-Role: A Study of Class Differences', *Journal of Health and Human Behaviour*, 3, 1962, 277-82; D. Phillips, 'Self-Reliance and the Inclination to Adopt the Sick-Role', *Social Forces*, 43, 1965, 555-63; G. Gordon, *Role Theory and Illness: A Sociological Perspective*, College and University Press (New Haven 1966).

45. For example: G. G. Kassebaum and B. O. Baumann, 'Dimensions of the Sick-role in Chronic Illness', *Journal of Health and Human Behaviour*, 6, 1965, pp. 16-27.

46. For example: G. Gordon, *Role Theory* (*op cit.*); J. R. Butler, 'Illness and the Sick-Role: An Evaluation in Three Communities', *British Journal of Sociology*, 21, 1970, pp. 241-61; A. C. Twaddle, 'Health Decisions and Sick-Role Variations: An Explanation', *Journal of Health and Social Behaviour*, 10, 1969, pp. 105-15.

47. D. G. Gilbert and D. J. Levinson, 'Ideology, Personality and Institutional Policy in the Mental Hospital', *Journal of Abnormal and Social Psychology*, 53, 1956, pp. 263-71.

48. Practical problems arising from these differences are discussed in: B. Bernstein, 'Social Class, Speech Systems and Psychotherapy', *British Journal of Sociology*, 15, 1964, pp. 54-64.

50. A great deal of research has been undertaken into problems of doctor/patient communication, which is excellently summarized in H. Waitzkin and J. Stoeckle, 'The Communication of Information about Illness: Clinical, Sociological and Methodological Considerations', *Advances in Psychosomatic Medicine*, 8, 1972, pp. 180-215.

FURTHER READING

SOCIOLOGY

A selection of introductory texts

P. L. Berger, *Invitation to Sociology: A Humanistic Perspective*, Penguin (Harmondsworth 1966).
P. L. Berger and B. Berger, *Sociology: A Biographical Approach*, Basic Books (New York, London 1972).
M. A. Coulson and D. S. Riddell, *Approaching Sociology: A Critical Introduction*, Routledge & Kegan Paul (London 1970).
S. Cotgrove, *The Science of Society: An Introduction to Sociology* (Revised Edition), Allen & Unwin (London 1972).
T. B. Bottomore, *Sociology: A Guide to Problems and Literature* (2nd Revised Edition), Allen & Unwin (London 1971).
K. Thompson and J. Tunstall, *Sociological Perspectives and Selected Readings*, Penguin in association with the Open University Press (Harmondsworth 1971).
P. Worsley (ed.), *Introducing Sociology*, Penguin (Harmondsworth 1970).
G. Hurd (ed.), *Human Societies*, Routledge & Kegan Paul (London and Boston, 1973).

SOCIOLOGY OF MEDICINE

Some basic texts

R. M. Coe, *Sociology of Medicine*, McGraw-Hill (New York 1970).
H. E. Freeman, S. Levine and L. G. Reeder, *Handbook of Medical Sociology* (2nd Edition), Prentice Hall (Englewood Cliffs, NJ, 1972).
E. Friedson and J. Lorber, *Medical Men and Their Work*, Aldine Atherton (Chicago and New York 1972).
E. G. Jaco (ed.), *Patients, Physicians and Illness*, Free Press (New York 1958).
D. Mechanic, *Medical Sociology: A Selective View*, Free Press (New York 1968).
D. Robinson, *Patients, Practitioners and Medical Care: Aspects of Medical Sociology*, Heinemann Medical Books (London 1973).
J. K. Skipper Jr and R. C. Leonard (eds), *Social Interaction and Patient Care*, J. B. Lippincott (Philadelphia and Toronto 1965).
M. W. Susser and W. Watson, *Sociology in Medicine* (2nd Edition), Oxford University Press (London 1971).

I | The sociology of illness and illness behaviour

1 | *Culture and symptoms: an analysis of patients' presenting complaints*

I. K. ZOLA

Physical disorder is often thought to be a fairly objective and relatively infrequent phenomenon. An examination of the literature reveals, however, that the empirical reality may be that illness, defined as the presence of clinically serious signs, is the statistical norm. Given that the prevalence of abnormalities is so high, the rate of acknowledgement so low, and the decision to seek aid unrelated to objective seriousness and discomfort, it is suggested that a socially conditioned selective process may be operating in what is brought for medical treatment. Two such processes are delineated and the idea is postulated that it might be such selective processes and not aetiological ones which account for many of the previously unexplained epidemiological differences between societies and even between subgroups within a society. A study is reported which illustrates the existence of such a selective process in the differing complaints of a group of Italian and Irish patients—a pattern of differences which is maintained even when the diagnosed disorder for which they sought aid is held constant.

THE CONCEPTION OF DISEASE

In most epidemiological studies the definition of disease is taken for granted. Yet today's chronic disorders do not lend themselves to such easy conceptualization and measurement as did the contagious disorders of yesteryear. That we have long assumed that what constitutes disease *is* a settled matter is due to the tremendous medical and surgical advances of the past half-century. After the current battles against cancer, heart disease, cystic fibrosis and the like have been won, Utopia, a world without disease, would seem right around the next corner. Yet after each battle a new enemy seems to emerge. So often has this been the pattern that some have wondered whether life without disease is attainable.[1]

Usually the issue of life without disease has been dismissed as a philosophical problem—a dismissal made considerably easier by our general assumptions about the statistical distribution of disorder. For though there is a grudging recognition that each of us must go sometime, illness is generally assumed to be a relatively infrequent, unusual, or abnormal phenomenon. Moreover, the general kinds of statistics used to describe

23

illness support such an assumption. Specifically diagnosed conditions, days out of work, and doctor visits do occur for each of us relatively infrequently. Though such statistics represent only treated illness, we rarely question whether such data give a true picture. Implicit is the further notion that people who do not consult doctors and other medical agencies (and thus do not appear in the 'illness' statistics) may be regarded as healthy.

Yet studies have increasingly appeared which note the large number of disorders escaping detection. Whether based on physicians' estimates[2] or on the recall of lay populations[3] the proportion of untreated disorders amounts to two thirds or three fourths of all existing conditions. (That these high figures of disorder include a great many minor problems is largely irrelevant. The latter are nevertheless disorders, clinical entities, and may even be the precursors of more medically serious difficulties.) The most reliable data, however, come from periodic health examinations and community 'health' surveys.[4] At least two such studies have noted that as much as 90% of their apparently healthy sample had some physical aberration or clinical disorder.[5] Moreover, neither the type of disorder nor the seriousness by objective medical standards differentiated those who felt sick from those who did not. In one of the above studies even of those who felt sick only 40% were under medical care.[6] (Consider the following computation of Hinkle *et al.* They noted that the average lower middle-class male between the ages of twenty and forty-five experiences over a twenty-year period approximately one life-endangering illness, twenty disabling illnesses, 200 non-disabling illnesses and 1,000 symptomatic episodes. These total 1,221 episodes over 7,305 days or one new episode every six days. And this figure takes no account of the duration of a particular condition, nor does it consider any disorder of which the respondent may be unaware. In short, even among a supposedly 'healthy' population scarcely a day goes by wherein they would not be able to report a symptomatic experience.)[7] It seems that the more intensive the investigation, the higher the prevalence of clinically serious but previously undiagnosed and untreated disorders.

Such data as these give an unexpected statistical picture of illness. Instead of it being a relatively infrequent or abnormal phenomenon, the empirical reality may be that illness, defined as the presence of clinically serious symptoms, is the statistical *norm*. What is particularly striking about this line of reasoning is that the statistical notions underlying many 'social' pathologies are similarly being questioned. A number of social scientists have noted that the basic acts or deviations, such as law-breaking, addictive behaviours, sexual 'perversions' or mental illness, occur so frequently in the population[8] that were one to tabulate all the deviations that people possess or engage in, virtually no one could escape the label of 'deviant'.

Why are so relatively few potential deviants labelled such, or more accurately why do so few come to the attention of official agencies? Perhaps the focus on how or why a particular deviation arose in the first place might be misplaced; an equally important issue for research might be the individual and societal reaction to the deviation once it occurs.[9] Might it then be the differential response to deviation rather than the prevalence of the deviation which accounts for many reported group and sub-group differences? A similar set of questions can be asked in regard to physical illness. Given that the prevalence of clinical abnormalities is so high and the rate of acknowledgement so low, how representative are 'the treated' of all those with a particular condition? Given further that what *is* treated seems unrelated to what would usually be thought the objective situation, i.e. seriousness, disability and subjective discomfort, is it possible that some selective process is operating in what gets counted or tabulated as illness?

THE INTERPLAY OF CULTURE AND 'SYMPTOMS'

Holding in abeyance the idea that many epidemiological differences may in fact be due to as yet undiscovered aetiological forces, we may speculate on how such differences come to exist, or how a selective process of attention may operate. Upon surveying many cross-cultural comparisons of morbidity, we concluded that there are at least two ways in which signs ordinarily defined as indicating problems in one population may be ignored in others. The first is related to the actual prevalence of the sign, and the second to its congruence with dominant or major value-orientations. (Here we are dealing solely with factors influencing the perception of certain conditions as symptoms. A host of other factors influence a second stage in this process, i.e., once perceived as a symptom, what, if anything, is done.[10] Such mechanisms, by determining whether or not certain conditions are treated, would also affect their over- or under-representation in medical statistics.)

In the first instance, when the aberration is fairly widespread this in itself might constitute a reason for its not being considered 'symptomatic' or unusual. Among many Mexican-Americans in the Southwestern United States diarrhoea, sweating and coughing are everyday experiences,[11] while among certain groups of Greeks trachoma is almost universal.[12] Even within our own society Koos has noted that although lower back pain is a quite common condition among lower-class women it is not considered symptomatic of any disease or disorder but part of their expected everyday existence.[13] For the population where the particular condition is ubiquitous, the condition is perceived as the normal state.[14] This does not mean that it is considered 'good' (although instances have been noted where not having the endemic condition was considered abnormal) but rather that it is natural and inevitable and thus to be ignored as being of no consequence. (For example, Ackerknecht[15] noted that pinto [dichromic spirochetosis], a skin disease, was so common among some South American tribes that the few single men who were not suffering from it were regarded as pathological to the degree of being excluded from marriage.) Because the 'symptom' or condition is omnipresent (it always was and always will be) there simply exists for such populations or cultures no frame of reference according to which it could be considered a deviation.

It is no doubt partly for this reason that many public health programmes flounder when transported *in toto* to a foreign culture. In such a situation, when an outside authority comes in and labels a particularly highly prevalent condition a disease, and, as such, both abnormal and preventable, he is postulating an external standard of evaluation which, for the most part, is incomprehensible to the receiving culture. To them it simply has no cognitive reality.

In the second process, it is the 'fit' of certain signs with a society's major values which accounts for the degree of attention they receive. For example, in some non-literate societies there is anxiety-free acceptance of and willingness to describe hallucinatory experiences. Wallace noted that in such societies the fact of hallucination *per se* is seldom disturbing; its content is the focus of interest. In Western society however, with its emphasis on rationality and control, the very admission of hallucinations is commonly taken to be a grave sign and in some literature regarded as the essential feature of psychosis.[16] (With the increased use of LSD, psychedelics, and so forth, within our own culture such a statement might have to be qualified.) In such instances it is not the sign itself or its frequency which is significant but the social context within which it occurs and within which it is perceived and understood. Even more explicit workings of this process can be seen in the interplay of 'symptoms' and social roles. Tiredness, for example, is a physical sign which is not only ubiquitous but a correlate of a vast number of disorders. Yet amongst a group of the author's students who kept a calendar noting all bodily states and conditions, tiredness, though often recorded, was rarely cited as a cause for concern. Attending school and being among peers who stressed the importance of hard work and achievement almost as an end in itself, tiredness, rather than being an indication of something being wrong, was instead positive proof that they were doing right. If they were tired, it must be because they had been working hard. In such a setting tiredness would rarely in itself be either a cause for concern, a symptom or a reason for action or seeking medical aid.[17] On the other hand, where arduous work is not gratifying in and of itself, tiredness would more likely be a matter for concern and perhaps medical attention. (Dr John D. Stoeckle, in a personal communication, has noted that such a problem is often the presenting complaint of the 'trapped housewife' syndrome.[18] We realize, of course, that tiredness here might be more related to depression than any degree of physical exertion. But this does not alter how it is perceived and reacted to once it occurs.)

Also illustrative of this process are the divergent perceptions of those bodily complaints often referred to as 'female troubles'.[19] Nausea is a common and treatable concomitant of pregnancy, yet Margaret Mead records no morning sickness among the Arapesh; her data suggest that this may be related to the almost complete denial that a child exists, until shortly before birth.[20] In a Christian setting, where the existence of life is dated from conception, nausea becomes the external sign, hope and proof that one is pregnant. Thus in the United States, this symptom is not only quite widespread but is also an expected and almost welcome part of pregnancy. A quite similar phenomenon is the recognition of dysmenorrhoea. While Arapesh women reported no pain during menstruation, quite the contrary is reported in the United States.[21] (As far as the Arapesh are concerned, Mead does note that this lack of perception may be related to the considerable self-induced discomfort prescribed for women during menstruation.) Interestingly enough the only consistent factor related to its manifestation among American women was a learning one—those that manifested it reported having observed it in other women during their childhood.[22]

The fact that one has to learn that something is painful or unpleasant has been noted elsewhere. Mead reports that in causalgia a given individual suffers and reports pain because she is *aware* of uterine contractions and not because of the occurrence of these contractions. Becker[23] and others studying addictive behaviours have noted not only that an individual has to learn that the experience is pleasurable but also that a key factor in becoming addicted is the recognition of the association of withdrawal symptoms with the lack of drugs. Among medical patients who had been heavily dosed and then withdrawn, even though they experience symptoms as a result of withdrawal, they may attribute them to their general convalescent aches and pains. Stanley Schaclter and Jerome Singer have recently reported a series of experiments where epinephrine-injected subjects defined their mood as euphoria or anger depending on whether they spent time with a euphoric or angry stooge.[24] Subjects without injections reported no such change in mood responding to these same social situations. This led them to the contention that the diversity of human emotional experiences stems from differential labelling of similar physical sensations.

From such examples as these it seems likely that the degree of recognition and treatment of certain gynaecological problems may be traced to the prevailing definition of what constitutes 'the necessary part of the business of being a woman'.[25] That such divergent definitions are still operative is shown by two recent studies. In the first, seventy-eight mothers of lower socio-economic status were required to keep health calendars over a four-week period. Despite the instruction to report *all* bodily states and dysfunctions, only fourteen noted even the occurrence of menses or its accompaniments.[26] A second study done on a higher socio-economic group yielded a different expression of the same phenomenon. Over a period of several years the author collected four-week health calendars from students. The women in the sample had at least a college education and virtually all were committed to careers in the behavioural sciences. Within this group there was little failure to report menses; very often medication was taken for the discomforts of dysmenorrhoea. Moreover, this group was so psychologically sophisticated or self-conscious that they interpreted or questioned most physical signs or symptoms as attributable to some psycho-social stress. There was only one exception—dysmenorrhoea. Thus, even in this 'culturally advantaged' group, this seemed a sign of a bodily condition so ingrained in what one psychiatrist has called 'the masochistic character of her sex' that the woman does not ordinarily subject it to analysis.

In the opening section of this paper, we presented evidence that a selective process might well be operating in what symptoms are brought to the doctor. We also noted that it might be this selective process and not an aetiological one which accounts for the many unexplained or over-explained epidemiological differences observed between and within societies. For example, Saxon Graham noted a significantly higher incidence of hernia among men whose backgrounds were Southern European (Italy or Greece) as compared with Eastern European (Austria, Czechoslavakia, Russia or Poland).[27] Analysis of the occupations engaged in by these groups revealed no evidence that the Southern Europeans in the sample were more engaged in strenuous physical labour than the Eastern Europeans. From what is known of tolerance to hernia, we suggest that, for large segments of the population, there may be no differences in the actual incidence and prevalence of hernia but that in different groups different perceptions of the same physical signs may lead to dissimilar ways of handling them. Thus the Southern Europeans in Graham's sample may have been more concerned with problems in this area of the body, and have sought aid more readily (and therefore appear more frequently in the morbidity statistics). Perhaps the Southern Europeans are acting quite rationally and consistently while the other groups are so threatened or ashamed that they tend to deny or mask such symptoms and thus keep themselves out of the morbidity statistics. (There may even be no 'real' differences in the prevalence rates of many deviations. In studying the rates of peptic ulcer among African tribal groups Raper[28] first confirmed the stereotype that it was relatively infrequent among such groups and therefore that it was associated, as many had claimed, with the stresses and strains of modern living. Yet when he relied not on reported diagnosis but on autopsy data, he found that the scars of peptic ulcer were no less common than in Britain. He concluded: 'There is no need to assume that in backward communities peptic ulcer does not develop; it is only more likely to go undetected because the conditions that might bring it to notice do not exist.') Such selective processes are probably present at all the stages through which an individual and his condition must pass before he ultimately gets counted as 'ill'. In this section we have focused on one of these stages, the perception of a particular bodily state as a symptom, and have delineated two possible ways in which the culture or social setting might influence the awareness of something as abnormal and thus its eventual tabulation in medical statistics.

SAMPLE SELECTION AND METHODOLOGY

The investigation to be reported here is not an attempt to prove that the foregoing body of reasoning is correct but rather to demonstrate the fruitfulness of the orientation in understanding the problems of health and illness. This study reports the existence of a selective process in what the patient 'brings' to a doctor. The selectiveness is analysed not in terms of differences in diseases but rather in terms of differences in responses to essentially similar disease entities.

Specifically, this paper is a documentation of the influence of 'culture' (in this case ethnic group membership) on 'symptoms' (the complaints a patient presents to his physician). The measure of culture was fairly straightforward. The importance of ethnic groups in Boston, where the study was done, has been repeatedly documented;[29] ethnicity seemed a reasonable urban counterpart of the cultures so often referred to in the previous pages. The sample was drawn from the out-patient clinics of the Massachusetts General Hospital and the Massachusetts Eye and Ear Infirmary: it was limited to those new patients of both sexes between eighteen and fifty who were white, able to converse in English, and of either Irish Catholic, Italian Catholic, or Anglo-Saxon Protestant background. (Ethnicity was ascertained by the responses to several questions: what the patients considered their nationality to be; the birthplaces of themselves, their parents, their maternal and paternal grandparents and, if the answers to all of these were American, they were also asked whence their ancestors originated.)[30] These were the most numerous ethnic groups in the clinics; together they constituted approximately 50% of all patients. The actual interviewing took place at the three clinics to which these patients were most frequently assigned (the three largest out-patient clinics): the Eye Clinic, the Ear, Nose and Throat Clinic and the Medical Clinic.

In previous research the specific method of measuring and studying

symptoms has varied among case record analysis, symptom check lists
and interviews. The data have been either retrospective or projective, that
is either requesting the subject to recall symptoms experienced during a
specific time period or to choose symptoms which would bother him
sufficiently to seek medical aid.[31] Such procedures do not provide data on
the complaints which people actually bring to a doctor, a fact of particular
importance in light of the many investigations pointing to the lack of and
distortions in recall of sickness episodes.[32] An equally serious problem is
the effect of what the doctor, medicine-man or health expert may tell the
patient about his ailment on the latter's subsequent perceptions and recall
of it.[33] We resolved these problems by restricting the sample to new
patients on their first medical visit to the clinics and by interviewing them
during the waiting period *before* they were seen by a physician. [This particular methodological choice was also determined by the nature of the
larger study, that is, how patients decided to seek medical aid, where the
above mentioned problems loom even larger. While only new admissions
were studied, a number of patients had been referred by another medical
person. Subsequent statistical analysis revealed no important differences
between this group and those for whom the Massachusetts General Hospital
or the Massachusetts Eye and Ear Infirmary was the initial source of
help.]

The primary method of data-collection was a focused open-ended
interview dealing with the patient's own or family's responses to his
presenting complaints. Interspersed throughout the interview were a number
of more objective measures of the patient's responses—checklists, forced-
choice comparisons, attitudinal items and scales. Other information
included a demographic background questionnaire, a review of the medical
record and a series of ratings by each patient's examining physician as to
the primary diagnosis, the secondary diagnosis, the potential seriousness
and the degree of clinical urgency (i.e. the necessity that the patient be seen
immediately) of the patient's presenting complaint.

THE PATIENT AND HIS ILLNESS

The data are based on a comparison between sixty-three Italians (thirty-
four female, twenty-nine male) and eighty-one Irish (forty-two female,
thirty-nine male), who were new admissions to the Eye, the Ear, Nose, and
Throat and the Medical Clinics of the Massachusetts General Hospital and
the Massachusetts Eye and Ear Infirmary, seen between July 1960 and
February 1961. [Forty-three Anglo-Saxons were also interviewed but are
not considered in this analysis. They were dropped from this report because
they differed from the Irish and Italians in various respects other than
ethnicity: they included more students, more divorced and separated, more

people living away from home, and more downwardly mobile; they were of higher socio-economic and educational level, and a majority were fourth generation and beyond.] The mean age of each ethnic group (male and female computed separately) was approximately thirty-three. While most patients were married there was in the sample a higher proportion of single Irish men—a finding of other studies involving the Irish[34] and not unexpected from our knowledge of Irish family structure.[35] Most respondents had between ten and twelve years of schooling, but only about 30% of the males claimed to have graduated from high school as compared with nearly 60% of the females. There were no significant differences on standard measures of social class, though in education, social class, occupation of the breadwinner in the patient's family and occupation of the patient's father the Irish ranked slightly higher. (In Warner's terms[36] the greatest number of patients was in class 5. Only a small proportion of new Irish and Italian patients were what might be traditionally labelled as charity cases, although by some criteria they were perhaps 'medically indigent'.) The Italians were overwhelmingly American-born children of foreign parents: about 80% were second generation while 20% were third. Among the Irish about 40% were second generation, 30% third, and 30% fourth.

With regard to general medical coverage there were no apparent differences between the ethnic groups. Approximately 62% of the sample had health insurance, a figure similar to the comparable economic group in the Rosenfeld survey of Metropolitan Boston.[37] Sixty per cent had physicians whom they would call family doctors. The Irish tended more than the Italians to perceive themselves as having poor health, claiming more often they had been seriously ill in the past. This was consistent with their reporting of the most recent visit to a doctor: nine of the Irish but none of the Italians claimed to have had a recent major operation (e.g. appendectomy) or illness (e.g. pneumonia). Although there were no differences in the actual seriousness of their present disorders (according to the doctor's ratings) there was a tendency for the examining physician to consider the Irish as being in more urgent need of treatment. It was apparent that the patients were not in the throes of an acute illness, although they may have been experiencing an acute episode. There was a slight tendency for the Irish as a group to have had their complaints longer. More significantly, the women of both groups claimed to have borne their symptoms for a longer time than the men.

In confining the study to three clinics, we were trying not only to economize but also to limit the range of illnesses. The latter was necessary for investigating differential responses to essentially similar conditions. [This is similar to Zborowski's[38] method, in his study of pain reactions, of confining his investigation to patients on certain specified wards.] Yet at best this is only an approximate control. To resolve this difficulty, after all initial comparisons were made between the ethnic groups as a whole the data were examined for a selected sub-sample with a specific control for diagnosis. This sub-sample consisted of matched pairs of one Irish and one Italian of the same sex, who had the same primary diagnosis and whose disorder was of approximately the same duration and was rated by the examining physician as similar in degree of 'seriousness'. Where numbers made it feasible, there was a further matching on age, marital status and education. In all thirty-seven diagnostically-matched pairs (eighteen female and nineteen male) were created; these constituted the final test of any finding of the differential response to illness. [These pairs included some eighteen distinct diagnoses: conjunctivitis; eyelid disease (e.g. blepharitis); myopia; hyperopia; vitreous opacities; impacted cerumen; external otitis; otitis media; otosclerosis; deviated septum; sinusitis; nasopharyngitis; allergy; thyroid; obesity; functional complaints; no pathology; psychological problems.

To give some indication of the statistical significance of these comparisons, a sign test was used. For the sign test, a 'tie' occurs when it is not possible to discriminate between a matched pair on the variable under study, or when the two scores earned by any pair are equal. All tied cases were dropped from the analysis, and the probabilities were computed only on the total N's excluding ties. In our study there were many ties. In the nature of our hypotheses, as will appear subsequently, a tie means that at least one member of the pair was in the predicted direction. Despite this problem, the idea of a diagnostically-matched pair was retained because it seemed to convey the best available test of our data. Because there were specific predictions as to the direction of differences, the probabilities were computed on the basis of a one-tailed test. This was used to retest the findings of Tables 1-6.[39]]

Table 1

Distribution of Irish and Italian Clinic Admissions by Location of Chief Complaint

Location of Complaint	Italian	Irish*
Eye, ear, nose or throat	34	61
Other parts of the body	29	17
Total	63	78

Note: $\chi^2 = 9 \cdot 31$, $P < \cdot 01$.
  * Since 3 Irish patients (two women, one man) claimed to be asymptomatic, no location could be determined from their viewpoint.

Location and quality of presenting complaints

In the folklore of medical practice, the supposed opening question is: 'Where does it hurt?' This query provides the starting-point of our analysis —the perceived location of the patient's troubles. Our first finding is that more Irish than Italians tended to locate their chief problem in either the eye, the ear, the nose, or the throat (and more so for females than for males). The same tendency was evident when all patients were asked what they considered to be the most important part of their body and the one with which they would be most concerned if something went wrong. Here too, significantly more Irish emphasized difficulties of the eye, the ear, the nose or the throat. That this reflected merely a difference in the conditions for which they were seeking aid is doubtful since the two other parts of the body most frequently referred to were heart and 'mind' locations, and these represent only 3% of the primary diagnoses of the entire sample. While there were a great many ties in the re-testing of these findings on diagnostically matched pairs, the general directions were still consistent. [For the prediction that the Irish would locate their chief complaint in eye, ear, nose or throat, and the Italians in some other part, eight matched diagnostic pairs were in favour of the hypothesis, one against, twenty-eight ties ($p=·02$); for the same with respect to most important part of the body there were twelve in favour of the hypothesis, two against, twenty-three ties ($p=·006$).] Thus even when Italians had a diagnosed eye or ear disorder, they did not locate their chief complaints there, nor did they focus their future concern on these locations.

Table 2

Distribution of Irish and Italian Clinic Admissions by Part of the Body Considered Most Important

Most Important Part of the Body	Italian	Irish
Eye, ear, nose or throat	6	26
Other parts of the body	57	55
Total	63	81

Note: $\chi^2 = 10·50$, $p < ·01$.

Table 3

Distribution of Irish and Italian Clinic Admissions by Presence of Pain in Their Current Illness

Presence of Pain	Italian	Irish
No	27	54
Yes	36	27
Total	63	81

Note: $\chi^2 = 10·26$, $p < ·01$.

Pain, the commonest accompaniment of illness, was the dimension of patients' symptoms to which we next turned. Pain is an especially interesting phenomenon since there is considerable evidence that its tolerance and perception are not purely physiological responses and do not necessarily reflect the degree of objective discomfort induced by a particular disorder or experimental procedure.[40] In our study not only did the Irish more often than the Italians deny that pain was a feature of their illness but this difference held even for those patients with the same disorder. [For the prediction that Italians would admit the presence of pain and the Irish would deny it, sixteen matched diagnostic pairs were in favour of the hypothesis, none against it, twenty-one ties (p=·001).] When the Irish were asked directly about the presence of pain, some hedged their replies with qualifications. ('It was more a throbbing than a pain ... not really pain, it feels more like sand in my eye.') Such comments indicated that the patients were reflecting something more than an objective reaction to their physical conditions.

While there were no marked differences in the length, frequency or noticeability of their symptoms, a difference did emerge in the ways in which they described the quality of the physical difficulty embodied in their chief complaint. Two types of difficulty were distinguished: one was of a more limited nature and emphasized a circumscribed and specific dysfunctioning; the second emphasized a difficulty of a grosser and more diffuse quality. [Complaints of the first type emphasized a somewhat limited difficulty and dysfunction best exemplified by something specific, e.g. an organ having gone wrong in a particular way. The second type seemed to involve a more attenuated kind of problem whose location and scope were less determinate, and whose description was finally more qualitative and less measurable.] When the patients' complaints were analysed according to these two types, proportionately more Irish described their chief problem in terms of specific dysfunction while proportionately more Italians spoke of a diffuse difficulty. Once again the findings for diagnostically matched pairs were in the predicted direction. [For the prediction that the Italians would emphasize a diffuse difficulty and the Irish a specific one, there were ten diagnostically-matched pairs in favour, none against, twenty-seven ties (p=·001).]

Diffuse versus specific reactions

What seems to emerge from the above is a picture of the Irish limiting and understating their difficulties and the Italians spreading and generalizing theirs. Two other pieces of information were consistent with this interpretation: first, an enumeration of the symptoms an individual presented—a phenomenon which might reflect how diffusely the complaint was perceived;

second, the degree to which each patient felt his illness affected aspects of life other than purely physical behaviour.

Table 4

Distribution of Irish and Italian Clinic Admissions by Quality of Physical Difficulty Embodied in Chief Complaint

Quality of Physical Difficulty	Italian	Irish*
Problems of a diffuse nature	43	33
Problems of a specific nature	20	45
Total	63	78

Note: $\chi^2 = 9 \cdot 44$, $p < \cdot 01$.

* Since 3 Irish patients (two women, one man) claimed to be asymptomatic no rating of the quality of physical difficulty could be determined from their viewpoint.

Table 5

*Distribution of Irish and Italian Clinic Admissions by Number of Presenting Complaints**

Number of Presenting Complaints	Italian	Irish
Zero	0	3
One	5	21
Two	15	22
Three	14	16
Four	10	7
Five	9	7
Six or more	10	5
Total	63	81

Note: $p < \cdot 001$

* The Mann-Whitney U-test was used. Probabilities were computed for one-tailed tests. They are, however, slightly 'conservative'; with a correction for ties, the probabilities or levels of significance would have been even lower. See Siegel, *op. cit.*, pp. 116-27.

The first measure of this specific/diffuse dimension—number of distinguishable symptoms [this number could be zero, as in a situation where the patient denied the presence of *any* difficulty, but others around him disagreed and so made the appointment for him or 'forced' him to see a doctor]—was examined in three ways: (i) the total number presented by each patient; (ii) the total number of different bodily areas in which the patient indicated he had complaints, e.g. back, stomach, legs; (iii) the total number of different qualities of physical difficulty embodied in the patient's presenting complaints. [Qualities of physical difficulty were categorized under nine headings.] The ethnic differences were consistent with the previous findings. Compared to the Irish the Italians presented significantly more symptoms, had symptoms in significantly more bodily locations and noted significantly more types of bodily dysfunction. [The distributions for these two tables closely resemble those of Table 5 (p=·018 for bodily locations; p=·003 for types of bodily dysfunctions).]

The second analysis, the degree to which a patient felt his illness affected his more general well-being, was derived from replies to three questions: (i) Do you think your symptoms affected how you got along with your family? (ii) Did you become more irritable? (iii) What would you say has bothered you most about your symptoms? [For the latter question, the patient was presented with a card on which were listed eight aspects of illness and/or symptoms which might bother him. One of these statements was, 'That it made you irritable and difficult to get along with.'] An admission of irritability scale was created by classifying an affirmative response to any of the three questions as an admission that the symptoms affected extra-physical performance. As seen in Table 6, the Irish were more likely than the Italians to state that their disorders had not affected them in this manner. Here again the asides by the Irish suggested that their larger number of negative responses reflected considerable denial rather than a straightforward appraisal of their situation.

To examine these conclusions in a more rigorous manner, we turned to our sub-sample of matched diagnostic pairs. In general, the pattern and direction of the hypotheses were upheld. [For the prediction that the Italians would have more symptoms in all instances there were: for total number, twenty-four matched diagnostic pairs in favour of hypothesis, seven against, six ties (p=·005); for number of different locations, sixteen in favour, five against, sixteen ties (p=·013); for number of different qualities of physical difficulties, twenty-two in favour, nine against, six ties (p=·025). For the prediction that Italians would admit irritability and Irish would deny it, there were seventeen in favour, six against, fourteen ties (p=·017).] Thus even for the same diagnosis the Italians expressed and complained of more symptoms, more bodily areas affected, and more kinds of dysfunctions than did the Irish, and more often felt that their symptoms affected their interpersonal behaviour.

Table 6

Distribution of Irish and Italian Clinic Admissions by Responses to Three Questions Concerning Admission of Irritability and Effect of Symptoms on Interpersonal Behaviour

Response Pattern	Italian	Irish
No on all three questions	22	47
Yes on at least one question	41	34
Total	63	81

Note: $\chi^2=7·62$, p<·01.

The following composite offers a final illustration of how differently these patients reacted to and perceived their illnesses. Each set of responses was given by an Italian and an Irish patient of similar age and sex with a disorder of approximately the same duration and with the same primary and secondary diagnosis (if there was one). In the first two cases the Irish patient focused on a specific malfunctioning as the main concern while the Italian did not even mention this aspect of the problem but went on to mention more diffuse qualities of his condition. The last four responses contrast the Italian and Irish response to questions of pain and interpersonal relations.

Diagnosis	Question of Interviewer	Irish Patient	Italian Patient
1. Presbyopia and hyperopia	What seems to be the trouble?	I can't see to thread a needle or read a paper.	I have a constant headache and my eyes seem to get all red and burny.
	Anything else?	No, I can't recall any.	No, just that it lasts all day long and I even wake up with it sometimes.
2. Myopia	What seems to be the trouble?	I can't see across the street.	My eyes seem very burny, especially the right eye.... Two or three months ago I woke up with my eye swollen. I bathed it and it did go away but there was still the burny sensation.
	Anything else?	I had been experiencing headaches, but it may be that I'm in early menopause.	Yes, there always seems to be a red spot beneath this eye....
	Anything else?	No.	Well, my eyes feel very heavy ... at night they bother me most.
3. Otitis externa A.D.	Is there any pain?	There's a congestion ... but it's a pressure, not really a pain.	Yes ... if I rub it, it disappears.... I had a pain from my shoulder up to my neck and thought it might be a cold.
4. Pharyngitis	Is there any pain?	No, maybe a slight headache but nothing that lasts.	Yes, I have had a headache a few days. Oh, yes, every time I swallow it's annoying.
5. Presbyopia and hyperopia	Do you think the symptoms affected how you got along with your family? Your friends?	No, I have had loads of trouble. I can't imagine this bothering me.	Yes, I have had a headache, I'm very irritable, very tense, very short-tempered.
6. Deafness, hearing loss.	Did you become more irritable?	No, not me ... maybe everybody else but not me.	Oh, yes ... the least little thing aggravates me ... and I take it out on the children.

SOCIO-CULTURAL COMMUNICATION

What has so far been demonstrated is the systematic variability with which bodily conditions may be perceived and communicated. Until now the empirical findings have been presented without interpretation. Most of the data are quite consistent with those reported by other observers.[41] Although no data were collected in our investigation on the specific mechanics of the interplay between a member of a specific sub-culture and the communication of 'symptoms', some speculation on this seems warranted.

In theorizing about the interplay of culture and symptoms particular emphasis was given to the 'fit' of certain bodily states with dominant value orientations. The empirical examples for the latter were drawn primarily from data on social roles. Of course, values are evident on even more general levels, such as formal and informal societal sanctions and the culture's orientation to life's basic problems. With an orientation to problems usually goes a preferred solution or way of handling them.[42] Thus a society's values may also be reflected in such preferred solutions. One behavioural manifestation of this is defence mechanisms—a part of the everyday way individuals have of dealing with their everyday stresses and strains.[43] We contend that illness and its treatment (from taking medicine to seeing a physician) is one of these everyday stresses and strains, an anxiety-laden situation which calls forth coping or defence mechanisms. That illness is almost an everyday problem is shown by the data in our opening section on the prevalence of illness. That illness and its concomitants are anxiety-laden is suggested by the findings of many studies on patient delay.[44] From this general reasoning, we would thus speculate that Italian and Irish ways of communicating illness may reflect major values and preferred ways of handling problems within the culture itself. Speculation as to why the Italians and the Irish, with similar problems of hardship and poverty, should develop dissimilar ways of handling such problems, is beyond the scope of this paper.

For the Italians, the large number of symptoms and the spread of the complaints, not only throughout the body but into other aspects of life, may be understood in terms of their expressiveness and expansiveness so often seen in sociological, historical, and fictional writing.[45] And yet their illness behaviour seems to reflect something more than lack of inhibition, and valuation of spontaneity. There is something more than real in their behaviour, a 'well-seasoned, dramatic emphasis to their lives'. In fact, clinicians have noted that this openness is deceptive. It only goes so far and then.... Thus this Italian overstatement of 'symptoms' is not merely an expressive quality but perhaps a more general mechanism, their special way of handling problems—a defence mechanism we call dramatization. Dynamically dramatization seems to cope with anxiety by repeatedly over-expressing it and thereby dissipating it. Anne Parsons delineates this process in a case study of a schizophrenic woman. Through a process of repetition and exaggeration she was able to isolate and defend herself from the destructive consequences of her own psychotic breakdown. Thus Anne Parsons concludes:

> ... rather than appearing as evidence for the greater acceptance of id impulses the greater dramatic expression of Southern Italian culture might be given a particular place among the ego mechanisms, different from but in this respect fulfilling the same function as the emphasis on rational mastery of the objective or subjective world which characterizes our own culture (U.S.A.)[46]

While other social historians have noted the Italian flair for show and spectacle, Barzini has most explicitly related this phenomenon to the covering up of omnipresent tragedy and poverty, a way of making their daily lives bearable, the satisfactory *ersatz* for the many things they lack.

> The most easily identifiable reasons why the Italians love their own show.... First of all they do it to tame and prettify savage nature, to make life bearable, dignified, significant and pleasant for others, and themselves. They do it then for their own private ends; a good show makes a man *simpatico* to powerful people, helps him get on in the world and obtain what he wants, solves many problems, lubricates the wheels of society, protects him from the envy of his enemies and the arrogance of the mighty—they do it to avenge themselves on unjust fate.[47]

Through many works on the Southern Italian there seems to run a thread —a valued and preferred way of handling problems shown in the tendency towards dramatization. The experience of illness provides but another stage.

But if the Italian view of life is expressed through its fiestas, for the Irish it is expressed through its fasts.[48] Their life has been depicted as one of long periods of plodding routine followed by episodes of wild adventure, of lengthy postponement of gratification of sex and marriage, interspersed with brief immediate satisfactions like fighting and carousing. Perhaps it is in recognition of the expected and limited nature of such outbursts that the most common Irish outlet, alcoholism, is often referred to as 'a good man's weakness'. Life was black and long-suffering, and the less said the better. [The ubiquitous comic spirit, humour, and wit for which the Irish are famous can be regarded in part as a functional equivalent of the dramatization by Italians. It is a cover, a way of isolating life's hardships, and at the same time a preventive of deeper examination and probing.[49] Also, while their daily life was endowed with great restrictions, their fantasy life was replete with great richness (tales of the 'wee folk').]

It is the last statement which best reflects the Irish handling of illness. While in other contexts the ignoring of bodily complaints is merely descriptive of what is going on, in Irish culture it seems to be the culturally prescribed and supported defence mechanism—singularly most appropriate for their psychological and physical survival. [Spiegel and Kluckhohn[49] state that the Irishman's major avenue of relief from his oppressive sense of guilt lies in his almost unlimited capacity for denial. This capacity they claim is fostered by the perception in the rural Irish of a harmonic blending between man and nature. Such harmonizing of man and nature is further interpreted as blurring the elements of causality, thus allowing for continually shifting the responsibility for events from one person to another, and even from a person to animistically conceived forces. Thus denial becomes not only a preferred avenue of relief but also one supported and perhaps elicited by their perception of their environment.] When speaking of the discomfort caused by her illness, one stated, 'I ignore it like I do most things'. In terms of presenting complaints this understatement and restraint was even more evident. It could thus be seen in their seeming reluctance to admit they have any symptoms at all, in their limiting their symptoms to the specific location in which they arose and finally in their contention that their physical problems affected nothing of their life but the most minute physical functioning. The consistency of the Irish illness behaviour with their general view of life is shown in two other contexts. First it helped perpetuate a self-fulfilling prophecy. Thus their way of communicating complaints, while doing little to make treatment easy, did assure some degree of continual suffering and thus further proof that life is painful and hard (that is 'full of fasts'). [Their 'fantasying' and their 'fasting' might be reflected in the serious illness they claim to have had in the past, and the dire consequences they forecast for their future. We do not know for a fact that the Irish *had* more serious illnesses than the Italians, but merely that they claimed to. The Italians might well have had similar conditions but did not necessarily consider them serious.] Secondly, their illness behaviour can be linked to the sin and guilt ideology which seems to pervade so much of Irish society. For, in a culture where restraint is the *modus operandi*, temptation is ever-present and must be guarded against. Since the flesh is weak, there is a concomitant expectation that sin is likely. Thus, when unexpected or unpleasant events take place, there is a search for what they did or must have done wrong. Perhaps their three most favoured locations of symptoms (the eyes, ears and throat) might be understood as symbolic reflections of the more immediate source of their sin and guilt—what they should not have seen; what they should not have heard; and what they should not have said.

In these few paragraphs, we have tried to provide a theoretical link between membership in a cultural group and the communication of bodily complaints. The illness behaviour of the Irish and the Italians has been explained in terms of two of the more generally prescribed defence mechanisms of their respective cultures—with the Irish handling their troubles by denial and the Italians theirs by dramatization. [The Anglo-Saxons complete the circle with an emphasis on neutralizing their anxiety.]

QUALIFICATIONS AND IMPLICATIONS

The very fact that we speak of trends and statistical significance indicates the tentativeness of this study. In particular, the nature of sample selection affected the analysis of certain demographic variables since the lack of significant differences in some cases may be due to the small range available for comparison. Thus, there were no Italians beyond the third generation and few in the total sample who had gone to college. When comparisons were made within this small range (for example, only within the second generation or only within the high school group) there were, with but one exception, no significant differences from previously reported findings. [The previously reported ethnic differences with respect to presenting complaints did begin to blur. The Italian and the Irish males tended to 'move' towards the 'middle position' of the Anglo-Saxon Protestant group. In many of the major comparisons of this study, the Anglo-Saxon group occupied a position midway between the responses of the two other ethnic groups, though generally closer to the Irish. For example, when asked about the presence of pain some 70% of the Irish males denied it, as compared to almost 60% of the Anglo-Saxon males, and 40% of the Italian males.] Despite the limitations cited, it can be stated with some confidence that of the variables capable of analysis socio-cultural ones were the most significant. When a correlational analysis (and within this, a cluster analysis) was performed on all the codable and quantifiable material (including the demographic data, the health behaviours and attitude scales) the variable which consistently correlated most highly with the 'illness behaviours' reported in this study was ethnic group membership.

There is one final remark about our sample selection which has ramifications not for our data analysis but rather for our interpretation. We are dealing here with a population who had decided to seek or were referred for medical aid at three clinics. Thus we can make no claim that in a random selection of Irish, they will be suffering primarily from eye, ear, nose and throat disorders or even locate their chief symptoms there. What we are claiming is that there are significant differences in the way people present and react to their complaints, *not* that the specific complaints and mechanisms we have cited are necessarily the most common ones. (We would, of course, be surprised if the pattern reported here did not constitute one of the major ones.) Another difficulty in dealing with this population is the duration of the patients' disorders. Since the majority of these patients have had their conditions for some time, one may wonder if similar differences in perception would exist for more acute episodes, or whether the very length of time which the people have borne their problems has allowed for colouration by socio-cultural factors. As a result of this we can only raise the issues as to whether the differences reported here between members of a cultural group exist only at a particular stage of their illness, or reflect more underlying and enduring cultural concerns and values.[50]

While there has long been recognition of the subjectivity and variability of a patient's reporting of his symptoms, there has been little attention to the fact that this reporting may be influenced by systematic social factors like ethnicity. Awareness of the influence of this and similar factors can be of considerable aid in the practical problems of diagnosis and treatment of many diseases, particularly where the diagnosis is dependent to a large extent on what the patient is able and willing, or thinks important enough, to tell the doctor.[51] The physician who is unaware of how the patient's background may lead him to respond in certain ways, may, by not probing sufficiently, miss important diagnostic cues or respond inappropriately to others.[52]

The documentation of socio-cultural differences in the perception of and concern with certain types of symptoms has further implications for work in preventive medicine and public health. It has been found in mental health research that there is an enormous gulf between lay and professional opinion as to when mental illness is present, as well as when and what kind of help is needed.[53] If our theorizing is correct such differences reflect not merely something inadequately learned (that is, wrong medical knowledge) but also a solidly embedded value system.[54] Such different frames of reference would certainly shed light on the failures of many symptom-based health campaigns. Often these campaigns seem based on the assumption that a symptom or sign is fairly objective and recognizable and that it evokes similar levels of awareness and reaction. Our study adds to the mounting evidence which contradicts this position by indicating, for example, the systematic variability in response to even the most minor aches and pains.

The discerning of reactions to minor problems harks back to a point mentioned in the early pages of this report. For, while sociologists, anthropologists, and mental health workers have usually considered socio-cultural factors to be aetiological factors in the creation of specific problems, the interpretative emphasis in this study has been on how socio-cultural background may lead to different definitions and responses to essentially the same experience. The strongest evidence in support of this argument is the different ethnic perceptions for essentially the same disease. While it is obvious that not all people react similarly to the same disease process, it is striking that the pattern of response can vary with the ethnic background of the patient. There is little known physiological difference between ethnic groups which would account for the differing reactions. In fact, the comparison of the matched diagnostic groups led us to believe that, should diagnosis be more precisely controlled, the differences would be even more striking.

The present report has attempted to demonstrate the fruitfulness of an approach which does not take the definition of abnormality for granted. Despite its limitations, our data seem sufficiently striking to provide further reason for re-examining our traditional and often rigid conceptions of health and illness, of normality and abnormality, of conformity and deviance. Symptoms or physical aberrations are so widespread that perhaps relatively few, and a biased selection at best, come to the attention of official treatment agencies like doctors, hospitals and public health agencies. There may even be a sense in which they are part and parcel of the human condition. We have thus tried to present evidence showing that the very labelling and definition of a bodily state as a symptom or as a problem is in itself part of a social process. If there is a selection and definitional process, then focusing solely on reasons for deviation (the study of aetiology) and ignoring what constitutes a deviation in the eyes of the individual and his society may obscure important aspects of our understanding and eventually our philosophies of treatment and control of illness.[55]

REFERENCES

1. Rene Dubos, *Mirage of Health*, Anchor (New York, Garden City 1961). On more philosophical grounds, William A. White, in *The Meaning of Disease*, Williams & Wilkin (Baltimore 1926) arrives at a similar conclusion.
2. R. J. F. H. Pinsett, *Morbidity Statistics from General Practice*, Studies of Medical Population, No. 14, HMSO (London 1962); P. Stocks, *Sickness in the Population of England and Wales, 1944-7*, Studies of Medical Population Subjects, No. 2, HMSO (London Dec. 1948); John and Elizabeth Horder, 'Illness in General Practice', *The Practitioner*, 173, August 1954, pp. 177-85.
3. Charles R. Hoffer and Edgar A. Schuler, 'Measurement of Health Needs and Health Care', *American Sociological Review*, 13, December 1948, pp. 719-24; Political and Economic Planning, *Family Needs and the Social Services*, George Allen & Unwin (London 1961); Leonard S. Rosenfeld, Jacob Katz and Avedis Donabedian, *Medical Care Needs and Services in the Boston Metropolitan Area*, Medical Care Evaluation Studies, Health, Hospitals and Medical Care Division, United Community Services of Metropolitan Boston (Boston 1957).
4. See, for example: Commission on Chronic Illness, *Chronic Illness in a Large City*, Harvard University Press (Cambridge, Mass., 1957); Kendall A. Elsom, Stanley Schor, Thomas W. Clark, Katherine O. Elsom and John P. Hubbard, 'Periodic Health Examination—Nature and Distribution of Newly Discovered Disease in Executives', *Journal of the American Medical Association*, 172, January 1960, pp. 55-61; John W. Runyan, Jr, 'Periodic Health Maintenance Examination—III. Industrial Employees', *New York State Journal of Medicine*, 59, March 1959, pp. 778-81; C. J. Tupper and M. B. Becket, 'Faculty Health Appraisal, University of

Michigan', *Industrial Medicine and Surgery*, 27, July 1958, pp. 328-32; Leo Wade, John Thorpe, Thomas Elias and George Bock, 'Are Periodic Health Examinations Worthwhile?', *Annals of Internal Medicine*, 56, January 1962, pp. 81-93.

For questionnaire studies, see: Paul B. Cornerly and Stanley K. Bigman, *Cultural Considerations in Changing Health Attitudes*, Department of Preventive Medicine and Public Health, College of Medicine, Howard University (Washington DC, 1961); and for more general summaries, see: J. Wister Meigs, 'Occupational Medicine', *New York Journal of Medicine*, 264, April 1961, pp. 861-7; George S. Siegel, *Periodic Health Examinations—Abstracts from the Literature*, Public Health Service Publications, No. 1010, US Government Printing Office (Washington DC, 1963).

5. See: Innes H. Pearce and Lucy H. Crocker, *The Peckham Experiment*, Allen & Unwin (London 1949); *Biologists in Search of Material*, Interim Reports of the Work of the Pioneer Health Centre, Peckham, Faber & Faber (London 1938); Joseph E. Schenthal, 'Multiphasic Screening of the Well Patient', *Journal of the American Medical Association*, 172, January 1960, pp. 51-64.

6. Pearce and Crocker, *Peckham*, 1949, *op. cit.*

7. Lawrence E. Hinkle, Jr, Ruth Redmont, Norman Plomer and Harold G. Wolff, 'An Examination of the Relation between Symptoms, Disability and Serious Illness in Two Homogeneous Groups of Men and Women', *American Journal of Public Health*, 50, September 1960, pp. 1327-36.

8. See Fred J. Murphy, Mary M. Shirley and Helen L. Witmer, 'The Incidence of Hidden Delinquency', *American Journal of Orthopsychiatry*, 16, October 1946, pp. 686-96; Austin L. Porterfield, *Youth in Trouble*, Leo Potishman Foundation (Fort Worth 1949); James F. Short and F. Ivan Nye, 'Extent of Unrecorded Delinquency', *Journal of Criminal Law, Criminology and Police Science*, 49, December 1958, pp. 296-302; James S. Wallerstein and Clement J. Wyle, 'Our Law-Abiding Law-Breakers', *Probation*, 25, April 1947, pp. 107-12; Alfred C. Kinsey, Wardell B. Pomeroy and Clyde C. Martin, *Sexual Behaviour in the Human Male*, W. B. Saunders (Philadelphia 1953); Stanton Wheeler, 'Sex Offences: a Sociological Critique', *Law and Contemporary Problems*, 25, Spring 1960, pp. 258-78; Leo Srole, Thomas S. Langer, Stanley T. Michael, Marvin K. Opler and Thomas A. C. Rennie, *Mental Health in the Metropolis*, McGraw-Hill (New York 1962); Dorothea C. Leighton, John S. Harding, David B. Macklin, Alistair M. MacMillan and Alexander H. Leighton, *The Character of Danger*, Basic Books (New York 1963).

9. As seen in the works of: Howard S. Becker, *Outsiders*, The Free Press (Glencoe, Ill., 1963); Kai T. Erikson, 'Notes on the Sociology of Deviance', *Social Problems*, 9, Spring 1962, pp. 307-14; Erving Goffman, *Stigma—Notes on the Management of Spoiled Identity*, Prentice Hall (Englewood Cliffs, NJ, 1963); Wendell Johnson, *Stuttering*, University of Minnesota Press (Minneapolis 1961); John I. Kitsuse, 'Societal Reaction to Deviant Behaviour: Problems of Theory and Method', in Howard S. Becker (ed.), *The Other Side*, The Free Press (Glencoe, Ill., 1964), pp. 87-102; Edwin M. Lemert, *Social Pathology*, McGraw-Hill (New York 1951); Thomas J. Scheff, 'The Societal Reaction to Deviance: Ascriptive Elements in the Psychiatric Screening of Mental Patients in a Midwestern State', *Social Problems*, 11, Spring 1964, pp. 401-13.

10. See, for example: Edward S. Suchman, 'Stages of Illness and Medical Care', *Journal of Health and Human Behaviour*, 6, Fall 1965, pp. 114-28.

11. Margaret Clark, *Health in the Mexican-American Culture*, University of California Press (Berkeley 1958).

12. Richard H. Blum, *The Management of the Doctor/Patient Relationship*, McGraw-Hill (New York 1960), p. 11.

13. Earl L. Koos, *The Health of Regionville*, Columbia University Press (New York 1954).

14. Erwin W. Ackerknecht, 'The Role of Medical History in Medical Education', *Bulletin of History of Medicine*, 21, March/April 1947, pp. 135-45; Allan B. Raper, 'The Incidence of Peptic Ulceration in Some African Tribal Groups', *Transactions*

of the Royal Society of Tropical Medicine and Hygiene, 152, November 1958, pp. 535-46.

15. Ackerknecht, 'Role of Medical History', *Bull. Hist. Med.*, 1947, *op. cit.*

16. Anthony F. C. Wallace, 'Cultural Determinants of Response to Hallucinatory Experience', *Archives of General Psychiatry*, 1, July 1959, pp. 58-69.

17. For the specific delineation of this process, I am grateful to: Barbara L. Carter, 'Non-Physiological Dimensions of Health and Illness', Brandeis University (Waltham 1965).

18. For detail on this syndrome, see: Betty Friedan, *The Feminine Mystique*, Dell (New York 1963); Richard E. Gordon, Katherine K. Gordon, and Max Gunther, *The Split-Level Trap*, Dell (New York 1962).

19. This section on 'female troubles' was suggested by the following readings: Simone de Beauvoir, *The Second Sex*, Knopf (New York 1957); Helene Deutsch, *The Psychology of Women*, Grune & Stratton (New York 1944); Margaret Mead, *Male and Female*, Morrow (New York 1949).

20. Margaret Mead, *Sex and Temperament in Three Primitive Societies*, Mentor (New York 1950).

21. Mead, *Male and Female*, 1949, *op. cit.*

22. Mead, *Male and Female*, 1949, *op. cit.*

23. Becker, *Outsiders*, 1963, *op. cit.*

24. Stanley Schachter and Jerome Singer, 'Cognitive, Social and Physiological Determinants of Emotional State', *Psychological Review*, 69, September 1962, pp. 379-87.

25. A term used by Drs R. Green and K. Dalton, as quoted in Hans Selye, *The Stress of Life*, McGraw-Hill (New York 1956), p. 177.

26. John Kosa, Joel Alpert, M. Ruth Pickering and Robert J. Haggerty, 'Crisis and Family Life: A Re-examination of Concepts', *The Wisconsin Sociologist*, 4, Summer 1965, pp. 11-19.

27. Saxon Graham, 'Ethnic Background and Illness in a Pennsylvania County', *Social Problems*, 4, July 1956, pp. 76-81.

28. Raper, 'Peptic Ulceration', *Trans. R. Soc. Trop. Med & Hyg.*, 1958, *op. cit.*

29. Oscar Handlin, *Race and Nationality in American Life*, Doubleday (Garden City, NY, 1957); Oscar Handlin, *Boston's Immigrants*, Harvard University Press (Cambridge, Mass., 1959).

30. For details, see: Irving Kenneth Zola, *Socio-cultural factors in the Seeking of Medical Aid*, unpublished doctoral dissertation, Harvard University, Department of Social Relations, 1962.

31. The range of methods includes: case research analysis, Berta Fantl and Joseph Schiro, 'Cultural Variables in the Behaviour Patterns and Symptom Formation of Fifteen Irish and Fifteen Italian Female Schizophrenics', *International Journal of Social Psychiatry*, 4, Spring 1959, pp. 245-53; check lists, Cornerly and Bigman, *Changing Health Attitudes*, 1961, *op. cit.*; standardized questionnaires, Sydney H. Croog, 'Ethnic Origins and Responses to Health Questionnaires', *Human Organization*, 20, Summer 1961, pp. 65-9; commitment papers, John B. Enright and Walter R. Jaeckle, 'Psychiatric Symptoms and Diseases in Two Subcultures', *International Journal of Social Psychiatry*, 9, Winter 1963, pp. 12-17; interview and questionnaire, Graham, 'Ethnic Background and Illness', *Soc. Prob.*, 1956, *op. cit.*; Mark Zborowski, 'Cultural Components in Response to Pain', *Journal of Social Issues*, 8, Fall 1952, pp. 16-30; interview and psychological tests, Marvin K. Opler and Jerome L. Singer, 'Ethnic Differences in Behaviour and Psychopathology: Italian and Irish', *International Journal of Social Psychiatry*, 2, Summer 1956, pp. 11-12; observation, Clark, *Mexican-American Culture*, 1958, *op. cit.*

32. See Jacob J. Feldman, 'The Household Interview Survey as a Technique for the Collection of Morbidity Data', *Journal of Chronic Diseases*, 11, May 1960, pp. 535-57; Theodore D. Woolsey, 'The Health Survey', presented at the session, 'The

Contributions of Research in the Field of Health', 1959 AAPOR Conference, May 1959, Lake George, New York.

33. Charles Kadushin, 'The Meaning of Presenting Problems: A Sociology of Defences', paper read at the 1962 annual meeting of the American Sociological Association.

34. Opler and Singer, 'Ethnic Differences', *Int. J. of Soc. Psych.*, 1956, *op. cit.*

35. Conrad M. Arensberg and Solon T. Kimball, *Family and Community in Ireland*, Harvard University Press (Cambridge, Mass., 1948).

36. W. Lloyd Warner, *Social Class in America*, Science Research Associates (Chicago 1949).

37. Rosenfeld *et al., Needs annd Services in Boston*, 1957, *op cit.*

38. Zborowski, 'Cultural Components', *J. Soc. Iss.*, 1952, *op. cit.*

39. See: Sidney Siegel, *Non-parametric Statistics for the Behavioural Sciences.* McGraw-Hill (New York 1956), pp. 68-75.

40. William P. Chapman and Chester M. Jones, 'Variations in Cutaneous and Visceral Pain Sensitivity in Normal Subjects', *Journal of Clinical Investigation*, 23, January 1944, pp. 81-91; James D. Hardy, Harold G. Wolff and Helen Goodell, *Pain Sensations and Reactions*, Williams & Wilkins (Baltimore 1952); Ronald Melzack, 'The Perception of Pain', *Scientific American*, 204, February 1961, pp. 41-9; Harry S. Olin and Thomas P. Hackett, 'The Denial of Chest Pain in Thirty-two Patients with Acute Myocardial Infection', *Journal of the American Medical Association*, 190, December 1964, pp. 977-81; Zborowski, 'Cultural Components', *J. Soc Iss.*, 1952, *op. cit.*

41. The whole specific/diffuse pattern and the generalizing/withholding illness behaviour dovetails neatly with the empirical findings of Opler and Singer, 'Ethnic Differences', *Int. J. of Soc. Psych.*, 1956, *op. cit.*, Fantl and Schiro, 'Cultural Variables', *Int. J. of Soc. Psych.*, 1959, *op. cit.*, and Paul Barrabee and Otto von Mering, 'Ethnic Variations in Mental Stress in Families and Psychotic Children', *Social Problems*, 1, October 1953, pp. 48-53. The specific emphasis on expressiveness has been detailed especially by Zborowski, 'Cultural Components', *J. Soc. Iss.*, 1952, *op. cit.* and the several studies of Italian mental patients done by Anne Parsons, 'Some Comparative Observations on Ward Social Structure: Southern Italy, England, and the United States', *Tipografia dell'Ospedale Psichiatrico*, Napoli, April 1959; 'Family Dynamics in Southern Italian Schizophrenics', *Archives of General Psychiatry*, 3, November 1960, pp. 507-18, 'Patriarchal and Matriarchal Authority in the Neapolitan Slum', *Psychiatry*, 24, May 1961, pp. 109-21. The contrast on number of symptoms has been noted by Groog, 'Ethnic Origins', 1961, *op. cit.*, and Graham, *op. cit.*

42. Florence R. Kluckhohn, 'Dominant and Variant Value Orientations', in Clyde Kluckhohn, Henry A. Murray and David M. Schneider (eds.), *Personality in Nature, Society and Culture*, Knopf, 2nd edition (New York 1956), pp. 342-57; Florence R. Kluckhohn and Fred L. Strodtbeck, *Variations in Value Orientations*, Row Peterson (Evanston, Ill., 1961); John Spiegel, 'Conflicting Formal and Informal Roles in Newly Acculturated Families', in *Disorders of Communication*, Vol. XLII, Research Publications, Association for Research in Nervous and Mental Disease, 1964, pp. 307-16; John P. Spiegel and Florence R. Kluckhohn, 'The Influence of the Family and Cultural Values on the Mental Health and Illness of the Individual', Unpublished progress report of Grant M-971, US Public Health Service.

43. Anna Freud, *The Ego and the Mechanisms of Defence*, Hogarth (London 1954).

44. Barbara Blackwell, 'The Literature of Delay in Seeking Medical Care for Chronic Illnesses', *Health Education Monographs*, 16, 1963, pp. 3-32; Bernard Kutner, Henry B. Malcover and Abraham Oppenheim, 'Delay in the Diagnosis and Treatment of Cancer', *Journal of Chronic Diseases*, 7, January 1958, pp. 95-120; 'Seeking Care for Cancer', *Journal of Health and Human Behaviour*, 2, Fall 1961, pp. 171-8.

45. In addition to the references cited in notes 41 and 42 above, we have drawn our picture from many sociological, literary and historical works. A complete bibliography is available on request. For the compilation and annotation of many of these references I am particularly indebted to Mrs Marlene Hindley.

46. Anne Parsons, 'Authority', *Psychiatry*, 1961, *op. cit.*, p. 26.

47. Luigi Barzini, *The Italians*, Bantam (New York 1965), p. 104.

48. In addition to the papers cited in note 41 above, Arensberg and Kimball, *Ireland*, 1948, *op. cit.*, remains the classic reference work.

49. Spiegel and Kluckhohn, 'Influence of the Family and Cultural Values', unpublished, *op. cit.*

50. Such a problem was explicitly stated and investigated by Ellen Silver, 'The Influence of Culture on Personality: A Comparison of the Irish and Italians with Emphasis on Fantasy Behaviour', mimeographed, Harvard University, 1958, in her attempted replication of the Opler and Singer work, 'Ethnic Differences', *Int. J. of Soc. Psych.*, 1956, *op. cit.*, and was emphasized by the somewhat ambiguous findings of Rena S. Grossman, 'Ethnic Differences in the Apperception of Pain', unpublished undergraduate honours thesis, Department of Social Relations, Radcliffe College, 1964, in her replication of Zborowski's findings, 'Cultural Components', *J. Soc. Iss.*, 1952, *op. cit.*, on a non-hospitalized population.

51. Several examples are more fully delineated in Irving Kenneth Zola, 'Illness Behaviour of the Working Class: Implications and Recommendations', in Arthur B. Shostak and William Gomberg (eds), *Blue Collar World*, Prentice Hall (Englewood Cliffs, NJ, 1964), pp. 350-61.

52. This may be done to such an extreme that it is the physician's response which creates epidemiological differences. Such a potential situation was noted using data from the present study and is detailed in Irving Kenneth Zola, 'Problems of Communication, Diagnosis, and Patient Care: The Interplay of Patient, Physician and Clinic Organization', *Journal of Medical Education*, 38, October 1963, pp. 829-38.

53. The explanations of such differences have, however, more often emphasized negative aspects of the respondents' background—their lower education, lower socio-economic status, lesser psychological sophistication, and greater resistance and anti-pathy—by virtue of their membership in certain racial and cultural minorities. See Bernard Bergen, 'Social Class, Symptoms, and Sensitivity to Descriptions of Mental Illness—Implications for Programmes of Preventive Psychiatry', unpublished doctoral dissertation, Harvard University, 1962; Elaine Cumming and John Cumming, *Closed Ranks: An Experiment in Mental Health Education*, Harvard University Press (Cambridge 1957); Howard E. Freeman and Gene G. Kassebaum, 'Relationship of Education and Knowledge to Opinions about Mental Illness', *Mental Hygiene*, 44, January 1960, pp. 43-47; Gerald Gurin, Joseph Veroff and Sheila Feld, *Americans View Their Mental Health*, Basic Books (New York 1960); Jum C. Nunnally, *Popular Conceptions of Mental Health*, Holt, Rinehart & Winston (New York 1961); Glenn V. Ramsey and Melita Seipp, 'Attitudes and Opinions Concerning Mental Illness', *Psychiatric Quarterly*, 22, July 1949, pp. 1-17; Elmo Roper and associates, *People's Attitudes Concerning Mental Health*, private publication (New York 1950); Shirley Star, 'The Public's Ideas about Mental Illness', paper presented to the annual meeting of the American Association for Public Opinion Research, Washington, DC., 1957; Julian L. Woodward, 'Changing Ideas on Mental Illness and Its Treatment', *American Sociological Review*, 16, August 1951, pp. 443-54.

54. This approach is evident in such works as: Stanley King, *Perceptions of Illness and Medical Practice*, Russell Sage Foundation, New York 1962, *op. cit.*; Clyde Kluckhohn, 'Culture and Behaviour' in Gardner Lindzey, *Handbook of Social Psychology*, Addison-Wesley (Cambridge 1954), Vol. 2, pp. 921-76; Walter B. Miller, 'Lower Class Culture as a Generating Milieu of Gang Delinquency', *Journal of Social Issues*, 14, July 1958, pp. 5-19; Marvin K. Opler, *Culture, Psychiatry and Human Values*, Charles C. Thomas (Springfield, Ill., 1956); Marvin K. Opler, *Culture*

and Mental Health, Macmillan (New York 1959); Benjamin D. Paul, *Health, Culture and Community—Case Studies of Public Reactions to Health Programmes*, Russell Sage Foundation (New York 1955); Lyle Saunders, *Cultural Differences and Medical Care*, Russell Sage Foundation (New York 1954); Henry J. Wegroski, 'A Critique of Cultural and Statistical Concepts of Abnormality', in Clyde Kluckhohn, Henry A. Murray and David M. Schneider, *Personality in Nature, Society and Culture*, Knopf, revised edition (New York 1956), pp. 691-701.

55. This is spelled out from various points of view in such works as: Samuel Butler, *Erewhon*, Signet (New York 1961); René Dubos, *Mirage of Health*, 1961, *op. cit.*, Josephine D. Lohman (participant), 'Juvenile Delinquency: Its Dimensions, its Conditions, Techniques of Control, Proposals for Action', subcommittee on Juvenile Delinquency of the Senate Committee on Labor and Public Welfare, 86th Congress, S. 765, S. 1314, Spring 1959, p. 268; Talcott Parsons, 'Social Change and Medical Organization in the United States: A Sociological Perspective', *Annals of the American Academy of Political and Social Science*, 346, March 1963, pp. 21-34; Edwin M. Schur, *Crimes without Victims—Deviant Behaviour and Public Policy*, Prentice Hall (Englewood Cliffs, NJ, 1965); Thomas Szasz, *The Myth of Mental Illness*, Hoeber-Harper (New York 1961); Thomas Szasz, *Law, Liberty and Psychiatry*, Macmillan (New York 1963); Irving Kenneth Zola, 'Problems for Research: Some Effects of Assumptions Underlying Socio-Medical Investigations', in Gerald Gordon (ed.), *Proceedings, Conference on Medical Sociology and Disease Control*, National Tuberculosis Association, 1966, pp. 9-17.

2 | *Values, social class and community health services*

N. MILIO

A distinction can be made between the value orientations of the middle and lower social classes. These distinctions are important with respect to variations in health attitudes and behaviour. A group of maternity patients was studied in order to increase understanding of the influence of social class membership on health activities during pregnancy. Middle-class women were found to adhere most closely to the 'ideal' prenatal regime recommended by their medical practitioners. Interestingly, however, although lower-class women were less likely to follow the 'ideal' regime, their pregnancies were relatively uneventful and they had healthy babies. This suggests that the medical profession's 'ideal' pattern of prenatal activities is influenced by dominant middle-class beliefs, rather than physiologically-based requirements. If lower-class patients are to receive relevant and appropriate medical care, a clear explication of the lower-class value system is required, attention being paid to the ordering of values contained therein and the ways in which these are related to patterns of living.

This paper presents an example of the way in which the value assumptions of the dominant social group, namely the middle classes, underlie the organization of the dominant social institutions and provide criteria for evaluating behaviour in those institutions. In this case it is the system of community health services and the prenatal care system in particular.

Awareness in the field of public health of rising rates of pre-maturity and infant deaths among low-income urban populations has stimulated increasing efforts to reduce these rates. The focus has been on the expansion of maternity services, that is, on the elaboration of the system as it exists. This study attempts to refocus the approach to maternity problems by asking what it is in the orientation of the lower-class population which devalues activities prescribed by the medical profession to ensure a healthy mother and baby.

THEORETICAL FOUNDATIONS

The frame of reference assumed is that of Parsons's theory of action.[1] Human behaviour is oriented to the attainment of valued states. The actor relates only to that part of theenvironment which has significance for him as focused by his value orientation.

Behaviour patterns and culture orientations

A variety of studies support the descriptions of middle-class values offered by Parsons and Florence Kluckhohn—that is of an activistic, rational mastery, future-time orientation to life.[2] These studies reflect a middle-class emphasis on the future, on planning, on the deferment of gratification and on education as the means for achievement.[3] Also consistent with the middle-class view is involvement in formal voluntary associations, the use of bureaucratic forms and elaborate networks of committees and confidence in 'experts' or professionals as rational means for manipulating the environment.[4]

A future-time orientation implies the importance of the next generation. Children are therefore considered a worthy investment.[5] They are planned for, and mothers are 'delighted' with their pregnancies.[6] They are reared without overt hostility and are taught to defer gratification and to see themselves as 'I', that is individualistically.[7] They become imbued with their parents' high aspirations for occupational and social success.[8]

The formal social institutions, generally reflective of this dominant culture value system, are readily accessible to the middle classes and are therefore supportive in perpetuating the dominant pattern.[9]

But under the conditions of 'anomie' described by Robert Merton where culturally-defined goals are inaccessible by socially-structured means the deprived group alters its focus.[10] The shift is from the dominant value system to a variant system of values, standards, and expectations achievable by the subordinate culture group.

Thus the lower classes, whose position in the social structure does not support a belief in the rational mastery of the world, tend to reflect a passive or at least non-achievement orientation, with a focus on adjustment rather than control.[11] Occurrences are viewed as 'luck' rather than as by rational design.[12] The emphasis is on the present and on the immediate gratification of needs, particularly in the concrete, physical realm.[13] Planning, education and involvement in organized activity are less important in this framework.[14] Peers rather than 'experts' or professionals are influential.[15]

Children, insofar as they represent the future, are therefore less central. They tend to be unplanned; mothers' feelings about them tend to be overtly expressed.[16] They are not reared in a rational, consistent manner as judged by paediatricians; the 'I' is not stressed; the present, not the future, becomes encapsulated in their speech; and they are thus equipped to think and live in the present.[17] Their aspirations are low.[18]

Health attitudes and culture orientations
Conceptions of health and well-being mirror social class orientations. Health, as 'the state of optimum capacity for the effective performance of valued tasks', means for the middle classes a level of functioning which will allow occupational achievement and social mobility.[19] In the lower classes the 'valued tasks' on which the person is evaluated occur in the present and are related to physical activity. 'Optimum capacity' means 'immediate ability' to gratify needs. Incapacity then becomes what is disruptive of immediate satisfaction or comfort and is dealt with when it occurs. Health thus has narrow, shorter-range requirements.

Maternity behaviour and culture orientations
Social-class orientation likewise provides the frame of reference in which women respond to the circumstance of pregnancy. A 'maternity activities pattern' (MAP) emerges. This is defined as the characteristic pattern of activities engaged in by women from their awareness of their pregnancy through delivery.

It is to be expected then that (i) the pattern of maternity activities prescribed by the obstetrical specialist as the ideal would be most closely adhered to by the middle classes; (ii) this ideal pattern of activities might not be essential in its entirety to ensure a normal birth; and (iii) the prenatal care system available to encourage this pattern would be based generally on middle-class assumptions. Thus, both the ideal pattern and the system of prenatal care become relatively inaccessible to the lower-class sub-culture.

METHOD

In order to determine this activity pattern the clinic and private physicians' prenatal records and the hospital delivery records of 569 women were examined. These women were the total number of patients in eight Detroit census tracts who gave birth to their babies in 1963 (except for an estimated seventy-seven illegitimate births which were not included in the data).

The subjects were divided into six social classes, from lower-lower to upper-middle, on the basis of Warner's Index of Status Characteristics consisting of occupation, source of income, and housing area.[20]

The maternity activities pattern was measured according to a three-part scale (Tables 1, 2, 3) intended to reflect (MAP I) the woman's physical condition in approaching the pregnancy (implying the level of health prior to pregnancy); (MAP II) her response to the pregnancy during its course (consisting of a range of activities over which she has some degree of control) and (MAP III) the outcome of the pregnancy which is presumably favourable if she follows the prescribed pattern.

Table 1

Criteria for MAP I score indicating physical condition on approach to pregnancy

Item	Criteria	Weight (Item Score)
1. Medical history[21]	History of Heart disease, high blood pressure, kidney disease, rheumatic fever, diabetes, cancer, venereal disease	0
	No history of above	1
2. Non-pregnant weight[22]	Less than 100 lbs	0
	100 to 165 lbs	1
	More than 165 lbs	0
3. Initial haemoglobin level[23]	Less than 10 Gm	0
	10-10·9 Gm	1
	11-11·9 Gm	2
	12-14 Gm	3
	14·1 Gm or more	4
	Maximum Score=6	

Table 2

Criteria for MAP II score indicating response to pregnancy

Item	Criteria	Weight (Item Score)
4. Initiation of prenatal care[24]	First trimester (weeks 1-13)	3
	Second trimester (weeks 14-26)	2
	Third trimester (weeks 27-40)	1
	No prenatal care	0
5. Number of prenatal visits[25]	9 or more	3
	5-8	2
	1-4	1
	0	0
6. Amount of weight gain[26]	Up to 24 lbs	2
	25-30 lbs	1
	Over 30 lbs	0
7. Rate of weight gain[27]	11 lbs or less in second trimester (or less than 15 lbs in trimesters 1 and 2)	1
	11 lbs or less in third trimester	1
8. Prenatal complications and missed appointments*	No complications	1
	Complications present, no missed appointments	1
	Complications present, missed appointments	0
9. Haemoglobin level at term[28]	Less than 10 Gm	0
	10-11 Gm	1
	11·1 Gm or more	2
10. Length of pregnancy	38 weeks or more	2
	28-37 weeks	1
	Less than 28 weeks	0
11. Place of delivery†	Planned	1
	Not planned	0
	Maximum Score=16	

* Conditions regarded as evidence of complications were vaginal bleeding; stated pre-eclampsia, eclampsia, or toxaemia; elevation of blood pressure over 140, blood pressure increase of more than 30 points, albuminuria, edema, scotomata, nausea and vomiting in the third trimester; severe respiratory or genito-urinary infection; premature rupture of membranes; blood incompatibility.[29]

† Hospital deliveries were considered to indicate some preparation; deliveries in ambulance, emergency room, or at home were considered unplanned.

The fifteen-item scale includes the generally accepted criteria of maternity care evaluation; each was weighted according to current medical data. The sum of the weighted items gave the MAP score. This score was evaluated in five gradations from excellent or ideal to very poor.

The excellent or ideal range (27-29) meant that the woman began prenatal care within the first three months of gestation and was in good health and of normal weight at the time; she made at least nine visits to the doctor prior to delivery, gained not more than twenty-four pounds in nine months and at a rate of not more than eleven pounds in each of the last two trimesters; if complications occurred, she missed no appointments and delivered in a hospital after thirty-eight weeks. There were no complications at delivery; the baby weighed over six and a half pounds and was in good condition.

Table 3

Criteria for MAP III score indicating response to pregnancy

Item	Criteria	Weight (Item Score)
12. Intrapartal Complications* (occurring at delivery)	If present	0
	If absent	1
13. Newborn weight†, ‡	6 lbs 9 oz or more	3
	5 lbs 9 oz-6 lbs 8 oz	2
	4 lbs 11 oz-5 lbs 8 oz	1
	2 lbs 10 oz-4 lbs 10 oz	1
	Less than 2 lbs 10 oz or deceased	0
14. Condition of baby§	Satisfactory	2
	Poor	1
	Deceased	0
15. Birth Anomalies or defects‖	If present	0
	If absent	1
	Maximum Score=7	

* Conditions regarded as complications were placenta previa, abruptio placenta, rupture of the uterus, intrapartal haemorrhage, dystocia, prolonged labour, cephalo-pelvic disproportion, uterine inertia, emergency Caesarian-section, prolapse of the cord, incompetent cervix.[30]

† In a study of ninety-seven surviving prematures weighing 3 lbs 4 oz or less at birth, there was found to be more frequent and more severe illness in the first 10 years of life in those with the lower birth weights. No significant correlation was found between obstetrical problems and birth weight. This finding is significant for the conclusions of the MAP Study also.[31]

‡ The risk of death is strongly influenced by birthweight. This risk increases rapidly as birthweight falls below 5 lbs 8 oz. Prematurity (as measured by a birthweight of 5 lbs 8 oz or less) is associated with increased risk of retarded mental development, neurologic disorders, etc. as a result of anoxic-producing prenatal or intrapartal conditions.[32]

§ As indicated by the physician on the delivery record.

‖ Conditions noted by the attending physicians on the delivery records included missing or extra digits, cleft lip and cleft palate, spina bifida, the meningoceles and club foot. The rationale for using this item was that although genetic factors play a large role in producing the above anomalies, other factors, such as the indiscriminate use of drugs or x-ray, and certain viruses and medical disorders, may be guarded against by adequate medical supervision in the prenatal period.[33]

A satisfactory score (17-21) meant that the woman began her prenatal care in the second trimester of pregnancy and might have been a little anaemic at the time; she made from five to eight visits to the doctor, probably gained from twenty-five to thirty pounds, may have had swollen ankles and missed an appointment or delivered between the twenty-eighth and thirty-seventh week of pregnancy. Delivery was in the hospital and the baby would have weighed between five and a half and six and a half pounds and was in good condition.

A poor or very poor score would have meant the woman was ill during pregnancy or began prenatal care very late or not at all, and the baby was premature and/or in poor or abnormal condition.

Table 4

Relationship between age, race, number of children and socio-economic status and maternity activities pattern score—N = 569

	MAP Score*	
Variable	*Coefficient of Correlation*	*t-value†*
Age	0·09	1·6844
Race	0·36	6·8158
No. of Children	−0·07	−1·3390
SES	0·45	8·8210

* The product-moment (Pearsonian) correlation coefficient was used. Fisher's *t* test statistic was used in addition to make meaningful comparisons among the social class categories, which were of uneven size. The correlation coefficients and *t*-values were calculated at the Wayne State University Computing and Data Processing Center.

† Significant above 1·960 on a two-tailed test at ≤P = 0·05.

Scores were analysed according to their distribution among the social classes and in other age and race groupings.

The small numbers in the higher social classes require that generalizations for those groups must be tentative, although the consistency of scores adds to their reliability.

The inclusion of illegitimate births, the vast majority of which occurred in the lower classes, would have presumably increased the differences between lower- and middle-class scores.

ANALYSIS

Maternity behaviour as a dominant culture pattern
Although certain statistically significant relationships were found between variables of age, race, number of children and various kinds of maternity activities, these relationships almost completely disappeared when examined

along social class lines. In other words, among the variable examined, a woman's place in society (SES) was the most influential factor in producing her pattern of maternity activities ($t=8\cdot821$; Table 4).

Table 5

Frequency and percentage distribution of the total maternity activities pattern scores by social class

		Total MAP score*				
Social class	Number	Very Poor Less than 14	Poor 14-16	Satisfactory 17-24	Good 22-26	Excellent or 'Ideal' 27-29
Lower-Lower	125	2 (1·6)	9 (7·1)	75 (59·5)	37 (29·3)	2 (1·6)
Middle-Lower	79	2 (2·5)	1 (1·2)	38 (48·5)	35 (44·3)	3 (3·7)
Upper-Lower	35	—	1 (2·8)	8 (22·8)	23 (65·7)	3 (8·5)
Lower-Middle	27	—	—	5 (18·5)	19 (70·3)	3 (11·2)
Middle-Middle	7	—	—	2 (28·5)	4 (57·1)	1 (14·4)
Upper-Middle	22	—	—	—	15 (68·1)	7 (31·9)
Total	295	4	11	128	133	19

* Figures in parentheses are percentage of number in each social class.

Examination of the distribution of the complete MAP Scores (Table 5) which were obtained on 295 women shows how the scores uniformly increased with socio-economic status. (Partial scores [I, II, III] were obtained and evaluated on 549 women. This was necessary because some of these fifteen items were missing from certain records. These scores were generally consistent with the complete scores.) In the lower-lower class (N=125), about 60% were satisfactory and 30% were good. In the middle-lower class (N=79), almost 50% were satisfactory and 44% good. Combining the next two social classes (N=62), 70% were good, and about 10% ideal; there were no very poor scores. Combining the two highest classes (N=29), 65% were good and 28% ideal, with no poor or very poor scores.

The second point that adherence to the ideal maternity activity pattern is not essential in its entirety to a normal delivery is also supported by the data. There is a stronger significant relationship between a woman's social class and the patterning of her activities in pregnancy ($t=8\cdot8210$—$p<0\cdot001$), than between those activities and the health of her baby, as indicated by birth weight ($t=7.470$—$p<0.001$). In other words, attaining just a 'satisfactory' score ensured a normal birth.

These findings concur with certain recent medical studies regarding the unrelatedness of aspects of prenatal care for producing a normal delivery.[34]

Thus the nonessential nature of the prescribed or ideal MAP further supports the hypothesis that it is a dominant culture pattern, and not a physiologically-based requirement.

The prenatal care system as a reflection of dominant culture

The health care system established to support the prescribed pattern of maternity activities would be expected to focus on the needs implied by the middle-class orientation. The prenatal care system as it exists assumes in effect the *same* hierarchy of needs (and therefore the same value hierarchy) for *all* pregnant women. In a sense, the fact of pregnancy in a woman's life, regardless of her life situation, is assumed to transform her into 'the pregnant woman'.

Such assumptions are reflected in statements by physicians who describe primary needs to be dealt with in prenatal care:

> In modern American culture, the expectant father feels more than a little lost. He has to put up with a lot of discomfort and privation, and he feels that he has no useful function....[35] [There is the anxiety and uncertainty of parents] about themselves and their behaviour, over the coming baby, and the new life after the baby comes.... [The pregnant woman manifests] dependent, regressive behaviour.... [These needs are] *universal and tend to follow a pattern in sequence and intensity*.[36] (The italics are ours.)

As such psychological needs are thus identified by the professions the prenatal care system evolves to meet them in for example 'preparation for childbirth' programmes and 'psychoprophylaxis' methods designed to 'refocus attention on the importance of emotional support during child-bearing'.[36] Consistent with this focus is the growth of associations to foster the 'natural childbirth movement' (the LaMaze Society). Akin to these with their middle and upper-middle class membership is LaLeche International which addresses itself to the new mother so that she can 'know that all over the country womanly women are breast feeding their babies and [that] ... advice and encouragement are available if you need them in learning this most womanly art.'[37]

Other structures in the prenatal care system are expectant parents' classes. The content of these classes is intended to reflect the 'concerns' of expectant parents; and the 'concerns' of expectant parents are derived from those who attend the classes—who are almost invariably the patients of private physicians.[38]

The organization of the system also assumes middle-class economic status. The cost of the predominant type of obstetrical care provided by the private physician has assumed the financial capacity of the middle-income family.

Where lower-cost clinic facilities exist, their central location in large cities assumes, unrealistically, ease of transportation for the lower-class woman; their location also unrealistically assumes a strong inclination for pregnant women to seek prenatal care. Such misplaced assumptions have resulted in an uneven distribution of prenatal care among social classes.

This situation illustrates Simmons's contention that the felt needs of the public (which is essentially the dominant social group) determine the appropriate foci of interest and activity in the field of public health.[39] Thus where there is a relative disparity of health care activity, it will occur in those health areas which pose no problem to the dominant social classes.

Finally, the attempts to improve the prenatal care system often reflect middle-class assumptions. The following is used as an illustration. At a conference in New York following observations gathered at twelve city clinics by public health personnel 'the question was raised as to why so many women fail to avail themselves of prenatal services *even though they have been told* how important early, continuing care is to their own *welfare* and that of their children. The conclusion was inescapable that *there are things in* our clinic systems which discourage mothers from registering early and persisting in care.'[40] (The italics are ours.)

This statement assumes that the women eligible to attend the New York City clinics (women in the lower classes) possess the same value hierarchy and attend to the same priorities in their life situations as pregnant women who seek a private obstetrician (women in the middle classes). It assumes that the concept of personal welfare and of essentials is the same. It therefore assumes that there are impediments in the clinic system which if removed would result in the desired behaviour; in other words lower-class women would begin to behave like middle-class women.

This approach then prevents seeing the system as based on cultural values which are alien to the women it is seeking to serve, and that it may be the system itself and the assumptions upon which it is based that are the real deterrents to the goal of relevant and appropriate prenatal care for the lower classes.

DISCUSSION

This statistical and illustrative data suggests that the pattern of maternity activities prescribed as ideal for all women who become pregnant is consistent with a rational-mastery, future-time orientation held by the dominant middle-class culture. The structures in the prenatal care system which function to support this pattern are based on and maintained under the same culture view of life.

However, this ideal pattern and the structures which support it are inaccessible to those who hold an alternative and opposing view of life, a view more tolerable within the limitations of their social status. The passive-adjustive, present-time orientation of the lower classes produces behaviour which does not uphold the ideal maternity activities patttern and which cannot readily make use of the health care system which has evolved to support that ideal.

As to the implications for the social sciences, it is apparent that clearer explication of the orientation of the lower classes is needed and in particular of the webs of variation that exist among low-income populations. This is especially needed at this time because of the dynamic being created by the goads of the civil rights movement and the anti-poverty programmes. More knowledge also is needed of the ranking of values, the informal social organization, and patterns of communication among lower-class groups.

As to the implications for service-oriented institutions, such as the public health services system, it is clear that (i) the health services provided for the lower classes ought to be based on physiological requirements (not on a middle-class mystique), and (ii) such services ought to be provided in a form consistent with the orientation and pattern of living of low-income populations. This would seem to include truly neighbourhood-based non-bureaucratic structures utilizing low-income people for staffing and evolving programmes which reflect *their* interests. These components would provide media of communication between the middle-class professional and the lower-class patient. Then, as contact occurs in such a setting, appropriate public health measures of a preventive or therapeutic nature can be instituted. Such an approach is being attempted by the Visiting Nurse Association of metropolitan Detroit.

If the profession of nursing is to fulfil its responsibility for the quality of care received by patients we must do more than simply acknowledge the inequities which exist in the care of low-income groups. We must recognize that *quality* of care cannot be separated from the *form* in which the care is given, that there is no one ideal form or approach, that we have as yet not found appropriate and relevant ways of serving many non-middle-class groups and that it is *our* responsibility to take the initiative in making attempts at innovation.

This obviously cannot be done by nursing alone. Where necessary we must involve the medical profession and other public health and helping professions.

Awareness of the knowledge available in the social sciences can provide guidelines for designing new ways to provide relevant preventive and therapeutic services to the urban poor. Such knowledge could be had through collaboration, for example between service-oriented agencies and the graduate or research faculty of a college of nursing (or of a liberal arts college). Using increasingly available experimental monies, new approaches could thus be tried and tested, and where effective, could be integrated into the programme of the service agency.

The difficulties of such collaboration have been described in the literature and are well known by those who have made attempts at it. These difficulties may be even more pronounced given the present stage of nursing as a profession. However rapid changes in the field of patient care continue. Choices about the direction of those changes are now being made. If we do not make the choices about the ways in which human beings are to be made and kept whole, those choices will be made for us.

REFERENCES

1. Talcott Parsons and E. A. Shils (eds), *Towards a General Theory of Action*, Harper Bros. (New York 1962), pp. 53-60.
2. Florence R. Kluckhohn, 'Dominant and Substitute Profiles of Cultural Orientations; Their Significance for the Analysis of Social Stratification', *Social Forces*, 28, May 1950, pp. 376-93.
3. O. B. Brim, Jr and Raymond Forer, 'A Note on the Relation of Values and Social Structure to Life Planning', *Sociometry*, 19, March 1956, pp. 54-60; Herbert Hyman, 'The Value Systems of Different Classes', in Reinhard Bendix and S. M. Lipset (eds), *Class, Status and Social Power*, Free Press (Glencoe, Ill., 1953), pp. 426-42; C. C. McArthur, 'Personalities of Public and Private School Boys', *Harvard Educational Review*, 24 (no. 4), 1954, pp. 256-61; M. A. Straus, 'Deferred Gratification, Social Class, and the Achievement Syndrome', *American Sociological Review*, 27, June 1962, pp. 326-35.
4. Morris Axelrod, 'Urban Structure and Social Participation', *American Sociological Review*, 21, February 1956, pp. 13-18; G. E. Lenski, 'Social Correlates of Religious Interest', *American Sociological Review*, 18, October 1953, pp. 533-44; Ashley Weeks *et al.*, 'Apathy of Families Towards Medical Care: An Exploratory Study', in Gartly Jaco (ed.), *Patients, Physicians and Illness; Sourcebook in Behavioural Science and Medicine*, Free Press (Glencoe, Ill., 1958), pp. 159-64.
5. Lee Rainwater *et al.*, *Workingman's Wife*, Oceana Publications (New York 1959), p. 99.
6. Gerald Handel and Lee Rainwater, 'Working-Class People and Family Planning', *Social Work*, 6, April 1961, pp. 18-25; H. Wortis *et al.*, 'Child-Rearing Practice in a Low Socio-Economic Group: The Mothers of Premature Infants', *Paediatrics*, 32, August 1963, pp. 298-307.
7. Basil Bernstein, 'Social Class, Linguistic Codes and Grammatical Elements', *Language and Speech*, 5, 1961, pp. 221-40; M. L. Kohn, 'Social Class and the Exercise of Parental Authority', *American Sociological Review*, 24, June 1966, pp. 352-66; Louis Scheider and Sverre Lysgaard, 'The Deferred Gratification Pattern: A Preliminary Study', *American Sociological Review*, 18, April 1953, pp. 142-7.
8. B. C. Rosen, 'Achievement Syndrome: A Psycho-cultural Dimension of Social Stratification', *American Sociological Review*, 21, April 1956, pp. 203-11.
9. Basil Bernstein, 'Social Class and Linguistic Development: A Theory of Social Learning', in A. H. Halsey *et al.* (eds.), *Education, Economy and Society*, Free Press (New York 1967), p. 305; Basil Bernstein, 'Social Class, Speech Systems and Psychotherapy', in F. Riessman *et al.* (eds), *Mental Health of the Poor*, Free Press (New York 1964), pp. 194-204; E. A. Suchman, 'Social Factors in Medical Deprivation', *American Journal of Public Health*, 55, November 1965, pp. 1725-6; E. A. Suchman and Daniel Rosenblatt, 'Under-utilization of Medical Care Services by Blue

Collarites', in A. B. Shostak and William Gomberg, *Bluecollar World*, Prentice-Hall (Englewood Cliffs, NJ, 1964), p. 346.

10. R. K. Merton, *Social Theory and Social Structure*, Free Press, revised and enlarged edition (New York 1957).

11. Hyman, 'Value Systems', in Bendix and Lipset (eds), *Class, Status and Power*, 1953, *op. cit.*; Rosen, 'Achievement Syndrome', *Amer. Sociol. Rev.*, 1956, *op. cit.*

12. Bernstein, 'Social Class and Linguistic Development', in Halsey *et al.*, *Education, op cit.*; P. B. Cornely and S. K. Bigman, 'Some Considerations in Changing Health Attitudes', *Children*, 10, January/February 1963, pp. 23-8.

13. Basil Bernstein, 'Language and Social Class', *British Journal of Sociology*, 11, September 1960, pp. 271-6; L. L. Leshan, 'Time Orientation and Social Class', *Journal of Abnormal and Social Psychology*, 47, July 1952, pp. 589-92; E. A. Suchman, 'Medical Deprivation', *Amer J. Public Health*, 1965, *op cit.*

14. Morris Axelrod, 'Urban Structure', *Amer. Sociol. Rev.*, 1956, *op. cit.*; Hyman, 'Value Systems', in Bendix and Lipset (eds), *Class, Status and Power*, 1953, *op. cit.*; G. E. Lenski, 'Religious Interest', *Amer. Sociol. Rev.*, 1953, *op. cit.*; MacArthur, 'Public and Private School Boys', *Harvard Educ. Rev.*, 1954, *op cit.*

15. Weeks *et al.*, 'Apathy', in Gartly Jaco (ed.), *Patients, Physicians and Illness*, 1958, *op. cit.*

16. Handel and Rainwater, 'Working-Class People', *Social Work*, 1961, *op. cit.*; W. R. Rosengren, 'Social Status, Attitudes Toward Pregnancy and Child-Rearing Attitudes', *Social Forces*, 41, December 1962, pp. 127-34.

17. Bernstein, 'Social Class', *Language and Speech*, 1961, *op. cit.*; Melvin Wallace and A. I. Rabin, 'Temporal Experience', *Psychological Bulletin*, 57, May 1960, pp. 213-36; Wortis *et al.*, 'Mothers of Premature Infants', *Paediatrics*, 1963, *op cit.*

18. R. J. Havighurst and Allison Davis, 'A Comparison of the Chicago and Harvard Studies of Social Class Differences in Child-Rearing', *American Sociological Review*, 20, August 1955, pp. 438-42; W. H. Sewell *et al.*, 'Social Status and Educational and Occupational Aspiration', *American Sociological Review*, 22, February 1957, pp. 67-73.

19. Talcott Parsons, 'Definitions of Health and Illness in the Light of American Values and Social Structure', in Gartly Jaco (ed.), *Patients, Physicians and Illness*, 1958, *op cit.*, p. 168.

20. William Warner *et al.*, *Social Class in America: A Manual of Procedure for the Measurement of Social Status*, Science Research Associates (Chicago 1949), pp. 123-54.

21. Massachusetts Medical Society, 'Minimum Standards of Obstetrician Care', *New England Journal of Medicine*, 252, 28 April 1955, p. 379.

22. W. T. Tompkins and D. G. Wiehl, 'Nutritional Deficiencies as a Causal Factor in Toxaemia and Premature Labour', *American Journal of Obstetrics and Gynaecology*, 62, October 1951, pp. 901, 916.

23. A. C. Beck, *Obstetrical Practice*, Williams & Wilkins, 4th edition (Baltimore 1947), p. 170; J. B. De Lee, *Principles and Practice of Obstetrics*, W. B. Saunders, 10th edition, J. D. Greenhill (ed.) (Philadelphia 1951).

24. R. A. Johnston *et al.*, 'Is Prenatal Care Beneficial or Necessary?', *Southern Medical Journal*, 57, April 1964, p. 400; Massachusetts Medical Society, 'Obstetric Care', *New Eng. J. Med.*, 1955, *op. cit.*

25. Massachusetts Medical Society, 'Obstetric Care', *New Eng. J. Med.*, 1955, *op. cit.*

26. S. A. Alexander and J. T. Downs, 'Influence of Weight Gain on Pregnancy: Review of 1000 Private Cases', *American Journal of Obstetrics and Gynaecology*, 66, December 1953, p. 1162.

27. F. J. Browne and J. C. M. Browne, *Antenatal and Postnatal Care*, Churchill, 9th edition (London 1960), p. 28; De Lee, *Obstetrics*, 1951, p. 86, *op. cit.*

28. Luella Klein, 'Premature Birth and Maternal Prenatal Anaemia', *American Journal of Obstetrics and Gynaecology*, 83, 1 March 1962, pp. 588-90.

29. B. Pasamanick and A. M. Lilienfeld, 'Association of Maternal and Fetal Factors with Development of Mental Deficiency: Abnormalities in the Prenatal and Paranatal (sic) Periods', *Journal of the American Medical Association*, 159, 17 September 1955, pp. 155-60.

30. J. P. Semmens and J. C. McGlamory, 'Teenage Pregnancies', *Obstetrics and Gynaecology*, 16, July 1960, pp. 31-43.

31. Lubchenco *et al.*, 'Premature Birth Evaluation', *American Journal of Diseases of Children*, 1963, *op. cit.*

32. R. V. Rider *et al.*, 'Associations between Premature Birth and Socio-economic Status', *American Journal of Public Health*, 45, August 1955, pp. 1022-8.

33. Barnes, 'Prevention of Clinical Anomalies', *American Journal of Obstetrics and Gynaecology*, 1964, *op. cit.*

34. A. C. Barnes, 'Clinical Approach to the Prevention of Congenital Anomalies', *American Journal of Obstetrics and Gynaecology*, 90 (Part 2), 1 December 1964, pp. 1242-50; E. P. Crump, *et al.*, 'Growth and Development, Part 4: Relationship Between Prenatal Maternal Nutrition and Socio-Economic Index, Weight of Mother and Birth Weight of Infant', *American Journal of Obstetrics and Gynaecology*, 77, March 1959, pp. 562-72; S. H. Kane, 'Significance of Prenatal Care', *Obstetrics and Gynaecology*, 24, July 1964, pp. 66-70; L. O. Lubchenco *et al.*, 'Sequelae of Premature Birth Evaluation of Premature Infants of Low Birth Weights at Ten Years of Age', *American Journal of Diseases of Children*, 106, July 1963, pp. 101-15.

35. Gerald Caplan, 'Psychological Aspects of Maternity Care', *American Journal of Public Health*, 47, January 1957, pp. 25-31.

36. Aline B. Auerbach, 'Meeting the Needs of New Mothers', *Children*, 11, November/December 1964, pp. 223-8.

37. LaLeche International, *Breast Feeding*, LaLeche International (Franklin Park, Ill., n.d.), p. 155.

38. Joyce French, *Summary of Expectant Parents Classes Questionnaires, Blodgett and Butterworth Hospitals, 1964-5* (Grand Rapids, Mich, 1965).

39. Ozzie Simmons, 'Implications of Social Class for Public Health', in Gartly Jaco (ed.), *Patients, Physicians and Illness*, 1958, *op. cit.*, p. 107.

40. Maternity Centre Association, *Report of Conference on Prenatal Clinic Care in New York City*, The Association (New York 1963). (Mimeographed.)

3 | *Socialization, command of performance and mental illness*

E. BECKER

The origins of some mental illnesses may lie in the early socialization process of the individual. Man differs from other members
of the animal kingdom in that he moves in a world of symbolic
meaning. The child is prepared for the world through the process
of socialization: by interaction and verbal communication with
others he learns appropriate and acceptable social behaviour.
This process is both delicate and tortuous; he must learn to
establish his own self-esteem, but not at the expense of others'
self-identities. This requires that a subtle balance be maintained
between avoidance and presentation, between defence and
demeanour. The genesis of some mental illnesses may lie in the
fracturing of this intricate and delicate process.

The essentials for a sociological understanding of behavioural malfunction
presented here underline a crucial but simple consideration which has not
been sufficiently stressed in discussions of mental illness.[1] It is clear that
whatever the origin of malfunction—in biological substrata or in conventional social definition of desirable norm—there are individuals who will
not meet the behavioural requirements of their fellows. But in addition to
this consideration, there is a less obvious one, namely, that to a self-
reflexive, symbol-using animal, the *purely symbolic, social definition of
normative behaviour is as crucial to action* as is instinctive patterning to
any lower organism. The basis for this conclusion is common knowledge
to the clinician. However, recapitulation of several crucial features of man's
uniqueness in the animal kingdom is warranted in the present context
inasmuch as these features become, as we shall review below, the central
problem in negotiating social action.

THE PECULIARITY OF HUMAN ACTION

Freud's genius has been credited with many discoveries, notably the dynamic
unconscious and the importance of infantile sexuality and the multifarious
effects of these on human behaviour. But it is becoming increasingly
obvious—or should be—that a comprehensive theory of human behaviour
will draw upon those discoveries of Freud which figure less prominently
in clinical matters and which are of more general import. I am referring
specifically to the genesis of the self and the ego, and to the fact of the

Oedipal transition—a transition from biological proximal relationship to a succouring figure to a distanced, symbolic relationship to the internalized values of that figure. These two general, universal developmental trends are crucial in the humanization of homo sapiens. It is important to underscore that they are based upon one continuous thread: the change from a stimulus-response reaction to primitive anxiety, to an ego-controlled reaction.[2] The latter interposes a series of complex mechanisms between anxiety and the organism, which we have come to know as the self-system.[3] The bootstraps, so to speak, by which man lifts himself above the other animals are those which enable him to handle primitive animal annihilation-anxiety with a durative defence. The self-system is an anxiety-buffering motor that is always idling.

Now it is well known that this unique development in the animal kingdom is possible for only one reason: the development of language, which permits a self-referential existence. As the infant learns 'mine, me, I' in that order, he fixes himself in a space-time world populated by named, identifiable objects. Sullivan referred to the self-system as largely a series of linguistic tricks by which the human conciliates his environment—allays his anxiety, that is. Thus self-reflexivity and anxiety avoidance are two sides of the same coin. They create symbolic action possibilities by making the world safe for a symbolic, self-reflexive animal.

THE SOCIOLOGICAL VIEW

Sociologists have tended to focus their attention not on the individual intra-psychic aspects of the defensive operations of this animal but rather on the fact that a symbolic animal must be fashioned from the symbols inculcated by other animals. Society cooperates in its instrumental dominance over the natural environment by a joint allegiance to a shared symbolic system of meaning. If the behavioural world of the self-reflexive animal is based on a pronominal 'I', then the 'I' must be separated from the 'not-I'. In other words, the motivational goals and the proper actions for reaching those goals must be jointly defined as more desirable than other alternatives.[4] The animal must have, in brief, a feeling of primary value in a world of meaningful objects. Culture, in this sense, is a symbolic fiction without which the psychological animal could not act. The basis of this fiction is a pattern of values which gives vital meaning and permits action.

The problem of human behaviour in social terms is nothing short of prodigious: how to bring the acutely anxiety-sensitive animals to act together, without endangering the fragile self-system of each. How, in other words, to confront a multitude of individuals with each other and still permit them all the conviction (the fiction) *that each is an object*

of primary value in a world of meaningful objects. In the social encounter
the indispensable internal sentiment of warm self-value that serves as an
anxiety buffer is exposed to possible undermining by the very same sentiments of all others. We miss the point completely when we consider 'face'
an idle preoccupation of a decrepit Chinese culture. The apt term 'face'
refers to the turning outward for public view and possible mishandling
of the anxiety-buffering self-esteem, so laboriously fashioned in the
process of humanization. Social interaction, in other words, is a potential
anarchy of psychological destruction.

When we say that an individual is properly socialized, we mean simply
that the process of formation of the self-system has been secure enough
to enable him to sustain interaction with someone other than the agents
of his immediate socialization. If he can do this, society provides him
with a conventional code of rules for interaction by which to sustain his
own face and to protect the face of others. The intricacies of this code
have been masterfully detailed by Erving Goffman in a series of land-
marking writings.[5] With his two central concepts of deference and
demeanour, he has shown how society provides for and even maximizes
the primary sense of self-value that the individual brings with him to social
encounters.

DEFENSIVE NEEDS VERSUS REQUIREMENTS
OF SOCIAL ACTION

The problem, from a social point of view, is to respect the privacy
and integrity of the individual and at the very same time to include him
in social interaction. Society does this by a series of conventions which
Goffman includes under two main headings: deferential rituals of avoidance and deferential rituals of presentation. The body privacy, separate-
ness, and the integral self of the individual must be accorded a degree
of avoidance behaviour. Avoidance implies that everyone has the right
to keep others at a certain distance and recognizes that the self is personal.
Presentation, on the other hand, implies that everyone has the right to
engage others, *if it is done properly*; the self is recognized as social. Thus,
all the conventions of salutation, farewell, quick formal smiles of acknowledgement, facile compliments, brief adjustments of another's tie or
brushing his clothing and so on, are presentation rituals which engage his
self in social intercourse. (The details of these rituals are infinite, and
nowhere better conceptualized than by Goffman. Each society, of course,
has its own conventions for laying social claim to the personal self. In
traditional Japan, for example, the self had to be available to society at
almost all times—to close one's door during the day was a community
offence.)

When we are slighted by a 'snub' we are simply protesting that someone did not acknowledge the social existence of our self. The 'Hi' makes electric contact and fuses two discrete selves into a social unity. The problem of deference is an extremely touchy one, precisely because self-esteem is at stake. We must exercise a social claim on each other and yet not seem to manipulate. The simple act of engaging someone by offering him a seat is fraught with possibilities of bungling. Rituals of farewell are delicately sensitive, because here the self is being released from a social situation. The release must be gentle and not an ejection into isolation. An Italian watching his friends pull away in a train will remain on the platform waving a handkerchief in farewell until they are well out of sight —one must not coarsely break off the social fusion of selves; the magic melting must be sustained until it becomes a thinnest thread. The members of a group long accustomed to being together develop subtle cues for taking leave and will melt apart at a slight signal, perhaps undetectable to an observer.

The further problem is that the gestures of presentation which engage the individuals in social intercourse must not encroach too much on their private selves; 'a peculiar tension must be maintained'[6] between avoidance and presentation rituals. The individual, in sum, must be assured that if he entrusts his fallible face to society, it will take good care of it for him. 'A social relationship ... can be seen as a way in which the person is more than ordinarily forced to trust his self-image and face to the tact and good conduct of others.'[7] If this all seems axiomatic, its simplicity is deceptive. It is only when we consider the complement to deference, the phenomenon of demeanour, that the fictional fabric of social life becomes transparently clear. Demeanour refers to the problem of social action from the point of view of the individual. Demeanour means proper deportment, dress, bearing—in a word, self-regard. The individual is tasked to respect and maintain a sense of self. For an individual to have a sense of self— and this is of fundamental importance—means sustaining a named, identifiable locus of symbolic causality, which can be counted on to communicate within the social conventions. Demeanour is the *obligation to have a self*, so that there is something *socially transactable*. But the self-contained locus of communication must behave in an expected manner, so that his inclusion within the larger plot is a matter of facility. Otherwise, people would endanger themselves in undertaking interaction with someone who does not present a socially viable self. They would expose their fragile self-esteem to an entirely capricious monstrosity.

Crucial to our understanding of the delicately staged plot of social actors within a social fiction of learned meanings, goals and values is this: an individual who engages us by manifesting the proper deference must have an equally appropriate sense of demeanour to make the deference socially

meaningful—he must present a credible stage personality. If our interlocutor does not have proper self-regard he threatens us at the very core
of our artificial action. It is fundamental to the implicit rules of social life
that there must be no hint or revelation of the unbelievably flimsy basis
for our impassioned life and death actions: the revelation that the self
is merely an attitude of self-regard and a learned set of arbitrary conventions designed to facilitate symbolic action. The hopeful injunction
that upholds the social fiction is: 'let us all protect each other by sincere
demeanour and convincing presentations, so that we can carry on the
business of living.' The self-esteem of plural numbers of anxiety-prone
animals must be protected so that symbolic action can continue. Not only
must it be protected, it must in fact be enhanced by an intricate web of
rituals for delicate handling of the self. Man must make provision for the
utmost sensitivity in social intercourse. This fine social sensitivity is, as
Goffman observes, largely what we mean when we speak of 'universal
human nature'. That marvellous performer, Goethe, who even in his old
age radiated an aura of indomitable selfhood, said that there was a 'courtesy
of the heart which is akin to love'. The courtesy is the delicate handling
of other selves. The love is the control of one's self so that social life
can go on.

The culture protects social action in two ways. By providing a strict
code of social ritual, it makes available an adaptational device designed
to prevent the contamination of social intercourse with private data. The
more or less 'proper' thing to say in each situation is provided. At the
same time, it protects the ongoing action situation by ablating the irrelevancies of private data. The socially awkward person is one who is not
'successfully' socialized from roughly two points of view: (i) his reaction-
sensitivity prevents effective communication, and the forward motion of
social action in a situation; (ii) he has not learned to use with facility
the social ritual rules for interaction. We can ask of an individual in this
context: 'how much "reaction-sensitivity" is present in his social presentation of face (of his positive-self valuation)?' 'To what extent do his needs
and susceptibilities risk contaminating the smooth flow of face-saving ritual
that the culture needs in order to function?' (For example, a schizophrenic
may be overperceptive, unable to shut out irrelevant definitions of the
interaction situation. Thus, by his inordinate sensitivity to his interlocutor's
genitals, for example, he upsets a comfortably singly defined situation with
his own private data.)

THE LINGUISTIC BASIS OF POWER

It is perhaps in the manipulation of the conversational gambits of polite-
ness that we see best the importance to the individual of learning to use

the ritual rules for interaction. It is not widely enough recognized that easy handling of the verbal context of action gives the possibility of direct exercise of power over others. The individual who uses with facility 'I'm *terribly* sorry', '*Good* show!' '*Good* to see you!' and so on, creates the context of action for his interlocutor, by his confident manipulation of the conventional ritual verbiage. The parent's injunction 'Say "thank you" to the man' is not an inculcation of obsequiousness so much as it is a training in control. It is now up to 'the man' to frame an appropriate response, or to end the social situation gracefully. The proper formula delivered defines the situation for the other and is the most direct means of power. The newly liberated slave's reluctance to relinquish his lifelong pattern of obsequious formulas of deference does not derive from his 'degenerate character'. Rather, the formulas are his only tools for confident manipulation of the interpersonal situation—proven methods of control for which substitutes are not easily learned. Furthermore, as mentioned above, by verbally setting the tone for action by the proper ritual formula, we permit complementary action by our interlocutor. Not only do we permit it, we compel it, if mutual face is to be sustained. Thus the subordinate not only calls the tune for his superior but by doing his part in permitting action to continue infuses the situation with meaning. Finally, since action within shared meaning provides the only framework for the continual social validation of the actors, we can understand that deference is the means we have of enhancing one another.[8] The ability to use its formulas with facility means the power to manipulate others by providing the symbolic context for their action. (The manic seems to make a frantic bid for this power. But his exaggerated manipulations of the verbal proprieties are shown to be unnatural by the discomfort they create—in place of the comfort they are supposed to create. Only the manic himself is bemusedly comfortable; and in a social context this discrepancy defines his deviance.)

Conversely, this power has a central role in the creation of the self. The simplest definition of identity is the experience of one's self as the subject and agent of one's powers.[9] Thus, the person who has not been able to exercise his powers has little experience of self, therefore, little identity. Now using the deference-demeanour model, we can see how identity and self-experience are socially created: only by exercising demeanour and experiencing deference does the person fashion and renew himself by purposeful action in meaningful contexts. Thus loneliness is not only a suspension in self-acquaintance, it is a suspension in the very fashioning of identity, because, cut off from one's fellows, one cannot exercise demeanour or experience deference. Therefore, he cannot experience his own powers and come to know himself as agent of them. In this sense, identity is simply the measure of power and participation of the individual in the joint cultural staging of self-enhancing ceremony. One might say that everyone should be a

talented *metteur en scène* to get along in social life. But he who is so
need-disposition sensitive that he fails to learn to manipulate the ritual
rules in his early peer contacts is seriously handicapped in building a strong
identity: he never feeds his own power and self-acquaintance with the
proper staging of demeanour, as well as with the fuel of deference from
his fellows.

It is important to realize that the delicate balance of avoidance and
presentation rituals is not an easy one to manipulate. In order to have
any skill at it at all, one needs a clear definition of the situation. It is
precisely this that is obscured by poor socialization. A clear definition of
the situation demands an apprehension of one's private self, a sensitivity
to needs and expectancies in the interaction, and last but not least, a
sure cognizance of self-other discreteness. Thus, in the simplest terms, we
might say that the basis for social ineptitude is the failure to form an
adequate phenomenological self. A feeling of primary value, separation,
and de-identification of self from the succouring figure, sure possession of
one's body—these have all to be under the individual's control if he is at
all to get started in the complicated game of role-playing. Otherwise, we
have the familiar gaucheries of an overdoing of avoidance ritual, as, for
example, by not allowing oneself to be touched when it is quite in order;
or overdoing of presentation ritual by overpersonal manipulations and
attentions. (Cf. manic kissing and overly intimate compliments and so on,
so upsetting to one's interlocutors. 'Oh, there's the doctor who was *so*
nice to me! Look everyone, there's the most wonderful doctor in the
world; Oh I love him, I do love him, he is so super-wonderful. Here let
me straighten your glasses, so you can look as handsome as you are
wonderful.')

The notorious attribution to children of 'cruelty' is simply a recognition
that they have not yet learned to use the face-preserving and mutually
enhancing social conventions. When a child first steps out into the peer
group, the selves of others are not yet recognized except as something to
be overcome rather than used. ('Cripple!' 'Fatty!' 'Four-eyes!') One still
basks in the parental omnipotence and has no need as yet to be socially
sustained and created. Actually, the early peer group contacts are crucial
in learning the social rituals. One result of role-taking practice is sensitivity
in sustaining a constant presentation of self against a variably responsive
background. Thus, the child learns to sustain his own sense of value even
in the face of negative responses. He learns whose evaluation to discount,
who is overly private; he sees others making improperly personal gambits
in the social situation. We all remember, hopefully, at least one such
person with whom we could compare ourselves favourably in early peer
interaction, and feel 'properly social' at a very early age. For example, there
was always one 'sore loser' who filled us with a sense of social righteousness.

Furthermore, in early peer contacts, the child may learn that he is justified in refusing a negative response as emanating solely from another's private evaluation, not from his own *improperly presented self*: 'Wasn't *I* right?' is a plea for reassurance that one is sustaining the social fiction with proper demeanour. By thus mastering early unjust evaluations in the early peer group, the child learns to sustain a steady self-valuation, without resorting to bolstering paranoid responses. He learns a realistic appraisal of the other's unwarranted privatization of the social context.

In the last analysis, *power over others* consists in presenting an infallible self and in commanding dextrous performance of deference. The power of the 'natural leader' resides perhaps in such fortunate socialization that a convincing self is invariably put forth, with sharp separation of personal and reality needs. By putting forth a convincing self, the actor obliges others to a more careful deference. The strong self forces others to make an effort at performance that may often be beyond their means. Thus, the aura of his infallibility is enforced as their performance stumbles or becomes painfully effortful. In this sense, everyone is a potential *metteur en scène* who fashions the plot and provides the cues for proper performance by others. Witness man's enormous expenditure of time in self-torture over having failed to say just the right thing at a particular point in conversation: 'If only I had said *that*!' 'If *only* I had said that.' The implication in this galling preoccupation is that it was at *that* point that one could have exercised majestic control over the interaction. Some are more fortunately endowed to set implicitly the tone for the performance by presenting a model self and an unshakeable command of the script. To continue the film analogy: one explanation for 'involutional' depression lies simply in the fact that an individual can realistically appraise his life as having fallen far short of hoped-for goals, and give up in the face of a bad job.[10] If a sixty-year span be calculated imaginatively as a fictional saga of sixty minutes, one can imagine the depressed *metteur en scène* who after forty minutes—forty years—of plot sees the whole thing as botched. He simply cannot pin a happy ending within twenty minutes on a forty-minute background which does not support the ending with any credulity. Therefore, the fictional meaning of the whole plot is undermined, and he can give it up as an insurmountable assignment by depressive withdrawal.

SOCIALIZATION AS TRAINING IN COMMAND OF PERFORMANCE

Socialization, then, is a preparation for *social performance* of the individual actor. Using this scheme (deference-demeanour) we might ask two key sociological questions of this individual preparation, questions familiar to the clinician:

'With what behavioural style has the individual *learned* to get his self-rights respected?' How, in other words, has the child obtained appreciation from significant adults of his discrete social self? The manner of obtaining respect for self would be his basic method of comportment, or demeanour. The other important question has to do with determining his basic pattern of orientation to deference: 'how has he learned to react to the hierarchialized status of others?' In other words, what kind of cognizance does he have of the plot, the fiction of social action in which he will be expected to perform? These two sets of questions are separated for conceptual purposes; actually they are part of the same judgement: *how has the actor been trained as a performer?* The social judgement of the individual can be phrased in stark terms of his rule-following ability.

Transference, understood sociologically, is simply rule-following ability as it is constricted within a narrow stylistic range. The artificial crystallization of this stylistic range is what takes place in psychoanalytic therapy. By analysing it, the analyst hopes to permit performance over a broader range: he presents the patient 'with the possibility of a greater number of choices'. (In this context, it is worth mentioning the usual fascination of youth for the theatre. Goethe, it will be remembered, thought of acting as an indispensable preparation for adult life. [Wilhelm Meister]. Theatrical acting is a vicarious freedom of acting *control* of a situation. Especially noteworthy of our attention here is that this control is gained merely by *properly saying the right things.* Perfect acting is a unique exercise in omnipotence; by infallible wielding of deference and demeanour, the actor is at one and the same time indisputed director. Those of us who have never performed theatrically have perhaps experienced the sheer power-control aspects of language in learning a foreign tongue. Facility in speaking a foreign language partakes somewhat of a kindred experience in psychotherapy: the individual may find that he is capable of utterances which usher others into appropriate complementary action; but which utterances, because they are new [and in a foreign tongue] he at first experiences as unreal and somewhat ego-alien. It is then that he can best 'watch himself perform' and see in action the power aspects of language. When the utterances are finally reduced to habit, the self-critical and the acting individual becomes more fused. One's first sojourn abroad may be a quasi-psychotherapeutic exercise in freedom and power.)

The individual we term schizophrenic may well be one who has never learned the simple bases for the possession of real power over his fellows by aptly wielding the verbal armament of social ritual. In Bateson's double-bind theory of schizophrenia, the individual is prevented by ambiguities and inconsistencies of the environment from forming a firmly oriented and consistently recognized self. From the outset, therefore, he does not have the wherewithal to play the ritual game on social terms.

He has nothing that he can consistently present to confront the potential threats and uncertainties of the environment (except perhaps a certain 'unanchored' symbolic dexterity to be satisfied in library halls; or, if illiterate, in shamanistic fantasies). The young schizophrenic may often provide the best example of failure to handle even the simple greeting. With a self-esteem brittle to the core, the threat of an encounter can be overwhelming. One schizophrenic at the beginning of his army career signalled his 'queerness' to other soldiers. He learned that a simple greeting used by all never failed to elicit a friendly response. He followed others around, even to the latrine, repeating the greeting again and again. Another learned, perhaps for the first time, a sure ritual of presentation, a reliable way to engage another in social intercourse, without eliciting a hostile response: one had only to offer a cigarette. But even this act has its appropriateness, and the others quickly became embarrassed by his incessant offerings of handfuls of cigarettes, often at inappropriate times.

One cannot overemphasize the fact that the basic pattern of deference-demeanour in a society is the necessary social nutrient for the continuing creation of the personal significance of the social actors—a sort of public manna in which everyone is rejuvenated and supplied. There is a continuing affirmation of meaning in deference-demeanour social transactions which although purely on a fictional-symbolic level of discourse seems vital to the very organization of the self. This symbolic sustenance in other words seems a sine qua non for creating and maintaining an integral symbolic animal. This idea in itself is certainly not new, but its consequences have still not been followed through broadly enough in psychiatry, nor with the requisite theoretical relentlessness: that we cogitate this whole problem on the organism's purely symbolic level of functioning.

Using his idea of deference and demeanour within the framework of a socially self-sustaining fiction, Goffman makes a bold attack upon the label 'mental illness'. It would refer simply to those individuals 'who are the least ready to project a sustainable self'.[11] Those, in other words, who most directly undermine the mutually sustaining fiction of social ceremonial and who thus prevent the peculiar type of self-justifying action necessary to the continual anxiety-buffering needs of the human animal. It is these individuals who frustrate by their ineptitude the best efforts of the other metteurs en scène to make the show go on. 'One of the bases upon which mental hospitals through the world segregate their patients is degree of easily apparent "mental illness". By and large this means that patients are graded according to the degree to which they violate ceremonial rules of social intercourse.'[12] However, it would be wrong to be misled by words like 'ceremonial' into thinking that failure to perform is anything but a vitally serious matter to a symbolic animal. Whether we use the word 'fictional' to describe the anxiety-buffering self-system that is created by artificial linguistic symbols, or 'ceremonial' to subsume the social means of protecting this fragile self-system, it is plain that we are not talking about inconsequential matters. These fictions are not superfluous creations that could be put aside so that the more serious business of life could continue. The flesh and blood action of lower animals is no more infused with seriousness than is the ethereal, shadowy, symbolic conduct with which man organizes his dominion over nature. We may deal with flimsier coin, but like the abstractness of high finance, the business is perhaps even the more serious for it.

CONCLUSION

The view that social life is a symbolic, fictional nutrient for a self-reflexive, symbolic animal represents one direct, theoretical approach to the problems of behavioural malfunction. Seen from the individual point of view, this problem presents itself in terms of the individual's ability to sustain a self of positive value in a world of meaning and to act according to the social conventions for sustaining and reinforcing that meaning by mutual support. When we realize that the action world of a symbolic animal is fictional and continually fabricated, nourished and validated, this does not diminish the importance of that world to the behaviour of homo sapiens. There remains the problem of individuals who *cannot* follow the social ritual rules. Questions to which behavioural specialists should be sensitized are: 'in what ways is the manner in which this individual has learned to handle anxiety a hindrance in his performance of the ceremonial that permits sustenance of the social fiction of shared meaning?' 'what are the rules for performance which society itself projects?' Alertness to questions such as these would lead to a more sensitive understanding of the variations in performance ability of the individual actors, and (as in existing research) the reasons for that variation. Finally, and not least important, it would contribute to a greater flexibility of appraisal of the conditions for social becoming in an open democratic society.[13]

REFERENCES

1. See, e.g.: D. P. Ausubel, 'Personality Disorder is Disease', *American Psychologist*, 16 (No. 2), February 1961, pp. 69-74; O. H. Mowrer, ' "Sin", the Lesser of Two Evils', *American Psychologist*, 15, 1960, pp. 301-4; T. S. Szasz, 'The Myth of Mental Illness', *American Psychologist*, 15, 1960, pp. 113-18, and his *The Myth of Mental Illness: Foundations of a Theory of Personal Conduct*, Paul B. Hoeber (New York 1961). See also my *The Birth and Death of Meaning: A Perspective in Psychiatric Anthropology*, Free Press (New York, forthcoming).
2. S. Freud, *The Problem of Anxiety*, W. W. Norton (New York 1936).
3. H. S. Sullivan, *The Interpersonal Theory of Psychiatry*, W. W. Norton (New York 1953).

4. A. I. Hallowell, *Culture and Experience*, University of Pennsylvania Press (Philadelphia 1955).

5. Erving Goffman, 'On Face-work, an Analysis of Ritual Elements in Social Interaction', *Psychiatry*, 18, 1955, pp. 213-31; 'The Nature of Deference and Demeanour', *American Anthropologist*, 58 (No. 3), 1956, pp. 473-502; *The Presentation of Self in Everyday Life*, Doubleday (Garden City, New York, 1959).

6. Goffman, 'Deference and Demeanour', *American Anthropologist*, 1956, *op. cit.*, p. 488.

7. Goffman, 'On Face-work', *Psychiatry*, 1955, *op. cit.*, p. 227.

8. Goffman, 'Deference and Demeanour', *American Anthropologist*, 1956, *op. cit.*, p. 493.

9. E. Fromm, *The Sane Society*, Rinehart (New York 1955).

10. Cf. E. Bibring, 'The Mechanism of Depression', in P. Greenacre (ed.), *Affective Disorders*, International Universities Press (New York 1953).

11. Goffman, 'Deference and Demeanour', *American Anthropologist*, 1956, *op. cit.*, p. 497.

12. Goffman, 'Deference and Demeanour', *American Anthropologist*, 1956, *op. cit.*

13. E. Becker, 'The Relevance to Psychiatry of Recent Research in Anthropology', *American Journal of Psychotherapy*, 16 (No. 4), 1962, pp. 600-17.

4 | *A social-psychological theory of neurosis*

A. M. ROSE

An interactionist perspective is applied to unravelling some of the significant casual factors operating in the aetiology of neuroses. A neurotic person is essentially one who holds a negative attitude towards himself. This negative self-image can be created and sustained through the interaction process with others. In a situation where a person is searching for an appropriate social role or identity, feelings of inadequacy and self-devaluation may be intense and seemingly exaggerated. This may engender negative responses from 'significant others', so intensifying feelings of social inadequacy and anxiety. Socio-psychological, as well as biological and other factors, need to be taken into account when constructing the complex matrix of causation relevant to the aetiology of mental illness.

The analysis of the causes of human behaviour of certain types has often been beset by two types of logical difficulties. One is the monistic explanation in which the search for causation is directed to only one set of determining forces. In the case of pathological behaviour (psychosis and neurosis), the monism has most frequently been that of biological determinism or of explanation in terms of disturbances in the transfer of libido (as analysed by Freud and his followers). The most diverse forms of mental disturbances in individuals with the most diverse life histories have been analysed in terms of the same set of causes. The effort to correct this error by means of a theory involving pluralistic causation has sometimes resulted in the second logical difficulty to be mentioned here. This is the procedure of discovering a list of causes without indicating their relative importance or their manner of interaction. It is not particularly helpful to know that biological, psychological, economic, cultural and social interactional forces underlie the diverse manifestations of mental disturbances, even though this may be a true statement. Logicians have found that useful causal theories distinguish between the one 'sufficient' cause and the several 'necessary' causes for a given type of phenomenon—thus gaining some of the advantages of a monistic explanation—and that causation generally involves a complex interplay of forces in which each is effective only when in certain relationship to others.

When now offering a social-psychological theory of neurosis, I wish to avoid both of these errors even though the theory does not yet have sufficient empirical grounding to allow me to be sufficiently detailed concerning the exact relationship of this factor to other causal factors. We must be able to conceive that a given behavioural disturbance has its roots in a given social/personal situation, but that this situation operates to cause the mental disturbance through the creation of physiological unbalances and that it is necessary to restore the physiological balance as well as the social/personal situation to remedy the mental disturbance. To use a perhaps overly simple example: a 'worry' induced by relatively insuperable objective social conditions may result in such a deprivation of sleep that the physiological changes ensuing produce mental disturbances. A necessary step in the treatment of this problem might very well be the administration of drugs to induce sleep, even though the 'cause' of the problem is a social one. It is difficult to get out of the theological habit of separating the mind from the body and to recognize that all mental processes are also body processes, so that nothing social or psychological ever happens without biological concomitants. Yet it is proper and necessary to make a social or psychological analysis. In other words, our theory does not claim to exhaust the causal statements that might legitimately be made concerning neurosis; it merely suggests one significant variable which is relatively amenable to control. We must also learn to conceive that a given theory may be highly appropriate for the understanding of one kind of mental disturbance, but quite inappropriate for another kind of mental disturbance. It is not necessary to claim that our hypothesis explains each and every manifestation of neurosis; we merely expect that it helps to explain most forms of neurosis, and we leave the explanation of marginal forms of neurosis to other theorists.

With these cautions before us, a specific social-psychological theory of neurosis will be set forth. Any claim that this theory covers all the varied forms of mental disturbance is specifically denied, although—because the dividing line between neurosis and psychosis is often thin or arbitrary—it might be that such borderline phenomena as 'involutional melancholia', at least in its mild form, are capable of being understood in terms of the theory. Our definition of neurosis will simply be 'inability to act reasonably effectively—within the material means and limitations present—for the achievement of socially acceptable and personally accepted goals, because of anxiety or because of compulsions which camouflage anxiety'. (What is reasonably effective action is, of course, not precise and somewhat arbitrary. The criterion is what the individual and his associates consider to be reasonably effective action. By 'socially acceptable' is meant acceptance by the valued associates of the individual—that is, his reference membership groups. By using the term 'acceptance' rather than 'desired' we imply that the groups are at least willing to tolerate the individual's goals, even if they do not always evaluate them highly. By juxtaposing 'socially acceptable' and 'personally accepted' we imply a modicum of harmony in goals between the individual and his society, not a perfect harmony or conformity.) The theory does not rule out the possibility of other factors being important in the aetiology of neurosis—as, for example, a traumatic experience which conditions an individual to certain hysterical behaviour. The theory further refers to only one social-psychological element in what must necessarily be a complicated matrix of causation. The theory applies only to the behaviour covered in our definition of neurosis; if another definition is used the theory may be rendered inappropriate.

Our theory is based on the social psychology of Charles H. Cooley and George H. Mead, who held that a 'self', reflecting the reactions of others towards it, is an important intervening variable in human conduct. Observations of human behaviour in a variety of settings have supported this conception and recently Manford Kuhn has undertaken laboratory experiments which demonstrate that one's opinion of onself is significantly influenced by a sharply negative reaction from others concerning oneself.

The hypothesis offered here takes up where Kuhn leaves off. A factor in the chain of events leading to neurotic behaviour is the induction of a person's negative attitude towards himself, and this may develop in a variety of ways—not only by sharply negative reactions from others. A significant and consistent pattern of self-deprecation, whether conscious or not, is the independent variable. The repression of this attitude may result in hysterical forms of neurosis, rather than the more direct anxiety symptoms. The individual's negative attitude towards himself is related in different degrees and ways to other people's reactions towards him. It is an essential element of Cooley's concept of the 'looking-glass self' and of Mead's concept of the 'me' that part of the self is a reflection—albeit sometimes distorted—of other people's reactions to the person in question. If the reaction of others is generally negative, and the individual gets a correct perception of this negative reaction, and if he accepts this negative evaluation, our proposition is that the individual becomes neurotic. In other words an element in the chain of causes leading to neurosis is held to be the social-psychological factor of psychological self-mutilation. The psychoanalyst Carl Jung recognized this in speaking of a sense of 'loss of significance' as a major factor in adult neurosis.[1] A depreciated or 'mutilated' self is a major factor in the development of neurosis, we hypothesize, because an individual's ability to accept strongly held values of any kind and to act effectively to achieve those values is a function of his conception of himself—a conception that he is an adequate, worthwhile, effective, and appreciated person. The mental state is similar to that of the person who commits what Durkheim calls 'egoistic' suicide. The difference lies solely in that the individual either retains a compunction against suicide or else is not sufficiently organized to engage in the act of suicide. The psychoanalyst Alfred Adler had a comparable self-image theory of neurosis, although he tended to limit the concept of a negative self-image to those who had an 'organ inferiority'.

Certain temporary phenomena should not be confused with the more permanent self-devaluation here considered. Some negative reactions from others, some erroneous interpretations of others' reactions as unfavourable to ourselves, occasional moods of mild depression, are a part of everyday experience and hardly incapacitate an individual except for a very short time. The acceptance of a negative attitude towards oneself has to occur over a period of time to produce a neurosis. There is one significant exception to this: a psychological trauma, a crippling single incident of sharp self-devaluation, may create a neurosis for a significant period of time, although the individual generally recovers if a chain of negative events does not follow.

It is clear that the interactional process is central in this theory of neurosis. Rejection and devaluation by others are probably the most important cause of devaluation of self, provided the individual is not so psychotic or psychopathic that he cannot perceive the opinions of others. (There are other sources of incorrect perceptions of the opinions of others—including institutionalized sources. We are referring here to grossly incorrect perceptions, which we believe to be associated with psychosis or psychopathy.) Of course, an accurately perceived negative evaluation from others may be rejected by the individual concerned, but in such a case the individual generally has accepted what is for him the higher, more valued opinion of a small select group—perhaps even a group not in immediate social contact with him. The 'looking-glass self' is not a mere reflection, it involves selection and evaluation, and hence the resulting self-image is far from being the image of the individual as seen by others with whom the individual interacts.

This selective and evaluative process can also give rise to a second type of self-disparagement—that in which the individual selects the negative reactions of others and gives them prime importance among the wide range of others' reactions to build his conception of himself. Persons who do this have a perfectionist attitude, and even slight blows to their egos are accorded a subjective importance out of all proportion to their objective importance (in the eyes of a neutral observer). Such a perfectionist or 'oversensitive' attitude probably grows out of certain childhood experiences of a harsh nature, and hence may be thought of as psychogenic. At any rate, the tendency to overrate the negative reactions of others serves to inflict regular blows on one's conception of self. Over the course of time, our hypothesis holds, this is a link in the chain of causes that produce neurosis.

It is to be noted that at first these two types of neurotics are able to communicate with and receive communications from others as well as non-neurotic people can. There is no immediate interruption of communication such as is generally associated with psychosis. In fact it is in the process of communication that the neuroses develop. However if the self-deprecation persists and becomes greatly exaggerated, communication becomes interrupted and/or distorted. The disturbed individual concentrates his attention on himself to the partial exclusion of all other external stimuli. His very preoccupation with the unworthiness, uselessness and hopelessness of his self tends to restrict communication with others. Others no longer have to carry on their deprecation from the outside—although they may tend to do so as the individual fails to conform to their social pressures—for the self-deprecatory process comes to be reinforced by itself. The individual's obvious unhappiness, which makes him unattractive to others, and his own concentration of attention on himself tend to isolate him. Thus there are certain tendencies towards an interruption of communication and a withdrawal from reality which are productive of a psychosis on the border of neurosis—usually called 'involutional melancholia', at least in its milder form. On the other hand, unless the individual withdraws himself physically from social relations, the usual stimuli of everyday life intrude on his attention and keep him in some touch with reality. Thus the neurotic is only partly out of touch with reality, in so far as he over-selects the negative responses of others to the relative exclusion of the positive ones and in so far as his attention is concentrated on himself to the partial exclusion of some external stimuli; but if the neurotic further withdraws himself from society and broods almost exclusively on his unhappy self and its psychic pains, an involutional process with melancholia as its external manifestation will result. Karl Menninger describes the similarity of involutional melancholia to the neuroses.

> In this condition [melancholia] sufficient contact with reality may be maintained so that the individual, for all his self-destructiveness, does not endanger the lives of others, and may even co-operate in efforts to redirect or reshape his own life. For this reason, melancholia is sometimes described as a neurosis rather than a psychosis. But some victims of melancholia abandon all loyalty to reality and may be extremely deluded and even homicidal. The mechanisms are the same as in the so-called neurotic form, but the surrender of object attachment and of reality testing here is much greater.[2]

Davidoff expresses the ambiguous distinction between neurosis and involutional melancholia by holding that there is a difference between 'the non-psychotic involutional syndrome' and 'the involutional psychosis'.[3]

The symptoms characteristic of involutional melancholia are those of extreme anxiety and depression. The melancholic individual is able to communicate with others, but in this communication he immediately makes it clear that he has a highly negative attitude towards himself. His inability, failure and unworthiness are drawn to exaggerated proportions. A melancholic man will typically emphasize his belief that his life has been a failure. A melancholic woman will typically emphasize that she is not capable of doing anything right. The bodily symptoms are appropriate to these attitudes: there is much weeping and whining, wringing of the hands, negative shaking of the head, 'long' expression on the face, high body tension. The melancholic's stated belief that nothing is worth while for him (except perhaps for something obviously unobtainable) is reflected in his activity: sometimes futile gestures are made in the direction of doing something constructive, but most of the time the melancholic seems 'content' to sit back and contemplate his miserable state in his usual agitated manner. Any slight incident of a mildly unpleasant sort is awarded great importance in the melancholic's thought and conversation; any incident of a pleasant sort is glossed over and quickly forgotten. Attempts at suicide are not uncommon.

Our examination of the statistical incidence of involutional melancholia, even recognizing the great inadequacy of most statistics on mental disorder, reveals two persistent facts: women are more likely to have involutional melancholia in our society than are men, and the women typically have their first onset between the ages of forty-five and fifty-five, while men have their onset between the ages of fifty-five and seventy.[4] These facts have led many psychiatrists to associate melancholia with glandular changes going on in the body in connection with the loss of sexual powers, particularly with the menopause in women and other physiological changes associated with ageing.[5] But the facts are equally compatible with a social-psychological theory about the changes of life roles. Women in our society typically lose their child-rearing function and much of their household-caring function during the fifth decade of their lives, and men—whose sexual potency has been declining gradually since the age of twenty—typically lose their occupational functions at about the age of sixty-five and begin to foresee this loss about ten years earlier. The 'normal' procedure at such a critical juncture is to assume a new life role, which is of course facilitated by some earlier preparation for taking on such a new life role. The process is easier for men, since the socially expected life role for men past the age of sixty-five is one of leisure (including hobbies, travel, pottering around the house). But it is more difficult for a woman at the age of forty-five to assume a new life role, because she is too young to retire (both in terms of her physical strength and in terms of social expectations). Our culture does not specify a 'typical' role for the middle-aged woman whose child-rearing days are over, and the choices before her involve new efforts and skills on her part: she can find a job commensurate with her social status and abilities, she can become regularly active in civic or social affairs, she can play a larger part in the lives of her husband or her now-grown children (who often do not want her 'interference'). Because of lack of previously acquired skill, because of the difficulty in engaging in these activities when one begins them at the age of forty-five, because of the outside world's frequent resistance, a woman may often fail to make a satisfactory transition to a new role. A man between the ages of fifty-five and sixty may also fail, if he thinks of himself as a failure in his occupation and finds that he cannot compete with younger men, and if he has never developed any skills or interests in the uses of leisure, or if he is especially unhappy about retiring from his occupational role. Our culture values highly the occupational role for men and the child-rearing role for women and when these are lost the individual's value goes down sharply unless he can find a new role for himself. In certain other societies a middle-aged person automatically takes on a new role of influence and prestige and there is no decline in the individual's sense of his own worth.

The relationship of these facts and interpretations to our theory of neurosis should now be apparent. People who for one reason or another fail to make a satisfactory role transition (which our culture requires at about the age of forty-five and fifty for women and sixty to sixty-five for men), especially if they find that their achievements have not been up to their expectations and hence cannot retire content with their laurels, are likely to develop persistent negative attitudes towards themselves. The central element in this negative attitude is that life is meaningless. This entails a sense of worthlessness, a loss of motivation, a belief in one's inability to achieve anything worth while. Such a complex tends to be persistent, as our culture does not offer any ready solution of the problem, and no happy accident is likely to change the situation (as might occur in other difficult problems of life). The individual feels himself aged or ageing, and this feeling adds to the sense of hopelessness. The result is a persistent psychological beating of the self with a circular intensification of the process. Soon the individual is no longer able to control his feelings of anxiety and depression. It is as though the individual commits suicide mentally, but forgets to do it, or loses the capacity to do it, physically. After deciding he is not going to have anything more to do with life he finds himself still alive, with the usual sorts of body needs. The latter naturally become very annoying; hence they tend to become the major object of attention and chief source of worry. Many such people do attempt suicide, but others have certain compunctions against it or fears of it.

This extreme form of neurosis is generally known to psychiatrists as involutional melancholia. Failure to make a subjectively satisfactory tran-sition in life role is not the sole cause of persistent self-deprecation, of course, but it may very well be the most frequent cause. Also there seem to be certain types of personalities who are especially susceptible to melancholia, personalities who are especially rigid and hence least able to find new life roles when the culture does not automatically offer them.[6]

The theory applies, of course, to milder forms of neurosis than involutional melancholia. In the case of compulsive-obsessive neuroses, the individual is hypothesized to seek reassurance—to combat his negative attitude towards himself—by some form of repetitive behaviour. Repetition of thought or behaviour provides a way of 'hanging on', of assuring oneself that something is stable even when one does not have confidence in one's perceptions, actions, or thought processes because he conceives of himself as generally inadequate. The specific compulsion or obsession is thus a mere symptom, although the choice of it is undoubtedly related to some significant experience in the life of the neurotic individual.

If reality is persistently bleak, it might be wiser for the individual not to face it completely, at least not for a certain period until a sense of self-confidence can be restored. People have to be taught to avoid persistent self-deprecation, as much as they have to be taught to face reality. Modern Western culture is weak in the social crutches which tend to compensate individuals for personal dissatisfaction with life: the belief in a just hereafter, the belief that God sets trials for people to test them, a strong family and church system which forces people into activity despite their personal disinclination. In the modern Western setting where these things are weak or non-existent the wise psychiatrist should function partly as a priest, not only in the sense that he can serve as a confessor to relieve guilt feelings and other repressions, but also in that he can help people to turn their minds temporarily from the misery of their personal lot. Such avoidance of reality is necessary if only to let the body restore its physiological balance, which is inevitably unbalanced by the persistent anxiety and depression.

Having a neurotic individual avoid reality is of course a temporary device, a first step, since—if our theory is correct—the cure of neurosis must involve changing his situation and/or getting him to redefine his situation. Both of these require contact with reality at least most of the time. If the basis of a neurosis is persistent self-deprecation because the individual is in an objectively unpleasant situation, such as having to face uniformly negative judgements on the part of others or finding oneself without a meaningful life role, a major part of treatment should not be psychotherapeutic but consist of helping the individual move into a more favourable situation. That is, the unfavoured individual should be brought into a new social environment, and the roleless individual should be taught a new role. An effective psychotherapy must be allied with these procedures, and should consist in helping the individual to redefine his relationship to his environment. If, on the other hand, the difficulty is not 'objective' but results from the neurotic person's tendency to interpret his social situation in personally unflattering terms, there is not any point to changing the situation, and psychotherapy is all-important. Part of the psychotherapy still consists, however, in helping the individual to redefine his situation—in this case, bringing the definition closer to reality. The problem of getting at the sources of the neurotic's tendency to interpret his social situation as more unfavourable to him than it objectively is, cannot be helped by our theory. Freudian or other familiar theories of neurosis would be more successful at this point in guiding psychotherapy. Shock or drug treatment has also been found to be successful in some cases in bringing the melancholic to recognize the social world around him and to realize his relationship to it, and this sometimes aids redefinition and hence at least is a partial 'cure'.[7] Our own contribution here limits itself to a psychotherapy of redefining the situation, redefining the self through a redefinition of the situation, and to a broader treatment process which involves changing the objective social situation. The goal is the development of a positive attitude towards the self, and a realistic recognition of the attainable ways in which the changing self can continue to function in a changing social environment.

This is not Couéism nor 'positive thinking'. The individual must *do* those things which are in accord with his own values and which reflect the values of some social group that he rates highly. He must be able to congratulate himself occasionally and receive congratulations from esteemed others. This involves his social actions and not merely his personal thoughts. The therapy, therefore, must include putting him into a situation where he can engage in self-satisfying action with some fair degree of success and where he can receive some degree of recognition by others for this success. If neither changing the situation nor redefining the situation is possible for a given neurotic individual—perhaps because of his advanced age—it may be that 'adjustment' can be achieved only by psychologically separating the individual from the stark reality of his life. For such an individual, self-delusion may be the only alternative to complete apathy and depression or suicide. The important thing is to maintain the integrity and the value of the self, even if—in the extreme instance—this means loss of contact with reality.

REFERENCES

1. C. G. Jung, *Modern Man in Search of a Soul*, Harcourt, Brace (New York 1933).
2. Karl A. Menninger, *Man Against Himself*, Harcourt, Brace (New York 1938), p. 213.
3. Eugene Davidoff, 'The Involutional Psychoses', in Oscar J. Kaplan (ed.), *Mental Disorders in Later Life*, Stanford University Press (Stanford, Calif., 1945), p. 189.

4. Philip Palatin and James F. MacDonald, 'Involutional Psychoses', *Geriatrics*, 6, 1951.

5. Davidoff, 'Involutional Psychoses', in Kaplan (ed.), *Mental Disorders*, 1945, *op. cit.*, pp. 187-204, esp. p. 188.

6. M. F. Brew and Eugene Davidoff, 'The Involutional Psychoses, Prepsychotic Personality and Prognosis', *Psychiatric Quarterly*, 14, 1940, p. 412; William Malamud, S. L. Sands and Irene T. Malamud, 'The Involutional Psychoses: A Socio-Psychiatric Study', *Psychosomatic Medicine*, 3, October 1941, pp. 410-26; William Malamud, S. L. Sands, Irene T. Malamud and P. J. P. Powers, 'The Involutional Psychoses: A Socio-Psychiatric Follow-up Study', *American Journal of Psychiatry*, 105, February 1949, p. 567; W. Titley, 'Prepsychotic Personality of Patients with Involutional Melancholia', *Archives of Neurology and Psychiatry*, 36, 1936, p. 19.

7. Isadore Leo Fishbein, 'Involutional Melancholia and Convulsive Therapy', *American Journal of Psychiatry*, 106, August 1949, pp. 128-35.

II | The sociology of the healing professions

5 | *Training for uncertainty*

R. C. FOX

The practising physician must learn to cope with a certain degree of doubt and uncertainty in the performance of his role. One type of uncertainty results from an incomplete and inadequate mastery of available knowledge; another type of uncertainty stems from the limitations in current medical science. These two causes contribute to a third source of uncertainty: the difficulty of distinguishing between, on the one hand, personal ignorance or ineptitude, and on the other hand, inadequacies in the present state of medical knowledge. This reading discusses the various types of uncertainty confronting the student as he progresses through his medical training, the different ways in which he responds to these, and the part played by the medical culture in preparing him to cope with the problematic nature of the medical task.

There are areas of experience where we know that uncertainty is the certainty. James B. Conant

Voluminous texts, crammed notebooks, and tightly-packed memories of students at Cornell University Medical College attest to the 'enormous amount'[1] of established medical knowledge they are expected to learn. It is less commonly recognized that they also learn much about the uncertainties of medicine and how to cope with them. Because training for uncertainty in the preparation of a doctor has been largely overlooked, the following discussion will be focused exclusively on this aspect of medical education, but with full realization that it is counterbalanced by 'all the material [students] learn that is as solid and real as a hospital building'.

There is of course marked variation among students in the degree to which uncertainty is recognized or acknowledged. Some students, more inclined than others to equate knowing with pages covered and facts memorized, may think they have 'really accomplished a lot ... gained valuable knowledge', and that what they have learned is 'firmly embedded and clear in their minds'. Other students are more sensitive to the 'vastness of medicine', and more conscious of ignorance and superficiality in the face of all they 'should know', and of all the 'puzzling questions' they glimpse but cannot answer. Many students fall somewhere between these two extremes, half aware in the course of diligent learning that there is much they do not understand, yet not disposed 'at this point to stop and lament'. Discussion will be limited to the training for uncertainty that seems to apply to the largest number of students, admitting at the outset that inferences from the data must be provisional.

THE KINDS OF UNCERTAINTY THAT THE DOCTOR FACES

In Western society, where disease is presumed to yield to application of scientific method, the doctor is regarded as an expert, a man professionally trained in matters pertaining to sickness and health and able by his medical competence to cure our ills and keep us well. It would be good to think that he has only to make a diagnosis and to apply appropriate treatment for alleviation of ills to follow. But such a utopian view of the physician is at variance with facts. His knowledge and skill are not always adequate, and there are many times when his most vigorous efforts to understand illness and to rectify its consequences may be of no avail. Despite unprecedented scientific advances, the life of the modern physician is still full of uncertainty. It is not only the doctor, of course, who must deal with the problem of uncertainty. To some extent this problem presents itself in all forms of responsible human action. The business executive or the parent, for example, has no assurance that his decisions will have the desired results. But the doctor is particularly subject to this problem for his decisions are likely to have profound and directly observable consequences for his patients.

Two basic types of uncertainty may be recognized. The first results from incomplete or imperfect mastery of available knowledge. No one can have at his command all skills and all knowledge of the lore of medicine. The second depends upon limitations in current medical knowledge. There are innumerable questions to which no physician, however well trained, can as yet provide answers. A third source of uncertainty derives from the first two. This consists of difficulty in distinguishing between personal ignorance or ineptitude and the limitations of present medical knowledge. It is inevitable that every doctor must constantly cope with these forms of uncertainty and that grave consequences may result if he is not able to do so. It is for this reason that training for uncertainty in a medical curriculum and in early professional experiences is an important part of becoming a physician.

An effort will be made to identify some experiences as well as some agencies and mechanisms in medical school that prepare students for uncertainty and to designate patterns by which students may gradually come to terms with uncertainty. In the initial inquiry we shall content ourselves with a general view of the sequence through which most students pass, but in a concluding section we shall suggest some variations that might be considered in further investigation of training for uncertainty.

THE PRECLINICAL YEARS

Learning to acknowledge uncertainty

The first kind of uncertainty which the student encounters has its source in his role as a student. It derives from the avoidance of 'spoon-feeding', a philosophy of the preclinical years at Cornell Medical College (as at many other medical schools).

> You will from the start be given the major responsibility for learning [students are told on the first day that they enter medical school]. Most of your undergraduate courses to date have had fixed and circumscribed limits; your textbooks have been of ponderable dimensions.... Not so with your medical college courses.... We do not use the comfortable method of spoon-feeding....[2] Limits are not fixed. Each field will be opened up somewhat sketchily.... You will begin to paint a picture on a vast canvas but only the centre of the picture will be worked in any detail. The periphery will gradually blur into the hazy background. And the more you work out the peripheral pattern, the more you will realize the vastness of that which stretches an unknown distance beyond.... Another common collegiate goal is to excel in competition with others.... [But] because an overly-competitive environment can hinder learning, student ratings are never divulged [in this medical school], except to the extent that once a year each student is privately informed as to which quarter of the class he is in.

From the first, the medical school rookie is thus confronted with the challenge of a situation only hazily defined for him. Information is not presented 'in neat packets';[3] precise boundaries are not set on the amount of work expected. Under these conditions the uncertainty which the beginning student faces lies in determining how much he ought to know, exactly what he should learn, and how he ought to go about his studies.

This uncertainty, great as it is, is further accentuated for the beginner by the fact that he does not receive grades, and therefore does not have the usual concrete evidence by which to discover whether he is in fact doing well.

> In college, if you decide to work very hard in a course, the usual result is that you do very well in it, and you have the feeling that studying hard leads to good grades. You may tell yourself that you don't give a damn about grades, but nevertheless they do give you some reassurance when you ask yourself if the work was worth it.... In medical school, there is no such relationship. Studying does not always lead to doing well—it is quite easy to study hard, but to study the wrong things and do poorly. And if you should do well, you never know it.... In my own case, I honestly think the thing that bothers me most is not the lack of grades, but rather the feeling that even after studying something in a given course I always end up knowing so little of what I should know about it.... Medicine is such an enormous proposition that one cannot help but fall short of what he feels he should get done....

Thus, it would seem that avoidance of spoon-feeding by the preclinical faculty encourages the student to take responsibility in a relatively unstructured situation, perhaps providing him with a foretaste of the ambiguities he may encounter when he assumes responsibility for a patient.

From the latter parts of the comment under review it would appear that the same teaching philosophy also leads to the beginning awareness of a second type of uncertainty: by making the student conscious of how vast medicine is, the absence of spoon-feeding readies him for the fact that even as a mature physician he will not always experience the certainty that comes with knowing 'all there is to know' about the medical problems with which he is faced. He begins to realize that no matter how skilled and well-informed he may gradually become, his mastery of all that is known in medicine will never be complete.

It is perhaps during the course of studying gross anatomy that the student experiences this type of uncertainty most intensely. Over the centuries this science has gradually traced out what one medical student describes as the 'blueprint of the body'. As a result of his struggle to master a 'huge body of facts', he comes to see more clearly that medicine is such an 'enormous proposition' he can never hope to command it in a way both encompassing and sure.

> ... Men have been able to study the body for thousands of years ... to dissect the cadaver ... and to work on it with the naked eye. They may not know everything about the biochemistry of the body, or understand it all microscopically ... but when it comes to the gross anatomy, they know just about all there is to know.... This vast sea of information that we have to keep from going out the other ear is overwhelming.... There's a sense in which even before I came to medical school I knew that I didn't know anything. But I never *realized* it before, if you know what I mean—not to the extent that it was actually a gripping part of me. Basically, I guess what I thought before was, sure, I was ignorant *now*—but I'd be pretty smart after a while. Well, at this point it's evident to me that even after four years, I'll still be ignorant.... I'm now in the process of learning how much there is to learn. ...

(Such a felt sense that there will always be more to learn in medicine than he can possibly make his own is the beginning of the medical student's acceptance of limitation. It might also be said that this same realization is often one of the attitudinal first signs of a later decision on the part of a student to enter a specialized medical field. This is of some relevance to the discussion of specialization by Patricia L. Kendall and Hanan C. Selvin.[4])

As in this case, the student's own sense of personal inadequacy may be further reinforced by the contrast he draws between his knowledge and that which he attributes to his instructors. Believing as he does that 'when it comes to the gross anatomy, they know just about all there is know', he is made increasingly aware of how imperfect his own mastery really is.

There are other courses and situations in preclinical years which acquaint the Cornell student with uncertainties that result not from his own inadequacies but from the limitations in the current state of medical knowledge. For example, standing in distinction to the amassed knowledge of a discipline such as gross anatomy is a science like pharmacology, which only in recent years has begun to emerge from a trial and error state of experimentation.

> Throughout the history of pharmacology, it would appear that the ultimate goal was to expedite the search for agents with actions on living systems and to provide explanations for these actions, to the practical end of providing drugs which might be used in the treatment of the disease of man. As a result of many searches there now exist such great numbers of drugs that the task of organizing them is a formidable one. The need for the development of generalizations and simplifying assumptions is great. It is to be hoped that laws and theories of drug action will be forthcoming, but the student should at this point appreciate that few of them, as yet, exist.[5]

The tentativeness of pharmacology as a science, then, advances the student's recognition that not all the gaps in his knowledge indicate deficiencies on his part. In effect, pharmacology helps teach medical students that because 'there are so many voids' in medical knowledge, the practice of medicine is sometimes largely 'a matter of conjuring ... possibilities and probabilities'.

> When Charles was over for dinner last week, I remarked at the time that I was coming to the conclusion that medicine was certainly no precise science, but rather, it is simply a matter of probabilities. Even these drugs today, for example, were noted as to their wide range of action. One dose will be too small to elicit a response in one individual; the same dose will be sufficient to get just the right response in another; and in yet another individual, the same dose will produce hyper-sensitive toxic results. So, there is nothing exact in this, I guess. It's a matter of conjuring the possibilities and probabilities and then drawing conclusions as to the most likely response and the proper thing to do. And Charles last week agreed that a doctor is just an artist who has learned to derive these probabilities and then prescribe a treatment.

In pharmacology (and in the other basic medical sciences as well) it is assumed that 'laws and theories will be forthcoming' so that the uncertainties which result from limited knowledge in the field will gradually yield to greater certainty. However, the 'experimental point of view' pervading much of early teaching at the Cornell Medical College promotes the idea that an irreducible minimum of uncertainty is inherent in medicine, in spite of the promise of further scientific advance. The preclinical instructors presenting this point of view have as a basic premise the idea that medical knowledge thus far attained must be regarded as no more than tentative, and must be constantly subjected to further inquiry. It is their assumption that few absolutes exist.

> If you were having a great deal of trouble finding some simple sort of cell in histology and you asked him about it, Dr A. always made a point to give you information from the experimental point of view. He would (i) point out that this cell has five different names; (ii) point out that this cell might actually be a ——— cell or a ——— cell that has undergone a transformation and that indeed, this cell might be able to change into almost anything; (iii) also mention that even though the cell has five names, it may not, in fact, exist in the first place—perhaps it's just an artefact.

> Or, take the way the bacteriology department pushes the theme of 'individual differences'—how one person will contract a disease he's been exposed to, while another one won't. The person may have a chill, or not; the agent may be virulent or not; and that determines whether pneumonia will occur or not.... 'The occurrence, progression and outcome of a disease is a function of the offence of the micro-organism and the defence of the host.' That's the formula they keep pounding home....

> ... In the course of the demonstration of drugs affecting respiration, Dr S. quoted Goodman and Gilman [a pharmacology textbook universally recommended and respected] as to the dramatic effect of one certain drug in respiratory failure. And then, they proceeded to show the falsity of that statement. So pharmacologists are now debunking pharmacologists! Heretofore they simply showed the drugs commonly used by many physicians had no effect. If this keeps up, we will all be first-class sceptics!

This is not to say, a student cautions, that we don't learn 'a lot of established facts ... tried and true things about which there is little or no argument'. But in course after course during the preclinical years at Cornell, emphasis is also placed on the provisional nature of much that is assumed to be medically known. The experimental point of view set forth by his teachers makes it more apparent than it might otherwise be that medicine is something less than a powerful, exact science, based on nicely invariant principles. In this way, the student is encouraged to acknowledge uncertainty, and, more than this, to tolerate it. He is made aware, not only that it is possible to act in spite of uncertainties, but that some of his teachers make such uncertainties the basis of their own experimental work.

Up to this point we have reviewed some of the courses and situations in the preclinical years at Cornell which make the beginning student aware of his own inadequacies and others which lead him to recognize limitations in current medical knowledge. The student has other experiences during the early years of medical school which present him with the problem of distinguishing between these two types of uncertainty—that is, there are times when he is unsure where his limitations leave off and the limitations of medical science begin. The difficulty is particularly evident in situations where he is called upon to make observations.

Whether he is trying to visualize an anatomical entity, studying gross or microscopic specimens in pathology, utilizing the method of percussion in physical diagnosis, or taking a personal history in psychiatry, the preclinical student is being asked to glean whatever information he can from the processes of looking, feeling, and listening. (The physician is called upon to use his sense of smell and of taste on occasion, too, but not as frequently as those of sight, touch, and hearing.) In all these situations, students are often expected to see before they know how to look or what to look for. For, the ability to 'see what you ought to see', 'feel what you ought to feel', and 'hear what you ought to hear', students assure us, is premised upon 'a knowledge of what you're supposed to observe', an ordered method for making these observations, and a great deal of practice in medical ways of perceiving. ('We see only what we look for. We look for only what we know,' the famous Goethe axiom goes.)

Nowhere does this kind of uncertainty become more salient for medical students during their preclinical years than in physical diagnosis.

> Physical diagnosis is the one course I don't feel quite right about. I still have a great deal of difficulty making observations, and I usually don't feel certain about them.... Dick and I had a forty-year-old woman as our patient this morning. Though I thought we were doing better than usual at the time, we nevertheless missed several important things—a murmur and an enlarged spleen....

'This sort of thing happens often in a course like physical diagnosis,' the same student continues, and 'it raises a question that gives me quite a bit of concern—*Why* do I have ... difficulty making observations?'

There are at least two reasons for which a student may 'miss' an important clinical sign, or feel uncertain about its presence or absence. On the one hand, his oversight or doubt may be largely attributable to lack of knowledge or skill on his part.

> One of the problems now is that we don't know the primary clinical signs of various disease processes.... For example, today we suspected subacute bacterial endocarditis, but we didn't know that the spleen is usually enlarged, and as a result, we didn't feel as hard as we should have....

On the other hand, missing a spleen, for example, or 'not being sure you hear a murmur' is sometimes more the 'fault of the field' (as one student puts it) than 'your own fault'. That is, given the limitations in current medical knowledge and technique, the enlargement of a spleen may be too slight, the sound of a murmur too subtle, for 'even the experts to agree upon it'.

The uncertainty for a student, then, lies in trying to determine how much of his own 'trouble ... hearing, feeling or seeing is personal', and how much of it 'has to do with factors outside of himself'. (Or, as another student phrases the problem: 'How do you make the distinction between yourself and objectivity?')

Generically, the student's uncertainty in this respect is no different from that to which every responsible, self-critical doctor is often subject. But because he has not yet developed the discrimination and judgement of a skilled diagnostician, a student is usually less sure than a mature physician about where to draw the line between his own limitations and those of medical science. When in doubt, a student seems more likely than an experienced practitioner to question and 'blame' himself.

His course in gross anatomy, it has been suggested, gives a Cornell student some awareness of his own inadequacies; pharmacology emphasizes the limitations of current medical knowledge; and his training in observation, particularly in physical diagnosis, confronts him with the problem of distinguishing between his own limitations and those in the field of medicine. But in his second year his participation in autopsies simultaneously exposes the student to all these uncertainties. The autopsy both epitomizes and summarizes various other experiences which together make up the preclinical student's training for uncertainty.

Before witnessing their first autopsy, second-year students may, on occasion, sound rather complacent about the questions which death poses. For example, speculating on the causes of death, one group of Sophomores decided to their satisfaction that the cessation of life could be explained in simple physiological terms and that, armed with this knowledge, the doctor stands a good chance of 'winning the fight' against death.

> We found that one very important matter could be traced back to one of two basic actions. The important matter—death. The two basic actions— the heart and respiration. For death is caused, finally, by the stopping of one of these two actions. As long as they both continue, there is life.... It's all a fight to keep the heart beating, the lungs breathing, and, in man, a third factor—the brain unharmed.... With all the multitude of actions and reactions which are found in this medical business, it seems strange and satisfying to find something that can really be narrowed down....

But the conviction that death 'can really be narrowed down' is not long-lasting. Only a short time later, commenting on an autopsy he had just witnessed, one of these same students referred to death with 'disquietude' as something you 'can't pinpoint' or easily prevent.

One of the chief consequences of the student's participation in an autopsy is that it heightens his awareness of the uncertainties that result from limited medical knowledge and of the implications these uncertainties have for the practising doctor. This is effected in a number of ways. To begin with, the experience of being 'on call' for an autopsy ('waiting around for someone to die') makes a student more conscious of the fact that, even when death is expected, it is seldom wholly predictable.

> In groups of three, we all watch at least one autopsy—and my group is the third one in line. The first group went in for theirs this morning; this means that ours may come any time now. You can't be sure when, though, so you have to stay pretty close to home where you can be reached....

In other words, although ultimate death is certain, medical science is still not far enough advanced so that the physicians can state with assurance exactly when an individual will die.

Of even greater importance, perhaps, in impressing the student with the limitations of current medical knowledge is the fact that, although the pathologist may be able to provide a satisfactory explanation of the patient's death, the student usually finds these 'causes of death' less 'dramatic' and specific than he expected them to be.

> While our case was unusual, it was a bit of a letdown to me, for there was nothing dramatic to be pointed to as the cause of death. The clinician reported that the patient had lost 1,000 cc of blood from internal bleeding in the G.I. tract.... Well, we saw no gaping hole there. There was no one place you could pinpoint and say: 'This is where the hemorrhage took place.' ... Rather, it was a culmination of a condition relating to various factors. I suppose most causes of death are this way. But still ... (though I'm not really sure why it should be) ... it was somewhat disquieting to me.

A third limitation of the field is implied in lack of control over death. For example, the student observes that 'the various doctors connected with the case being autopsied ... wander in while the procedure is going on'. This serves to remind him that the 'body on the autopsy table' belongs to a patient whose death no physician was able to prevent.

It it not only the limits of the field which are impressed upon the student during his participation in an autopsy. This experience also serves to make him aware of the personal limitations of even the most skilled practitioners. For instance, an autopsy gives a student an opportunity to observe that 'the doctors aren't always sure what caused the patient's death'; rather, as one student puts it, 'they come ... to find out what was really wrong'. Furthermore, the student may be present at an autopsy in which the pathologist's findings make it apparent that the physician was mistaken in his diagnosis (when, for example, the pathologist 'doesn't find any of the things in the doctors' diagnoses'). From experiences such as these the student learns that not only he but also his instructors have only an imperfect mastery of all there is to know in medicine.

These varied aspects of the autopsy, in other words, give it central significance in the student's training for uncertainty.

Learning to cope with uncertainty

In describing the various kinds of uncertainty to which a student is exposed during his preclinical years at Cornell, we do not mean to portray him as groping helplessly around in the midst of them. On the contrary, as time goes on, a student begins to develop effective ways of dealing with these forms of uncertainty, so that, gradually, he becomes more capable of meeting them with the competence and equipoise of a mature physician.

To begin with, as a student acquires medical knowledge and skill, some of his uncertainty gives way. 'A more complete and satisfying picture of the organism takes shape' in his mind. Gradually, 'the missing jig-saw puzzle pieces seem to fall into place, and [he] sees interconnections and inter-relationships between all subjects'. The student also feels more at home looking in a microscope; he finds it easier to draw slides; he begins to have more confidence in what he sees and hears in physical diagnosis; and he becomes more adept at talking to patients. In all these respects, cognitive learning and a greater sense of certainty go hand in hand.

Growing competence and more experience decrease the student's uncertainty about his personal knowledge and skills; this, in turn, modifies his attitude towards the uncertainties which arise from limitations in the current state of medical knowledge. It will be remembered that, at first, the preclinical student goes through a period in which he is inclined to regard his uncertainty as reflecting his personal inadequacy. During his early days in physical diagnosis, for example, a student is likely to dismiss the uncertainty he may feel about 'how much percussion tells [him]' in a particular instance, by saying that he thinks he is 'probably wrong' to have doubts in the first place and that giving vent to these doubts might make him 'look like a fool'.

> For example, I can see that percussion *does* tell you a lot, and that in most cases, the borders of the heart *can* be percussed. What it amounts to really is not that I doubt it, but that I can't do it.... It's all very well and good [to express your doubt], but if it turns out that you're the only one who seems to be having so much trouble, you begin to look like a fool after a while if you do.... We don't really know enough yet so that we can afford not to take a positive stand....

With the growth of his knowledge and skill, however, and the widening and deepening of his experience, a student's perspective on his own uncertainty changes. Now that he 'knows a little more' and is 'a little more sure of himself', a student says, he realizes that although some of his uncertainty is attributable to his 'ignorance', some of it is 'really well justified'. By this he means that he is better able to distinguish between

those aspects of his uncertainty that derive from his own lack of knowledge and those that are inherent in medicine. He is therefore less apt
to think of his uncertainty as largely personal and now considers it more
appropriate to give voice to the doubts he feels.

This more 'affirmative attitude' towards doubting (as one student calls
it) is not only a product of book knowledge and skill in the techniques of
physical diagnosis. It also results from what a student learns about the
uncertainties of medicine through his daily contact with members of the
faculty. From time to time in the classroom, for example, a student will
ask what he considers a 'well chosen question' only to discover that his
teacher 'does not have immediate command of the known medical facts
on that point' or to be told that the problem into which he is enquiring
'represents one of the big gaps in medical knowledge at present'. In the
autopsy room, as we have seen, a student is struck by the fact that the
pathologist cannot always explain the causes of death and that, although
the 'doctors' diagnoses are often right, they can also be wrong'. Examining
patients under the supervision of clinical faculty, a student discovers that
when 'different instructors listen to (or feel or see) the exact same thing,
they frequently come up with different impressions ... and have to consult
one another before they reach a final conclusion'.

In short, observing his teachers in various classroom and clinical situations makes a student more aware of the fact that they are subject to
the same kinds of uncertainty that he himself is experiencing. Furthermore,
the student notes that when his instructors experience these uncertainties,
they usually deal with them in a forthright manner, acknowledging them
with the consistency of what one student has termed a 'philosophy of
doubting'. Thus, a student's relationship to the faculty, like his advances
in knowledge and skill, encourages him to accept some of his uncertainty
as 'inevitable' and thoroughly 'legitimate' and to handle that uncertainty
by openly conceding that he is unsure.

Another process by which the student learns to face up to uncertainty
in an unequivocal manner is connected with his membership in the 'little
society' of medical students, for a medical school class is a closely-knit,
self-regulating community, with its own method of 'tackling a big problem'
like that of uncertainty.

Through a process of 'feeling each other out', the group first establishes
the fact that uncertainty is experienced by 'everyone', thereby reassuring
a student that his own difficulties in this regard are not unique. 'As always,
the biggest lift comes from talking to other students and finding that they
have felt the same way. You may do this by a few casual jokes, but you
know there is more to it than that. . . .'

Secondly, out of the more than 'casual joking, asking around and talking
to others' that constantly go on among students, a set of standards for

dealing with uncertainty gradually emerges—standards that tend to co-incide with those of the faculty.

> Suppose I should talk real enthusiastically about the job of dissection I did [a freshman explains]. Well, Earl will say, 'Gee, I'm a great guy, too, you know', or something to that effect. From that remark, I can tell I'm bragging too much. That cues me in, so I make a mental note not to brag so much the next time.... Because you don't talk about your successes to the group as a whole. It's sort of understood that you don't try to impress each other.... A lot of the fellows belittle themselves.... I mean, a fellow will say, for example, that he thought a certain structure was a lymph node and that it turned out to be something entirely different. Then he and every-one else will laugh a lot over that....

If he acts presumptuously about his knowledge, a student will be reproached by his classmates whereas an admission of ignorance on his part may evoke their approval. From their positive and negative reactions, a student learns that his classmates, like his teachers, expect him to be uncertain about what he knows and candid about his uncertainty. (As one student puts it, 'It really isn't fashionable to believe much or to be overly sure.')

'Summing up is pretty tough,' a Sophomore writes, taking stock as his second year draws to a close.

> The uncertainty of first year is missing. You feel now as though you have a very shaky hold on a great deal of knowledge. You rather expect that the next two years will be spent getting a better hold on the things you are already familiar with.... We are half way through. To some people this is quite a milestone.... The realization that one day we will be doctors—finished with medical school—is now in the back of our minds. But few people have a definite idea of what they want to do.... For the most part, I think our class is looking forward to the third year, although there is a certain uneasiness about the idea of presenting yourself to the patient as a doctor....

In some respects confident and knowing, in others uneasy and not sure, a student feels variously certain and uncertain as he makes the transition from the preclinical to the clinical years of medical school.

THE CLINICAL YEARS

The kinds of uncertainty facing the third-year student
The kinds of uncertainty experienced by a third-year student are qualita-tively the same as those he encountered in his preclinical years. First, there is the uncertainty that comes with realizing that, despite all the medicine a student has mastered and all he will learn, he can never hope to 'shovel out more than a corner of what there is to know'.

Studying medicine is a lot like digging a hole in the sand. You get down there and start digging, but it seems as though for every shovelful you toss out, some more slides in. And of course, when you dig *any* hole, you never get to the bottom.... If you were to ask me how I felt about medicine now, and you happened to catch me in a moment of honesty, I'd tell you that I'm completely overwhelmed by a feeling of lack of knowledge....

Secondly, when he meets clinical problems that 'even stump the experts', a third-year student is confronted with uncertainty that derives from the limitations of medical science.

Ted and I got to talking about some of the revelations of third year, and one of the things that has struck him is that there isn't a diagnosis for everything. He has more or less assumed that there was always a diagnosis that could be made, and especially that a resident or attending should have no trouble making one. But this year, he has discovered that even a sharp attending like Dr ——— can be stumped....

Uncertainty over how to distinguish his own inadequacies from those which are general to the field continues to pose a problem for the student. If he has trouble with a venipuncture, for example, or does what he considers a 'hack job' in 'working up' a patient, a student wonders if 'it's mostly due to the fact that [his] talents just don't run towards being a doctor' or if his difficulty is largely attributable to the poor condition of the patient's veins and to the objective intricacy of her case.

But if the uncertainties of third year are like those with which a student is already acquainted and to which he has become partly inured, there is a sense in which the third year at Cornell seems to intensify the *degree* of uncertainty. As one student puts it, 'starting third year is a little like starting medical school all over. Everything is new, and you don't know what to expect or plan for....' Because the third year represents a major transition point in a student's training—it is the beginning of his total immersion in clinical medicine—the uncertainties he encounters at first seem greater to him than those he encountered as a Sophomore. (Within the limited confines of this paper, we have chosen to treat the third year as a unit—for the most part ignoring the fact that it is actually made up of a series of microcosms. The third year at Cornell is divided into three terms (i) medicine; (ii) surgery; (iii) obstetrics-gynaecology; paediatrics; public health; psychiatry. And the class itself is divided into three groups that rotate through these various terms—some taking medicine first, some surgery, some obstetrics-gynaecology, etc. Further, these three groups are in turn subdivided—half taking their medical clerkships at New York Hospital first, half at Bellevue first (and then interchanging); half taking paediatrics first, half obstetrics-gynaecology first (and interchanging too). Again, within each of these terms, even more subdivisions take place. For example, the students go two by two to the palpation clinic while on obstetrics-gynaecology; on medicine, they are broken up into tutorial groups containing five students apiece, and so on. In the section that follows, we will only allude to the differences between the trimesters of the year and the wide dispersion of the student group. Though our discussion of it here is cursory, the effect that the 'geometry' of third year has on students merits future study.)

In spite of his enthusiasm over working on the wards and in the clinics of the hospital, a third-year student looks back somewhat wistfully on what he regards as the relative 'organization and continuity of the academic classroom'. How do you 'approach learning', he wonders,[6] 'now that things are no longer grouped by courses—and the choice of what to study is so completely your own? For example, suppose you want to read up on headache.... You can read a two-page section in the Merck Manual, a five-page section in Cecil,[6] a thirty-page section in a book called *Signs and Symptoms*, or recent articles in the journals.... Which is best is very hard to decide.' Part of the student's difficulty in evolving a plan of study lies in the fact that what he is really seeking is nothing less than an organized way of learning to think like a doctor. During the third year at Cornell the student reaches out to make the process of differential diagnosis and the logic of rational treatment more conclusively his own.

As a student quickly discovers, however, the way of thought of the doctor is something other than a sum total of the ideas he has already mastered. Neither the principles he has learned in the basic medical sciences nor his book knowledge of disease processes automatically equip him to think like a doctor.

> The basic principles of medicine are very difficult things to catch hold of [a third-year student writes]. In engineering, once you really understand a principle, it stays with you, and you feel confident you will be able to use it in attacking a wide range of new problems. If you really understand mechanics, you can do anything with it, and you don't have to worry so much about whether certain things are true in one case and not in another.... The problems may be new tomorrow, but the basic principles don't change (much).... With medicine, it's different... There are as many exceptions as there are rules ... and the important things in one case don't count in another.... You can't read the chapter and 'figure out the problem' in medicine. And it is the greatest folly to argue with an instructor (a good one) with only the chapter behind you. You can say, 'Cecil says ...' but if he's seen patients with such-and-such for twenty years, then he probably has you. In other words, years of experience don't modify the principles of the engineering book, but in medicine they do....

Along with the change in organization and the different way of thought, the divided nature of the third year augments the uncertainty to which a student is subject. 'The class is pretty split up these days.... Lunch is the only time you see friends you are otherwise completely out of contact with. You are all doing different things, and it is really very nice to get a chance to eat together and talk about them. . . .' Separated from some of the people on whom he depended for confirmation and support and now asked to see patients alone, a third-year student is called upon to meet uncertainty in a more solitary fashion. 'Last year, if you thought you felt a liver, for instance, but you weren't quite sure, there were always two or three other fellows there, and you could ask them if they felt it too. But this year, we see patients alone. So we're more on our own now. . . .' Perhaps most important of all in quickening a student's sense of uncertainty is his conviction that 'third year is the year when the whole jump is made, and you learn to be a doctor'. What is called for now, he says, is 'knowing enough to do justice to your patients. . . . You get to the point where you say I should know these things. . . . Otherwise I'll be cheating my patients. . . . In that respect, I feel like a doctor already. . . .'

In general then the uncertainty of third year is compounded for a student by his 'developing sense of responsibility'. As he becomes aware of the imminence of his doctorhood, 'gaps in [his] knowledge' or unsureness on his part seem more serious to a beginning third-year student than they formerly did.

The certitude of the third-year student
Although a student may tell you at the outset of the third year that he feels 'a little bit like a pea on a griddle' (dwarfed by medicine and alone in some ways), he does not continue to sound so unsure of himself. As the year unfolds, a student's initial uncertainty gradually gives way to a manner of certitude. One gains the impression that students are more uncertain during the first part of the third year than they were before, but that they become less uncertain than before during the later part of the third year. There seem to be several reasons for this.

In the atmosphere of the 'clinical situation', a student can feel his medical knowledge take root. The 'chance to see many of the things [he] has read about' reinforces what he has previously learned; and the fact that 'there is a patient lying there in bed proves' to him that what he is currently learning is 'really important'.

However, the growing assurance of a third-year student does not result only from his greater knowledge and his conviction that what he is doing is important. It results also from the fact that in the third year he is relatively insulated from some of the diagnostic and therapeutic uncertainties he will encounter later. For one thing, the acute illnesses he sees on the wards and the explicit problems he handles in the clinics are often 'classic' or so manifest that he says they seem almost 'obvious' to him. For another, the responsibilities a third-year student is asked to assume are carefully circumscribed. Although he now has more responsibility than he did when he was a preclinical student, he has considerably less than he will have later, as a fourth-year student or practising physician. His duties on the wards do not go beyond taking a history, doing a physical examination, and carrying out indicated laboratory tests. When it comes to the problems of treating a patient, the student is largely an onlooker. He does not have to decide upon medicaments and other therapeutic procedures— weighing the potential risks involved against the possible benefits that may accrue to his patients. A student's responsibilities in the clinic are equally limited and specific. In the surgery speciality clinics, for example, his diagnoses are restricted to those facets of a patient's problems that are encompassed by the particular speciality he is representing at the time. The only therapy for which he is responsible is 'fairly simple and concrete': treating infections, removing sutures, and dressing wounds, for example, such as he does on minor surgery.

In effect, the delimited nature of his responsibilities frees a student from the necessity of coping with diagnostic and therapeutic uncertainties that fall outside a narrow orbit. (One of the factors that may persuade a student to enter a specialized field within medicine is that narrowing the scope of practice also narrows the range of potential uncertainty with which he will have to deal as a doctor.) Even in the general surgery clinic where he deals with a wider range of medical problems in a more comprehensive way, the student is protected from many clinical uncertainties. In general surgery (and in his other clinics as well) a student rarely sees a patient more than once. It is usually only in retrospect that he catches a glimpse of the uncertainties he might have encountered had his relationship with patients been continuous. For example, reviewing the charts of patients he examined in general surgery as a junior, a fourth-year student was 'amazed to discover' that some of the cases he saw were never resolved.

> ... One poor woman had a negative GB series (I thought she had gall bladder disease); was seen by someone else and had a negative GI series (he thought she had an ulcer); was seen by someone else and had a negative proctoscopy and Ba. enema (he thought she had Ca. of the colon). She then went to another clinic and had two more negative GI series because someone there thought she had a Meckel's diverticulum. On her last visit, someone wrote down 'irritable colon' and treated her with 'reassurance'....

His close relationship to the clinical faculty is another source of a third-year student's increasing assurance.

> During the first two years it was possible to remain completely removed from the faculty and yet still do OK by reading and going to lectures. While some departments made an effort to develop a close student/faculty relationship, you never had to depend on this to get the things you were supposed to. But now only 50% of what we need can come from books.

The other 50% has to come from the teachers we work with. And so, there is a 180 degree shift in the class's relation to the faculty....

Because he finds that listening to experienced doctors reason out loud is the only way he can get 'a sense of how to approach clinical problems', the third-year student welcomes the opportunity to learn through direct contact with his instructors. Meeting with members of the faculty or house staff in small intimate groups and discussing patients with them is 'the heart of clinical medical education', so far as a student is concerned. Sessions like these, he says, 'give [him] insight into how a doctor organizes and uses his information', and a 'real sense of colleagueship'. ('You catch the feeling you must have in a craft: the father passing the secrets of the craft on to the son.') The closeness of his relationship to the faculty in the third year helps a student to think and feel more like a doctor, and consequently fosters his sense of certainty.

In these respects, the student acquires greater assurance during the course of his third year at Cornell. He also adopts a *manner* of certitude, for he has come to realize that it may be important for him to 'act like a savant' even when he does not actually feel sure. From his instructors and patients alike a student learns this lesson: that if he is to meet his clinical responsibilities, he cannot allow himself to doubt as openly or to the same extent that he did during his preclinical years. Instead, he must commit himself to some of the tentative judgements he makes, and move decisively on behalf of his patients.

Dr T's philosophy goes something like this.... 'You boys are to handle the case as you see best. I put no restrictions on you from this point of view. You do the work-up, decide what's to be done, and whatever you decide is all right. But I insist on this much—you must stand up for your decisions, never apologize for what you are doing, and never start getting humble and say you don't know....'

The third-year student learns from his instructors that too great a display of unsureness on his part may elicit criticism; from his patients he learns that it may evoke alarm.

To say that the patient 'searches your face' for clues is no overstatement. An example—while on O.B. when trying to palpate a baby once, I got a little confused and frowned in puzzlement. Sensed at once that the mother saw the frown and was alarmed. So, I reassured her that everything was all right. I have always tried to remember not to do it again....

Yielding to the point of view of his instructors who enjoin him to be 'firm and take a position', to the desire of his patients to be assured, and to his own 'need for definiteness' as well, a third-year student generally makes it his policy to 'believe'.

I'm sure that on the higher levels of medicine you *do* admit your ignorance and avoid stereotyped thinking. But we are at the point now where you have to believe in the rule rather than the exception.... Perhaps this is a phase you must pass through on the way up, just as you must learn that the heart *does* have a pacemaker before you learn that it *doesn't*....

In sum, the assurance of a third-year student results from his progress in learning and his unawareness of many clinical uncertainties. He assumes a sure manner also because of his belief that 'it is a mistake for a medical student at [his] stage of the game to doubt too much'.

Training for uncertainty in the comprehensive care and teaching programme

The sense of sureness expressed by students about to complete their third year at Cornell is, in some respects, premature. At any rate, the fourth-year student's perspective on the uncertainties of medicine is usually different from that of a junior.

Experience makes you less sure of yourself, [a Senior explains]. What you realize is that even when you've been out of medical school twenty years, there'll be many times when you won't be able to make a diagnosis or cure a patient.... Instead of looking for the day, then, when all the knowledge you need will be in your possession, you learn that such a day will never come....

A fourth-year student who faces up to uncertainty in this way has departed considerably from his third-year self. Part of this change seems attributable to experiences in the comprehensive care and teaching programme. (Though the fourth year at Cornell is made up of three terms, we will discuss only the medicine semester [comprehensive care] in this paper. The qualitative data [diaries, interviews, and observations] are not sufficient to do justice to the surgery and obstetrics-gynaecology terms that also form part of the fourth year.) A central feature of the programme is the extensive responsibility for patients which it allows students. Each student is assigned a number of patients who are defined as *his* patients, and he is expected to deal with all the problems that each case presents.[8] Stemming from this degree of responsibility are varied situations and experiences which make the fourth-year student more aware of the uncertainties of medicine. The types of uncertainties a student encounters in the comprehensive care and teaching programme seem to be like those he has dealt with recurrently since his days as a freshman. However, it is no longer so easily possible to distinguish which fourth-year experiences are salient for which types of uncertainty. Rather, in the situations in which the fourth-year student finds himself all types of uncertainty seem to converge and to be inter-twined. For this reason we have found it necessary here to modify the pattern set in earlier sections of this paper, and we talk now largely in terms of undifferentiated uncertainties.

One important way in which students exercise the broad responsibility offered them is by following their patients over a period of months. This gives them more insight into the prevalence of uncertainties in the practice of medicine. What began as the 'classical case' of Mrs B., for example, illustrates this fact. 'My new patient arrived first ... Mrs B., a thirty-two year old housewife and mother of two children, who had a sudden onset of typical thyroid symptoms complete with the physical findings to go with them.... I ordered several diagnostic tests for her and advised her to return in a week....' In this initial contact, the student-physician considered Mrs B.'s case 'typical', and the tests which he ordered were presumably intended merely to confirm his diagnosis. There is no indication that he anticipated special difficulty in handling Mrs B.'s problems.

On the second visit the student and the attending physician who was supervising him agreed that Mrs B.'s case was clear-cut, and that surgery would be appropriate. But they did not reckon with the response of the patient to that proposal.

By the time I got to my second re-visit, Mrs B., my toxic thyroid case, she had been waiting some time.... She gave me the story of continuation of her previous symptoms with shaking even more apparent at present. Of the tests ordered, only the BMR came back, but this was conclusive, being 59% above normal. I informed her that all her problems were related to these findings, and after discussing her with Dr D. told her that hospitalization and surgery were her best chance for a permanent cure. At this she broke down in tears, and after composing herself, made many arguments against surgery.... Dr D. and I quickly agreed that I should treat her with propylthiouracil on an ambulatory basis until she has quieted down. This is an unnatural response to hospitalization and surgery, and I'll be interested in seeing if she becomes more logical with the quiescence of her toxic symptoms....

The patient's fear of an operation forced the student and the attending physician to adopt a plan of therapy which they believed was less effective than the one they originally set forth.

On a later visit the full complexity of Mrs B.'s case became more apparent.

I went in to see Mrs B. and found that the threat of her husband's quitting his job was related to her hysterical crying most of the day. She admitted that her reaction wasn't wholly because of her disease state, but that she had been easily unnerved prior to this. I assured her that although this might be so, her thyroid was making it much worse, and that we would shortly be rid of part of it.... She mentioned that a lump on her daughter's wrist was bothering her, and I suggested that she bring her in on the next visit.... We discussed surgery at her initiation, and arrived at the same conclusion as before: my insisting that surgery was the best solution to her problem, and her insisting that she, her husband and friends all agree that if a cure is possible without surgery, that is to be embarked on....

Mrs B.'s emotional response to the diagnosis and recommendation made by the student-physician, her eagerness to accept the anti-surgical opinions of her family and friends, her anxiety over her husband's job and her daughter's health all proved relevant to the appraisal and management of her case. With each visit it became more apparent to the student-physician that Mrs B.'s problems were psychological as well as physical, and this realization evoked new questions. Was Mrs B.'s long-standing nervousness wholly attributable to her disease state? Would it be possible to 'ever get this woman over some of her anxious moments', and thus ready her for a needed operation? 'I'm not too certain about any of these things,' Mrs B.'s student-physician reported at the end of his third visit with her. But had he seen her only once, this student would not have had any reason to alter his original impression that the case of Mrs B. was diagnostically and therapeutically 'clearcut'.

The continuous nature of his contact with patients in the programme, then, alerts a student to some of the clinical uncertainties that lie beyond first medical judgements and the appearance of things. Furthermore, it confronts him with the problem of managing a long-term doctor/patient relationship in the face of these uncertainties. For example:

I saw Mr T. again and gave him the sad news—no ulcer demonstrated. What could this be if it wasn't an ulcer? I tried my best to put him off so that I wouldn't be obligated to further diagnostic procedures which would be useless and expensive. I did my best to convince him that it sounded like nothing but ulcer, and that we planned to treat it as such because not all ulcers are demonstrated by X-ray. This wasn't good enough....

Mrs J. puts up a pretty good front, but I think she worries a good deal about her problem. And today she asked me what she had. I was kind of up a tree.... I told her that what she had was somewhat different in that it didn't respond to the usual therapy—but that we had many other weapons and she shouldn't be concerned....

With every re-visit, the need for a solution may grow more intense in both the patient and the student-physician. Mr T., for example, becomes harder to convince or reassure. Mrs J. shows evidence of worrying a great deal and begins to press her doctor for an explanation of her problem. And the student, feeling responsible for the welfare of this man and woman (defined by the programme as *his* patients), is likely to feel frustrated and disappointed by his inability to resolve their cases.

These frustrations may be all the more provoking because the student has not been completely prepared for them by his earlier experiences. His

relatively brief and circumscribed contact with patients in the third year
had led him to assume that a good doctor ought to be able to arrive at
a 'definitive diagnosis' and to evolve a successful plan of treatment for
most of the cases with which he deals. But the broad and continuous
experience provided by the programme teaches a student that cases like
those of Mr T. and Mrs J. are more widespread than he had supposed
them to be.

Not only do his continuing relationship with patients and the growing
magnitude of his responsibility for them increase a student's awareness
of the uncertain aspects of the cases with which he deals; they often lead
to his being deeply affected by these uncertainties. Because he is working
with patients in a sustained way, a student is more susceptible to positive
and negative counter-transference than he was before entering the programme. As time goes on, he may become attached to some patients and
alienated from others. Furthermore, the relatively large degree of responsibility assigned to him by the programme makes a student feel more
accountable for what happens to patients than he formerly did. As a result,
the uncertainties that a student experiences in the programme 'make an
emotional impact on [him]', so that he is sometimes inclined to react
subjectively to the uncertain features of cases he cannot bring to a satisfactory conclusion. Usually these reactions involve the placing of 'blame',
either on himself or on his patient:

> I blame myself, not Mrs H. [her student-physician declares]. I can't get her
> to reduce, and I don't know what I'm doing wrong. I have remained pleasant
> and sympathetic, but have applied strong urging and have registered
> disappointment (not wrath) at her failure to cooperate.... The reason I find
> her so difficult is that I feel if someone else were handling her, he could get
> the pounds off her....

> Mrs C. has caused me quite a bit of consternation [another student asserts].
> Though we have taken adequate physical measures to ascertain that her
> difficulty is on an emotional basis, she's still showing bodily over-concern....
> She complains of pains in her legs; that her arms are too weak; that she's
> tired; that she feels pressure in her abdomen.... And then, these gripes
> about her husband. I can understand them in a way—because he's the type
> of man who comes home from work, picks up his paper, looks at TV for
> a while, and then goes to bed without saying a word.... But she makes
> no effort to do anything about the situation.... She just sits there and tells
> me, 'that's the way he is....' Another thing about this woman is, in all
> instances she will discontinue whatever treatment you prescribe and proceed
> on her own conception....

The 'failure' is his, the first student claims; it's the 'fault' of the patient
and her environment, says the second.

As the cases of Mrs H. and Mrs C. suggest, a student is particularly

apt to respond in one or the other of these affectual ways when the uncertainty he faces concerns either the social and psychological aspects
of a patient's illness, or his own management of the doctor/patient relationship. Partly because psychiatry and the social sciences are in a more
embryonic stage of development than the disciplines from which medicine
derives its understanding of the human body, the student encounters
uncertainty more frequently in trying to handle the emotional and environmental components of his patient's disorder than in trying to cope with
problems that are largely physical in nature. The classification of psychological disturbances thus far evolved, for example, is not precise enough
to permit a high degree of diagnostic exactitude. The relationship between
social factors and illness is only beginning to be systematically explored.
And most of the available methods for treating socio-psychological difficulties are still grossly empirical, their relative merits and demerits a focus
of present-day medical controversy, interest and concern.

Intellectually, a student is aware of these things before he enters the
comprehensive care programme; but he has not yet fully learned to acknowledge the uncertainties and limitations in this realm, or to proceed
comfortably within the framework of such a realization. This is partly
because, prior to his semester in the programme, a student has had little
opportunity to take active responsibility for the 'personal problems' of his
patients. In the third year, for example, as we have seen, a student's work
centres primarily on physical diagnosis. The only personal therapy he has
occasion to administer to his patients is a simple and limited form of
reassurance, which, on the whole, he judges to be effective. His success
in this respect he deems 'understandable' for he is inclined to feel that the
so-called art of medicine skills are based not so much on trained experience as they are on personal qualities. Such an attitude is reflected, for
example, in the way that a number of third-year students look upon their
psychiatry instructors. 'There is a general feeling of great respect for
most of the psychiatry people we have come in contact with [one student
tells us]. We are impressed to note that the psychiatrist almost always
suggests the honest, straightforward, direct approach to things ... and most
of us feel these people make sense....'

Yet 'the regard we have for psychiatrists is not the same as the respect
we have for surgeons,' this student goes on to say. In the case of surgery,
'it's a matter of respecting skill', in the case of psychiatry, 'respecting
common sense'.

This distinction is one that students carry with them into the programme.
It helps explain the observed tendency of many students in comprehensive
care to reproach themselves when they are unable to formulate the 'human
aspects of a patient's case' or to decide upon an effective way of dealing
with those aspects. ('I can't get Mrs H. to reduce ... and I don't know

what I'm doing wrong.') For a student who tends to regard problems like 'getting the patient to lose weight' as more contingent on personal attributes than on learned skill, the case of Mrs H. may seem to represent a personal failure on his part.

The more common tendency of a student to blame the patient under such circumstances is a different manifestation of the same emotional involvement. In the face of medical uncertainties that may impede his attempts to be decisive about the socio-psychological dimensions of the case he handles, a student often projects his own sense of inadequacy upon the patient. In comprehensive care, for example, students frequently apply the epithet 'crock' to 'patients who do not have an organic lesion' or whose behaviour appears to be 'psycho-neurotic'. 'The central feature in all these patients we call "crocks" is that they threaten our ability as doctors,' one student points out. This is both because such patients do not respond to the diagnostic and therapeutic efforts of the student-physician in the way he would like ('You don't get a foothold anywhere and do something to give them a better adjustment...') and because the student is emotionally 'more vulnerable when thinking about the human aspects of a case, rather than just the strict medical problems involved'.

> Whether you're conscious of it or not, a lot of the things disturbed patients talk to you about are the kinds of things you're likely to react to very strongly in a positive or negative way.... I mean, it's all very well to say you're not judging these people, for instance. But you can get annoyed as heck with some of them, or lose your sympathy even though you know they're psychoneurotic....

To sum up: the fourth-year student is repeatedly impressed by the diagnostic and therapeutic uncertainties he encounters in dealing with patients during his semester in comprehensive care. Some of these uncertainties, he realizes, result from his own lack of medical knowledge and some from the limitations of medicine itself. In this respect, they are no different from those he has met at earlier points in his training. However, the physician-like responsibilities ascribed to him by the programme, along with the continuing and holistic nature of his relationship to patients, magnify the problem of uncertainty for the student, and make it harder for him to deal with it in a dispassionate way. In turn, the student's emotional involvement increases the difficulty he has in distinguishing between those uncertainties that grow out of his personal ignorance and those that stem from the current limitations of medical science. It is particularly when he feels unsure about how to classify the ulcer-like symptoms of a Mr T., or what to do about the obesity of a Mrs H., that a student 'doesn't know whether [his] uncertainty is a reflection of his lack of knowledge and technique or whether such cases would be perplexing' even to more experienced physicians. As we have seen, a student is at first more apt to blame himself, or by projection, the patient, than he is to attribute his uncertainty to gaps in medical science.

Coming to terms with uncertainty in comprehensive care

The student's increased awareness of uncertainties in medicine is of course not the chief by-product of his term in comprehensive care. The same experiences which lead to such awareness also enlarge his skills in the realms of diagnosis and patient management. From the absence of expected findings in a case like that presented by Mr T., for example, he learns how to appraise conflicting evidence in arriving at a diagnosis. From the complex problems of Mrs B. he learns something of the connection between emotional stress and physical illness and gains some experience in dealing with patients who are under such stress. When he leaves the programme the student, therefore, has considerably more confidence about his ability to cope with these problems than he did six months before.

Moreover, the fourth-year student finds ways of adjusting to his remaining uncertainties. The organization of the comprehensive care programme and some of its precepts help the student to recognize that he shares part of his uncertainty with fellow classmates and instructors. This enables him to meet his uncertainty with greater confidence and equipoise.

An indication of the marked increase in confidence is contained in a simple statistical result. In May 1955 all four classes at Cornell were asked how capable they felt about dealing with a number of problems encountered by practising physicians. One of these problems concerned 'the uncertainties of diagnosis and therapy that one meets in practice'. The class by class distribution of replies on this item was as follows.

	Percentage of each class			
Problem of 'uncertainties'	First year	Second year	Third year	Fourth year
Quite sure I can deal with this	10	11	21	25
Fairly sure I can deal with this	52	61	60	72
Not sure I can deal with this	38	28	19	3
No. of students	(82)	(82)	(85)	(85)

In contrast to the many small groups into which the class is divided during the third year, half of the senior class is enrolled in comprehensive care at one time, spending a continuous six months together in the programme. This arrangement facilitates that kind of interchange between students which from the earliest days of medical school provided them with mutual aid and the supportive knowledge that 'others feel the way [they] do'.

In the process of a routine physical, I performed a pelvic and rectal, and the glove specimen of the stool was strongly guaiac positive! And I didn't quite know what to do. The patient lives in upstate New York and can come to the city only when her husband drives in once a month. A decent GI workup would require her spending four full days at the hospital. To further complicate matters, I wasn't sure of the significance of the positive test. I had rinsed my glove between pelvic and rectal, but the possibility of a positive test from blood in the vagina remains.... In the course of describing this experience at lunch ... one of my classmates suggested that it was a crime to let her out of the building without a GI series, Ba. enema, and proctoscopy. He felt that even if subsequent stool examinations are negative, such a workup is obligatory.... This is the sort of decision I would prefer to force on someone else. I would feel foolish if such a workup showed nothing and subsequent stools were negative, but I'd feel worse if she showed up with an inoperable cancer a few months hence.... The lunch table of four was evenly divided on the question of what one should do if such a circumstance arose in general practice.... This problem is a real threat to the young physician....

Although uncertainties such as these are 'threatening', the student can perhaps find some reassurance in the fact that his classmates experience the same difficulties in deciding on appropriate action.

The opportunity to work as coequal with the attending physicians of comprehensive care also gives the student a chance to see that, at times, expert doctors are not more facile than he in making a diagnosis or deciding upon a course of treatment.

My second case was a three-year-old girl with a swollen, red, warm left hand, which seemed to itch more than it hurt. No signs of infected wound— only history of a possible insect bite. I felt this was a contact dermatitis. The pediatrician felt it was obvious cellulitis, but insisted we call in a surgeon to confirm him. The surgeon leaned toward my diagnosis—and we called in a dermatologist who felt this was definitely infection—which was very amusing....

Finally, the experimental milieu of the programme also furthers the student's realization that neither his classmates nor his instructors have sure and easy answers to some of the questions he finds puzzling. Because one of the primary aims of the programme is self-critically to develop a more comprehensive type of medical care, students and staff are continuously engaged in a process of inquiry. Conjoined by a living experiment, they openly express their feelings of doubt and uncertainty, and systematically try to resolve them. In one of the weekly comprehensive care conferences, for example, we can see this process taking place. A fourth-year student is presenting the history of the Gonzales family, whom he serves as general physician.

The Gonzales family is a Puerto Rican family that has been in this country for sixteen months. It consists of eight members: Mr Gonzales, a thirty-

eight year old unskilled labourer; Mrs Gonzales, his twenty-five year old
uneducated wife; and their six children.... They live in a three room
unheated apartment on 60th Street. From the outset of our contact with
this family it was obvious that there were a number of interrelated sociological, economic and medical problems, all of which could not be treated
at the same time. We have tried to proceed in the most logical manner, but
often our efforts had to be sidetracked by the appearance of new problems.
First, there was the real possibility of the family breaking up under the
existing stresses. This immediate crisis passed. Then, there was the problem
of tuberculosis with the diagnosis of Anna's active case, the question
of Mrs Gonzales' status, and the necessity of evaluating other members of
the family. Coincidental with this investigation was the series of upper
respiratory infections, otitis medias, episodes of gastro-enteritis and pyelitis,
Carlo's seizure disorder, and finally Mr Gonzales' admission to the hospital.
Many of the family are known to be anaemic, so following our satisfaction
that none of the other children had tuberculosis, it was agreed that the known
parasitic infections should be next attacked.... It seems certain that poor
nutrition is another contributing factor to the anaemias, and we have taken
steps along this line as well... One of the family's food difficulties has been
the inability to shop properly. Previous to our contact with them, they
purchased all of their groceries from a store uptown where Spanish was
spoken, and high prices asked. On our advice, Mr Gonzales now does most
of his shopping at the A & P.... The situation has been in a constant state
of flux since we first came in contact with the family, and shows every
evidence of continuing in the same state.... All our efforts still leave
many of the major problems of the family unsolved.... We will welcome
any suggestions and opinions you may have....

A series of student comments followed upon his presentation, gradually
crystallizing around one of the major ideas of the programme. ('There is
consensus that adequate care must include preventive, emotional, environmental, and familial aspects if it is to offer the most that modern knowledge
can supply in the management of those who are ill.'[9] But it has not yet
been determined how inclusive 'adequate care' can and should be.)

I was thinking as I sat there listening to the Gonzales case ... is it or isn't
it part of the doctor's job to be concerned with such things as where his
patients buy their food?

Theoretically, I guess it's part of the doctor's job.... But from my own
point of view, I'm afraid that if I had a family like this, all I'd want to do
is throw up my hands completely....

As far as the question of whether or not the doctor is obligated to look
into such matters as the food people buy is concerned, I'd say yes ... so long
as those things pertain to medical illness. And in this particular family, it's
especially important because they're all anaemic.... But as for the social
problems of this Puerto Rican family, they're beyond the scope of an
everyday doctor to crack, in my opinion....

What we have here is a group of Americans coming from highly sordid conditions to live in highly sordid conditions.... Well, I think it's part of our responsibility to do something about this problem....

We had another case in a session on Thursday that bears on this. This is an Irish woman who's tied down with arthritis and who has a number of problems in addition. Among them is the fact that she lives in a one room flat—dirty and with no heat. Well, the question arose as to whether it's the doctor's responsibility to get her another apartment and encourage her to move ... or whether it's beyond the scope of the physician's work....

The variety of opinion voiced in the course of such a conference provides a student with intimations that not only his classmates, but his instructors and physicians in general, are as perplexed as he is by questions about such matters as the boundaries of the doctor's professional task and the unsolved problems of patients like the Gonzales family. In the words of a faculty member who spoke up at the end of this conference, 'These questions don't only concern students.... They concern doctors as well.... There just aren't many "ground rules" in this area....'

CONCLUSION

This paper reviews some experiences which acquaint the medical student with the different types of uncertainty he will encounter later as a practising physician, and some of the ways in which he learns to deal with these uncertainties.

Because this is a preliminary description of what, it turns out, are rather complex processes, we have not organized the analysis around several basic distinctions that could be made. But it seems appropriate to introduce these now so that lines of a more systematic analysis can begin to emerge.

One basic type of uncertainty distinguished at the outset is that deriving from limitations in the current state of medical knowledge. Clearly, the different medical sciences vary in this respect. It has been indicated, for example, that limitations in a field like pharmacology are now considerably greater than they are in, say, anatomy. There are comparable differences among the clinical sciences. There would probably be general agreement that gaps in psychiatric knowledge are considerably greater than those in the field of obstetrics and gynaecology. Such distinctions would provide a focus for further and more rigorous study of training for uncertainty. The different fields would be arranged according to the degree of uncertainty which characterizes them in order to see whether this ranking is paralleled by what the student learns from his different courses about the uncertainties of medicine. Are students made most aware of uncertainties when they are exposed to fields in which these uncertainties are greatest? More important, perhaps, is the question whether those fields in which limitations of knowledge are particularly prominent offer more or fewer means of coming to terms with uncertainty.

The second type of uncertainty, resulting from imperfect mastery of what is currently known in the various fields of medicine, was not analysed in terms of its variability. We chose rather to concentrate on the 'typical' or 'modal' student at different phases of his medical school career. But obviously there are significant individual differences and these could provide a second focus in a more systematic study of training for uncertainty. Students vary in the level of skill which they achieve at any particular stage of their training. For example, those who find it easy to memorize details may have an advantage over their classmates in the study of anatomy; those whose manual dexterity is highly developed may not experience the same degree of personal inadequacy as the less adroit students when they begin to carry out surgical procedures; extraverted students may find it easier to get along with patients than introverted classmates. These variations in aptitudes, skill and knowledge may lead to individual differences in the extent to which students experience the uncertainties which derive from limitations of skill and knowledge. Students probably differ also in awareness of their own limitations and in response to these limitations. Some may be more sensitive than others to their real or imagined lack of skill. Some may be more able than others to tolerate the uncertainties of which they are aware. As we have seen, distinctions such as these would have to be considered in a more precise investigation of training for uncertainty. Are relatively skilled students less likely than relatively unskilled students to become aware of those uncertainties that derive from limits on medical knowledge? Are students especially sensitive to the uncertainties which confront them better able than less sensitive classmates to cope with such uncertainties? Or, to raise a somewhat different sort of problem, do students with a low level of tolerance for such uncertainty perform less effectively in their medical studies than students who are able to accommodate themselves to uncertainty? The level of tolerance might also affect the choice of a career: for example, do students who find it difficult to accept the uncertainties which they encounter elect to go into fields of medicine in which there is less likelihood of meeting these uncertainties?

A third distinction involves the experiences through which the student becomes acquainted with the uncertainties of medicine. Some of them are directly comparable with those which a mature physician would encounter. For example, when he meets the tentative and experimental point of view of pharmacologists or when inconsistent findings make a definitive diagnosis problematic, the student is faced with exactly the same sort of unsurenesses met by a practising physician. But other experiences seem to derive their elements of uncertainty from the teaching philosophies or curricular organization of the medical school. For instance, the uncertainties which a student experiences as a result of the avoidance of spoon-feeding by the basic science faculty at Cornell or the atomistic division of his class in the third year are by-products of particular conditions in the medical school, although they may have their analogues in actual practice. This distinction would consequently have to be incorporated into a more detailed analysis of training for uncertainty. Which type of experience is more conducive to recognition of the uncertainties in medicine? Which is more easily handled by students? In view of the wide range of experiences in medical school which have a bearing on training for uncertainty, what is the relative balance between those experiences which are inherent in the role of physician and those which inhere in the role of student?

This concluding section is clearly not a summary of what has gone before. Instead, we have chosen this opportunity to make explicit some of the variables and distinctions which were only implicit in earlier pages in order to indicate further problems for the more systematic qualitative analysis of a process like training for uncertainty.

REFERENCES

1. Unless otherwise indicated, all the quoted phrases and passages in this paper are drawn from the diaries that eleven Cornell students at various points along the medical school continuum have kept for us over the course of the past three years; from interviews with these student diarists and some of their classmates; and from close to verbatim student dialogue recorded by the sociologist who carried out day by day observations in some of the medical school situations cited in this paper.

2. This particular sentence was taken from the 'Address of Welcome to the Class of 1957' delivered by Dr Lawrence W. Hanlon. Everything else in the paragraph quoted is extracted from 'Some Steps in the Maturation of the Medical Student', a speech delivered by Dr Robert F. Pitts at Opening Day Exercises, September 1952.

3. Pitts, speech, *op. cit.*

4. Patricia L. Kendall and Hanan C. Selvin, 'Tendencies Toward Specialization in Medical Training', in R. K. Merton *et al.* (eds), *The Student Physician*, Oxford University Press (London 1957).

5. Joseph A. Wells, 'Historical Background and General Principles of Drug Action', in Victor A. Drill (ed.), *Pharmacology in Medicine*, McGraw-Hill (New York 1945), p. 6.

6. Russell L. Cecil, Robert F. Loeb *et al.*, *Textbook of Medicine*, W. B. Saunders (Philadelphia 1955).

7. See, for further discussion: Kendall and Selvin, 'Specialization in Training', in Merton *et al.* (eds), *Student Physician*, 1957, *op. cit.*

8. For a more detailed description of the comprehensive care and teaching programme, and the kinds of experiences which students have in it, see: George G. Reader, 'The Cornell Comprehensive Care and Teaching Programme', and Margaret Olencki, 'Range of Patient Contacts in the Comprehensive Care and Teaching Programme', in Merton *et al.* (eds), *Student Physician*, 1957, *op. cit.*

9. *Report of the Comprehensive Care and Teaching Programme to the Commonwealth Fund*, 30 March 1954.

6 Professional socialization as subjective experience: the process of doctrinal conversion among student nurses

F. DAVIS

The training of student nurses is taken as an example of professional socialization: the process by which the student passes from identification with a 'lay' to a 'professional' culture. This socialization model emphasizes the changes in self-identification experienced by the student nurse, her subjective awareness of this process, and the socio-psychological factors involved in the change. It is postulated that the professional socialization process for the student nurse occurs in six sequential stages: (i) initial innocence, (ii) labelled recognition of incongruity, (iii) 'psyching out', (iv) role simulation, (v) provisional internalization, (vi) stable internalization. The student is required to move from a 'lay' conception of the appropriate role of the nurse, to a more expanded and professional definition. In this reading her feeling states are sensitively traced: from the early stages when she is searching for an appropriate identity, to the latter stage when she emerges with a self-conscious awareness and confident acceptance of her professional role.

One might say that the learning of the medical role consists of a separation, almost an alienation, of the student from the lay medical world; a passing through the mirror so that one looks out on the world from behind it, and sees things as in mirror writing. In all of the more esoteric occupations we have studied we find the sense of seeing the world in reverse.

The period of initiation into the role appears to be one wherein the two cultures, lay and professional, interact within the individual. Such interaction undoubtedly goes on all through life, but it seems to be more lively—more exciting and uncomfortable, more self-conscious and yet perhaps more deeply unconscious—in the period of learning and initiation. . . .

In the process of change from one role to another there are occasions when other people expect one to play the new role before one feels completely identified with it or competent to carry it out; there are others in which one overidentifies oneself with the role, but is not accepted in it by others. These and other possible positions between roles make of an individual what is called a marginal man; either he or other people or both do not quite know to what role (identity, reference group) to refer him. We need studies which will discover the course of passage from the laymen's estate to that of the professional, with attention to the crises and the dilemmas of role which arise. Everett Hughes, *Men and Their Work.*[1]

As those who have the privilege to study under him come quickly to know, it is the hallmark of the thought and personal style of Everett C. Hughes to unerringly detect mind-jolting similarities among species of social life which to the rest of us seem at first glance wholly disparate and unrelated, if not outrightly farfetched. This gift for comparative thinking in depth, for seeing around the conventional symbols and adornments by which men try to distinguish their stations and achievements from those of their fellow men, is everywhere evident in Hughes's writing, most especially in his lifelong preoccupation with the life of work; ergo, the intriguing, almost inexhaustibly provocative comparisons of the janitor and the physician, the prostitute and the psychiatrist, the jazz musician and the lawyer, to cite but a few which have long since become staples in courses on the sociology of occupations and professions.

But to assume that the drawing of such 'exotic' comparisons nearly begins to encompass the scope of Hughes's contribution to sociology would be as sadly in error as to dismiss them as mere 'playthings' of a lively imagination. On the contrary, the place they occupy in his work must be viewed as surface reflections—grace notes, as it were—of a much deeper analytical and humane strain. This is one which seeks tenaciously to assay the common dilemmas, contradictions, ambiguities, and ambivalences—in short, the exquisite and disconcerting apprehensions of self—which everywhere assail men as they try somehow to wend their way through the labyrinth of statuses, roles, organizations, and institutions to which they are heir. It is by virtue of this profoundly humane perspective on social action that the reader comes to appreciate that, even when not explicitly or obviously comparative, Hughes's writing achieves that breadth of understanding, detachment, and yet sympathy which we associate with the best work in that genre. In sum, his words bear the stamp of all truly great and complex sociological writing: sacrificing nothing by way of clarity, they say more than they appear to.

It was then not in the least unusual or startling when in the course of preparing the present essay I again came across the vaguely remembered passage from *Men and Their Work* quoted above, only to realize now that they held a quintessential relevance for my own work that had escaped me previously. Indeed, if the truth must out, the quoted passage more faithfully captures the sociological substance of what follows than any of several summaries and conclusions I had written for earlier drafts. Yet, characteristically enough, though I write here solely of student nurses, the passage is taken from Hughes's *The Making of a Physician*,[2] a kind of sociological prospectus he prepared in 1955 for the then barely initiated study of medical students he was later to complete with Howard S. Becker, Blanche Geer, and Anselm Strauss. What more apt illustration of his facility to inform the particular with the generic?

In this essay I mean to take seriously the injunction of the quotation's last sentence that 'we need studies which will discover the course of passage from the laymen's estate to that of the professional, *with attention to the crises and the dilemmas of role which arise*' (italics mine). In doing so I shall of necessity write mainly from the vantage point of those undergoing this kind of status passage rather than in the language of such familiar, phenomenologically exterior sociological constructs as 'value change', 'attitudinal fit', or 'the pattern variable structure of the professional role'.[3] Hence the title's designation of professional socialization as *subjective experience*. In particular I aim to pay close attention to those feeling states, inner turning points and experiential markings which from the perspective of the subject impart a characteristic tone, meaning and quality to his status passage. But recognizing that it would be a practical impossibility to capture, much less convey, the full flow of subjective experience contained in the transition from layman to professional, I shall focus specifically on *doctrinal conversion*, which as Hughes so aptly notes, constitutes perhaps the most crucial and problematic dimension in becoming a professional. By this I mean simply the social psychological process whereby students come to exchange their own lay views and imagery of the profession for those the profession ascribes to itself.

The research materials on which I base my discussion come from a five-year study of professional socialization among collegiate nursing students at a university school of nursing. For three of these years my colleagues and I gathered extensive and intensive data on five succeeding classes of students through the methods of observational field work, longitudinal questionnaire survey, and panel depth interview. Because of the extensive, space-consuming documentation that would be required, in the body of this paper I will forego citing specific evidence for this or that statement and instead present a summary version of some of our major findings that bear on the subjective experience of becoming a nurse.[4]

Some preliminary words are in order concerning the characteristics of this student nurse population and the kind of training its members receive. With a few exceptions, they are all young women in their late teens and early twenties who arrive at the school of nursing following two years of undergraduate liberal arts studies elsewhere, most from a nearby state university noted for its high academic standards. They remain at the school for three years, taking mainly clinical and theoretical courses in the various branches of nursing practice as well as a few additional required and elective courses in the natural and social sciences. At the end of the three years, assuming they have successfully completed their studies (as nearly 80% typically do), they receive a Bachelor of Science degree and are fully qualified to take state board examinations for licensing as professional registered nurses. By and large these are girls of middle and upper-middle class background,[5] reared in large metropolitan areas and medium-sized cities and though not for the most part strongly church oriented affiliated predominantly with the more socially prestigious Protestant denominations —Episcopal, Congregational, Presbyterian. Less than 15% are of working-class background and an equally small proportion is Catholic. Except for a handful of oriental students and even fewer Negroes, all are white.

In setting out to delineate the subjective side of the process of doctrinal conversion these students undergo, I do not wish to leave the implication that professional socialization everywhere, even as it may be reified through some set of formal categories, proceeds in like fashion. Much more comparative research among and within professions must be done before so rash a claim could be justified. Moreover, it must be remembered that these students are young women in what is overwhelmingly a female profession and hence subject, as we have had repeated occasion to note,[6] to career and life contingencies far different from those obtaining in such predominantly male fields as for example medicine and law. The somewhat distinctive doctrinal emphases of contemporary American nursing education generally and of this school in particular may also act to impart a more or less unique stamp and trajectory to their professional socialization. Rather, therefore, than presuming to deduce a set of universal categories by which to analyse doctrinal conversion in professional socialization wherever and whenever it occurs, in what follows I wish merely to sensitize the reader to certain common social psychological issues which are of necessity implicated in the process, albeit to a greater or lesser degree. Essentially, what I mean to suggest is that although certain of the broad social psychological questions relating to professional socialization may be the same irrespective of field, the answers are likely to be quite different depending on whom it is one studies, and where and when he studies them.

OCCUPATIONAL IMAGERY OF BEGINNER AND GRADUATE

Before describing the succession of feeling-states, role postures, and self-concepts that subjectively comprise the process of doctrinal conversion, it may be helpful to first convey some idea of what it is, substantively speaking, students move *from* and what it is they move *to*. I begin, therefore, with a brief sketch of the lay imagery of nursing with which students characteristically arrive at the school, followed immediately by a description of the 'institutionally approved' imagery with which nearly all depart three years later. In the remaining and major portion of the paper I will present a stage by stage sequential analysis of how students come to discard the former for the latter.

The lay imagery of the beginning student

This consists mostly of a simplistic exemplification of what Talcott Parsons has somewhere termed the core American value of 'instrumental activism': actively *doing* on behalf of some socially worthy purpose through a direct, tangible, means-end manipulation of tools and procedures which, to ensure successful outcomes, are seen as requiring technical mastery of a high order. Intimately infused with this commonsense version of instrumentalism, there exists a somewhat amorphous, though nonetheless deeply felt, Christian-humanitarian conviction that love, care and a desire to help others constitute a sufficient motivational wellspring in themselves to assure the moral efficacy of the nurse's ministration and to shield her from the transgressions that an unmitigated instrumentalism might entail. The student rhetoric—the verbal scheme of purposes, means, and causal processes—sustaining this orientation may in simple declarative terms be paraphrased as follows.

> Sick people require care and attention for them to feel comfortable and get well. It is the nurse's job to provide this care and attention. I am a caring person by nature, upbringing and conviction. If I am to become a nurse— that is, a person who can effectively demonstrate the care I feel for others— I must learn the many nursing skills, techniques and procedures by which patients are made comfortable and well. Through my demonstrating my proficiency at these, patients will immediately recognize that I care and thereby accord me the emotional and spiritual gratifications that the helpless customarily grant the helpful.

The 'institutionally approved' imagery of the graduating student

While it perhaps derives ultimately from the same moral and philosophical sources as the nurses' statement above, the school's ethos of nursing departs in several significant respects from the simplistic lay imagery of the student novice. Three major thematic emphases in the institutionally approved definition particularly deserve comment.

(i) The patient is defined as someone who is more than merely sick, he or she is someone with 'health problems'. Furthermore, if his health problems are to be satisfactorily resolved, intervention by the nurse is, whenever feasible, called for at all phases of his illness history (before he gets to the hospital, once there, and after he leaves) and at many levels in addition to that of the physical malfunctioning resulting from his illness. The patient's attitudes towards illness, his health practices, and even his social environment, insofar as it is thought to contribute to the pathology, all become legitimate objects of therapeutic nursing intervention according to the doctrine of the school. In sum, the scope of nursing practice as well as the variety of interests subsumed therein are greatly expanded in this definition of the professional nurse's role.

(ii) The beginning student's simplistic assumption that satisfactory nursing performance entails little more than a kind and caring attitude in league with an instrumental ability 'to do for' the patient is replaced by a perspective which views the nurse's very relationship to the patient in problematic terms. According to this perspective, rapport with the patient, for example, is not treated as the automatic by-product of unwitting and unexamined attitudes of helpfulness, necessary though these may be at bottom. Instead, the many interpersonal components that go into forming the relationship with the patient—his feelings and attitudes, the nurse's own along with their respective sources in personality and culture—are all made topics of explicit scrutiny and are thus seen as amenable to 'rational' alteration or manipulation. Ergo, the relationship to the patient, much as in psychotherapy, is strenuously 'objectified'; the student is enjoined to view her own person as a purposeful instrument in the therapeutic process, not merely as some benignly disposed vehicle through whom pre-formulated nursing procedures and techniques are dispensed.

(iii) As for the mastery of technical skills and procedures which as I have noted so preoccupies the beginning student, although not rejected as such by the school's ideology, it nevertheless receives a very different con-textual emphasis. Rather than treating technical proficiency as the essence of the student's performance, the school places vastly more emphasis on her learning the 'principles of nursing care' upon which such skills are said to be based. Technical mastery in itself can, it is asserted regularly, always be acquired through repeated exposure to situations in which it will have to be exercised. In the meantime, because nursing techniques and proce-dures are forever changing and because it is important to guard against their rote-like application with different patients whose needs and circum-stances may differ, much more is to be gained ultimately by focusing on 'why it's done' rather than on 'how it's done'.

STAGES IN THE PROCESS OF DOCTRINAL CONVERSION

What, then, is the subjective process by which students come to discard the pronounced lay imagery they bring with them for these school-approved definitions and perspectives on nursing practice? The process consists of six successive stages: (i) *Initial innocence*, (ii) *labelled recognition of incongruity*, (iii) *'psyching out'*, (iv) *role simulation*, (v) *provisional internalization*, and (vi) *stable internalization*. Before turning to the salient features of each stage, let me note that I regard the postulation of stages as an analytical device rather than an exact rendering of all that is of subjective significance for students during a particular segment of socialization time. There are numerous problems of chronology, transition points and inter-subject consistency which inevitably play havoc with almost any sequential model of a complexly articulated social process. Nevertheless, as a first approximation of the social psychological dynamics that underlie the subjective process of doctrinal conversion in professional socialization, the model does perhaps have heuristic value, much as it may flatten the actual contours of the process or impart to it an excessively undeviating trajectory.

Initial innocence

The controlling cognitive framework of this stage is the above-sketched lay imagery of nursing which students bring with them: a strong instrumental emphasis on *doing* alongside a secularized Christian-humanitarian ethic of care, kindness and love for those who suffer. But because instructors do so little to support this lay conception of nursing and choose instead to emphasize such seemingly inconsequential matters as the psychological scrutiny of the nurse/patient relationship, students rather quickly find themselves at a loss to know what to make of what is being taught them and what is expected of them. While they look forward eagerly to mastering such 'practical' techniques and procedures as the giving of injections, the preparation and administration of medications or the operation of a catheter, they are enjoined instead to go on to the wards and 'observe' patients and learn how to 'communicate' with them.

Their lay imagery makes very little sense of this. As one student remarked during her second month of school, 'the only things we've learned around here so far is how to make a bed and give a bath. All that other stuff on communication and psychological care is just so much fluff.' When during these first months students are occasionally taught a 'doing' kind of technique or procedure, a flurry of class enthusiasm ensues. This fades in short order, however, given the casualness with which faculty treats such 'small accomplishments'.

Typically, the students' encounters with patients during this initial period are filled with feelings of embarrassment, uselessness and personal inadequacy. Despite assurances of instructors to the contrary, 'just standing around observing and talking' with patients does not, in the students' lay lexicon, constitute *doing*; and because they cannot *do*, many feel they have no legitimate right to be at the patient's bedside. Because they feel they cannot act as they imagine a 'real nurse' would, some try to compensate for their sense of role deprivation by relating to patients in the guise of an indulgent daughter, favoured niece, or attentive domestic. All the more galling then when, as happens often enough, the patient responds to them in these terms, thereby further negating the student's wish to be treated as a nurse.

In sum, the stage of initial innocence is one which abounds in feelings of worry, disappointment, frustration, and heightened self-concern for students. Notwithstanding the repeated failure of lay imagery to supply satisfactory answers to their dilemma, they constantly appeal to it in the hope that it can provide some cogent reason for performing as the faculty seems to want them to perform. So pervasive is the hold of lay imagery at this stage that even the powerful disquiet that many students experience is treated as if it were a purely individual phenomenon. Thus, in private interview many a student confided to us the belief that she alone suffered feelings of bewilderment, disappointment, and inadequacy. Certain publicly acknowledged events engaging the group as a whole had first to transpire before students could achieve a collective definition of their problem. In the present instance, perhaps the most important of these was the first round of student evaluations held midway into the first semester. This, more than anything, seemed to trigger a collective transition to the second stage.

Labelled recognition of incongruity

Deriving from the familiar teacher/student interaction of mid-term evaluations with their grades, reprimands and cautious notes of encouragement, students begin to articulate and collectively label what it is that troubles them. They characteristically remark, 'nursing school is not what we expected'. Although it is not always easy for them to specify the precise respects in which it is not, judging from the repetitiveness of certain prominent complaints, the key points at issue may be paraphrased as follows.

> We thought we'd be learning many concrete procedures and skills which we could perform on patients, but we are not.
> We thought that our instructors would always be able to show us what to do and how to do it, but instead they tell us to find out for ourselves, i.e., 'to engage in problem-solving on our own'.
> We thought that by now we'd be able to *do* enough for patients so that they could appreciate us as nurses and not simply as persons who can chit-chat ('communicate') with them, run errands for them and in general 'be social' with them; instead, we find that so much of our contact with patients is exactly of this nature.

This is perhaps the most problematic stage for students during the whole of their nursing school career. With but the vaguest insight into the ideological and pedagogical rationale of the school's curriculum, large numbers of them begin to question openly their choice of nursing and to contemplate, some actively, other occupations still open to them.[7]

Overall, this is the stage when students as a group begin to recognize and define their situation as involving a gross misalignment between their own initial expectations and those which faculty directs at them. The felt incongruity is sufficiently acute as to lead them to search for ways to reduce the dissonance.[8] Several avenues are of course open, the most drastic and obvious being the decision a number of them make at about this time to resign from the school. Of these students I shall say no more. For the vast majority who continue to hold this alternative in abeyance, other means of accommodation and adjustment must be devised. This ushers in the third stage, one which in actual experience flows directly from the group-labelled recognition of incongruity.

'Psyching out'

This is the term students themselves use to designate the arts of divining what instructors expect of them and of how best to go about satisfying such expectations. As far as these student nurses are concerned, this is a particularly crucial stage in the subjective process of 'becoming a nurse'. As will soon become evident, it is here that the cognitive framework for the students' later internalization of school-approved perspectives assumes a certain rudimentary shape.

First it should be noted that whereas isolated instances of psyching out by a few sophisticated students occur very early in the game (well before the period of which I speak) it does not emerge as a *collective* response sooner, since prior to this time the student group as a whole is fixated on assessing performances and their motivational adequacy in terms of the lay imagery they bring with them. Not until the values and norms implicit in this imagery are rendered incongruous—the achievement of the second stage—can psyching out assume the status of an institutionally adaptive mechanism.

Students of course differ greatly in the finesse and imagination they bring to the task of psyching out instructors. Some, perhaps the largest number, resort to frontal tactics, putting straightfaced didactic questions to the instructor concerning what she expects of them and the precise respects in which their performances fall short of or meet her criteria. But at this early point in the curriculum it is primarily an attitude, a kind of working doctrinal stance, which instructors seek to inculcate. It is therefore the rare instructor who can clearly communicate to students precisely what she expects of them. Other, more subtle practitioners of psyching out make a point of empathically noting in their everyday interaction with faculty when an instructor 'lights up', when she perfunctorily passes by one student's recitation to linger over that of another in the hope that something of value will be forthcoming. These more artful students can it seems begin to fashion valued performances earlier and with greater success than their more interrogatively predisposed peers.

It should be noted in passing that it is not wholly a random, fortuitous or purely individual matter as to which students evidence one as against the other style of psyching out instructors. Our strong impression is that the more cosmopolitan girl, usually one of upper-middle-class background, is considerably more adept at utilizing subtle styles of indirection with instructors. Closely associated with this ability one observes frequently a higher degree of verbal facility and even more important, well-cultivated feminine skills and sensitivities in what may be termed the diplomatic niceties in interpersonal relations.

Yet, despite its emergence as a collective mechanism at this stage, there remain some students who throughout their nursing school career never evidence any conscious awareness or appreciation of psyching out and who in their ingenuousness never employ it. While greatly handicapped in certain respects from this peculiar want of talent (or perhaps want of peculiar talent), it would be wrong to conclude that such students are forever destined to remain innocents or bumblers. Themselves bereft of psyching out talents, they nevertheless are secondhand beneficiaries of the insights gained by more adroit classmates. The 'valued performances' which the latter are able to construct as a result of psyching out soon emerge—by virtue of their tangible, immediately visible, and patently successful attributes—as generalized performance models for the student group as a whole. Thus through emulation even the more laggard student can in time enact valued performances with sufficient verisimilitude to satisfy instructors, albeit perhaps with a certain stereotype which on occasion betrays their secondhand derivation.

At the same time, both for students who are adept at psyching out and those less so, a certain quality of moral discomfort and ego alienation—inauthenticity, in the existentialist sense—attaches itself to the act. I shall have more to say on this in the next section; here I merely note that in trying to divine in a calculating fashion the wishes of a superior seemingly for the sole purpose of gaining the academic rewards which it is in her power to bestow, students occasionally catch glimpses of themselves as amoral manipulators, as persons prepared to discredit convictions which have formed a part of their innermost selves. Perhaps to relieve the guilt that attaches to these small betrayals of self, as well as to assure peers that they are not *truly* as they represent themselves before faculty, students will frequently joke among themselves about 'putting on a front' before instructors.

Role simulation

Role simulation is but the performance implementation of psyching out and as such is hardly distinguishable from it temporally. Nevertheless for analytical purposes it is worth treating separately.

By role simulation I refer to that genre of highly self-conscious, manipulative behaviour of students which aims at constructing institutionally valued performances of a particular role,[9] in this instance, of course, that of nurse as defined by school faculty. What distinguishes role simulation from the ordinary mundane enactment of social roles are those qualities of self-consciousness, ego alienation and, at times, play-acting which in the actor's mind are felt to adhere to his performance. In common parlance, he is uncomfortable with and unsure of his performance, although, as we shall see, this does not necessarily communicate itself to those before whom he enacts the role.

By this point in time (roughly the end of the first semester and the start of the second), the nursing students had learned that to enact their lay conceptions of nursing with patients and others would win them little favour with instructors. Psyching out had revealed that a holistic conception of the patient, a psychotherapeutically tinged objectification of one's relationship to him, and a concern for health teaching in the context of comprehensive health care were what instructors wanted and were prepared to reward. Students, particularly the more socially sensitive and intellectually flexible among them, began, therefore, to turn their attention to the problem of fashioning performances on the wards and in class which would elicit favourable responses from instructors. This transpired despite the strong misgivings many continued to feel concerning the school's doctrinal emphases.

In examining role simulation as an interactional stratagem two orders of psychological disjunction need to be distinguished from each other. The first is that occurring between the actor and himself; the second between the actor and his alters.[10] The first touches on the sense of ego alienation or inauthenticity to which I have referred, namely the self-conscious enactment of constructed performances whose legitimacy and efficacy are doubted or questioned by the actor himself. Hence, the feelings of guilt, hypocrisy and role illegitimacy that typically hover over such performances; or as students themselves were wont to put it much later in their school career, 'during my first year here all I did was "play nurse", I wasn't a real nurse.'

Such feelings however would last interminably—the actor could never become convinced of the authenticity of his performances in the new role— were it not for a favourable resolution of the second-order psychological disjunction to which I have referred: that between the actor's perception of his constructed performance and alters' perception of it. Here, much as in the theatre itself, the archetypal dilemma confronting the actor is whether the lack of conviction and quality of inauthenticity he feels about his performance will somehow communicate itself to the audience and 'give the show away'. In other words, will the audience dismiss his performance as 'mere front' or 'show' and accordingly view him as inept and untrustworthy? If such followed inevitably whenever an actor lacked conviction concerning the authenticity of his performance, it is doubtful whether new social roles could ever be assimilated into the existential fabric of one's being. But it is because prior knowledge (or rather, prior feeling) exists that it is possible to convince another of what oneself is in doubt: that, indeed, some persons possess a shameless facility at this, that in the everyday world one's alters characteristically take one at face value,[11] that persons find the courage to enact new and unfamiliar roles.

The paradoxical thing about this kind of role simulation is that the more successful the actor is at it, the less he feels he is simulating, the more he gains the conviction that his performances are authentic. As the symbolic interactionist would analyse it,[12] this transformation occurs by virtue of the actor's ability to adopt towards himself the favourable responses which his performances of the new role elicit from others. Thus, the sense of alienation from self which shrouds his beginning efforts—the first order discrepancy between his constructed performances and his conviction concerning their authenticity—grows less poignant with time as he learns that despite his own misgivings others can and do regard him as trustworthy, competent and legitimate; in short, he is that status which his performances claim him to be.

So it was that the nursing students could gradually fashion performances before instructors, patients, staff nurses and others in their role set which were more in accord with the doctrinal emphases of the school; performances which, though they violated numerous tenets of the residual lay imagery to which many still felt attached,[13] nevertheless brought in their wake sufficient reward and sense of accomplishment as to gradually dissipate the feelings of hypocrisy and inauthenticity that besieged them at first. Moreover, having lived through the beguiling process of 'becoming nurse' through 'playing at it', the cognitive groundwork was laid for a less stressful, more wholehearted internalization of the 'institutionally approved' version of nursing practice which the school sought to inculcate.

Provisional internalization

The four preceding stages are, with some qualifications and exceptions, encountered and surmounted by students by the end of the first year. The subjective focus of the remaining two years is characterized by a continuous, fairly imperceptible, and subjectively uneventful transition from what I have termed *provisional internalization* of institutionally approved perspectives to their *stable internalization*. These last stages bear much the same relationship to each other as that given by Piaget in his studies of cognitive development among children: a preparatory sub-stage followed by a behaviourally integrated consummatory stage.[14]

The distinguishing feature of *provisional internalization* is a recurrent, episodic failure at integration among the cognitions, percepts and role orientations which guide the institutionally significant behaviour of the student. Though not nearly as unsettling psychologically as the students' earlier recognition of incongruity between their lay imagery and faculty expectations, this state nevertheless evidences much vacillation between commitment to the new and a subterranean attachment to the old, a frequent though progressively muted reawakening of feelings of doubt concerning their suitability for nursing and of the practical value of what they are being taught, and a labile tendency alternately to evidence strong loyalty to the school's doctrinal emphasis and to inveigh against it as either excessive, misguided or inconsistent.

In view of this subjective lack of integration among cognitions and effects, how do students finally achieve that state of relatively secure conviction and assured performance which I have termed *stable internalization*? Two phenomena are especially noteworthy in this connection: (i) the functions served by professional rhetoric and (ii) the emergence within the student group of relatively unambiguous positive and negative reference models of the professional nurse.

The matter of professional rhetoric—by which I refer here specifically to the massive infusion in recent years of psychotherapeutic, educationist, and social science terms into the working vocabulary of advanced sectors of the American nursing profession—is something the philosophical materialist and incidentally students themselves tend to make light of, assuming the question is considered at all. From the students' vantage point the self-conscious use of non-layman, school-approved rhetoric is usually interpreted as little more than a self-serving attempt 'to please the instructor' in order to 'get good grades'. Indeed, it was interesting how when speaking among themselves students would frequently accompany the utterance of such phrases as 'patient needs', 'continuity of patient care' and 'health teaching' with a hand gesture imitative of quote marks, as if to say, 'these are the words they want us to use, but which we don't necessarily buy ourselves.' Be that as it may, the employment of professional rhetoric serves the function, to make the obvious point, of cognitively delineating and structuring the operational field for the student, or defining for her which of its events are central and which peripheral, and of providing her with the interpretative schema for appraising her performances and for communicating their 'meaning' to significant others, most notably her instructors and fellow students. All of this is part and parcel of the subjective process of socialization in which a cognitively coherent map emerges from the fragments of what had earlier seemed to be discrete and unrelated experiences.

Coincidentally, and serving to reinforce the socializing influence stemming from the school's professional rhetoric, there develops among the students a clearcut differentiation of positive and negative reference models

from which to fashion and evaluate their own and others' nursing performances. In the school we studied, the positive model was furnished by the
students' clinical instructors, these being after all the persons upon whom
they were dependent for grades. More important for the process of
doctrinal conversion, however, these were the persons whose rhetoric and
professional outlooks they had begun to assimilate. The negative reference
model was furnished by the many, typically less well-educated, non-
collegiate staff RN's whom the students encountered on the wards, and in
the clinics and agencies to which they were assigned.[15] Since the latter
rarely exemplified the advanced nursing ideals propagated by faculty, and
since by this time students could enact creditable nursing performances
more nearly in accord with these ideals, a strong bond of ideological affinity
grew up between students and instructors, one made all the stronger by
the now palpably negative examples of 'bad nursing practice' furnished by
near at hand staff RN's.

Stable internalization

Having arrived at this point in the subjective process of doctrinal conversion, there remains little to say concerning the last stage. Despite occasional
residual misgivings which hark back to the initial lay imagery, the self-
image of students is by now rather firmly that of professional nurses of a
particular doctrinal persuasion. Specifically, the distinguishing features of
this stage are a relatively, if not yet wholly, assured stance towards their
nursing performance even when beset by difficulties not encountered before,
an ease at articulating the kind of nursing practice they believe in and
in pointing out how it differs from prevailing modes of practice and, most
revealing for the social psychologist, a tendency to reinterpret retrospec-
tively the traumas, personal doubts and gripes which had assailed them
at the beginning and midpoints of their school career. For the most part
such reconstructions take the narrative form of depicting one's beginning
professional self as but a mere miniaturization of the presently conceived
version. In other words, students selectively ignore those features of the
self's past which might now be construed as contradicting or belying that
which the self has become; they suppress the frequently jarring and ego-
alienating alterations in attitude and perception which, as I have tried to
point out, are actually entailed in the becoming process.

The attainment of stable internalization should not, however, suggest
that the subjective forging of a professional identity ceases with the student's
completion of her professional education, crucial though this career phase
doubtless is. The doctrinal identity that comes to be stabilized over this
span of time is, after all, only relative to the institutional context in which
it is fashioned. Once away from the controlling influences of school, it is
only reasonable to expect further revisions, transformations, or even

regressions in the student's doctrinal identity, depending not only on the particular career pattern she stakes out for herself but on other life contingencies as well.[16] It would be futile, however, to speculate further on this question, inasmuch as our data thus far barely touch on the post-graduation phases of the students' careers.

CONCLUSION

In this paper, I have described and analysed the subjective facets of doctrinal conversion in becoming a nurse as these evidenced themselves in our study of professional socialization among several successive classes of collegiate student nurses. Despite certain simplifications and omissions, perhaps enough of the process has been presented to confirm Hughes's seminal observation that the learning of a professional role is like 'passing through the mirror ... [to create] ... the sense of seeing the world in reverse'. Indeed, the interaction of lay and professional imagery which 'undoubtedly goes on all through life' *is* 'more lively, more exciting and uncomfortable, more self-conscious and yet perhaps unconscious in the period of learning and initiation'.[17] If this be so, it remains for sociology to follow the lead of Hughes and to generate models of professional socialization that are far more faithful to this picture of thinking, feeling, ever-responding and calculating *human* actors groping their way through the ambiguities posed by the confluence of their lived pasts and imagined futures; models, in other words, which in their sociological richness and complexity transcend the dominant one available today—that of neutral, receptive vessels into whom knowledgeable, expert members of a profession pour approved skills, attitudes, and values.[18]

REFERENCES

1. Everett C. Hughes, *Men and Their Work*, The Free Press (Glencoe, Ill., 1958), pp. 119-20.
2. 'The Making of a Physician—General Statement of Ideas and Problems', *Human Organization* (Winter 1956), pp. 21-5.
3. For some earlier efforts at such a reconceptualization, see: Anselm Strauss, *Mirrors and Masks*, The Free Press (Glencoe, Ill., 1959); Howard S. Becker and James Carper, 'The Elements of Identification with an Occupation', *American Sociological Review*, 21, 1956, pp. 341-8.
4. For further documentation, see: Fred Davis and Virginia L. Olensen, 'Initiation into a Woman's Profession', *Sociometry*, 26, 1963, pp. 89-101; Fred Davis and Virginia L. Olesen, 'Baccalaureate Students' Images of Nursing', *Nursing Research*, 13, 1964, pp. 8-15; Elvi W. Whittaker and Virginia L. Olesen, 'The Faces of Florence Nightingale', *Human Organization*, 23, 1964, pp. 123-30; Fred Davis and Virginia L. Olesen, 'The Career Outlook of Professionally Educated Women', *Psychiatry*, 28, 1965, pp. 334-45; Fred Davis, Virginia L. Olesen and Elvi W. Whittaker, 'Problems and Issues in Collegiate Nursing Education', in Fred Davis (ed.), *The Nursing Profession*, John Wiley (New York 1966); Virginia L. Olesen and Fred Davis, 'Baccalaureate

Students' Images of Nursing: A Follow-up Report', *Nursing Research*, 15, 1966, pp. 151-8; Virginia L. Olesen and Elvi W. Whittaker, 'Instant Life', *Journal of the National Association of Women's Deans and Counsellors*, 29, Spring 1966, pp. 131-5; Virginia L. Olesen and Elvi W. Whittaker, 'Adjudication of Student Awareness in Professional Socialization', *Sociological Quarterly*, 7, Summer 1966, pp. 381-96.

5. According to the Hollingshead Index of Social Position. See August B. Hollingshead and Frederick C. Redlich, *Social Class and Mental Illness*, John Wiley (New York 1958), pp. 387-97.

6. Davis and Olesen, 'Initiation into a Woman's Profession', *Sociometry*, 1963, *op cit.*, and 'The Career Outlook of Professionally Educated Women', *Psychiatry*, 1965, *op. cit.*

7. Davis and Olesen, 'Initiation into a Woman's Profession', *Sociometry*, 1963, *op. cit.*

8. Leon A. Festinger, *A Theory of Cognitive Dissonance*, Harper (New York 1957).

9. Cf. Erving Goffman, *The Presentation of Self in Everyday Life*, Doubleday Anchor (New York 1959); Sheldon Messinger, 'Life as Theatre: Some Notes on the Dramaturgic Approach to Social Reality', *Sociometry*, 25, 1962, pp. 98-110.

10. Gustav Icheiser, *Misunderstandings in Human Relations*, University of Chicago Press (Chicago 1949).

11. Alfred Schutz, *The Problem of Social Reality*, collected papers vol. 1, Nijhoff (The Hague 1962), pp. 3-47.

12. The discussion here obviously draws on the approach of George H. Mead, *Mind, Self and Society*, University of Chicago Press (Chicago 1934).

13. Davis and Olesen, 'Baccalaureate Students' Images of Nursing', *Nursing Research*, 1964, *op. cit.*

14. John H. Flavell, *The Developmental Psychology of Jean Piaget*, Van Nostrand (Princeton, NJ, 1963), pp. 237-66.

15. Davis, Olesen and Whittaker, 'Problems and Issues in Collegiate Nursing Education', in Davis (ed.), *Nursing Profession*, 1966, *op. cit.*

16. Davis and Olesen, 'The Career Outlook of Professionally Educated Women', *Psychiatry*, 1965, *op. cit.*

17. Everett C. Hughes, *Men and Their Work*, 1958, *op. cit.*, pp. 119-20.

18. For a fuller discussion of this theme, see: Virginia L. Olesen and Elvi W. Whittaker, *The Silent Dialogue*, Jossey-Bass (San Francisco 1968), chapter 1.

7 | *Practice orientations among general practitioners in England and Wales*

D. MECHANIC

This study is concerned with the correlates of two indices of practice orientations based on data obtained from a national sample of general practitioners in England and Wales. The doctor's scientific orientation is measured by his reported use of nineteen diagnostic procedures during the previous two weeks. The doctor's social orientation to medicine is measured by questions which define his views on the proper scope of medical practice. Moderns (high on both measures) and technicians (high on diagnostic use) are overrepresented in smaller communities, are more likely to have bed access, to be in partnership or group practice, to have an appointment system, to take course work, and to have professional contact with other doctors. Many other findings are reported and discussed.

The appropriate role of the general practitioner is a major issue within the context of modern medical care. With the development of advanced technology and specialized knowledge, there has been some movement in all medical systems away from general practice as the common mode of meeting the medical needs of the population. In the United States, where the proliferation of medical specialization has been pronounced, there is growing scepticism concerning the viability of general practice. Most medical students in the United States now specialize, and few choose an unrestricted general practice following the completion of their training.

In contrast, the English National Health Service through its structure has continued to support a general practice approach. Implicit in this approach is the concept of a family doctor who not only meets the more routine medical needs of the population but who also is concerned with the wider family and community ramifications of illness, who views the problem of disease in a broad social context, and who takes a preventive approach to the patient. The rejection of a medical approach based on growing specialization is clear in the following statement from a committee of the Royal College of General Practitioners.[1]

Those who visit countries where the family doctor has disappeared find that the first effect is a complete loss of the services of a personal doctor who looks on his patient as an individual in the context of a family and the community; the patient then becomes uncertain and confused in his relations with the medical service. The second effect is that care provided by specialists does not include the broader outlook and perspectives of the general practitioner and with it the abilities to protect and guide the patient through the medical jungle. The third effect is that the front-line of medical care is pushed right back to the doors of the hospitals; medical care becomes an expensive and impersonal matter, creating fresh problems for hospitals, doctors and patients alike. We can briefly state that the roles of the general practitioner include those of a personal, family and community doctor; of protector of his patients from wrong or unnecessary hospitalization, protector of hospitals from the wrong type of cases and protector of the community by saving money; of coordinator of all available medical and social services; and of manipulator of the patient's personal, social and medical environments, whether in the family, at work or elsewhere.

Numerous committees, including the Royal Commission on Medical Education[2] and the Subcommittee of the Medical Advisory Committee of the Central Health Services Council,[3] have adopted a similar position.

Although ideal descriptions of general practice involve many aspects, at least two dimensions run through all discussions of the proper role of the general practitioner. First, his medical competence is assumed; i.e. he is expected to have sufficient scientific know-how to locate cases requiring more detailed appraisal and care and to refer them to an appropriate consultant. Moreover, he is expected on his own to diagnose and treat more common acute disorders and to manage the care of many chronic patients. Second, it is assumed that the general practitioner will have a wide scope of concern, involving himself not only with the patient's illness but with the implications of health and disease for work, family life and the patient's general welfare. In short, the general practitioner is also expected to exercise a social orientation that views *dis-ease* in its wider community context.

The purpose of this report is to examine the characteristics of doctors and the modes in which they practise that can be compared to these ideals. In 1966, data were obtained from a random national sample of general practitioners in England and Wales, selected by the Ministry of Health from a sampling frame of all general practitioners with unrestricted practices as of 1 October 1964. Sixty per cent of eligible respondents completed a long questionnaire, and an additional 13% completed a shorter form. The analysis in this paper is based on 772 respondents of the 813 respondents who completed the long form. To facilitate the analysis, forty-one doctors were excluded from the sample because they failed to respond to 10% or more of the questions. In the remaining cases, where data on a particular question were missing, the respondent was assigned to the mean response of those replying to that question. The demographic profile of the sample used in this analysis was almost identical to the profile of all respondents, and the sample profile was remarkably similar to that of all general practitioners in England and Wales with unrestricted practices. A detailed description of the sample in relation to the total population of general practitioners is provided elsewhere.[4] Some of the descriptive details from the survey are available.[5, 6]

MEASURES OF PRACTICE ORIENTATIONS

In a general survey it is impossible to measure directly the quality of general practice. In this study, we have attempted to assess indirectly and crudely the practice orientations of general practitioners. In doing this we have tried to measure two components of their practice—the use of diagnostic and laboratory aids, and the degree of the doctor's acceptance of a social role.

Diagnostic use

In this analysis the assumption is made that the extent of the doctor's use of diagnostic and laboratory aids reflects his scientific and technical orientation to medical practice. Although the indiscriminate and improper use of laboratory aids reflects poor scientific practice, it is reasonable to expect in the British situation, where the use of diagnostic and laboratory aids is modest, that the level of use roughly depicts the doctor's orientation to medicine as a technical activity. We thus asked respondents if they used each of the following procedures during the previous two weeks: full size chest X-rays, bone and joint X-rays, bacteriologic examination of the urine, glucose tolerance tests, haemoglobin, white blood count, red blood count, routine urinalysis, erythrocyte sedimentation rate, blood sugar, prothrombin activity, serum cholesterol, blood culture, liver function test, serum electrolytes, BMR, CSF micro and culture and chemistry, radioactive iodine and electrocardiogram. Of the nineteen possible procedures, 19% of respondents reported using three or less, 45% reported using four to seven, 21% reported using eight or nine, and 16% reported using ten or more. (Because of rounding errors, percentages do not always equal one hundred. Thus, slight variations in the total percentage of doctors having various characteristics will occur in subsequent analysis.) We cannot assume that the answers to this question accurately portray behaviour during the two-week period in question; all we need assume is that the answers in general reflect the extent of use of these procedures.

Social orientations to medicine

We roughly depict the general practitioner's social orientation through responses to two questions. The first question asks the doctor whether he believes it is proper for patients to consult their GP for each of the following problems: family financial troubles, disobedience of children, marital difficulties, how to handle behaviour such as drunkenness in a relative, children's poor school performance, birth control advice, problems with drinking too much, general feelings of unhappiness, anxieties about child care, and obesity. Respondents were given the options of 'yes', 'sometimes' and 'no' for each item. The second question, correlated with the first, was: 'some medical commentators have recently argued that there is a growing tendency for people to bring less serious disorders to doctors and more readily seek help for problems in their family lives. In general do you feel that this is a good or bad trend, given present conditions of medical practice?' Doctors were given the options of responding that it was a 'very good', 'good', 'rather disturbing' and 'very disturbing' trend. The question included the phrase 'present conditions of medical practice' because we wished to separate those who endorse the idea in general from those who feel it is a good trend even under the conditions of limited medical manpower. Each doctor in the sample received a score on social orientations based on their responses to the two questions.

RESULTS

It is commonly believed that a technical and a social orientation are not fully compatible; thus the first issue we face is the relationship between these two orientations. An examination of Table 1 shows that this contention is not supported. Indeed, doctors who use the smallest number of procedures are overrepresented among those with the lowest social orientation scores, and the group with the highest use of procedures has the largest proportion of doctors with high social orientation scores. Overall the relationship between these two variables is a very modest one, indicating considerable independence between these two orientations.

Table 2 presents data relating various factors to the use of diagnostic and laboratory procedures. As an examination of the table will show, those who use more procedures, in contrast to those using less, have practices in smaller communities, and they are more likely to have direct access to NHS beds and hospital appointments. Such doctors, with higher use of procedures, also have a tendency to organize their practices differently. They are more likely to be part of larger groups or to have partners, to use an appointment system, to take supplementary course work, and to do some regular psychotherapy. These doctors include more younger practitioners and less older ones, and they are more likely to be members of the Royal College of General Practitioners. On the average they devote more time to their practices than doctors using fewer procedures, they have more private patients and they read more professional journals, although these differences tend to be small. Finally they tend to view a smaller proportion of their patients' consultations as trivial, inappropriate or unnecessary, and are more satisfied with their access to medical facilities.

Table 1

The relationship between diagnostic use and a social orientation to medicine among 772 British general practitioners

	Report of number of procedures used during the previous two weeks							
Social orientation to medicine	5 or less		6 or 7		8 or 9		10 or more	
	%	N	%	N	%	N	%	N
High (scores of 1-3)	23	(57)	26	(60)	18	(29)	36	(43)
Medium high (scores of 4-5)	34	(87)	42	(98)	46	(74)	32	(39)
Medium low (scores of 6-7)	27	(68)	24	(57)	31	(50)	24	(29)
Low (scores of 8 or 9)	16	(41)	09	(21)	06	(9)	08	(10)
Total	100	(253)	101	(236)	101	(162)	100	(121)

Table 3 presents some findings concerning factors associated with a social orientation to medicine. As one might reasonably expect, doctors who are higher on the social orientation variable are more likely to report that they seek out patient problems, that it is the doctor's responsibility to manage psychiatric patients and that they do psychotherapy. Such doctors also, as one might expect, report less of their case load as trivial, unnecessary or inappropriate. Although social orientation is not clearly related to access to NHS beds, those who fall lowest on social orientation have considerably less access to beds. Those with a high social orientation score are more likely to be members of the Royal College of General Practitioners, to have taken supplementary course work during the five years previous to the survey, to have had some special training in psychiatry, social medicine, or the behavioural sciences and to have more contact with other doctors relating to professional matters.

Doctors who report a high social orientation to medicine tend to be much higher than other doctors on most of our measures of satisfaction, and they appear to take a more favourable attitude towards general practice and the health service in general. They tend more than other doctors to believe that it is possible to practise high quality medicine under present conditions of practice. They are somewhat more positive towards Health Ministry standards and controls. Doctors low on social orientation are less likely to accept the view that doctors must sacrifice their own interests relative to those of patients.

Since the assumption of the paper is that it is essential that doctors maintain scientific and social orientations simultaneously, Table 4 combines these two variables. In each case, we have dichotomized each distribution at the median category. Doctors who report using eight or

Table 2

Factors associated with use of diagnostic and laboratory procedures

Aspects of doctors and their practices	Report of number of procedures used during the previous two weeks				
	5 or less (N=253)	6 or 7 (N=236)	8 or 9 (N=162)	10 or more (N=121)	r*
	%	%	%	%	
(a) Practices in a community of:					
Less than 25,000 population (N=233)	23	30	35	40	
25,000 to 99,999 population (N=276)	30	37	38	40	−22
100,000 or more population (N=263)	47	32	27	20	
(b) 40 years of age or less (N=272)	25	34	48	41	
41-55 years of age (N=378)	53	50	43	49	−20
56 years of age or older (N=122)	22	17	09	10	
(c) Has direct access to NHS beds (N=420)	43	53	60	74	−22
(d) Has an appointment on staff of NHS hospital (N=269)	23	34	41	51	−21
(e) Uses an appointment system (N=261)	20	29	52	46	−23
(f) Has taken supplementary course work in past five years (N=507)	55	65	80	71	17
(g) Member of the Royal College of General Practitioners (N=216)	19	27	35	39	−17
(h) Solo practice (N=160)	27	22	14	13	
Two or three partners (N=533)	64	69	75	71	16
Four or more partners (N=79)	08	09	10	16	
(i) Above median category in total practice time spent during day previous to interview (N=332)	42	45	48	50	16
(j) Median category or above in satisfaction with access to medical facilities (N=427)	48	56	58	66	−18
(k) Reports 26 or more private patients (N=148)	14	22	18	26	15
(l) Does some regular psychotherapy (N=172)	17	19	29	34	−14
(m) Reports reading three or more professional journals (N=229)	24	32	35	36	13
(n) Reports that 50% or more of surgery consultations are for trivial, unnecessary or inappropriate reasons (N=187)	30	26	15	19	10

* Product moment correlation coefficient for use of diagnostic procedures and measure of the independent variable. All r's reported are statistically significant at the ·05 level.

more procedures are classified as high diagnostic use, while those using seven or less are classified as low diagnostic use. Similarly, doctors with a social orientation score of 1-4 are classified as high social orientation, while those with scores of 5-9 are classified as low social orientation. Combining these two categorizations yields four groups with the following number of cases: low social orientation/low diagnostic use (N=275); low social orientation/high diagnostic use (N=149); high social orientation/low diagnostic use (N=214); and high social orientation/high diagnostic use (N=134). For convenience we shall label them as withdrawers, technicians, counsellors, and moderns.

Table 3

Factors associated with social orientation to medicine

	Scores on social orientation to medicine index				
Aspects of doctors and their practices	*High (scores of 1-3) (N=189)*	*Medium high (scores of 4-5) (N=298)*	*Medium low (scores of 6-7) (N=204)*	*Low (scores of 8-9) (N=81)*	*r**
	%	%	%	%	
(a) Has direct access to NHS beds (N=420)	60	54	56	38	10
(b) Reports that 50% or more of surgery consultations are for trivial, unnecessary or inappropriate reasons (N=187)	10	22	29	52	−34
(c) Reports that he seeks patient's problems and provides supportive treatment regardless of whether patient asks for help (N=465)	75	64	49	37	−26
(d) Agrees that in all cases it is the GP's responsibility to manage psychiatric patients released from the hospital (N=264)	43	36	28	23	24
(e) Does some regular psychotherapy (N=172)	32	24	15	10	18
(f) Member of the Royal College of General Practitioners (N=216)	36	27	25	19	−17
(g) Has taken supplementary course work in past five years (N=507)	72	69	64	44	−14
(h) Above median category on contact with other doctors on professional matters (N=333)	62	42	43	28	−12
(i) Has any training following medical school relating to social and family medicine, psychiatry or behavioural sciences (N=189)	30	27	22	12	−11
(j) General satisfaction with general practice—above median category (N=362)	62	48	38	30	26
(k) Median category or above in belief that high quality practice is possible under present conditions (N=436)	66	60	50	36	−20
(l) Above median category on willingness to sacrifice own interests scale (N=307)	46	41	39	23	−12
(m) Above median category on willingness to accept authority of Health Ministry (N=248)	38	31	31	25	−17

* Product moment correlation coefficient for social orientation to medicine score and measure of the independent variable. All r's reported are statistically significant at the ·05 level.

Table 4
Factors associated with general practice orientations

Aspects of doctors and their practices	Withdrawers (N=275)	Technicians (N=149)	Counsellors (N=214)	Moderns (N=134)
	%	%	%	%
(a) Has direct access to NHS beds (N=420)	45	65	52	66
(b) Hospital appointment (N=269)	28	25	25	23
(c) Reports that 50% or more of surgery consultations are for trivial, unnecessary or inappropriate reasons (N=187)	38	24	16	10
(d) Reports that he seeks patient's problems and provides supportive treatment regardless of whether patient asks for help (N=465)	51	51	68	77
(e) Agrees that in all cases it is the GP's responsibility to manage psychiatric patients released from the hospital (N=269)	25	38	37	43
(f) Does some regular psychotherapy (N=172)	14	21	23	39
(g) Solo practice (N=160)	24	13	26	15
Two or three partners (N=533)	68	72	65	75
Four or more partners (N=79)	09	15	09	10
(h) Reports 26 or more private patients (N=148)	16	17	20	26
(i) Above median category in total practice time spent during day previous to interview (N=332)	38	53	40	48
(j) Uses an appointment system (N=261)	23	52	26	48
(k) Member of the Royal College of General Practitioners (N=216)	21	30	26	44
(l) Overall satisfaction with general practice (N=362)	38	40	58	56
(m) Forty years of age or less (N=272)	35	52	22	38
Forty-one to fifty-five years of age (N=378)	48	43	55	48
Fifty-six years of age or older (N=122)	17	05	22	14
(n) Has taken supplementary course work in past five years (N=507)	58	72	61	81
(o) Above median category on contact with other doctors on professional matters (N=333)	33	55	44	49
(p) Median category or above in belief that high quality practice is possible under present conditions (N=436)	51	53	60	66
(q) Has any training following medical school relating to social and family medicine, psychiatry, or behavioural science (N=189)	17	28	24	35
(r) Reports reading three or more professional journals (N=229)	24	34	29	37
(s) Above median category on willingness to sacrifice own interests scale (N=307)	35	42	43	41
(t) Above median category on willingness to accept authority of Health Ministry (N=248)	31	29	36	33
(u) Practices in a community of: Less than 25,000 population (N=233)	24	37	29	37
25,000 to 99,999 population (N=276)	36	38	31	41
100,000 or more population (N=263)	40	26	40	22
(v) Median category or above in satisfaction with access to medical facilities (N=427)	49	56	56	55

As an examination of Table 4 will show, there is a tendency for results reported previously to persist without very large interactions between diagnostic use and social orientations. There were, however, some interactions of considerable interest. Cartwright[7] has shown that doctors' reports of the proportion of their practices concerned with trivial and inappropriate complaints is indicative of a wide range of other responses. While 38% of withdrawers in our sample reported that 50% or more of their patients presented trivial, unnecessary or inappropriate complaints, only 10% of moderns gave a similar response. Another indication of a modern orientation was the practice of some psychotherapy; while approximately two fifths of the moderns reported doing some psychotherapy, only from 14-23% of the other groups reported doing as much. One of the most impressive findings is the high proportion of members of the Royal College of General Practitioners in the modern group—44%. Only 21% of the withdrawers were members of the college. Although very few of the doctors in our sample were members of the Royal Society of Medicine, more than half of these doctors were in the modern group. Another indication of orientation was the reading of *Lancet*, a highly sophisticated journal dealing with medical issues of general interest. Only seventy-seven doctors indicated that they either read *Lancet* selectively or in whole. While 19% of moderns reported reading this journal, only 6% of withdrawers, 8% of counsellors, and 11% of technicians gave a similar report.

It is interesting to note that 37% of technicians and moderns are found in communities of less than 25,000 population, in contrast to 24% of withdrawers and 29% of counsellors. In contrast, 40% of withdrawers and counsellors are found in areas of 100,000 or more of population as compared with 26% of technicians and 22% of moderns. Although access to NHS beds and hospital appointments are greater in smaller communities, diagnostic use is not associated with hospital appointments, although it is with access to NHS beds. With the concentration of hospitals and consultants in larger urban areas, doctors in such areas apparently are more likely to depend on the hospital to do much of the diagnostic work.

Distribution of doctors with varying practice orientations

Although we lack much data on the individual personality and background characteristics of doctors, we do have information on where they attended medical school and we know where they practise. These data provide some indication of where doctors of different orientations come from and how they are distributed around the country. Since the members of our sample come from a large number of medical schools, for some we have an insufficient number of cases. In Table 5, we report only on medical schools from which fifteen or more doctors in our sample had graduated. These data must be regarded with great caution since medical school graduates from varying schools may differ on a variety of characteristics which predict practice orientation, and it must not be assumed that the differences observed among schools are necessarily a product of the training they provide. (Another problem with these data is that they describe doctors who graduated from medical school during the past half century. Medical education has changed dramatically during this period, and individual schools may have been very different during varying periods.)

As an examination of Table 5 shows, among doctors with modern practice orientations, there was an overrepresentation of doctors who had graduated from Guys, University of Bristol, St Mary's, Newcastle upon Tyne, Middlesex, University of Edinburgh and University of Glasgow. Only in the case of the first two was the difference of more than ten percentage points, and because of the small sample sizes involved, these differences must be interpreted with great caution. Among doctors classified as counsellors, there was an overrepresentation of doctors from University College (London), University of Birmingham, and St Thomas's. Among technicians, there was an overrepresentation of doctors from Guys, Kings College, St Bartholomew, King's, Newcastle upon Tyne and the University

Table 5

Source of medical education and general practice orientations

Medical school background	General practice orientations			
	Withdrawers	Technicians	Counsellors	Moderns
	36% of total sample	19% of total sample	28% of total sample	17% of total sample
	%	%	%	%
Guys (N=47)	21	34	17	28
King's College (N=26)	35	27	31	08
London Hospital (N=38)	42	21	24	13
Middlesex (N=31)	26	23	29	23
St Bartholomew (N=46)	26	33	22	20
St Mary's (N=24)	42	21	13	25
St Thomas's (N=29)	35	14	34	17
University College, London (N=16)	19	13	50	19
University of Birmingham (N=36)	22	22	36	19
University of Bristol (N=16)	22	22	22	33
Leeds (N=38)	45	18	29	08
University of Liverpool (N=16)	31	25	31	13
Victoria University (N=32)	47	09	31	13
Newcastle upon Tyne (N=26)	25	29	21	25
University of Sheffield (N=15)	53	13	20	13
University of Aberdeen (N=18)	33	33	17	17
University of Edinburgh (N=50)	36	12	30	22
University of Glasgow (N=31)	35	16	26	23
University of Dublin (N=27)	50	25	13	13
No answer (N=110)	40	12	38	10

of Aberdeen. Finally, among withdrawers, there was an overrepresentation of doctors from the University of Dublin, University of Sheffield, Victoria University and Leeds.

Table 6 shows the distribution of practice orientation among executive council areas. For the most part, practice orientations are well distributed. There is an overrepresentation of doctors in the Southern Region who are moderns but it is only nine percentage points. Similarly, doctors from the Midlands Region are overrepresented among counsellors and doctors from the East and West Riding Region among withdrawers, but these differences are also modest.

DISCUSSION

Overall we have not been particularly successful in accounting for differences in practice orientations among doctors. It is quite clear that the dominant orientation among younger doctors is the technical role while older doctors are overrepresented among the counsellors. The modern orientation—the one we have defined as the most desirable one—corresponds fairly closely to the age distribution of the entire sample of doctors. Both technicians and moderns tend to predominate in communities of less than 100,000 population in contrast to counsellors and withdrawers, two fifths of whom are located in areas of more than 100,000 population. One wonders whether the presence of large hospitals close by in more urbanized areas—particularly teaching hospitals—discourages doctors from assuming a wider medical responsibility for their patients. Moderns and technicians are more likely to have access to hospital beds than counsellors and withdrawers, and these are more readily available in smaller community hospitals than in the major urban hospitals.

By most definitions of modernity, technicians and moderns appear more advanced in their practices than counsellors and withdrawers. They are both more likely than counsellors and withdrawers to be part of a partnership or group practice, to have an appointment system, to take supplementary course work, to have contact with other doctors on professional matters and to do more professional reading. One of the most impressive findings was the extent to which moderns held membership in the Royal College of General Practitioners. When the data were collected, special qualifications were not required for membership, yet more than twice as many moderns in contrast to withdrawers held such membership, and moderns were also much more likely to be members than either technicians or counsellors. Whether the educational programme and values of the college influence the way doctors practise, or whether doctors who are more committed to certain ways of practising select themselves into membership, cannot be answered by our data. It seems reasonable to expect, however, that the educational pro-

Table 6

Distribution of doctors with varying practice orientations among executive council areas

	General practice orientations			
	Withdrawers	Technicians	Counsellors	Moderns
Executive Council Area	*36% of total sample*	*19% of total sample*	*28% of total sample*	*17% of total sample*
	%	%	%	%
Northern Region (N=57)	40	18	30	12
East and West Riding Region (N=72)	47	08	31	14
North Midland Region (N=58)	28	22	31	19
Eastern Region (N=88)	33	26	22	19
London and Southeastern Region (N=142)	35	23	23	20
Southern Region (N=61)	30	18	26	26
Southwestern Region (N=70)	34	23	23	20
Midland Region (N=87)	34	13	38	15
Northwestern Region (N=95)	41	19	32	08
Welsh Region (N=42)	31	21	26	21

gramme of the college, which emphasizes many of the aspects of practice associated with modernity, has some effect on doctors.

An issue of some concern is the relatively large number of younger doctors in the technician group. These doctors who are less committed to the social aspects of practice appear to be in many respects as disgruntled as the withdrawers. On most measures of dissatisfaction, for example, they rate as a relatively unhappy group. More than twice as many technicians as moderns feel that 50% or more of their surgery consultations are for trival and unnecessary reasons, and many of the patients they are likely to see in general practice require other than a traditional technical approach. It is interesting to note that the technicians have not had, on average, less training specific to social science and psychiatry than other groups, and indeed they appear to be comparable to the other types in their acknowledgement of the GP's responsibility for managing psychiatric patients released from the hospital. In a sense this too is a technical task requiring special skills and knowledge of drugs. It is primarily the more common psychological and social complaints of patients that they seem to frown on treating.

The issue remains as to what other factors might contribute to practice orientations since we found that much of the variance remains unexplained. Part of this is due to measurement error, but it is also likely that the value orientations and personality characteristics of doctors also play some part in defining how doctors orient themselves to their practices and how they deal with their daily tasks.

REFERENCES

1. College of General Practitioners, London, *Report of a Symposium on the Art and the Science of General Practice*; or, *The Problems of General Practice*, held at the Wellcome Building, London, 22 November 1964, Devonshire Press (Torquay 1965).

2. *Royal Commission on Medical Education, 1965-8 Report*, HMSO (London 1968); Cmnd. 3569.

3. Ministry of Health, *The Field of Work of the Family Doctor*, HMSO (London 1963).

4. R. Faich, 'Social and Structural Factors Affecting Work Satisfaction: A Case Study of General Practitioners in the English Health Service', PhD dissertation, University of Wisconsin (Madison, Wis., 1969).

5. D. Mechanic, 'General Practice in England and Wales: Results From a Survey of a National Sample of General Practitioners', *Medical Care*, 6, 1968, p. 245.

6. D. Mechanic, 'General Medical Practice in England and Wales: Its Organization and Future', *New England Journal of Medicine*, 279, 1968, p. 680.

7. A. Cartwright, *Patients and Their Doctors: a Study of General Practice*, Routledge (London 1967).

8 | *The doctors' dilemma—a sociological viewpoint*

M. JEFFERYS

Some 'division of labour' within the medical profession is both necessary and inevitable. The doctors' dilemma refers to the choice that has to be made between alternative organizational structures. General practitioners are generally acknowledged to be the least satisfied section of the profession. A sociological perspective is used to examine the reasons for the dissatisfaction: in the light of this analysis, several changes in the training and organization of general practice are suggested. Official recommendations aim at improving the status of the general practitioner by equipping him with more specialized skills; this, however, may not be sufficient to increase his prestige within the community he serves. It is suggested that greater emphasis should be placed on the social, as opposed to the technical, content of medical practice—more attention being directed in medical education to the part played by social and psychological factors in the aetiology of disease.

INDICATIONS OF DISSATISFACTION

The dilemmas which I want to consider are those faced by one section of the medical profession—namely, the general practitioners.

There is considerable evidence to suggest that in the opinion of many of those who have qualified in medicine general practice does not provide a satisfying career. For example, the shortage of applicants for vacancies in general practices in many parts of the country;[1] the low prestige accorded general practice by many medical students as compared to other forms of medical practice;[2] the substantial number of emigrants from among recently qualified doctors;[3] and the spate of complaining letters from general practitioners in medical journals[4] can all be interpreted as indications that this branch of medical practice is failing to attract, keep or satisfy sufficient numbers of British trained doctors to maintain in the future the viability of the present system of primary medical care. Incidentally, it is not only in this country that the viability of a system of care in which the physician of primary contact is a generalist has been called in question. In the major cities of the USA, the general practitioner as the primary and main source of medical contact for people of both sexes, all ages and all social classes has long since disappeared.[5]

There is no comparable evidence, be it noted, of any massive discontent with the system among the consumers of primary medical care in this country. On the contrary, there is no substantial defection of patients of any class from the National Health Service to private practice,[6] and surveys which have been undertaken of patients' attitudes to their doctors present a picture of a generally contented, largely uncritical population.[7] One suspects that the feelings of overwhelming gratitude to doctors who have relieved them of painful symptoms or disquieting fears of death or chronic disablement, may have made most of those who have been questioned in surveys reluctant to criticize doctors or the conditions under which they have been treated. They may fear that any criticism would seem unwarranted and churlish. Indeed, the difficulty of finding out from patients and their relatives in the course of a relatively structured survey interview the true nature and extent of the anxieties associated with illness, because of their feelings of gratitude to the doctor if their condition has finally improved or of continued dependency on him if it has not, has perhaps permitted greater complacency with the quality of the care provided both in and outside hospital than is really warranted. Certainly, some small scale intensive questioning of relatives of patients with conditions in which the prognosis was one of continuing severe handicap has suggested that there was considerable dissatisfaction (although often unfairly attributed to the doctor) with the care and understanding which they had obtained from doctors.[8]

HOW CAN MEDICAL CARE BE DIVIDED ORGANIZATIONALLY AND PROFESSIONALLY?

If, however, we take the signs of doctors' current dissatisfactions with general practice as an indication that change is needed, we then come to the crux of the problem. What kinds of change are possible, which of them are most desirable or least undesirable and how can they best be achieved?

Before we can answer these questions, we must conduct a much more searching examination than has so far taken place of the present system of dividing the provision of medical care of all kinds between doctors of first contact who are not specialists in any branch of medicine and those who specialize in the diseases of systems or age groups. I for one was disappointed because both the Gillie report on *The Field of Work of the Family Doctor* in 1963[9] and the report of the Todd Royal Commission on Medical Education[10] seemed to me to shy away from this examination. Neither really stated whether there was, in their view, a discrete body of knowledge, mastery of which through academic study and practical application would distinguish general practitioners from specialists in all other branches of medicine. They both indicated, however, that general practitioners should continue to provide the *first* point of contact for all patients in need of medical advice or treatment and by implication, the *only* point of contact for those whose medical conditions were acute but relatively easily diagnosed and treated. They also saw, although less explicitly, the general practitioner as a 'continuity' man helping to relieve the pain and discomfort of the chronic sick and to maximize their potentiality for satisfying activities and relationships. And, in order to give this work the status which they believed it deserved in the community and among the medical fraternity as a whole, they suggested it should be called a speciality. The Gillie report, for example, suggested that general practice 'became a speciality in its own right, if only as that branch of medicine which did not specialize but provided a personal medical service for the "whole" patient in his total environment',[11] i.e. its speciality was to be its lack of speciality. One feels that Lewis Carroll might have made hay with the logic of such a position.

Turning to the Todd Commission, its report recommends for the general practitioners three years of postgraduate training through appointments in a wide range of specific specialities—including mainly obstetrics and gynae-cology, general medicine, paediatrics, psychiatry; but, as well, in anaesthetics, dermatology, geriatrics, ophthalmology, otorhinolaryngology, physical medicine and therapeutics, as well as appointments in general practice, and if possible in local authority—or occupational health-based services.[12] One might well ask 'What is left out?' (there was no mention of heart transplant!) After a further period of two years in general practice in a training post, the doctor would then be deemed competent to exercise independent clinical judgement as 'in effect, a "specialist" in general practice'.[13]

It is interesting to note however that designation as 'specialist' is the height of the career to which the Commission considered it possible for the general practitioner to aspire. They did not envisage the experienced or specially gifted general practitioner becoming eventually, after a period of further intensive training, a consultant, as they did the similarly able 'specialist' in other branches of medicine. Indeed, they could not envisage what further training there could be in this speciality which would warrant the further promotion to consultant status.[14] One is tempted to ask whether without this comparable career prospect general practice can expect to be accorded parity of esteem with other specialities, or whether the Todd Commission's expectation 'that our proposals, if implemented will considerably raise the status of general practice' will be realized.[15]

It is at this stage that a sociological analysis of the determinants of 'status', in the sense of 'prestige', may be useful. When applied to the situation I have just described, such as analysis suggests that the Todd proposals for general practice by themselves may not be enough to ensure greater prestige for it, even if they are allied, as the Commission thought they must be, with improvements in the conditions of service and increases in rewards for those who can demonstrate that they have been pursuing the practices currently regarded as 'good' from the professional viewpoint (e.g. by employing receptionists and secretaries, accepting attachments from local health authority workers, improving surgery and waiting room equipment, running well-baby and geriatric clinics, attending postgraduate courses, etc.).

THE STATUS OF GENERAL PRACTICE

In all known societies, adults rank positions in the occupational structure in some hierarchial order of prestige or standing. An analysis of prestige ranking shows that many factors enter into it. For example, occupations are judged not only on their material rewards but on the extent to which they are thought to involve scholarship or learning. Recently, a rating study among professional workers in the USA suggests that the higher the supposed scientific content of an occupation the greater the prestige attached to it.[16] This may help to explain the relative prestige attached by students to different specialities in medicine. At least on this count, the proposals to lengthen the training required for general practice and to give it a more 'scientific' content (at least in therapeutics) are likely to go some way to improve its prestige.

Yet another factor in determining prestige is the extent to which the occupation permits individuals to exercise 'charismatic authority', i.e. a type of authority 'to which the governed submit because of their belief in the extraordinary quality of the specific person'.[17] In other words, occupations which allow scope for the individual to shine, because they provide opportunities for securing the loyalty and respect of those with whom they work, tend to be ranked highly. One thinks in this context of film directors, of politicians, of company directors. But such occupations are not lacking in medicine. For example, they are to be found in the field of spare-part surgery and in fundamental pathological research where team activities are a necessity for success and call for leadership qualities as well as intellectual ability. By contrast, the opportunities of exercising this kind of 'charismatic authority' are relatively speaking small in general practice activities as they are at present practised and as they are still envisaged for the future, it seems, in the form of one to one relationships between doctor and patient.

Again, occupations which include posts where authority can be exercised directly or indirectly over others are usually accorded more prestige than those where the authority is more limited. The hospital-based doctor, directing a team of physicians, nurses, social workers and others, is in this sense more likely to acquire a high ranking than a doctor in general practice who is seldom a team leader. Or, if he does lead a team, it may not be so obvious to the participants that he does. For example, he has no ward round or lecture theatre rostrum to demonstrate his authority. If a case conference is called to discuss a patient's case, he may not appear to be the most authoritative individual.

Again, prestige will ordinarily attach to occupations whose practitioners are felt by public opinion generally to be of great value to the community at large. Thus in war time, the rating of the armed forces, from commander-in-chief down to private soldier, increases relative to that of civilians.[18] This factor may account for a large part of the explanation for the universally high rating accorded the medical profession in all societies.[19] (And this applies to traditional healers in East Africa as well as to the practitioners of scientific medicine.) But the public may make invidious value judgements and one expects that more value is attached to the prolongation of a few lives by dramatic surgical triumphs than to the improvement in health and happiness of mothers and children which follow from the inspired practice of preventive medicine, including health and sex education, or prompt primary care in the general practitioner's surgery.

To sum up, the relative prestige of occupations depends upon a number of factors, and the Todd proposals for improving that of general practice *vis à vis* other branches of medicine seem to touch upon only some of the important factors in the matrix. Given the strength of countervailing factors which also enter into that matrix, the proposals may be ineffective.

POLICIES FOR IMPROVING THE ATTRACTIVENESS OF
GENERAL PRACTICE

If this analysis is correct, there seem to be several possible courses of action. One can try, for example, to deal with all or some of the countervailing factors which enter into the matrix, in an effort to raise the prestige of the occupation; one can also try to determine whether there are ways, other than by raising the prestige of the occupation, of attracting sufficient numbers of doctors of the right quality to it and of retaining their services. One can also consider, once again, what functions it is intended that a general practitioner should perform, whether these functions are essential to the objectives of a health service and, if so, whether they could be performed, more or as effectively by any other kind of doctor or other kind of worker.

Take first, for example, the exploration of other ways of increasing the prestige of general practitioners *vis à vis* other branches of medical practice. If my analysis is correct, the standing of general practice would rise if it involved team work with other doctors and medical workers, and if, further, it gave opportunities for individuals to become recognized and revered leaders of inter-professional teams. The question we have to ask is whether it is justifiable to alter the organization of general practice in this way, which would certainly lead to conflict with other tenets which have guided general practice in the past, for example with the exclusivity of the doctor/ patient relationship and the tacit assumptions that general practitioners must not intervene in or criticize the professional practices or judgements of their peers, and that medical practitioners are members of a fraternity and not of a hierarchy, an assumption which incidentally has been partially abandoned in hospital medicine and which both the recent reports on hospital staffing from the Ministry of Health[20] and the Scottish Home and Health Department[21] and the Todd Commission's recommendations for the appointment of departmental chiefs suggest should be further undermined.

Moreover, it is sometimes said that general practice attracts the kind of individual who acts best when independent of other members of his profession. This may well be so. A study which is being carried out among general practitioners in the London Borough of Camden certainly suggests that some single-handed practitioners there would not like to work in teams of any kind and cherish their independence. The desire for independence can stem from various motivations, some good and some not so good. Some lone wolves choose their isolation not so much because they feel it will enable them to do better work, but because they know it will not expose them to the critical judgement of their peers. One cannot deliberately gear general practice organization to the psychological needs of the few individuals who may do their best work when working on their own. This is not to say, however, that there is not also a possible danger of creating work units which are too large and where the work of individuals may suffer because they feel they have lost their own identity in a depersonalized institution.

Secondly, the status of general practice might be raised if activities of its practitioners were to be more highly valued both by the profession and by the general public. Changing value systems is usually very difficult, if not impossible, if one has to work against the values inculcated by the mass media. Nevertheless, we may be much too defeatist about our chances of doing so. Through health education in schools and elsewhere the public image of the work which the general practitioner can do in preventing sickness and maintaining the chronic sick can be improved. A new approach to community medicine in medical schools, such as that which is being pioneered in Newcastle, may well alter radically the comparative values which medical students learn to attach to the medicine practised in the different settings of the hospital and of the local authority health or group practice centres. The increasing emphasis which the Todd Commission suggests should be given to the teaching of the behavioural sciences in the preclinical degree in medical sciences may also help, in the sense that students may come to understand how their own values are influenced by the cultural climate of their environment and be more ready therefore to question these values. Nevertheless, it would be foolish to underestimate the enormous difficulties of changing the established value system of the medical school, particularly at a time when the great advances in medical knowledge seem to be coming from fundamental biological research rather than from sociological or psychological research.

This suggests, therefore, that in addition to attempts to manipulate the factors which enter into the determination of the status of general practice, other measures might be considered of attracting doctors to this branch of medicine.

Those which need serious consideration are also bound up with the selection and training of medical students. Many would-be applicants for medical training are young men and women who see in the profession an opportunity to give individuals a fuller and happier life by helping to over-come sickness and premature death, which are the source of so much human misery. During the course of medical training, learning about the techniques of diagnosing and dealing with sickness becomes all-absorbing, and students are encouraged, tacitly rather than explicitly, to forget the more fundamental reason for their initial motivation. Indeed, it is argued that, unless they do so, their scientific capacity which rests upon emotional detachment may be impaired.

But suppression of this interest does have some deleterious results, because it ultimately affects students' views both of what is interesting in the study of medicine and of what branches of medicine are most worth-while practising. Moreover, by largely ignoring the social and psychological components in the aetiology of illness, and in its treatment, prognosis and outcome (sometimes on the grounds that there is little known in this field so far which can be scientifically validated), medical schools limit unneces-sarily the competence which the doctor should have in them when he begins to practise medicine. This loss, while affecting all doctors, falls most heavily on general practitioners, both because the social and psychological components loom large in the spectrum of illness which they see and treat, and because, as physicians of primary contact whose patients are not in hospital beds, they are in a better position than hospital-based physicians to see and investigate these components of illness. Another unfortunate result of the disinterest in the social aspects of illness and medical care is that little encouragement is given to able students to research in this field, and scientific research is badly needed to make good the gaps in our knowledge.

The Todd proposals for teaching the behavioural sciences at undergraduate level will, if done with imagination, go some way to meeting the problem which the present emphasis in medical education creates. But they may not go far enough and the syllabuses which are set out in Appendices 10 and 11 of the report may not meet the purpose.

However, the proposals made by the Commission for general professional training in general practice are inadequate in this regard. Indeed, one of the most important components in general practice training is missing from it altogether, namely a period of serious study in an academic department of the social and psychological components in the 'illnesses' with which patients approach the physician of first contact. Such a period might well include placements in social welfare agencies where the relationship of illness to other forms of social pathology can be observed, for 'illness', in its consequences at least, may be as much a form of social pathology or deviance as crime, malingering, child neglect, marital disharmony or family breakdown—with which it is often allied.

At this point, however, one has to remember that the scope of general professional training which the Todd Commission suggested as the basis for general practice was already almost ludicrously heavy, and these proposals would only make it heavier. This is an added reason for asking whether it is realistic to assume that a general practitioner, acting as the doctor of first contact (and in most cases of only contact) for every kind of individual who opts to register with him, can maintain 'all across the board', the high quality of practice expected of him by his peers.

A very strong argument for suggesting that general practice should continue to be general is that the health and sickness of any individual is related to that of others in his domestic group, and that a doctor's knowledge of the whole group will increase his competence in dealing with the individual. Doctors who restrict their role of primary care physicians to a single age band would not have the same opportunities to take into consideration the patient's whole domestic group, which usually includes people of different ages and both sexes.

On the other hand, we must recognize that the cake of medical care has to be divided at some place, and that every division will carry with it some disadvantages as well as advantages. Hence the dilemma which forms the title of this paper. It is clear that careful consideration must be given to the costs and benefits which would accrue from the form of medical care organization envisaged by Professor McKeown, in which the task of primary care is divided between physicians who restrict their practice to individuals of certain ages, a restriction which he considers would enable the physician to play a more substantial part in the total medical care required by that age group than the general practitioner is now able to do.

How should the dilemma be resolved? Careful analyses of the present characteristics of our medical care organization and, in particular, of the social and psychological components in illness and illness behaviour on the one hand and practitioners' response to that behaviour on the other can help us decide which horn of the dilemma to grasp. Moreover, this analysis must take into account the possible contribution to medical care of workers trained in the other disciplines which bear on medicine, in particular, nursing, midwifery, health visiting, medical social work and psychiatric social work. But equally important is the need for careful experimentation with different forms of medical care organization, and this involves, of course, careful evaluation of the experiments. We might find that one kind of organization was better than the other in achieving one kind of objective, and the other kind of organization superior in another regard. If we did, it might be wiser to allow different forms of care to develop rather than insist on a monolithic pattern.

REFERENCES

1. Ministry of Health, *Annual Report for the Year 1966*, HMSO (London 1967), Cmnd. 3326, pp. 204-5.
2. Cf. F. M. Martin and F. A. Boddy, 'Career Preferences of Medical Students', *Sociological Review Monograph*, No. 5, 1962. However in 1966 final year students were more likely than first-year students to give general practice as their first preference. Cf. *Report of the Royal Commission on Medical Education* (Todd Report), HMSO (London 1968), Cmnd. 3569, pp. 358-60.
3. R. Ash and H. D. Mitchell, 'Doctor Migration 1962-4', *British Medical Journal*, 1968, p. 569.
4. See for example the correspondence columns of the *BMJ*, *The Lancet*, and even the daily press.
5. B. Abel Smith, 'The Major Pattern of Financing and Organization of Medical Services that have Emerged in Other Countries', *Medical Care*, 3, 1965, pp. 33-40.
6. Ann Cartwright estimated that in 1965 only 3% of the population had some or all of their front-line medical care other than through the National Health Service. Ann Cartwright, *Patients and Their Doctors*, 1967, pp. 11, 275.
7. Cartwright, *Patients and Their Doctors*, 1967, *op. cit.*, pp. 216-17; Gordon Forsyth, 'Is the Health Service Doing Its Job?', *New Society*, 19 October 1967; Political and Economic Planning, *Family Needs and the Social Services*, Allen & Unwin (London 1961).
8. Enid Mills, *Living with Mental Illness*, 1962.
9. Gillie Report, *The Field Work of the Family Doctor*, HMSO (London 1963).
10. Todd Report, 1968, *op. cit.*
11. Gillie Report, 1963, *op. cit.*, p. 8.
12. Todd Report, 1968, *op. cit.*, p. 61.
13. Todd Report, 1968, *op. cit.*, p. 62.
14. Todd Report, 1968, *op. cit.*, p. 62.
15. Todd Report, 1968, *op. cit.*, p. 62.
16. J. E. Gerstl and L. K. Cohen, 'Dissensus, situs and Egocentrism in Occupational Ranking', *British Journal of Sociology*, 15, 1964, pp. 254-61.
17. M. Weber, *Essays in Sociology*, edited by Gerth and Mills, 1962 edition.
18. M. Young and P. Willmott, 'Social Grading by Manual Workers', *British Journal of Sociology*, 7, 1956, pp. 337-450.
19. J. B. Montague and B. Pustelnik, 'Prestige Ranking of Occupations', *British Journal of Sociology*, 5, 1954, pp. 154-61.

20. DHSS, *The Organization of Medical Work in Hospitals*, HMSO (London 1967).
21. DHSS, *Organization of Medical Work in the Hospital Service*, HMSO (London 1967).

9 | *The British National Health Service: professional determinants of administrative structure*

D. G. GILL

It is contended that divisions within the medical profession and conflict between the various branches of the profession and the government have had a stronger influence on modifying the pattern of medical care in Great Britain today than the adoption and extension of the principle of social insurance. A fully integrated and free system of medical care was envisaged but the strength and power of two branches of the profession forced the government to accept certain modifications. Primary and secondary medical care and public health activities were all organized separately at the operational level, giving rise to a 'tripartite' structure, and a limited amount of private practice persists.

The form in which medical care is provided in Great Britain today is the culmination of a process whose roots are to be found in the nineteenth century. Three stages may be distinguished.

(i) 1834-1911. The earlier part of the period was typified by a limited provision of medical care for the poverty-stricken and those on the threshold of pauperism based upon the principles of laissez-faire, limited eligibility, and self-help; the latter half of the period was characterized by arguments in favour of a limited introduction of the social insurance principle.

(ii) 1911-48. A gradual extension of the social insurance principle to include the less well-off, but such provision restricted to primary medical care through general practitioners.

(iii) 1948-present day. The extension of the concept of social insurance until the state takes full responsibility for the provision of all medical services, and an almost continuous debate over both the quality and quantity of medical care which the National Health Service provides.

During the process of development there have occurred situations of vigorous conflict both between groups within the profession and between the profession and central and local government. These situations of conflict and the potential and actual schisms to which they gave rise have affected and are still affecting the way in which medical care is provided in Great Britain. The intention here is to examine the way in which these divisions

155

and conflicts have affected the structure and organization of a state-run system of medical care. It will be necessary to consider the consequence of divisions within the profession, specialization and generalism, variations in status and power, and conflict, conflict resolution and compromise. It will then be possible to assess the extent to which the forces referred to above, rather than the principles of social insurance and its ultimate development, 'socialized medicine', have affected the pattern of medical care in Great Britain today.

CONFLICT BETWEEN POOR LAW GUARDIANS AND
POOR LAW MEDICAL OFFICERS

The Poor Law Reform Bill of 1834 was the culmination of a protest movement launched by the landed aristocracy and gentry to reduce what they considered to be the outrageous cost of the poor rate. 'Between 1815 and 1820 condemnation of the poor laws as they then existed was all but universal in England except for the partisans of the emerging working-class movement.'[1] It is in this climate of opinion that medical services for the poor were subsequently developed. Deterrence, through the concept of limited eligibility, was the dominant principle of the Bill and this was to be accomplished through a denial of outdoor relief to the able-bodied pauper. While the sick and mentally defective were theoretically exempt from this order, in practice some local Boards of Guardians refused to give any outdoor medical relief.[2] From the Poor Law Medical Officer's point of view this was not always an obstacle to effective medical care, because the insanitary conditions and lack of amenities of many paupers' homes were so appalling that treatment of illness in such a situation was practically impossible and removal to the workhouse or its attached infirmary might be an advantage. Nevertheless the injunction to eliminate or at least reduce outdoor relief impinged upon the doctor's freedom of choice; criteria other than medical factors influenced the decision on where a course of treatment could be provided.

Conflict between the Poor Law Boards of Guardians and their medical officers was not, however, restricted to this single example of potential disagreement. The post of medical officer was often filled by competitive tender, creating a situation where persons offering the cheapest service were appointed rather than those with the best qualifications. The Apothecaries Act of 1815 had introduced a licensurate scheme whereby the Society of Apothecaries granted licences to practise to those who met their requirements; yet many boards refused to acknowledge that possession of this certificate was a desirable qualification for Poor Law medical officers. Moreover, medical officers were often required to renegotiate their contracts annually, creating uncertainty and insecurity of tenure, a practice hardly conducive to good relations between doctor and employer. The doctor's position *vis à vis* his employer was further weakened by the former's lack of understanding of illness and disease, and the small range and limited efficacy of treatment regimens available to the early nineteenth-century medical practitioner. Medical officers were well aware of the association between poverty—and its correlates of malnutrition and insanitary conditions—and disease, but they were unable to establish on acceptable theoretical grounds the nature of the relationship. Consequently, while medical officers were convinced of the usefulness of prescribing 'medical necessities' —nourishing food and drink—the Poor Law Boards were less inclined to accept the view that such 'treatment' was medically appropriate. More importantly, if this form of 'treatment' became general, then the cost of providing medical relief to the poor would increase dramatically.[3]

The Poor Law medical officer was, therefore, in a relatively powerless position in relation to his employers. The Boards of Guardians certainly influenced if not controlled the circumstances under which patients could be treated, and limited or even denied the doctor's freedom to prescribe 'medical necessities', one of the most effective palliatives available to the early nineteenth-century medical practitioner. Indeed the Poor Law medical officer was not in a position to exercise even the minimum degree of control necessary for the establishment of functional autonomy in relation to medical practice, '... the exclusive competence to determine the proper content and effective method of performing (his) task'.[3] In this context conflict between a particular group of medical practitioners, the Poor Law medical officers, and an arm of the establishment, the Boards of Guardians, was inevitable and it continued in various forms over a whole range of issues associated with conditions of service and treatment mechanisms throughout the nineteenth century.

DIVISIONS WITHIN THE MEDICAL PROFESSION

As the century progressed the lines of demarcation between physicians and surgeons, apothecaries/general practitioners, and public health practitioners became more apparent. These divisions stemmed in part from the different social class of origin of the categories of doctors but more importantly they were a reflection of the social class composition of the groups treated by the branches of the profession. Traditionally the physician provided medical care for the urban rich and the hospitalized poor, and was himself a member of the upper class with the advantages of a university education from the older seats of learning.[4] With the introduction of aseptic techniques, anaesthetics, and the development of the germ theory of disease, physicians and surgeons gained in status and prestige. They gained increasing control of the voluntary hospitals and of the emerging specialist hospitals, laying the foundations for their subsequent dominance within the medical pecking order as the possessors of specialist knowledge.

The apothecary/general practitioner was in a much less satisfactory position, at least until the establishment of the Medical Act of 1858 which created an official council, now the General Medical Council, whose purpose, among others, was to regulate the standards of existing examining bodies. These medical practitioners faced fierce, and in their view unfair, competition from unqualified quacks who were free to treat any patients they could attract. 'The extent of competition from the unqualified can be seen in Census and Medical Directory figures. The Census of 1841 showed over thirty thousand doctors, while the first directories twelve years later listed only eleven thousand *qualified* practitioners.'[5]

But the act of 1858, although it relieved the pressure from unqualified practitioners, did little to establish cooperation between general practitioners and physicians and surgeons. The latter, as the sophistication and extent of medical scientific knowledge improved, turned the hospitals into institutions more attractive to the middle and upper classes. The new specialist hospitals were often used to treat relatively minor conditions of middle-class patients, presumably because such practice offered considerable financial rewards to the hospital doctors. Moreover the expansion of teaching, combined with the voluntary hospitals' tradition of treating the seriously ill poor, led to an increase in the treatment of the medically indigent in out-patient departments. General practitioners stood to lose patients from both ends of the social scale.[6] The latter type of patient the general practitioner could well afford to lose. Many of the sick clubs and friendly societies which had emerged in the second half of the century were hopelessly under-capitalized, with risks spread over too small a group, so that the returns to the doctor for the treatment of episodes of lengthy illness were often below the actual cost of the care delivered. Middle-class patients were however a much more important clientele not only because they could pay for their care. General practitioners were concerned to see that their profession was identified with the status of a gentleman and one way of achieving this was to become a doctor to the emerging middle class. By the third quarter of the nineteenth century the British Medical Association (BMA) had become the general practitioner's trade union. The association through its ethical committee campaigned vigorously on the part of its members until agreement was reached with the specialists and consultants for the establishment of the 'referral system'. 'The physician and surgeon retained the hospital, but the general practitioner retained the patient.'

The publication of Chadwick's *Report on the Sanitary Condition of the Labouring Population of Great Britain* in July 1848, in which the contributions and investigations made by a large number of medical practitioners played no small part,[7] laid the foundation for the development of a third branch of the profession: public health. The sanitary reform movement and the subsequent Public Health Acts of 1848, 1866, 1872, and 1875 were among the undoubted successes of social reform in the nineteenth century; yet the medical officers of health, whose major responsibility it was to implement the acts, gained little in terms of status and prestige either from the public or their colleagues in the other branches of the medical profession.[8] Public health was and is still concerned with collectivities rather than individuals and it is this basic characteristic which distinguishes it from other forms of medical practice. Moreover the medical officer of health is dependent upon civil and sanitary engineers, water board officials, and tradesmen (wholesalers, retailers, and distributors) for the successful performance of his duties. While the public health acts contributed as much if not more to Britain's improved health status in the nineteenth century than improvements in surgical technique and the individual treatment of patients, these successes were of a much less dramatic and noticeable kind. Accordingly the profession did not seem to be disposed to honour its public health practitioners in the same way that successful hospital practice was rewarded. Nor could the medical officer of health expect to be accepted by the industrialists and other influential members of the middle class. Many of the regulations, whose provisions he was required to enforce, entailed considerable financial losses to the owners of slum houses, noxious and odious factories, and the proprietors of inefficient water boards and offensive burial grounds. The major beneficiaries of the public health practitioners' work were the urban working class, the group least able to confer status and prestige upon the medical officers of health.

Clearly the divisions within the profession and the precedents set by the experience of mistrust and conflict, generated out of the disagreements between the profession and both central and local government throughout much of the nineteenth century, paved the way for further vigorous disputes in the next century. The tripartite structure which was to characterize the National Health Service half a century later was further presaged by the relative isolation of the public health practitioner from the other two branches of the profession.

THE HEALTH INSURANCE ACT, 1911

This act provided a limited degree of medical care, initially to groups of workingmen earning under £2 per week, but subsequently extended to cover other occupational categories. The scheme entitled the beneficiaries to only free treatment and care by a general practitioner; hospital services were not included. In this sense only one branch of the profession, the general practitioners, was affected by the act although it had a number of indirect consequences for hospital practice.

Again the BMA acted as the GPs' trade union in the negotiations with the government which preceded the act. The initial formulation of the bill had placed the control of medical benefit in the hands of the friendly societies, did not allow for choice of doctor and did not give the medical profession representation on administrative committees. After a number of conferences between the BMA and the government these points were all reversed and GPs entered the service practically on their own terms. The BMA's 'six cardinal points'—(i) an upper income limit for those entitled to medical benefit, (ii) free choice of doctor, (iii) benefits to be administered by local health committees, not by friendly societies, (iv) choice of method of remuneration by doctors, (v) remuneration to be what the profession considered to be adequate for the work performed, and (vi) adequate medical representation among the insurance commissioners who administered the scheme and on the local health committees—all were in large measure accepted by the government, although clause (v) gave rise to considerable conflict which extended into the first few months of the act's implementation. Clearly the profession and its organization, the BMA, had emerged as a powerful and influential pressure group which in its dealings with the government could insist upon conditions of practice satisfactory to its own membership rather than passively accepting the establishment's views. Indeed the conditions under which general practitioners undertook to serve under the Health Insurance Act served to emphasize the profession's growing status and prestige. The six cardinal points further enhanced the functional autonomy of the profession, and established the right, in this case, of the general practitioner '... to determine the proper content and effective method of performing [his] task' (cf. p. 157). Strong representation of medical practitioners on the central advisory committee and on the local health insurance committees ensured that the profession's voice would continue to be heard on various administrative and operational issues as the insurance scheme got under way.

While the act of 1911 represented the first stage of transition from a system of medical care based upon a mixture of charity, philanthropy and minimal local tax support (the poor rate) to a system of social insurance and state support, it had no direct impact on hospital services or on preventive medicine. Yet, in some respects, the problems the hospital service faced in providing medical care were exacerbated. The voluntary hospitals were starved of an injection of new funds from a new source, the state, just when general practitioners were reaping the benefits of a scheme which ensured some regular financial return for the treatment of working-class patients. Moreover, the general practitioner could refer difficult cases (those requiring sophisticated diagnostic techniques or extended treatment) to the out-patient departments of the voluntary or the local authority hospitals. Under the 'panel' system the general practitioner was paid on a capitation basis—a fixed sum per annum for each insured person registered with him. Clearly it was advantageous to send patients whose care was likely to be costly to an out-patient department if the general practitioner wished to maximize the profitability of his practice, and also to reduce his work load.[9] Outright condemnation of the general practitioner who off-loaded his more expensive working-class patients in this way must nevertheless be tempered by a realistic appraisal of the general practice situation following the implementation of the 1911 act. Payments to the doctor under the insurance scheme were less than generous, and general practitioners and the hospitals who generally operated on a means test basis had in effect to overcharge middle-class patients to continue with what amounted to subsidized provision for working-class patients.[10] This first stage in the introduction of the social insurance principle into medical care, while improving the quality of care available to the less well-off sections of the working class, tended to increase the cost of both primary and secondary care to the middle class.

THE NATIONAL HEALTH SERVICE*

Throughout the twentieth century, improvements in scientific knowledge and understanding of disease conditions have further enhanced the status and power of the medical profession in general and of the hospital-based doctors in particular. Improvements in diagnostic and treatment techniques frequently necessitate improved and more expensive ancillary equipment such as X-ray machines. The expense of such equipment and the skills necessary to operate it virtually ensure that these services can only be provided by practitioners who operate from an organizational base that can take advantage of the economies of scale—the hospital. While one in three general practitioners in the inter-war period had some affiliations with a hospital, these links were often with municipal or cottage hospitals, not the large teaching or voluntary hospitals where the real revolution in medical technique was taking place. Inevitably the social and professional distance between the generalist and the specialist became greater with the former suffering a further decline in status and power, a situation which disadvantaged the general practitioners in their subsequent negotiations with the

---

* The circumstances surrounding the introduction of the National Health Service and subsequent changes in the administration and financial rewards of doctors are well documented in sources already referred to, e.g. Forsyth[5], Stevens[6], and Eckstein[10]. A detailed history of these processes will not be attempted here. Other valuable sources are A. Lindsay, *Socialised Medicine in England & Wales*[11], H. Eckstein, *Pressure Group Politics*[12], and A. J. Willcocks, *The Creation of the National Health Service.*[13]

government before the introduction of the National Health Service.

There had been changes in the conditions of employment and responsibilities of medical officers of health, but these did not affect the status and prestige of public health practitioners relative to the other two branches of the profession. From 1929 the chief medical officer of health had to be a full-time employee of the Local Authority, and a number of new tasks in the area of maternity and child welfare services had become his responsibility. It is therefore from these different bargaining positions and differing traditions of medical practice that the three branches of the profession entered into the discussions with the government which preceded the establishment of the National Health Service.

Unfortunately, in accordance with the principle of obscurantism or even secrecy which characterizes governmental decision-making in Great Britain, the bulk of the discussion and argument between the profession and the government is not available for scrutiny. However, some information (particularly from Willcocks's book) can be pieced together to outline the main points of dispute. The Brown 'plan' of March 1943, possibly drawn up by civil servants who had had experience of local government medical services, '... envisaged a unified health service, all the services being the responsibility of one administrative unit, based on a system of regional local government units or possibly joint authorities. The voluntary hospitals would be "utilized" although what this meant is not clear.... General practitioners were, apparently, to be full-time salaried servants within this administrative system.' With the exception of the Socialist Medical Association, all other medical groups were opposed to these proposals. General practitioners and specialists were united in their condemnation of the plan, if for no other reason than they feared it would limit the profession's functional autonomy. Specialists and consultants clearly wished to maintain control of the hospital service, and general practitioners were well aware of the nineteenth-century precedent of open conflict between the Poor Law medical officers and the representatives of local government, the Poor Law Guardians. Full-time salaried service under a system of medical care administered by regional or local government units was perceived as a threat to the doctor's freedom of action.

It may also be hypothesized that the medical profession was desperately concerned to maintain its prestige within the overall social structure of British society, particularly when it is remembered that the profession's high esteem is of relatively recent origin. As the century progressed the tendency for the general public to follow, to acknowledge and to accept the almost mystical omnipotence of 'doctor's orders' became more and more apparent. By the start of the Second World War Freidson's third condition for the establishment of functional autonomy, 'general public belief in the consulting occupation's competance, in the value of its professional knowledge and skill' was firmly established. One of the profession's main concerns in the discussions with the various ministers of health was to confirm and to consolidate this public acknowledgement of the qualified medical practitioners' dominance in matters relating to health and illness. Was this achieved, and if so what enabled the medical profession to influence the way in which the National Health Service was structured and organized? Which branches of the profession had the highest degree of success in their negotiations with the government?

There is little doubt that the specialists and consultants were the most successful group in their negotiations with the Minister and his advisers in moulding the hospital service to their liking. Conditions of service, pay, permission to continue with private practice including access to National Health Service hospital beds, a high degree of control over appointments and promotion, and control over the merit awards system were all negotiated successfully by the representatives of the medical élite, the English and Scottish Royal Colleges. The negotiations between the specialists and consultants and the government proceeded with good will, with both sides adopting a flexible approach. If the National Health Service was to operate successfully it was essential for the government to obtain the collaboration and cooperation of the specialists and consultants whose scarce and irreplaceable skills were in such short supply. In terms of exchange theory the specialists and consultants were in a most advantageous bargaining position. Moreover, by acceding to this group's requests, the government could also make use of the élite's acquiescence to its plans in its own negotiations with the general practitioners. Thus it became increasingly difficult for this latter group to argue in favour of retaining the right to sell the goodwill of a practice when the specialists had apparently accepted a less commercial basis for their terms of contract with the National Health Service, part-time or full-time salaried positions. The general practitioners' bargaining position was further undermined by the lack of a clear definition of what the GP's role should be under the envisaged National Health Service structure.

After the failure of the Brown plan, the successive Ministers of Health and the act's final architect, Aneurin Bevan, had all abandoned any real attempt to introduce an integral health service. The phrases in the 1946 Act relating to the provision of health centres in which it was proposed that primary and secondary medical care and preventive services would be combined became little more than a pious hope since the local authorities, who were supposed to provide the buildings, were permitted to ignore their responsibilities because of the country's economic condition and the shortage of building materials. General practitioners also lacked enthusiasm for work in health centres, since such a setting threatened the GP's perception of himself as an independent entrepreneur and raised again the bogey of salaried service being introduced by the back door.[14] With the collapse of the arguments in favour of a fully integrated service and the general practitioners' reluctance to accept any form of service which did not maintain their traditional independence, it was not surprising that the form and structure of primary care under the National Health Service simply represented an extension of the previous panel system to all sections and social classes.

The role which public health practitioners played during the negotiations preceding the introduction of the National Health Service is much less clearly documented in the basic sources. The earlier Brown plan clearly contained, if indirectly, the views of men who in their previous work experience had had first hand experience in public health practice. However, the failure of the movement for an integrated health service probably represented for public health practitioners the defeat of this branch of medicine's basic objective, the requirement to link preventive and curative services. Once the specialists and generalists had accepted an operational and an organizational distinction between primary and secondary medical care, any attempt to argue the case in favour of integrating preventive and curative services was probably doomed to failure. Surely too, the relative lack of status and prestige of public health practitioners compared with other branches of the profession and their isolation from other medical practitioners tended to reduce their bargaining power. If they could not claim the attention and support of their medical colleagues, then it was most unlikely that the public health movement would be successful in influencing the government's decisions concerning the future National Health Service structure.

The National Health Service therefore emerged as a tripartite structure, with the three arms of the service reflecting the divisions within the medical profession that had emerged out of the conditions of nineteenth-century medical practice.

When the government abandoned the principle of integration for the system of medical care to be provided, this was not the only concession made to the profession. During negotiations the profession insisted upon and the government conceded the right of medical practitioners to continue to provide medical care on a fee for service basis. Private practice in both primary and specialist care areas was to continue. Aneurin Bevan was not in favour of a continuation of private practice, but it was estimated by both his advisers and the professional groups that the number of patients who could afford and would be disposed to pay for care and treatment would be quite small. Had the government insisted that private practice should cease to exist, then there is little doubt that the profession's objection to the National Health Service would have continued with sufficient force to make it impossible to implement the 1946 act. The government therefore took the view that the existence of a limited private practice sector was a small price to pay for the profession's cooperation in the establishment of a predominantly state-run system of care. While the nature and extent of private practice in Britain since 1948 has been fairly limited,[15] it still represents a considerable breach of the principle of so-called 'socialized medicine'. For those who can afford either direct payments to their private practitioner, or who subscribe to private medical insurance schemes, such as the British United Provident Association, the advantages, real or apparent, of a financial component associated with the doctor/patient relationship can be maintained.

In fact, the introduction of a state-financed system of medical care supported largely from general tax revenues increased even further the degree of functional autonomy enjoyed by the profession. General practitioners could afford to treat illness conditions not in accordance with the individual's ability to pay but as the disease, the current state of medical knowledge, and the doctor's awareness of contemporary treatment techniques suggested. To this extent the general practitioner's degree of professional freedom was enhanced. Under such conditions the doctor can provide the best care of which he is capable without reference to the personal circumstances of the patient. Indeed under the National Health Service the primary physician has become less dependent upon his clients. The doctor/patient relationship, in which the doctor's remuneration is determined on a fee for service basis and where the patient is responsible for the payment, reduces the power of the professional in lay/professional interaction. The doctor, when providing care and treatment, must respond if only at a minimal level to the patient's wishes. He is dependent upon the opinions of his patients for his good standing and indeed for his continuing or growing prosperity. Patients of general practitioners under the National Health Service arrangements do not in any direct sense 'pay the piper' and are less able to call any part of the tune. (Under the National Health Service patients have complete freedom to choose the doctor with whom they wish to be registered and they can change doctors if they so desire. In practice very few seem to choose a particular general practitioner when they first register and even more rarely do patients switch from one general practitioner to another.) This new situation is reflected at least in part by the increasing tendency for general practitioners to arrange their work situation to their own, rather than to their patients' advantage. On the other hand, private patients are able to insist that consultations should take place in the patient's home, that office appointments should be made at the patient's rather than the doctor's convenience and are perhaps more likely to demand and receive an adequate explanation of their condition and its treatment in terms that the layman can understand. Clearly the retention of private practice at the level of primary medical care represents a limitation upon the doctor's independence, a reduction of functional autonomy. However private patients represent a relatively small proportion of the average general practitioner's practice. Cartwright's 1967 study of general practice[16] showed that just under one-third of general practitioners had no private patients, 60% had less than fifty, and only 9% had fifty or more such patients.

Private practice in the hospital sector on the other hand would appear to be a rather more important phenomenon. An estimate made in the early sixties suggested that approximately three million persons or 6% of the population were potential users of private hospital care. In 1964 part-time consultants (those who combined salaried hospital service with private practice) accounted for 69% of those employed in National Health Service hospitals in England and Wales. Their average incomes were higher than their full-time colleagues', reflecting partly the higher prevalence of merit awards among part-time compared with full-time personnel, but mainly because of the extra income derived from private practice. Consultants in branches such as pathology and radiology are unable to supplement their National Health Service salaries, since their specialities do not lend themselves to private practice.

Moreover this branch of private medicine would appear to be expanding. A precise estimate of the number of private patients is difficult to get, but the British United Provident Association, the biggest organization in the field, had more than 1,500,000 subscribers in 1969, suggesting that something like 5,000,000 were covered by the scheme. The association has also had considerable success with promotion efforts directed towards group schemes for company staffs, professional and trade groups and the like. What are the factors associated with this limited but nevertheless significant success? Clearly middle and upper-class businessmen and professionals appreciate the better facilities (e.g. telephones, television and flexible visiting hours) which can be made available in private wards or rooms, but these advantages are probably not the only ones. Businessmen and professionals may derive considerable benefit from being able to choose when they attend for surgery or treatment at their convenience, rather than that of the hospital. A further advantage may stem from the possibility that private patients can in effect jump the queue for hospital beds. No statistics are available for the average length of time a private patient has to wait for a hospital bed compared with a non-paying patient, but the chairman of the Junior Hospital Doctors' Association is reported as saying '... that the abuse of the National Health Service by consultants led to (amongst other things) preferential admission to National Health Service hospitals for private patients in need of surgical treatment.'[17]

The continued existence of private practice, while it caters to a relatively small proportion of the population, has nevertheless altered the character of the state-run system of medical care. It represents a breach of the principle of a uniform and universal system of care. Those with the ability to pay can purchase a number of advantages which they clearly consider to be worthwhile and even if the preferential treatment so obtained is more imagined than real the continued existence of private practice clearly contravenes the politico-moral concept of social equality. Private practice has had and still has its advocates and apologists, but even a brief examination of the impact of the private sector upon the overall medical care system leads to the conclusion that it simply serves to confer advantages upon the 5,000,000 or so potential private patients.

Private medical practice and the extra income it generates is for the benefit of those doctors able to attract private patients. It neither creates new resources nor does it stimulate, through competition, the state sector to improve the service. A small number of nursing homes and private hospitals operate outside the state system, but these units are largely unable to deal with conditions which require highly sophisticated treatment techniques or surgical intervention. Such conditions have to be treated in the private beds of the public hospitals and the quality of care is therefore dependent upon the techniques and equipment available to the public sector. The private patients of general practitioners are largely paying for the doctor's time. In this sense they are competing for a scarce resource and like the phenomenon of 'queue jumping', said to be one of the advantages of private arrangements for hospital care, achieve preferential treatment because of the private patient's willingness and ability to pay extra for more of the scarce resources than are available to the National Health Service patient. Private patients are, of course, drawn from that group of the population who not only have the ability to pay for treatment but are often powerful and articulate and therfore those most likely to complain about inadequate services and to be listened to by the establishment. If there were no alternative to state medicine, then it is just possible that the group now able to avoid the frustrations and delays of the public sector would direct their energies towards attempts to pressurize the government into improving the conditions under which medical care is provided.

THE PROFESSION, PATIENTS, AND POLITICS

In Britain the extension of the concept of social insurance until the state takes complete responsibility for the provision of medical care has had the effect of introducing a third party to the doctor/patient relationship, the government. Yet in the nineteenth century the government, through the Poor Law Boards of Guardians, was already intervening between doctor and patient. Nevertheless the Medical Act of 1858 and subsequent amendments confirmed the profession's demand for the establishment of an effective monopoly over the treatment of disease and created the first condition for the establishment of medicine's functional autonomy, the outlawing of unqualified practitioners. This freedom from state intervention only lasted until the first decade of the twentieth century. In 1911 and again in 1948, the state decided that the freedom of doctor and patient to reach whatever agreement they could achieve in relation to treatment and payment needed to be constrained. Sequentially then, and with particular reference to generalists, three steps can be recognized.

(i) Until 1858, when the state and its local bodies were the employers of some general practitioners (Poor Law medical officers), their freedom of action was limited. Paradoxically, however, in this earlier part of the nineteenth century, the state was not prepared to protect its employees or the profession in general from the competition of unqualified quacks.

(ii) Between 1858 and 1911, once the state had accepted the profession's demand for protection and had established a monopoly in relation to the practice of medicine, the degree to which the state intervened between doctor and patient was minimal.

(iii) In 1911, and more extensively in 1948, the state again intervened, in effect determining the nature and the conditions under which the doctor/patient relationship would operate for the vast majority of the population.

Specialists and consultants remained relatively free from government control until 1948 and were able to maintain rather more freedom of operation than their colleagues in general practice. By capitalizing upon the divisions within the profession and through their effective control over scarce resources and skills, they were able to bargain most effectively with the government and enter the National Health Service, if not on their own terms, then under conditions which preserved much of their functional autonomy established only ninety years ago.

The branch of the profession least able to exercise control over its work content and work situation, public health practitioners, came under the control of the government almost as soon as its recognition as a medical speciality had been achieved. Lacking status and prestige within the profession, and already at least in part an arm of the establishment, it is not surprising that public health practitioners apparently played little part in the negotiations which preceded the establishment of the National Health Service.

Today both the quality and quantity of medical care available to the British population is dependent upon decisions taken by Treasury officials in particular and politicians in general. Expenditure upon the Health Service has to compete with other government expenditure on other equally desirable services—housing, social welfare, education, and the like. Any attempt to shift more of the cost of the National Health Service on to direct rather than indirect payments is surely misguided. The principle of a uniform standard of service has already been breached by the continued existence of a private sector. Prescription charges, payment for dentures, spectacles, and so forth represent a further charge upon those least able to pay for treatment, given that mechanisms for reimbursement of such expenditure tend to be ineffective. Any further steps designed to increase the proportion of direct payments for health care are likely to reduce both the quality and quantity of medical care available to the less affluent.

REFERENCES

1. H. Perkin, *The Origins of Modern English Society, 1750-1880*, Routledge & Kegan Paul (London 1969), p. 190.
2. R. G. Hodgkinson, *The Origins of the National Health Service: the Medical Services of the New Poor Law, 1834-1871*, Wellcome Historical Medical Library (London 1967), pp. 6-7.
3. E. Freidson, *Profession of Medicine*, Dodd, Mead & Company (New York 1970), p. 10.
4. A. M. Carr-Saunders and P. A. Wilson, *The Professions*, Part I, Clarendon Press (Oxford 1933), p. 65.
5. G. Forsyth, *Doctors and State Medicine: A Study of the British Health Service*, Pitman Medical Publishing (London 1966), p. 5.
6. R. Stevens, *Medical Practice in Modern England*, Yale University Press (New Haven and London 1966), pp. 31-3.
7. E. Chadwick, *Report on the Sanitary Condition of the Labouring Population of Great Britain*, edited by M. W. Flinn, Edinburgh University Press (1965), pp. 18-26.
8. D. G. Gill, 'Status and Prestige within the Medical Profession: Some Speculations', Paper presented at the British Sociological Association's Medical Society Group Meeting, Blackpool, 1970. (Mimeographed.)
9. M. I. Roemer, 'On Paying the Doctor and the Implications of Different Methods', in W. Scott and E. H. Volkart (eds), *Medical Care*, John Wiley & Sons (New York 1965), pp. 140-41.
10. H. Eckstein, *The English Health Service*, 2nd edition, Harvard University Press (Cambridge, Mass, 1964), p. 9.
11. A. Lindsay, *Socialized Medicine in England and Wales*, Oxford University Press (London 1962).
12. H. Eckstein, *Pressure Group Politics*, George Allen & Unwin (London 1960).
13. A. J. Willcocks, *The Creation of the National Health Service*, Routledge & Kegan Paul (London 1967).
14. M. Ryan, 'Health Centre Policy in England and Wales', *British Journal of Sociology*, 19 (No. 2), 1968, pp. 34-46.
15. S. Mencher, *Private Practice in Britain*, chapter 1. Occasional Papers on Social Administration, No. 24, G. Bell & Sons (London 1967).
16. A. Cartwright, *Patients and Their Doctors*, Routledge & Kegan Paul (London 1967), p. 12.
17. D. Herbstein, 'Consultants "neglect NHS patients" ', *The Sunday Times* (London 6 June 1971).

10 | *Medicine as an institution of social control**

I. K. ZOLA

Relationships between beliefs regarding illness, responsibility, accountability and moral judgement are discussed, and the increasing pervasiveness of the institution of medicine as a form of social control is analysed in terms of (i) the expansion of those areas of life deemed to be relevant to the good practice of medicine, (ii) the retention of absolute control over certain technical procedures, (iii) the retention of access to certain 'taboo' (intimate and very personal) areas of life and (iv) the expansion of medical involvement in what is deemed relevant to the good practice of life. Some implications of the 'medicalizing of society' are mentioned with reference to drug safety, genetic counselling and automated multiphasic testing, highlighting some of the central ethical and social problems. In conclusion, Zola raises fundamental questions concerning the relationships between values, knowledge and the power of decision-makers.

The theme of this essay is that medicine is becoming a major institution of social control, nudging aside, if not incorporating, the more traditional institutions of religion and law. It is becoming the new repository of truth, the place where absolute and often final judgements are made by supposedly morally neutral and objective experts. And these judgements are made, not in the name of virtue or legitimacy, but in the name of health. Moreover, this is not occurring through the political power physicians hold or can influence, but is largely an insidious and often undramatic phenomenon accomplished by 'medicalizing' much of daily living, by making medicine and the labels 'healthy' and 'ill' *relevant* to an ever increasing part of human existence.

Although many have noted aspects of this process, by confining their concern to the field of psychiatry, these criticisms have been misplaced.[1] For psychiatry has by no means distorted the mandate of medicine, but indeed, though perhaps at a pace faster than other medical specialities, is

* This paper was written while the author was a consultant in residence at the Netherlands Institute for Preventive Medicine, Leiden. For their general encouragement and the opportunity to pursue this topic I will always be grateful.

It was presented at the Medical Sociology Conference of the British Sociological Association at Weston-Super-Mare in November 1971. My special thanks for their extensive editorial and substantive comments go to Egon Bittner, Mara Sanadi, Alwyn Smith, and Bruce Wheaton.

170

following instead some of the basic claims and directions of that profession. Nor is this extension into society the result of any professional 'imperialism', for this leads us to think of the issue in terms of misguided human efforts or motives. If we search for the 'why' of this phenomenon, we will see instead that it is rooted in our increasingly complex technological and bureaucratic system—a system which has led us down the path of the reluctant reliance on the expert.[2]

Quite frankly, what is presented in the following pages is not a definitive argument but rather a case in progress. As such it draws heavily on observations made in the United States, though similar murmurings have long been echoed elsewhere.[3]

AN HISTORICAL PERSPECTIVE

The involvement of medicine in the management of society is not new. It did not appear full-blown one day in the mid-twentieth century. As Sigerist[4] has aptly claimed, medicine at base was always not only a social science but an occupation whose very practice was inextricably interwoven into society. This interdependence is perhaps best seen in two branches of medicine which have had a built-in social emphasis from the very start— psychiatry[5] and public health/preventive medicine.[6] Public health was always committed to changing social aspects of life—from sanitary to housing to working conditions—and often used the arm of the state (i.e. through laws and legal power) to gain its ends (e.g. quarantines, vaccinations). Psychiatry's involvement in society is a bit more difficult to trace, but taking the histories of psychiatry as data, then one notes the almost universal reference to one of the early pioneers, a physician named Johan Weyer. His, and thus psychiatry's, involvement in social problems lay in the objection that witches ought not to be burned; for they were not possessed by the devil, but rather bedevilled by their problems—namely they were insane. From its early concern with the issue of insanity as a defence in criminal proceedings, psychiatry has grown to become the most dominant rehabilitative perspective in dealing with society's 'legal' deviants. Psychiatry, like public health, has also used the legal powers of the state in the accomplishment of its goals (i.e. the cure of the patient) through the legal proceedings of involuntary commitment and its concomitant removal of certain rights and privileges.

This is not to say, however, that the rest of medicine has been 'socially' uninvolved. For a rereading of history makes it seem a matter of degree. Medicine has long had both a *de jure* and a *de facto* relation to institutions of social control. The *de jure* relationship is seen in the idea of reportable diseases, wherein if certain phenomena occur in his practice the physician is required to report them to the appropriate authorities. While this seems

somewhat straightforward and even functional where certain highly contagious diseases are concerned, it is less clear where the possible spread
of infection is not the primary issue (e.g. with gunshot wounds, attempted
suicide, drug use and what is now called child abuse). The *de facto* relation
to social control can be argued through a brief look at the disruptions of the
last two or three American Medical Association conventions. For there
the American Medical Association members—and really all ancillary health
professions—were accused of practising social control (the term used by
the accusers was genocide) in first, *whom* they have traditionally treated
with *what*—giving *better* treatment to more favoured clientele; and secondly,
what they have treated—a more subtle form of discrimination, in that with
limited resources by focusing on some disease others are neglected. Here
the accusation was that medicine has focused on the diseases of the rich
and the established—cancer, heart disease, stroke—and ignored the diseases
of the poor, such as malnutrition and still high infant mortality.

THE MYTH OF ACCOUNTABILITY

Even if we acknowledge such a growing medical involvement, it is easy to
regard it as primarily a 'good' one—which involves the steady destigmati-
zation of many human and social problems. Thus Barbara Wootton was
able to conclude:

> Without question ... in the contemporary attitude toward antisocial
> behaviour, psychiatry and humanitarianism have marched hand in hand.
> Just because it is so much in keeping with the mental atmosphere of a
> scientifically-minded age the medical treatment of social deviants has been
> a most powerful, perhaps even the most powerful, reinforcement of
> humanitarian impulses; for today the prestige of humane proposals is
> immensely enhanced if these are expressed in the idiom of medical science.[7]

The assumption is thus readily made that such medical involvement in
social problems leads to their removal from religious and legal scrutiny
and thus from moral and punitive consequences. In turn the problems are
placed under medical and scientific scrutiny and thus in objective and
therapeutic circumstances.

   The fact that we cling to such a hope is at least partly due to two cultural-
historical blind spots—one regarding our notion of punishment and the
other our notion of moral responsibility. Regarding the first, if there is
one insight into human behaviour that the twentieth century should have
firmly implanted, it is that punishment cannot be seen in merely physical
terms, nor only from the perspective of the giver. Granted that capital
offences are on the decrease, that whipping and torture seem to be dis-
appearing as is the use of chains and other physical restraints, yet our
ability if not willingness to inflict human anguish on one another does not

seem similarly on the wane. The most effective forms of brain-washing deny any physical contact and the concept of relativism tells much about the psychological costs of even relative deprivation of tangible and intangible wants. Thus, when an individual because of his 'disease' and its treatment is forbidden to have intercourse with fellow human beings, is confined until cured, is forced to undergo certain medical procedures for his own good, perhaps deprived forever of the right to have sexual relations and/or produce children, *then* it is difficult for that patient *not* to view what is happening to him as punishment. This does not mean that medicine is the latest form of twentieth century torture, but merely that pain and suffering take many forms, and that the removal of a despicable inhumane procedure by current standards does not necessarily mean that its replacement will be all that beneficial. In part, the satisfaction in seeing the chains cast off by Pinel may have allowed us for far too long to neglect examining with what they had been replaced.

It is the second issue, that of responsibility, which requires more elaboration, for it is argued here that the medical model has had its greatest impact in the lifting of moral condemnation from the individual. While some sceptics note that while the individual is no longer condemned his disease still *is*, they do not go far enough. Most analysts have tried to make a distinction between illness and crime on the issue of personal responsibility.[8] The criminal is thought to be responsible and therefore accountable (or punishable) for his act, while the sick person is not. While the distinction does exist, it seems to be more a quantitative one rather than a qualitative one, with moral judgements but a pinprick below the surface. For instance, while it is probably true that individuals are no longer directly condemned for being sick, it does seem that much of this condemnation is merely displaced. Though his immoral character is not demonstrated in his having a disease, it becomes evident in what he does about it. Without seeming ludicrous, if one listed the traits of people who break appointments, fail to follow treatment regimen, or even delay in seeking medical aid one finds a long list of 'personal flaws'. Such people seem to be ever ignorant of the consequences of certain diseases, inaccurate as to symptomatology, unable to plan ahead or find time, burdened with shame, guilt, neurotic tendencies, haunted with traumatic medical experiences or members of some low status minority group—religious, ethnic, racial or socio-economic. In short, they appear to be a sorely troubled if not disreputable group of people.

The argument need not rest at this level of analysis, for it is not clear that the issues of morality and individual responsibility have been fully banished from the aetiological scene itself. At the same time as the label 'illness' is being used to attribute 'diminished responsibility' to a whole host of phenomena, the issue of 'personal responsibility' seems to be re-emerging within medicine itself. Regardless of the truth and insights of the concepts of stress and the perspective of psychosomatics, whatever else they do they bring man *not* bacteria to the centre of the stage and lead thereby to a re-examination of the individual's role in his own demise, disability and even recovery.

The case, however, need not be confined to professional concepts and their degree of acceptance, for we can look at the beliefs of the man in the street. As most surveys have reported, when an individual is asked what caused his diabetes, heart disease, upper respiratory infection, etc., we may be comforted by the scientific terminology if not the accuracy of his answers. Yet if we follow this questioning with the probe: 'why did you get X now?' or 'of all the people in your community, family etc. who were exposed to X, why did you get ...?', then the rational scientific veneer is pierced and the concern with personal and moral responsibility emerges quite strikingly. Indeed the issue 'why me?' becomes of great concern and is generally expressed in quite moral terms of what they did wrong. It is possible to argue that here we are seeing a residue and that it will surely be different in the new generation. A recent experiment I conducted should cast some doubt on this. I asked a class of forty undergraduates, mostly aged seventeen, eighteen and nineteen, to recall the last time they were sick, disabled or hurt and then to record how they did or would have communicated this experience to a child under the age of five. The purpose of the assignment had nothing to do with the issue of responsibility and it is worth noting that there was no difference in the nature of the response between those who had or had not actually encountered children during their 'illness'. The responses speak for themselves.

The opening words of the sick, injured person to the query of the child were:
'I feel bad'
'I feel bad all over'
'I have a bad leg'
'I have a bad eye'
'I have a bad stomach ache'
'I have a bad pain'
'I have a bad cold'
The reply of the child was inevitable:
'What did you do wrong?'
The 'ill person' in no case corrected the child's perspective but rather joined it at that level.
On bacteria:
'There are good germs and bad germs and sometimes the bad germs ...'
On catching a cold:
'Well you know sometimes when your mother says, "Wrap up or be careful or you'll catch a cold", well I ...'
On an eye sore:

'When you use certain kinds of things (mascara) near your eye you must be
very careful and I was not ...'
On a leg injury:
'You've always got to watch where you're going and I ...'

Finally to the treatment phase:
On how drugs work:
'You take this medicine and it attacks the bad parts ...'
On how wounds are healed:
'Within our body there are good forces and bad ones and when there is
an injury, all the good ones ...'
On pus:
'That's the way the body gets rid of all its bad things ...'
On general recovery:
'If you are good and do all the things the doctor and your mother tell you,
you will get better.'

In short, on nearly every level from getting sick to recovery a moral
battle raged. This seems more than the mere anthropomorphizing of a
phenomenon to communicate it more simply to children. Frankly it seems
hard to believe that the English language is so poor that a *moral* rhetoric
is needed to describe a supposedly amoral phenomenon—illness.

In short, despite hopes to the contrary, the rhetoric of illness by itself
seems to provide no absolution from individual responsibility, accountability and moral judgement.

THE MEDICALIZING OF SOCIETY

Perhaps it is possible that medicine is not devoid of a potential for
moralizing and social control. The first question becomes: 'what means
are available to exercise it?' Freidson has stated a major aspect of the
process most succinctly: 'The medical profession has first claim to jurisdiction over the label of illness and *anything* to which it may be attached,
irrespective of its capacity to deal with it effectively.'[9] For illustrative purposes this 'attaching' process may be categorized in four concrete ways:
first, through the expansion of what in life is deemed relevant to the good
practice of medicine; secondly, through the retention of absolute control
over certain technical procedures; thirdly, through the retention of near
absolute access to certain 'taboo' areas; and finally, through the expansion
of what in medicine is deemed relevant to the good practice of life.

*The expansion of what in life is deemed relevant to the good practice
of medicine*
The change of medicine's commitment from a specific aetiological model of
disease to a multi-causal one and the greater acceptance of the concepts
of comprehensive medicine, psychosomatics, etc., have enormously

expanded that which is or can be relevant to the understanding, treatment and even prevention of disease. Thus it is no longer necessary for the patient merely to divulge the symptoms of his body, but also the symptoms of daily living, his habits and his worries. Part of this is greatly facilitated in the 'age of the computer', for what might be too embarrassing, or take too long, or be inefficient in a face to face encounter can now be asked and analysed impersonally by the machine, and moreover be done before the patient ever sees the physician. With the advent of the computer a certain guarantee of privacy is necessarily lost, for while many physicians might have probed similar issues, the only place where the data were stored was in the mind of the doctor, and only rarely in the medical record. The computer on the other hand has a retrievable, transmittable and almost inexhaustible memory.

It is not merely, however, the nature of the data needed to make more accurate diagnoses and treatments, but the perspective which accompanies it—a perspective which pushes the physician far beyond his office and the exercise of technical skills. To rehabilitate or at least alleviate many of the ravages of chronic disease, it has become increasingly necessary to intervene to change permanently the habits of a patient's lifetime—be it of working, sleeping, playing or eating. In prevention the 'extension into life' becomes even deeper, since the very idea of primary prevention means getting there *before* the disease process starts. The physician must not only seek out his clientele but once found must often convince them that they must do something *now* and perhaps at a time when the potential patient feels well or not especially troubled. If this in itself does not get the prevention-oriented physician involved in the workings of society, then the nature of 'effective' mechanisms for intervention surely does, as illustrated by the statement of a physician trying to deal with health problems in the ghetto: 'Any effort to improve the health of ghetto residents cannot be separated from equal and simultaneous efforts to remove the multiple social, political and economic restraints currently imposed on inner city residents.'[10]

Certain forms of social intervention and control emerge even when medicine comes to grips with some of its more traditional problems like heart disease and cancer. An increasing number of physicians feel that a change in diet may be the most effective deterrent to a number of cardiovascular complications. They are, however, so perplexed as to how to get the general population to follow their recommendations that a leading article in a national magazine was entitled 'To Save the Heart: Diet by Decree?'[11] It is obvious that there is an increasing pressure for more explicit sanctions against the tobacco companies and against high users to force both to desist. And what will be the implications of even stronger evidence which links age at parity, frequency of sexual intercourse, or the lack of male circumcision to the incidence of cervical cancer, can be left to our imagination!

Through the retention of absolute control over certain technical procedures
In particular this refers to skills which in certain jurisdictions are the very operational and legal definition of the practice of medicine—the right to do surgery and prescribe drugs. Both of these take medicine far beyond concern with ordinary organic disease.

In surgery this is seen in several different sub-specialities. The plastic surgeon has at least participated in, if not helped perpetuate, certain aesthetic standards. What once was a practice confined to restoration has now expanded beyond the correction of certain traumatic or even congenital deformities to the creation of new physical properties, from size of nose to size of breast, as well as dealing with certain phenomena—wrinkles, sagging, etc.—formerly associated with the 'natural' process of ageing. Alterations in sexual and reproductive functioning have long been a medical concern. Yet today the frequency of hysterectomies seems not so highly correlated as one might think with the presence of organic disease. (What avenues the very possibility of sex change will open is anyone's guess.) Transplantations, despite their still relative infrequency, have had a tremendous effect on our very notions of death and dying. And at the other end of life's continuum, since abortion is still essentially a surgical procedure, it is to the physician-surgeon that society is turning (and the physician-surgeon accepting) for criteria and guidelines.

In the exclusive right to prescribe and thus pronounce on and regulate drugs, the power of the physician is even more awesome. Forgetting for the moment our obsession with youth's 'illegal' use of drugs, any observer can see, judging by sales alone, that the greatest increase in drug use over the last ten years has not been in the realm of treating any organic disease but in treating a large number of psycho-social states. Thus we have drugs for nearly every mood: to help us sleep or keep us awake; to enhance our appetite or decrease it; to tone down our energy level or to increase it; to relieve our depression or stimulate our interest. Recently the newspapers and more popular magazines, including some medical and scientific ones, have carried articles about drugs which may be effective peace pills or anti-aggression tablets, enhance our memory, our perception, our intelligence and our vision (spiritually or otherwise). This led to the easy prediction: 'We will see new drugs, more targeted, more specific and more potent than anything we have.... And many of these would be for people we would call healthy.'[12] This statement incidentally was made not by a visionary science fiction writer but by a former commissioner of the United States Food and Drug Administration.

Through the retention of near absolute access to certain 'taboo' areas

These 'taboo' areas refer to medicine's almost exclusive licence to examine
and treat that most personal of individual possessions—the inner workings
of our bodies and minds. My contention is that if anything can be shown
in some way to affect the workings of the body and to a lesser extent the
mind, then it can be labelled an 'illness' itself or jurisdictionally 'a medical
problem'. In a sheer statistical sense the import of this is especially great
if we look at only four such problems—ageing, drug addiction, alcoholism
and pregnancy. The first and last were once regarded as normal natural
processes and the middle two as human foibles and weaknesses. Now
this has changed and to some extent medical specialities have emerged to
meet these new needs. Numerically this expands medicine's involvement
not only in a longer span of human existence, but it opens the possibility
of medicine's services to millions if not billions of people. In the United
States at least, the implication of declaring alcoholism a disease (the possible
import of a pending Supreme Court decision as well as laws currently
being introduced into several state legislatures) would reduce arrests in
many jurisdictions by 10-50% and transfer such 'offenders' when 'discovered' directly to a medical facility. It is pregnancy, however, which
produces the most illuminating illustration. For, again in the United States,
it was barely seventy years ago that virtually all births and the concomitants
of birth occurred outside the hospital as well as outside medical supervision. I do not frankly have a documentary history, but as this medical
claim was solidified, so too was medicine's claim to a whole host of related
processes : not only to birth but to prenatal, postnatal, and paediatric care;
not only to conception but to infertility; not only to the process of repro-
duction but to the process and problems of sexual activity itself; not only
when life begins (in the issue of abortion) but whether it should be allowed
to begin at all (e.g. in genetic counselling).

Partly through this foothold in the 'taboo' areas and partly through the
simple reduction of other resources, the physician is increasingly becoming
the choice for help for many with personal and social problems. Thus a
recent British study reported that within a five-year period there had been
a notable increase (from 25 to 41%) in the proportion of the population
willing to consult the physician with a personal problem.[13]

*Through the expansion of what in medicine is deemed relevant to the
good practice of life*

Though in some ways this is the most powerful of all the 'medicalizing
of society' processes, the point can be made simply. Here we refer to the
use of medical rhetoric and evidence in the arguments to advance any
cause. For what Wootton attributed to psychiatry is no less true of medicine.

To paraphrase her, today the prestige of *any* proposal is immensely enhanced, if not justified, when it is expressed in the idiom of medical science. To say that many who use such labels are not professionals only begs the issue, for the public is only taking its cues from professionals who increasingly have been extending their expertise into the social sphere or have called for such an extension.[14] In politics one hears of the healthy or unhealthy economy or state. More concretely, the physical and mental health of American presidential candidates has been an issue in the last four elections and a recent book claimed to link faulty political decisions with faulty health.[15] For years we knew that the environment was unattractive, polluted, noisy and in certain ways dying, but now we learn that its death may not be unrelated to our own demise. To end with a rather mundane if depressing example, there has always been a constant battle between school authorities and their charges on the basis of dress and such habits as smoking, but recently the issue was happily resolved for a local school administration when they declared that such restrictions were necessary for reasons of health.

THE POTENTIAL AND CONSEQUENCES OF MEDICAL CONTROL

The list of daily activities to which health can be related is ever growing and with the current operating perspective of medicine it seems infinitely expandable. The reasons are manifold. It is not merely that medicine has extended its jurisdiction to cover new problems,[16] or that doctors are professionally committed to finding disease,[17] nor even that society keeps creating disease.[18] For if none of these obtained today we should still find medicine exerting an enormous influence on society. The most powerful empirical stimulus for this is the realization of how much everyone has or believes he has something organically wrong with him, or put more positively, how much can be done to make one feel, look or function better.

The rates of 'clinical entities' found on surveys or by periodic health examinations range upwards from 50-80% of the population studied.[19] The Peckham study found that only 9% of their study group were free from clinical disorder. Moreover, they were even wary of this figure and noted in a footnote that, first, some of these 9% had subsequently died of a heart attack, and secondly that the majority of those without disorder were under the age of five.[20] We used to rationalize that this high level of prevalence did not, however, translate itself into action since not only are rates of medical utilization not astonishingly high but they also have not gone up appreciably. Some recent studies, however, indicate that we may have been looking in the wrong place for this medical action. It has been noted in the United States and the United Kingdom that within a given twenty-four to thirty-six hour period, from 50-80% of the adult population have taken one or more 'medical' drugs.[21]

The belief in the omnipresence of disorder is further enhanced by a reading of the scientific, pharmacological and medical literature, for there one finds a growing litany of indictments of 'unhealthy' life activities. From sex to food, from aspirins to clothes, from driving your car to riding the surf, it seems that under certain conditions, or in combination with certain other substances or activities or if done too much or too little, virtually anything can lead to certain medical problems. In short, I at least have finally been convinced that living is injurious to health. This remark is not meant as facetiously as it may sound. But rather every aspect of our daily life has in it elements of risk to health.

These facts take on particular importance not only when health becomes a paramount value in society, but also a phenomenon whose diagnosis and treatment has been restricted to a certain group. For this means that that group, perhaps unwittingly, is in a position to exercise great control and influence about what we should and should not do to attain that 'paramount value'.

Freidson in his recent book *Profession of Medicine* has very cogently analysed why the expert in general and the medical expert in particular should be granted a certain autonomy in his researches, his diagnosis and his recommended treatments.[22] On the other hand, when it comes to constraining or directing human behaviour *because* of the data of his researches, diagnosis, and treatment, a different situation obtains. For in these kinds of decisions it seems that too often the physician is guided not by his technical knowledge but by his values, or values latent in his very techniques.

Perhaps this issue of values can be clarified by reference to some not so randomly chosen medical problems: drug safety, genetic counselling and automated multiphasic testing.

The issue of drug safety should seem straightforward, but both words in that phrase apparently can have some interesting flexibility—namely what is a drug and what is safe. During Prohibition in the United States alcohol was medically regarded as a drug and was often prescribed as a medicine. Yet in recent years, when the issue of dangerous substances and drugs has come up for discussion in medical circles, alcohol has been officially excluded from the debate. As for safety, many have applauded the AMA's judicious position in declaring the need for much more extensive, longitudinal research on marijuana and their unwillingness to back legalization until much more data are in. This applause might be muted if the public read the 1970 Food and Drug Administration's 'Blue Ribbon' Committee Report on the safety, quality and efficacy of *all* medical drugs commercially and legally on the market since 1938.[23] Though appalled at the lack and quality of evidence of any sort, few recommendations were made for the withdrawal of drugs from the market. Moreover there are no recorded cases of anyone dying from an overdose or of extensive adverse side effects from marijuana use, but the literature on the adverse effects of a whole host of 'medical drugs' on the market today is legion.

It would seem that the value positions of those on both sides of the abortion issue needs little documenting, but let us pause briefly at a field where 'harder' scientists are at work—genetics. The issue of genetic counselling, or whether life should be allowed to begin at all, can only be an ever increasing one. As we learn more and more about congenital, inherited disorders or predispositions, and as the population size for whatever reason becomes more limited, then inevitably there will follow an attempt to improve the quality of the population which shall be produced. At a conference on the more limited concern of what to do when there is a documented probability of the offspring of certain unions being damaged, a position was taken that it was not necessary to pass laws or bar marriages that might produce such offspring. Recognizing the power and influence of medicine and the doctor, one of those present argued: 'There is no reason why sensible people could not be dissuaded from marrying if they know that one out of four of their children is likely to inherit a disease.'[24] There are in this statement certain values on marriage and what it is or could be that, while they may be popular, are not necessarily shared by all. Thus, in addition to presenting the argument against marriage, it would seem that the doctor should—if he were to engage in the issue at all —present at the same time some of the other alternatives:

> Some 'parents' could be willing to live with the risk that out of four children, three may turn out fine.
> Depending on the diagnostic procedures available they could take the risk and if indications were negative abort.
> If this risk were too great but the desire to bear children was there, and depending on the type of problem, artificial insemination might be a possibility.
> Barring all these and not wanting to take any risk, they could adopt children.
> Finally, there is the option of being married without having any children.

It is perhaps appropriate to end with a seemingly innocuous and technical advance in medicine, automatic multiphasic testing. It has been a procedure hailed as a boon to aid the doctor if not replace him. While some have questioned the validity of all those test results and still others fear that it will lead to second class medicine for already underprivileged populations, it is apparent that its major use to date and in the future may not be in promoting health or detecting disease to prevent it. Thus three large institutions are now or are planning to make use of this method, not to treat people, but to 'deselect' them. The armed services use it to weed out the physically and mentally unfit, insurance companies to reject 'uninsurables' and large industrial firms to point out 'high risks'. At a recent conference representatives of these same institutions were asked what responsibility they did or would recognize to those whom they have just informed that they have been 'rejected' because of some physical or mental anomaly. They calmly and universally stated: none—neither to provide them with any appropriate aid nor even to ensure that they get or be put in touch with any help.

CONCLUSION

C. S. Lewis warned us more than a quarter of a century ago that 'man's power over Nature is really the power of some men over other men, with Nature as their instrument'. The same could be said regarding man's power over health and illness, for the labels health and illness are remarkable 'depoliticizers' of an issue. By locating the source and the treatment of problems in an individual, other levels of intervention are effectively closed. By the very acceptance of a specific behaviour as an 'illness' and the definition of illness as an undesirable state, the issue becomes not whether to deal with a particular problem, but *how* and *when*.[25] Thus the debate over homosexuality, drugs or abortion becomes focused on the degree of sickness attached to the phenomenon in question or the extent of the health risk involved. And the more principled, more perplexing, or even moral issue of *what* freedom an individual should have over his or her own body is shunted aside.

As stated in the very beginning this 'medicalizing of society' is as much a result of medicine's potential as it is of society's wish for medicine to use that potential. Why then has the focus been more on the medical potential than on the social desire? In part it is a function of space, but also of political expediency. For the time rapidly may be approaching when recourse to the populace's wishes may be impossible. Let me illustrate this with the statements of two medical scientists who, if they read this essay, would probably dismiss all my fears as groundless. The first was commenting on the ethical, moral, and legal procedures of the sex change operation:

> Physicians generally consider it unethical to destroy or alter tissue except in the presence of disease or deformity. The interference with a person's natural procreative function entails definite moral tenets, by which not only physicians but also the general public are influenced. The administration of physical harm as treatment for mental or behavioral problems—as corporal punishment, lobotomy for unmanageable psychotics and sterilization of criminals— is abhorrent in our society.[26]

Here he states, as almost an absolute condition of human nature, something which is at best a recent phenomenon. He seems to forget that there are laws promulgating just such procedures through much of the twentieth century, that within the past few years at least one Californian jurist ordered the sterilization of an unwed mother as a condition of probation, and that such procedures were done by Nazi scientists and physicians as part of a series of medical experiments. More recently, there is the misguided patriotism of the cancer researchers under contract to the United States Department of Defence who allowed their dying patients to be exposed to massive doses of radiation to analyse the psychological and physical results of simulated nuclear fallout. True the experiments were stopped, but not until they had been going on for *eleven* years.

The second statement is by Francis Crick at a conference on the implications of certain genetic findings: 'Some of the wild genetic proposals will never be adopted because the people will simply not stand for them.'[27] Note where his emphasis is: on the people, not the scientist. In order, however, for the people to be concerned, to act and to protest, they must first be aware of what is going on. Yet in the very privatized nature of medical practice, plus the continued emphasis that certain expert judgements must be free from public scrutiny, there are certain processes which will prevent the public from ever knowing what has taken place and thus from doing something about it. Let me cite two examples.

> Recently, in a European country, I overheard the following conversation in a kidney dialysis unit. The chief was being questioned about whether or not there were self-help groups among his patients. 'No,' he almost shouted, 'that is the last thing we want. Already the patients are sharing too much knowledge while they sit in the waiting room, thus making our task increasingly difficult. We are working now on a procedure to prevent them from ever meeting with one another.'

The second example removes certain information even further from public view.

> The issue of fluoridation in the US has been for many years a hot political one. It was in the political arena because, in order to fluoridate local water supplies, the decision in many jurisdictions had to be put to a popular referendum. And when it was, it was often defeated. A solution was found and a series of state laws were passed to make fluoridation a public health decision and to be treated, as all other public health decisions, by the medical officers best qualified to decide questions of such a technical, scientific and medical nature.

Thus the issue at base here is the question of what factors are actually of a solely technical, scientific and medical nature!

To return to our opening caution, this paper is not an attack on medicine so much as on a situation in which we find ourselves in the latter part of the twentieth century; for the medical area is the arena or the example *par excellence* of today's identity crisis—what is or will become of man.

It is the battleground, not because there are visible threats and oppressors, but because they are almost invisible; not because the perspective, tools and practitioners of medicine and the other helping professions are evil, but because they are not. It is so frightening because there are elements here of the banality of evil so uncomfortably written about by Hannah Arendt.[28] But here the danger is greater, for not only is the process masked as a technical, scientific, objective one, but one done for our own good. A few years ago a physician speculated on what, based on current knowledge, would be the composite picture of an individual with a low risk of developing atherosclerosis or coronary-artery disease. He would be:

> ... an effeminate municipal worker or embalmer completely lacking in physical or mental alertness and without drive, ambition, or competitive spirit; who has never attempted to meet a deadline of any kind; a man with poor appetite, subsisting on fruits and vegetables laced with corn and whale oil, detesting tobacco, spurning ownership of radio, television, or motorcar, with full head of hair but scrawny and unathletic appearance, yet constantly straining his puny muscles by exercise. Low in income, blood pressure, blood sugar, uric acid and cholesterol, he has been taking nicotinic acid, pyridoxine, and long term anti-coagulant therapy ever since his prophylactic castration.[29]

Thus I fear with Freidson: 'A profession and a society which are so concerned with physical and functional wellbeing as to sacrifice civil liberty and moral integrity must inevitably press for a 'scientific' environment similar to that provided laying hens on progressive chicken farms—hens who produce eggs industriously and have no disease or other cares.'[30]

Nor does it really matter if instead of the above depressing picture we were guaranteed six more inches in height, thirty more years of life or drugs to expand our potentialities and potencies; we should still be able to ask, what do six inches matter, in what kind of environment will the thirty additional years be spent, or who will decide what potentialities and potencies will be expanded and what curbed.

I must confess that given the road down which so much expertise has taken us, I am willing to live with some of the frustrations and even mistakes that will follow when the authority for many decisions becomes shared with those whose lives and activities are involved. For I am convinced that patients have as much to teach to their doctors as do students their professors and children their parents.

REFERENCES

1. T. Szasz, *The Myth of Mental Illness*, Harper & Row (New York 1961); R. Leifer, *In the Name of Mental Health*, Science House (New York 1969).
2. E.g. A. Toffler, *Future Shock*, Randon House (New York 1970); and P. E. Slater, *The Pursuit of Loneliness*, Beacon Press (Boston 1970).
3. Such as B. Wootton, *Social Science and Social Pathology*, Allen & Unwin (London 1959).

4. H. Sigerist, *Civilization and Disease*, Cornell University Press (New York 1943).

5. M. Foucault, *Madness and Civilization*, Pantheon (New York 1965); and Szasz, *op. cit.*

6. G. Rosen, *A History of Public Health*, MD Publications (New York 1955); G. Rosen, 'The Evolution of Social Medicine', in H. E. Freeman, S. Levine and L. G. Reeder (eds), *Handbook of Medical Sociology*, Prentice Hall (Englewood Cliffs, NJ, 1963), pp. 17-61.

7. Wootton, *Social Science and Social Pathology*, 1959, *op. cit.*, p. 206.

8. Two excellent discussions are found in V. Aubert and S. Messinger, 'The Criminal and the Sick', *Inquiry*, 1, 1958, pp. 137-60; and E. Freidson, *Profession of Medicine*, Dodd-Mead (New York 1970), pp. 205-77.

9. Freidson, *op. cit.*, p. 251.

10. J. C. Norman, 'Medicine in the Ghetto', *New England Journal of Medicine*, 281, 1969, p. 1271.

11. 'To Save the Heart; Diet by Decree?', *Time Magazine* (10 January 1968), p. 42.

12. J. L. Goddard quoted in the *Boston Globe* (7 August 1966).

13. K. Dunnell and A. Cartwright, *Medicine Takers, Prescribers and Hoarders*, Routledge & Kegan Paul, London 1972.

14. E.g. S. Alinsky, 'The Poor and the Powerful', in *Poverty and Mental Health*, No. 21 of the American Psychiatric Association, January 1967; and B. Wedge, 'Psychiatry and International Affairs', *Science*, 157, 1961, pp. 281-5.

15. H. L'Etang, *The Pathology of Leadership*, Hawthorne Books (New York 1970).

16. Szasz, *op cit.*; Leifer, *op. cit.*

17. Freidson, *Profession of Medicine*, 1970, *op. cit.*; T. Scheff, 'Preferred Errors in Diagnoses', *Medical Care*, 2, 1964, pp. 166-72.

18. R. Dubos, *The Mirage of Health*, Doubleday (Garden City, NY, 1959); and R. Dubos, *Man Adapting*, Yale University Press (1965).

19. E.g. the general summaries of J. W. Meigs, 'Occupational Medicine', *New England Journal of Medicine*, 264, 1961, pp. 861-7; G. S. Siegel, *Periodic Health Examinations—Abstracts from the Literature*, Public Health Service Publication, No. 1010 US Government Printing Office (Washington, DC, 1963).

20. I. H. Pearse and L. H. Crocker, *Biologists in Search of Material*, Faber & Faber (London 1938); and I. H. Pearse and L. H. Crocker, *The Peckham Experiment*, Allen & Unwin (London 1949).

21. Dunnell and Cartwright, *Medicine Takers*, *op. cit.*; and K. White, A. Andjelkovic, R. J. C. Pearson, J. H. Mabry, A. Ross and O. K. Sagan, 'International Comparisons of Medical Care Utilization', *New England Journal of Medicine*, 277, 1967, pp. 516-22.

22. Freidson, *op. cit.*

23. *Drug Efficiency Study—Final Report to the Commissioner of Food and Drugs*, Food and Drug Adm. Med. Nat. Res. Council, National Academy of Sciences (Washington, DC, 1969).

24. Reported in L. Eisenberg, 'Genetics and the Survival of the Unfit', *Harper's Magazine*, 232, 1966, p. 57.

25. This general case is argued more specifically in I. K. Zola, *Medicine, Morality, and Social Problems—Some Implications of the Label Mental Illness*, paper presented at the American Ortho-Psychiatric Association, 20-23 March 1968.

26. D. H. Russell, 'The Sex Conversion Controversy', *New England Journal of Medicine*, 279, 1968, p. 536.

27. F. Crick reported in *Time Magazine*, 19 April 1971.

28. H. Arendt, *Eichmann in Jerusalem—A Report on the Banality of Evil*, Viking Press (New York 1963).

29. G. S. Myers quoted in L. Lasagna, *Life, Death and the Doctor*, Alfred Knopf (New York 1968), pp. 215-16.

30. Freidson, *op. cit.*, p. 354.

III | The sociology of the Health Service organizations

11 | *The inverse care law*

J. TUDOR HART

The availability of good medical care tends to vary inversely with the need for it in the population served. This inverse care law operates more completely where medical care is most exposed to market forces, and less so where such exposure is reduced. The market distribution of medical care is a primitive and historically outdated social form, and any return to it would further exaggerate the maldistribution of medical resources.

INTERPRETING THE EVIDENCE

The existence of large social and geographical inequalities in mortality and morbidity in Britain is known, and not all of them are diminishing. Between 1934 and 1968, weighted mean standardized mortality from all causes in the Glamorgan and Monmouthshire valleys rose from 128% of England and Wales rates to 131%. Their weighted mean infant mortality rose from 115% of England and Wales rates to 124% between 1921 and 1968.[1] The Registrar General's last *Decennial Supplement on Occupational Mortality* for 1949-53 still showed combined social classes 1 and 2 (wholly non-manual) with a standardized mortality from all causes 18% below the mean, and combined social classes 4 and 5 (wholly manual) 5% above it. Infant mortality was 37% below the mean for social class 1 (professional) and 38% above it for social class 5 (unskilled manual).[2]

A just and rational distribution of the resources of medical care should show parallel social and geographical differences, or at least a uniform distribution. The common experience was described by Titmuss in 1968.

We have learnt from fifteen years' experience of the Health Service that the higher income groups know how to make better use of the service; they tend to receive more specialist attention; occupy more of the beds in better equipped and staffed hospitals; receive more elective surgery; have better maternal care and are more likely to get psychiatric help and psychotherapy than low-income groups—particularly the unskilled.[3]

These generalizations are not easily proved statistically, because most of the statistics are either not available (for instance, out-patient waiting-lists by area and social class, age and cause specific hospital mortality rates by area and social class, the relation between ante-mortem and post-mortem diagnosis by area and social class, and hospital staff shortage by area) or else they are essentially use rates. Use rates may be interpreted

189

either as evidence of high morbidity among high users, or of disproportionate benefit drawn by them from the National Health Service. By piling up the valid evidence that poor people in Britain have higher consultation and referral rates at all levels of the NHS, and by denying that these reflect actual differences in morbidity, Rein[4, 5] has tried to show that Titmuss's opinion is incorrect, and that there are no significant gradients in the quality or accessibility of medical care in the NHS between social classes.

Class gradients in mortality are an obvious obstacle to this view. Of these Rein says:

> One conclusion reached ... is that since the lower classes have higher death rates, then they must be both sicker or less likely to secure treatment than other classes ... it is useful to examine selected diseases in which there is a clear mortality class gradient and then compare these rates with the proportion of patients in each class that consulted their physician for treatment of these diseases....

He cites figures to show that high death rates may be associated with low consultation rates for some diseases, and with high rates for others, but, since the pattern of each holds good through all social classes, he concludes that:

> a reasonable inference to be drawn from these findings is not that class mortality is an index of class morbidity, but that for certain diseases treatment is unrelated to outcome. Thus both high and low consultation rates can yield high mortality rates for specific diseases. These data do not appear to lead to the compelling conclusion that mortality votes can be easily used as an area of class-related morbidity.

This is the only argument mounted by Rein against the evidence of mortality differences, and the reasonable assumption that these probably represent the final outcome of larger differences in morbidity. Assuming that 'votes' is a misprint for 'rates', I still find that the more one examines this argument the less it means. To be fair, it is only used to support the central thesis that 'the availability of universal free-on-demand, comprehensive services would appear to be a crucial factor in reducing class inequalities in the use of medical care services'. It certainly would, but reduction is not abolition, as Rein would have quickly found if his stay in Britain had included more basic fieldwork in the general practitioner's surgery or the out-patient department.

NON-STATISTICAL EVIDENCE

There is massive but mostly non-statistical evidence in favour of Titmuss's generalizations. First of all there is the evidence of social history. James[6] described the origins of the general practitioner service in industrial and coalmining areas, from which the present has grown.

The general practitioner in working-class areas discovered the well-tried business principle of small profits with a big turnover where the population was large and growing rapidly; it paid to treat a great many people for a small fee. A waiting-room crammed with patients, each representing 2s 6d for a consultation ... not only gave a satisfactory income but also reduced the inclination to practise clinical medicine with skilful care, to attend clinical meetings or to seek refreshment from the scientific literature. Particularly in coalmining areas, workers formed themselves into clubs to which they contributed a few pence a week, and thus secured free treatment from the club doctor for illness or accident. The club system was the forerunner of health insurance and was a humane and desirable social development. But, like the 'cash surgery', it encouraged the doctor to undertake the treatment of more patients than he could deal with efficiently. It also created a difference between the club patients and those who could afford to pay for medical attention ... in these circumstances it is a tribute to the profession that its standards in industrial practices were as high as they were. If criticism is necessary, it should not be of the doctors who developed large industrial practices but of the leaders of all branches of the profession, who did not see the trend of general practice, or, having seen it, did nothing to influence it. It is particularly regrettable that the revolutionary conception of a National Health Service, which has transformed the hospitals of the United Kingdom to the great benefit of the community, should not have brought about an equally radical change in general practice. Instead, because of the shortsightedness of the profession, the NHS has preserved and intensified the worst features of general practice....

This preservation and intensification was described by Collings[7] in his study of the work of 104 general practitioners in fifty-five English practices outside London, including nine completely and seven partly industrial practices, six months after the start of the NHS. Though not randomly sampled, the selection of practices was structured in a reasonably representative manner. The very bad situation he described was the one I found when I entered a slum practice in Notting Hill in 1953, rediscovered in all but one of five industrial practices where I acted as locum tenens in 1961 and found again when I resumed practice in the South Wales valleys. Collings said:

The working environment of general practitioners in industrial areas was so limiting that their individual capacity as doctors counted very little. In the circumstances prevailing the most essential qualification for the industrial GP ... is ability as a snap diagnostician—an ability to reach an accurate diagnosis on a minimum of evidence ... the worst elements of general practice are to be found in those places where there is the greatest and most urgent demand for good medical service.... Some conditions of general practice are bad enough to change a good doctor into a bad doctor in a very short time. These very bad conditions are to be found chiefly in industrial areas.

In a counter-report promoted by the British Medical Association, Had-field[8] contested all of Collings's conclusions, but, though his sampling was much better designed, his criticism was guarded to the point of compla-cency, and most vaguely defined. One of Collings's main criticisms—that purpose-built premises and ancillary staff were essential for any serious upgrading of general practice—is only now being taken seriously; and even the present wave of health centre construction shows signs of finishing almost as soon as it has begun, because of the present climate of political and economic opinion at the level of effective decision. Certainly in indus-trial and mining areas health centres exist as yet only on a token basis, and the number of new projects is declining. Aneurin Bevan described health centres as the cornerstone of the general practitioner service under the NHS, before the long retreat began from the conceptions of the service born in the 1930s and apparently victorious in 1945. Health centre con-struction was scrapped by ministerial circular in January 1948, in the last months of gestation of the new service; we have had to do without them for twenty-two years, during which a generation of primary care was stunted.

Despite this unpromising beginning, the NHS brought about a massive improvement in the delivery of medical care to previously deprived sections of the people and areas of the country. Former Poor Law hospitals were upgraded and many acquired fully trained specialist and ancillary staff and supporting diagnostic departments for the first time. The backlog of untreated disease dealt with in the first years of the service was immense, particularly in surgery and gynaecology. A study of 734 randomly sampled families in London and Northampton in 1961[9] showed that in 99% of the families someone had attended hospital as an out-patient, and in 82% someone had been admitted to hospital. The study concluded:

> When thinking of the Health Service mothers are mainly conscious of the extent to which services have become available in recent years. They were more aware of recent changes in health services than of changes in any other service. Nearly one third thought that more money should be spent on health services, not because they thought them bad but because 'they are so important', because 'doctors and nurses should be paid more' or because 'there shouldn't be charges for treatment'. Doctors came second to relatives and friends in the list of those who had been helpful in times of trouble.

Among those with experience of pre-war services, appreciation for the NHS, often uncritical appreciation, is almost universal—so much so that although most London teaching hospital consultants made their opposition to the new service crudely evident to their students in 1948 and the early years, and only a courageous few openly supported it, few of them appear to recall this today. The moral defeat of the very part-time, multi-hospital consultant, nipping in here and there between private consultations to see how his registrar was coping with his public work, was total and permanent; lip service to the NHS is now mandatory. At primary care level, private practice ceased to be relevant to the immense majority of general practitioners, and has failed to produce evidence of the special functions of leadership and quality claimed for it. On the other hand, despite the massive economic disincentives to good work, equipment and staffing in the NHS until a few years ago, an important expansion of well-organized, community-oriented and self-critical primary care has taken place, mainly through the efforts of the Royal College of General Practitioners; the main source of this vigour is the democratic nature of the service—the fact that it is comprehensive and accessible to all, and that clinical decisions are therefore made more freely than ever before. The service at least permits, if it does not yet really encourage, general practitioners to think and act in terms of the care of a whole defined community, as well as of whole persons rather than diseases. Collings seems very greatly to have underestimated the importance of these changes, and the extent to which they were to overshadow the serious faults of the service—and these were faults of too little change, rather than too much. There have in fact been very big improvements in the quality and accessibility of care both at hospital and primary-care level, for all classes and in all areas.

SELECTIVE REDISTRIBUTION OF CARE

Given the large social inequalities of mortality and morbidity that undoubtedly existed before the 1939-45 war, and the equally large differences in the quality and accessibility of medical resources to deal with them, it was clearly not enough simply to improve care for everyone: some selective redistribution was necessary, and some has taken place. But how much, and is the redistribution accelerating, stagnating or even going into reverse?

Ann Cartwright's study of 1370 randomly sampled adults in representative areas of England, and their 552 doctors,[10] gave some evidence on what had and what had not been achieved. She confirmed a big improvement in the quality of primary care in 1961 compared with 1948, but also found just the sort of class differences suggested by Titmuss. The consultation rate of middle-class patients at ages under forty-five was 53% less than that of working-class patients, but at ages over seventy-five they had a consultation rate 62% higher; and between these two age groups there was stepwise progression. I think it is reasonable to interpret this as evidence that middle-class consultations had a higher clinical content at all ages, that working-class consultations below retirement age had a higher administrative content, and that the middle class was indeed able to make more effective use of primary care. Twice as many middle-class patients were critical of consulting-rooms and of their doctors, and three times as many of waiting-rooms, as were working-class patients; yet Cartwright and Marshall[11] in another study found that in predominantly working-class areas 80% of the doctors' surgeries were built before 1900, and only 5% since 1945; in middle-class areas less than 50% were built before 1900, and 25% since 1945. Middle-class patients were both more critical and better served. Three times as many middle-class patients were critical of the fullness of explanations to them about their illnesses; it is very unlikely that this was because they actually received less explanation than working-class patients, and very likely that they expected, sometimes demanded, and usually received, much more. Cartwright's study of hospital care showed the same social trend for explanations by hospital staff.[12] The same study looked at hospital patients' general practitioners, and compared those working in middle-class and in working-class areas: more middle-class area GPs had lists under 2000 than did working-class area GPs, and fewer had lists over 2500; nearly twice as many had higher qualifications, more had access to contrast-media X-rays, nearly five times as many had access to physiotherapy, four times as many had been to Oxford or Cambridge, five times as many had been to a London medical school, twice as many held hospital appointments or hospital beds in which they could care for their own patients, and nearly three times as many sometimes visited their patients when they were in hospital under a specialist. Not all of these differences are clinically significant; so far the record of Oxbridge and the London teaching hospitals compares unfavourably with provincial medical schools for training oriented to the community. But the general conclusion must be that those most able to choose where they will work tend to go to middle-class areas, and that the areas with highest mortality and morbidity tend to get those doctors who are least able to choose where they will work. Such a system is not likely to distribute the doctors with highest morale to the places where that morale is most needed. Of those doctors who positively choose working-class areas, a few will be attracted by large lists with a big income and an uncritical clientele; many more by social and family ties of their own. Effective measures of redistribution would need to take into account the importance of increasing the proportion of medical students from working-class families in areas of this sort; the report of the Royal Commission on Medical Education[12] showed that social class 1 (professional and higher managerial), which is 2·8% of the population, contributed 34·5% of the final-year medical students in 1961, and 39·6% of the first-year students in 1966, whereas social class 3 (skilled workers, manual and non-manual), which is 49·9% of the population, contributed 27·9% of the final year students in 1961 and 21·7% of the first-year in 1966. The proportion who had received state education was 43·4% in both years, compared with 70·9% of all school-leavers with three or more A-levels. In other words, despite an increasing supply of well-qualified state-educated school-leavers, the over-representation of professional families among medical students is increasing. Unless this trend is reversed, the difficulties of recruitment in industrial areas will increase from this cause as well, not to speak of the support it will give to the officers/other ranks' tradition in medical care and education.

The upgrading of provincial hospitals in the first few years after the Act certainly had a geographical redistributive effect, and, because some of the wealthiest areas of the country are concentrated in and around London, it also had a socially redistributive effect. There was a period in which the large formerly local authority hospitals were accelerating faster than the former voluntary hospitals in their own areas, and some catching-up took place that was socially redistributive. But the better-endowed, better-equipped, better-staffed areas of the service draw to themselves more and better staff, and more and better equipment, and their superiority is compounded. While a technical lead in teaching hospitals is necessary and justified, these advantages do not apply only to teaching hospitals, and even these can be dangerous if they encourage complacency about the periphery, which is all too common. As we enter an era of scarcity in medical staffing and austerity in Treasury control, this gap will widen, and any social redistribution that has taken place is likely to be reversed.

Redistribution of general practitioners also took place at a fairly rapid pace in the early years of the NHS, for two reasons. First, and least important, were the inducement payments and area classifications with restricted entry to over-doctored areas. These may have been of value in discouraging further accumulation of doctors in the Home Counties and on the coast, but Collings was right in saying that 'any hope that financial reward alone will attract good senior practitioners back to these bad conditions is illusory; the good doctor will only be attracted into industrial practice by providing conditions which will enable him to do good work'. The second and more important reason is that in the early years of the NHS it was difficult for the increased number of young doctors trained during and just after the 1939-45 war to get posts either in hospital or in general practice, and many took the only positions open to them, bringing with them new standards of care. Few of those doctors today would choose to work in industrial areas, now that there is real choice; we know that they are not doing so. Of 169 new general practitioners who entered practice in under-doctored areas between October 1968 and October 1969, 164 came from abroad.[14] The process of redistribution of general practitioners ceased by 1956, and by 1961 had gone into reverse; between 1961 and 1967, the proportion of people in England and Wales in under-doctored areas rose from 17% to 34%.[15]

INCREASING LIST SIZE

The quality and traditions of primary medical care in industrial and particularly in mining areas are, I think, central to the problem of persistent inequality in morbidity and mortality and the mismatched distribution of medical resources in relation to them. If doctors in industrial areas are to reach take-off speed in reorganizing their work and giving it more clinical content, they must be free enough from pressure of work to stand back and look at it critically. With expanding lists this will be for the most part impossible; there is a limit to what can be expected of doctors in these circumstances, and the alcoholism that is an evident if unrecorded occupational hazard among those doctors who have spent their professional lives in industrial practice is one result of exceeding that limit. Yet list sizes are going up, and will probably do so most where a reduction is most urgent. Fry[16] and Last[17] have criticized the proposals of the Royal Commission on Medical Education[18] for an average annual increase of 100 doctors in training over the next twenty-five years, which would raise the number of economically active doctors per million population from 1181 in 1965 to 1801 in 1995. They claim that there are potential increases in productivity in primary care, by devolution of work to ancillary and para-medical workers and by rationalization of administrative work, that would permit much larger average list sizes without loss of intimacy in personal care, or decline in clinical quality. Of course, much devolution and rationalization of this sort is necessary, not to cope with rising numbers but to make general practice more clinically effective and satisfying, so that people can be seen less often but examined in greater depth. If clinically irrelevant work can be devoluted or abolished, it is possible to expand into new and valuable fields of work such as those opened up by Balint and his school,[19] and the imminent if not actual possibilities of presymptomatic diagnosis and screening, which can best be done at primary care level and is possible within the present resources of NHS general practice.[20] But within the real political context of 1971 the views of Last, and of Fry from his experience of London suburban practice which is very different from the industrial areas discussed here, are dangerously complacent.

Progressive change in these industrial areas depends first of all on two things, which must go hand in hand: accelerated construction of health centres, and the reduction of list sizes by a significant influx of the type of young doctor described by Barber in 1950:[21]

so prepared for general practice, and for the difference between what he is taught to expect and what he actually finds, that he will adopt a fighting attitude against poor medicine—that is to say, against hopeless conditions for the practice of good medicine. The young man must be taught to be sufficiently courageous, so that when he arrives at the converted shop with the drab battered furniture, the couch littered with dusty bottles, and the few rusty antiquated instruments, he will make a firm stand and say 'I will not practise under these conditions; I will have more room, more light, more ancillary help, and better equipment.'

Unfortunately, the medical ethic transmitted by most of our medical schools, at least the majority that do not have serious departments of general practice and community medicine, leads to the present fact that the young man just does not arrive at the converted shop; he has more room, more light, more ancillary help and better equipment by going where these already exist, and no act of courage is required. The career structure and traditions of our medical schools make it clear that time spent at the periphery in the hospital service, or at the bottom of the heap in industrial general practice, is almost certain disqualification for any further advancement. Our best hope of obtaining the young men and women we need lies in the small but significant extent to which medical students are beginning to reject this ethic, influenced by the much greater critical awareness of students in other disciplines. Some are beginning to question which is the top and which the bottom of the ladder, or even whether there should be a ladder at all; and in the promise of the Todd report, of teaching oriented to the patient and the community rather than towards the doctor and the disease, there is hope that this mood in a minority of medical students may become incorporated into a new and better teaching tradition. It is possible that we may get a cohort of young men and women with the sort of ambitions Barber described, and with a realistic attitude to the battles they will have to fight to get the conditions of work and the buildings and equipment they need, in the places that need them; but we have few of them now. The prospect for primary care in industrial areas for the next ten years is bad; list sizes will probably continue to increase, and the pace of improvement in quality of primary care is likely to fall.

RECRUITMENT TO GENERAL PRACTICE IN SOUTH WALES

Although the most under-doctored areas are mainly of the older industrial type, the South Wales valleys have relatively good doctor/patient ratios, partly because of the declining populations, and partly because the area produces an unusually high proportion of its own doctors, who often have kinship ties nearby and may be less mobile on that account. (In Williams's survey of general practice in South Wales 72% of the 68 doctors were born in Wales and 43% had qualified at the Welsh National School of

Medicine.[22]) On 1 January 1970, of thirty-six South Wales valley areas listed, only four were designated as under-doctored. However, this situation is unstable; as our future becomes more apparently precarious, as pits close without alternative local employment, as unemployment rises, and out-migration that is selective for the young and healthy increases, doctors become subject to the same pressures and uncertainties as their patients. Recruitment of new young doctors is becoming more and more difficult, and dependent on doctors from abroad. Many of the industrial villages are separated from one another by several miles, and public transport is withering while as yet comparatively few have cars, so that centralization of primary care is difficult, and could accelerate the decay of communities. These communities will not disappear, because most people with kinship ties are more stubborn than the planners, and because they have houses here and cannot get them where the work is; the danger is not the disappearance of these communities, but their persistence below the threshold of viability, with accumulating sickness and a loss of the people to deal with it.

WHAT SHOULD BE DONE?

Medical services are not the main determinant of mortality or morbidity; these depend most upon standards of nutrition, housing, working environment, and education, and the presence or absence of war. The high mortality and morbidity of the South Wales valleys arise mainly from lower standards in most of these variables now and in the recent past, rather than from lower standards of medical care. But that is no excuse for failure to match the greatest need with the highest standards of care. The bleak future now facing mining communities, and others that may suffer similar social dislocation as technical change blunders on without agreed social objectives, cannot be altered by doctors alone; but we do have a duty to draw attention to the need for global costing when it comes to policy decisions on redevelopment or decay of established industrial communities. Such costing would take into account the full social costs and not only those elements of profit and loss traditionally recognized in industry.

The improved access to medical care for previously deprived sections under the NHS arose chiefly from the decision to remove primary care services from exposure to market forces. The consequences of distribution of care by the operation of the market were unjust and irrational, despite all sorts of charitable modifications. The improved possibilities for constructive planning and rational distribution of resources because of this decision are immense, and even now are scarcely realized in practice. The losses predicted by opponents of this change have not in fact occurred; consultants who no longer depend on private practice have shown at least as much initiative and responsibility as before, and the standards attained in the best NHS primary care are at least as good as those in private practice. It has been proved that a national health service can run quite well without the profit motive, and that the motivation of the work itself can be more powerful in a decommercialized setting. The gains of the service derive very largely from the simple and clear principles on which it was conceived: a comprehensive national service, available to all, free at the time of use, non-contributory, and financed from taxation. Departures from these principles, both when the service began (the tripartite division and omission of family-planning and chiropody services) and subsequently (dental and prescription charges, rising direct contributions, and relative reductions in financing from taxation), have not strengthened it. The principles themselves seem to me to be worth defending, despite the risk of indulging in unfashionable value judgements. The accelerating forward movement of general practice today, impressively reviewed in a symposium on group practice held by the Royal College of General Practitioners,[23] is a movement (not always conscious) towards these principles and the ideas that prevailed generally among the minority of doctors who supported them in 1948, including their material corollary, group practice from health centres. The doctor/patient relationship, which was held by opponents of the Act to depend above all on a cash transaction between patient and doctor, has been transformed and improved by abolishing that transaction. A general practitioner can now think in terms of service to a defined community, and plan his work according to rational priorities.

Godber[24] has reviewed this question of medical priorities, which he sees as a new feature arising from the much greater real effectiveness of modern medicine, which provides a wider range of real choices, and the great costliness of certain forms of treatment. While these factors are important, there are others of greater importance which he omits. Even when the content of medicine was overwhelmingly palliative or magical—say, up to the 1914-18 war—the public could not face the intolerable facts any more than doctors could, and both had as great a sense of priorities as we have; matters of life and death arouse the same passions when hope is illusory as when it is real, as the palatial Swiss tuberculosis sanatoria testify. The greatest difference, I think, lies in the transformation in social expectations. In 1914 gross inequality and injustice were regarded as natural by the privileged, irresistible by the unprivileged, and inevitable by nearly everyone. This is no longer true; inequality is now politically dangerous once it is recognized, and its inevitability is believed in only by a minority. Diphtheria became preventable in the early 1930s, yet there were 50,000 cases in England and Wales in 1941 and 2400 of them died.[25] I knew one woman who buried four of her children in five weeks during an outbreak of diphtheria in the late 1930s. No systematic national campaign of immunization was begun until well into the 1939-45 war years, and, if such a situation is unthinkable today, the difference is political rather than technical. Godber rightly points to the planning of hospital services during the war as one starting-point of the change; but he omits the huge social and political fact of 1945: that a majority of people, having experienced the market distribution of human needs before the war, and the revelation that the market could be overridden during the war for an agreed social purpose, resolved never to return to the old system.

Perhaps reasonable economy in the distribution of medical care is imperilled most of all by the old ethical concept of the isolated one doctor/one patient relationship, pushed relentlessly to its conclusion regardless of cost —or, to put it differently, of the needs of others. The pursuit of the very best for each patient who needs it remains an important force in the progress of care; a young person in renal failure may need a doctor who will fight for dialysis, or a grossly handicapped child one who will find the way to exactly the right department, and steer past the defeatists in the wrong ones. But this pursuit must pay some regard to human priorities, as it may not if the patient is a purchaser of medical care as a commodity. The idealized, isolated doctor/patient relationship, that ignores the needs of other people and their claims on the doctor's time and other scarce resources, is incomplete and distorts our view of medicine. During the formative period of modern medicine this ideal situation could be realized only among the wealthy, or in the special conditions of teaching hospitals among those of the unprivileged with 'interesting' diseases. The ambition to practise this ideal medicine under ideal conditions still makes doctors all over the world leave those who need them most and go to those who need them least, and it retards the development of national schools of thought and practice in medicine, genuinely based on the local content of medical care. The ideal isolated doctor/patient relation has the same root as the nineteenth-century preoccupation with Robinson Crusoe as an economic elementary particle; both arise from a view of society that can perceive only a contractual relation between independent individuals. The new and hopeful dimension in general practice is the recognition that the primary care doctor interacts with individual members of a defined community. Such a community-oriented doctor is not likely to encourage expensive excursions into the twenty-first century, since his position makes him aware, as few specialists can be, of the scale of demand at its point of origin, and will therefore be receptive to common-sense priorities. It is this primary care doctor who in our country initiates nearly every train of causation in the use of sophisticated medical care, and has some degree of control over what is done or not done at every point. The commitment is a great deal less open-ended than many believe; we really do not prolong useless, painful or demented lives on the scale sometimes imagined. We tend to be more interested in the people who have diseases than in the diseases themselves, and that is the first requirement of reasonable economy and a humane scale of priorities.

RETURN TO THE MARKET?

The past ten years have seen a spate of papers urging that the NHS be returned wholly or partly to the operation of the market. Jewkes,[26] Lees,[27] Seale,[28] and the advisory planning panel on health services financing of the British Medical Association[29] have all elaborated on this theme. Their arguments consist in a frontal attack on the policy of removing health care from the market, together with criticism of faults in the service that do not necessarily or even probably depend on that policy at all, but on the failure of Governments to devote a sufficient part of the national product to medical care. These faults include the stagnation in hospital building and senior staffing throughout the 1950s, the low wages throughout the service up to consultant level, over-centralized control, and failure to realize the objective of social and geographical equality in access to the best medical care. None of these failings is intrinsic to the original principles of the NHS; all have been deplored by its supporters, and with more vigour than by these critics. The critics depend heavily on a climate of television and editorial opinion favouring the view that all but a minority of people are rich enough and willing to pay for all they need in medical care (but not through taxation), and that public services are a historically transient social form, appropriate to indigent populations, to be discarded as soon as may be in favour of distribution of health care as a bought commodity, provided by competing entrepreneurs. They depend also on the almost universal abdication of principled opposition to these views on the part of its official opponents. The former Secretary of State for Social Services, Mr Richard Crossman, has agreed that the upper limit of direct taxation has been reached, and that 'we should not be afraid to look for alternative sources of revenue less dependent on the Chancellor's whims.... I should not rule out obtaining a higher proportion of the cost of the service from the Health Service contribution.'[30] This is simply a suggestion that rising health costs should be met by flat-rate contributions unrelated to income—an acceptance of the view that the better-off are taxed to the limit, but also that the poor can afford to pay more in proportion. With such opposition, it is not surprising that more extravagant proposals for substantial payments at the time of illness, for consultations, home visits and hospital care, are more widely discussed and advocated than ever before.

Seale (see Ref. 28) proposed a dual health service, with a major part of hospital and primary care on a fee-paying basis assisted by private insurance, and a minimum basic service excluding the 'great deal of medical care which is of only marginal importance so far as the life or death or health of the individual is concerned. Do those who want the Health Service to provide only the best want the frills of medical care to be only the best or have they so little understanding of the nature of medical care that they are unaware of the existence of the frills?' Frills listed by Seale are: 'time, convenience, freedom of choice and privacy'. He says that 'it is precisely these facets of medical care—the "middle-class" standards—which become more important to individuals as they become more prosperous'. Do they indeed? Perhaps it is not so much that they (and other frills such as courtesy, and willingness to listen and to explain, that may be guaranteed by payment of a fee) become more important, as that they become accessible. The possession of a new car is an index of prosperity; the lack of one is not evidence that it is not wanted. Real evidence should be provided that it is possible to separate the components of medical care into frills that have no bearing on life, death, or health, and essentials which do. Life and happiness most certainly can hang on a readiness to listen, to dig beneath the presenting symptom, and to encourage a return when something appears to have been left unsaid. And not only the patient —*all* patients—value these things; to practise medicine without them makes a doctor despise his trade and his patients. Where are the doctors to be found to undertake this veterinary care? It need not be said; those of us who already work in industrial areas are expected to abandon the progress we have made towards universal, truly personal care and return to the bottom half of the traditional double standard. This is justified in anticipation by Seale:

> Some doctors are very much better than others and this will always be so, and the standard of care provided by them will vary within wide limits ... the function of the state is, in general, to do those things which the individual cannot do and to assist him to do things better. It is not to do for the individual what he can well do for himself.... I should like to see reform of the Health Service in the years ahead which is based on the assumption of individual responsibility for personal health, with the state's function limited to the prevention of real hardship and the encouragement of personal responsibility.

Lees's (see Ref. 27) central thesis is that medical care is a commodity that should be bought and sold as any other, and would be optimally distributed in a free market. A free market in houses or shoes does not distribute them optimally; rich people get too much and the poor too little, and the same is true of medical care. He claims that the NHS violates 'natural' economic law, and will fail if a free market is not restored, in some degree at least, and that in a free market 'we would spend more on medical care than the government does on our behalf'. If the 'we' in question is really all of us, no problem exists; we agree to pay higher income tax and/or give up some million-pound bombers or whatever, and have the expanding service we want. But if the 'we' merely means 'us' as opposed to 'them', it means only that the higher social classes will pay more for their own care, but not for the community as a whole. They will then want value for their money, a visible differential between commodity care and the utility brand; is it really possible, let alone desirable, to run any part of the health service in this way? Raymond Williams[31] put his finger on the real point here:

> We think of our individual patterns of use in the favourable terms of spending and satisfaction, but of our social patterns of use in the unfavourable terms of deprivation and taxation. It seems a fundamental defect of our society that social purposes are largely financed out of individual incomes, by a method of rates and taxes which makes it very easy for us to feel that society is a thing that continually deprives and limits us—without this we could all be profitably spending.... We think of 'my money' ... in these naive terms, because parts of our very idea of society are withered at root. We can hardly have any conception, in our present system, of the financing of social purposes from the social product....

Seale[32] thinks the return to the market would help to provide the continuous audit that is certainly necessary to intelligent planning in the health service:

> In a health service provided free of charge efficient management is particularly difficult because neither the purpose nor the product of the organization can be clearly defined, and because there are few automatic checks to managerial incompetence.... In any large organization management requires quantitative information if it is to be able to analyse a situation, make a decision, and know whether its actions have received the desired result. In commerce this quantitative information is supplied primarily in monetary terms. By using the simple, convenient, and measurable criterion of profit as both objective and product, management has a yardstick for assessing the quality of the organization and the effectiveness of its own decisions.

The purposes and desired product of medical care are complex, but Seale has given no evidence to support his opinion that they cannot be clearly measured or defined; numerous measures of mortality, morbidity and cost and labour effectiveness in terms of them are available and are (insufficiently) used. They can be developed much more easily in a comprehensive service outside the market than in a fragmented one within it. We already know that we can study and measure the working of the National Health Service more cheaply and easily than the diverse and often irrational medical services of areas of the United States of comparable population, though paradoxically there are certain techniques of quality control that are much more necessary in America than they are here. Tissue committees monitor the work of surgeons by identifying excised normal organs, and specialist registration protects the public from spurious claims by medical entrepreneurs. The motivation for fraud has almost disappeared from the NHS, and with it the need for certain forms of audit. A market economy in medical care leads to a number of wasteful trends that are acknowledged problems in the United States. Hospital admission rates are inflated to make patients eligible for insurance benefit, and according to Fry: [33]

> In some areas, particularly the more prosperous, competition for patients exists between local hospitals, since lack of regional planning has led to an excess of hospital facilities in some localities. In such circumstances hospital administrators are encouraged to use public relations officers and other means of self-advertisement.... This competition also leads to certain hospital 'status symbols', where features such as the possession of a computer, the possession of a 'cobalt bomb' unit, the ability to perform open-heart surgery albeit infrequently, and the listing of a neurosurgeon on the staff are all current symbols of status in the eyes of certain groups of the public. Even small hospitals of 150–200 beds may consider such features as necessities.

And though these are the more obvious defects of substituting profit for the normal and direct objectives of medical care, the audit by profit has another and much more serious fault; it concentrates all our attention on tactical efficiency, while ignoring the need for strategic social decisions. A large advertising agency may be highly efficient and profitable, but is this a measure of its socially useful work? It was the operation of the self-regulating market that resulted in a total expenditure on all forms of advertising of £455 million in 1960, compared with about £500 million on the whole of the hospital service in the same year.[34] The wonderfully self-regulating market does sometimes show a smaller intelligence than the most ignorant human voter.

All these trends of argument are gathered together in the report of the BMA advisory planning panel on health services financing (see Ref. 29), which recommends another dual service, one for quality and the other for minimum necessity. It states its view with a boldness that may account for its rather guarded reception by the General Medical Services Committee of the BMA.

The only sacrifice that would have to be made would be the concept of equality within the National Health Service ... any claim that the NHS has achieved its aim of providing equality in medical care is an illusion. In fact, absolute equality could never be achieved under any system of medical care, education or other essential service to the community. The motives for suggesting otherwise are political and ignore human factors.

The panel overlooks the fact that absolute correctness of diagnosis or absolute relief of suffering are also unattainable under any system of medical care; perhaps the only absolute that can be truly attained is the blindness of those who do not wish to see, and the human factor we should cease to ignore is the opposition of every privileged group to the loss of its privilege.

THE INVERSE CARE LAW

In areas with most sickness and death, general practitioners have more work, larger lists, less hospital support and inherit more clinically ineffective traditions of consultation than in the healthiest areas; and hospital doctors shoulder heavier case-loads with less staff and equipment, more obsolete buildings, and suffer recurrent crises in the availability of beds and replacement staff. These trends can be summed up as the inverse care law: that the availability of good medical care tends to vary inversely with the need of the population served.

If the NHS had continued to adhere to its original principles, with construction of health centres a first priority in industrial areas, all financed from taxation rather than direct flat rate contribution, free at the time of use, and fully inclusive of all personal health services, including family planning, the operation of the inverse care law would have been modified much more than it has been; but even the service as it is has been effective in redistributing care, considering the powerful social forces operating against this. If our health services had evolved as a free market, or even on a fee for item of service basis prepaid by private insurance, the law would have operated much more completely than it does; our situation might approximate to that in the United States,[35] with the added disadvantage of smaller national wealth. The force that creates and maintains the inverse care law is the operation of the market, and its cultural and ideological superstructure which has permeated the thought and directed the ambitions of our profession during all of its modern history. The more health services are removed from the force of the market, the more successful we can be in redistributing care away from its 'natural' distribution in a market economy; but this will be a redistribution, an intervention to correct a fault natural to our form of society, and therefore incompletely successful and politically unstable, in the absence of more fundamental social change.

REFERENCES

1. J. T. Hart, *Journal of the Royal College of General Practitioners*.
2. These figures are brought up to the 1959-63 occupational mortality supplement in the paper 'Data on Occupational Mortality, 1959-63', *The Lancet*, 1, 1972, p. 172.
3. R. M. Titmuss, *Commitment to Welfare* (London 1968).
4. M. Rein, *Journal of the American Hospital Association*, 43, 1969, p. 43.
5. M. Rein, *New Society*, 20 November 1969, p. 807.
6. E. F. James, *The Lancet*, 1, 1961, p. 1361.
7. J. S. Collings, *The Lancet*, 1, 1950, p. 555.
8. S. J. Hadfield, *British Medical Journal*, 2, 1953, p. 683.
9. *Family Needs and Social Services*, Political and Economic Planning (London 1961).
10. A. Cartwright, *Patients and their Doctors* (London 1967).
11. A. Cartwright and J. Marshall, *Medical Care*, 3, 1965, p. 69.
12. A. Cartwright, *Human Relations and Hospital Care* (London 1964).
13. Todd Report, *Report of the Royal Commission on Medical Education, 1965-8*. (London 1968), Cmnd. 3569, p. 331.
14. Department of Health and Social Security, *Annual Report for 1969* (London 1970).
15. *General Practice Today*, Office of Health Economics, paper no. 28 (London 1968).
16. J. Fry, *Journal of the Royal College of General Practitioners*, 17, 1969, p. 355.
17. J. M. Last, *The Lancet*, 2, 1968, p. 166.
18. Todd Report, 1968, *op. cit.*, p. 139.
19. M. Balint, *The Doctor, His Patient and the Illness* (London 1964).
20. J. T. Hart, *The Lancet*, 2, 1970, p. 223.
21. G. Barber, *The Lancet*, 1, 1950, p. 781.
22. W. O. Williams, *A Study of General Practitioners' Workload in South Wales, 1965-6*, Royal College of General Practitioners, reports from general practice no. 12 (January 1970).
23. *Journal of the Royal College of General Practitioners*, 20, 1970, suppl. 2.
24. G. Godber, *Journal of the Royal College of General Practitioners*, 20, 1970, p. 313.
25. J. N. Morris, *Uses of Epidemiology* (London 1967).
26. J. Jewkes and S. Jewkes, *The Genesis of the British National Health Service* (Oxford 1961).
27. D. S. Lees, *Health Through Choice: An Economic Study of the British National Health Service*, Hobart paper no. 14, Institute of Economic Affairs (London 1961).
28. J. Seale, *British Medical Journal*, 2, 1961, p. 476.
29. *Report of the Advisory Panel of the British Medical Association on Health Services Financing*, British Medical Association (London 1970).
30. R. H. S. Crossman, *Paying for the Social Services*, Fabian Society (London 1969).
31. R. Williams, *The Long Revolution* (London 1961).
32. J. Seale, *The Lancet*, 2, 1961, p. 476.
33. J. Fry, *Medicine in Three Societies* (Aylesbury 1969).
34. *The Observer*, 19 March 1961.
35. R. M. Battistella and R. M. F. Southby, *The Lancet*, 1, 1968, p. 581.

12 | *'Disability' and rehabilitation: some questions of definition*

M. BLAXTER

'Disability', like sickness, is a relative concept. Official attempts
to define categories of persons as 'disabled' have serious implications with respect to welfare provision and the 'rehabilitation'
process. Traditionally, medical and welfare agencies have
operated with somewhat arbitrary and limiting definitions, based
on humanitarian and economic considerations and influenced
by administrative expediency. A modification to a simple static
model of 'disability' is suggested, attention being focused on
the interplay of clinical, social welfare, economic and other social
factors. Emphasis on the dynamics involved in the definitional
process highlights the changes in social status to which the
individual is subjected.

Disability, like sickness, is a relative concept which is difficult to define
objectively. As there is a continuum between sickness and health, so most
people are physically disabled to some degree, and the place on the continuum that the individual finds similarly depends on factors of perception,
identification, cultural concepts of normality, social and family environment and individual factors of personality, as well as on clinical 'facts'.
Who is defined as disabled, and by whom, and in what context: a manual
worker with chronic bronchitis, or a professional man who has lost a
leg; a young woman with a facial disfigurement, or a middle-aged housewife with angina; a man suffering from an ill-defined condition which he
feels prevents him from working, or a man labelled 'epileptic' to whom
no one will give a job? Reflection upon the variables involved in such a
list demonstrates the complexity of 'disablement'. Rehabilitation, defined
in a common-sense way as the best possible readjustment—medical, vocational and social—of a patient within the limits of a long-term or
permanent impairment, is similarly a relative process. A given impairment
may or may not result in functional disablement, and if it does the disabled
person may or may not need (or want) rehabilitative help.

All this is very obvious. But in the past, arbitrary definitions of disability
have been at large in the community, and have left their legacy in legisla-
tion and welfare provision. The history of provision for the handicapped
in most industrialized societies shows the interaction of two not always
compatible social movements: humanitarian concern for the most visibly

207

and 'innocently' disabled (crippled children, or the blind) and economic pressures towards the rehabilitation of potential wage-earners. Early provision tended to define the handicapped by their disabling condition (deaf, crippled) or by the cause of their impairment (war injury, industrial injury). Increasingly, however, it is being realized that disablement cannot be defined by causes or clinical categories, and that rehabilitation has a wider significance than simply returning to gainful employment.

The definitions of the medical profession have, in the past, been equally narrow. The simple model of medical rehabilitation has involved an acute illness or trauma, followed by a gradual re-adaptation to reach a stable level of functioning within the residual limitations. This model is fitted to the type of condition (such as the results of crippling accidents) to which the concept of rehabilitative medicine was first applied—conditions which are identifiable at an early stage and can be expected to have stable and predictable outcomes. Increasingly, however, it is being realized that this concept ought to be applied equally to other types of impairment, where the onset is not clear, the prognosis uncertain, and the residual limitation progressive or fluctuating—chronic lung disease, cancer, metabolic or neurological disorders, mental illness, an unnecessary degree of deterioration in old age.

The sociological study of disability and rehabilitation has at times seemed to be falling into the trap of adopting without critical consideration these earlier arbitrary definitions. Studies of social attitudes towards those people with visible, stigmatized physical impairments (which are, of course, of socio-psychological interest in their own right) have been generalized as studies of 'disability'. Evaluative studies of rehabilitation processes, necessarily dealing with the very selected populations whom agencies have chosen to define as their clients, have tended to accept the agencies' own definitions of the rehabilitation process and its 'success' or 'failure'. A major criticism of such studies, made for instance by Myers,[1] is that the disability which is the starting point is rarely clearly measured (except sometimes on clinical criteria) and it is assumed that any change found is necessarily due to the rehabilitation programme.

More recently, however, both medical and administrative definitions of disability have widened and loosened, and the sociology of rehabilitation has taken new directions. Administratively, there is a new emphasis on a holistic approach to social welfare: thus, for instance, in the British system an Act has been passed to promote the welfare of the 'disabled' *and* the 'chronic sick', with no distinction made between their needs; an 'invalidity pension' has been introduced which acknowledges some other state existing between 'sick', a temporary state, and 'disabled', a permanent condition. In the medical context, surveys following patients from the hospital setting have demonstrated that medical rehabilitation is of limited value unless co-ordinated with social and vocational help.[2]

Sociology has now begun to ask the relevant questions. In the context of these current changes, whom does society define as disabled, and why? The pattern of development which has been sketched has several implications. As concern for disability and chronic sickness grows, and services widen, more and more institutional systems become involved, administrative categories become more and more important. Because of the weight of the residue of older definitions remaining in welfare systems, they may move only sluggishly in response to the newer social concepts. In this field of welfare, as in others, services rarely catch up with potential need, especially at a time when concepts of need are widening. Clients must be chosen, and the looser the definition of the agency's mandate, the more important informal, organizationally-created definitions of the clients will become.

In Britain, as a result of a long history and a pragmatic approach, administrative responsibility for disability and rehabilitation is fragmented at both governmental and local levels. Some services are statutory, some permissive, and some charitable. Some are financed from central funds, and some from local. At the local level, general medical practitioners, hospital staff, health visitors, district nurses, physiotherapists, occupational therapists, medical social workers, local authority social workers, voluntary welfare societies, the local authority housing department, the home-help service, and the local 'labour exchange' and social security office, may all be involved. It is formally possible—though in practice unlikely—for a disabled person to be in contact with every one of these agencies.

Therefore, as agencies proliferate and their scope widens, it becomes more and more relevant to consider the factors which affect their definition of their clients. How congruent are the labels applied by agencies and the ways in which the disabled perceive themselves? Are there structural incompatibilities between the defining processes of the agencies of 'health' and those of 'welfare'? How do agencies find their clients, and what stereotypes do they have of disability and rehabilitation? Agencies necessarily have their own definition of their proper clients, and the goal of the rehabilitation process which is envisaged, explicitly or implicitly, may vary from agency to agency, and between agency and client. These varying definitions may be crucial to the career of the disabled person, for his pathway is dependent on the way in which he is defined.

These questions will be considered, first, at the level of the formal definitions of the administrative system, and then at the level of the informal definitions of agencies.

FORMAL DEFINITIONS

The most specific definitions of the disabled are those official and legal categorizations which have practical consequences, particularly with regard to compensatory or welfare benefits. In Britain, as in most countries with a long history of changing patterns of welfare, the administrative categories available in the system are often confused, anomalous and full of historical hangover.

The deep division between the economically active and potentially valuable, whom society must rehabilitate in its own interest and as a matter of social justice, and the rest, to whom society owes only charity, is still obvious in the structure of services. The Beveridge Report itself (and the National Insurance Act 1946), while introducing a new concept of rehabilitation service as a right 'for all disabled persons who can profit by it irrespective of the cause of their disability', still used economic value as the paramount argument. Rehabilitation was defined as the process by which the disabled became 'producers and earners', and the difference between industrially-induced disease or injury and that produced by other causes was perpetuated and solidified.

Recompense for disablement, in this country as in most others, still varies according to the *cause* of the disability (whether or not acquired in the armed services or in the course of working life, for instance), as well as according to its *effects*. Operational measures of the extent of disability are difficult to develop and unlikely to be equitable, as Townsend[3] and Sainsbury[4] have pointed out. Assessments of 'loss of faculty' bear little relationship to what a man can actually do: there are, for instance, service-disabled men who have been assessed as 100% handicapped who are in full-time employment. The principle of 'compensation', deeply embedded in welfare systems, matches poorly with current attempts to apply a holistic concept of 'need'. Where a man is injured during working hours, for instance, or while serving in the armed forces, his income may vary by a factor of three for the rest of his life, depending upon whether or not he was judged to be 'on duty' at the time of the accident which crippled him.

Assessment criteria at once so particularistic about the disability itself (the exact position of an amputation, for instance) and so vague about its actual effect on the individual's capacity to work, or consequences for his social life, in his particular circumstances, naturally breed disagreement about definitions. The elaborate structure of insurance officers, medical boards, local legal Appeal Tribunals, medical Appeal Tribunals, and industrial injuries commissioner, erected to deal with disputed industrial injury cases, bears eloquent witness to this. It is firmly believed by many who have to deal with them that the industrially injured tend to exaggerate their disabilities: they would certainly be foolish to belittle them.

The decision-making process, even where explicit criteria exist, is hardly clear-cut. Empirical evidence on this subject was provided in the United States by Nagi, for whose studies three clinical teams, working in separate areas, examined the criteria on which disability was officially measured, rehabilitation potential assessed, and eligibility for benefits determined.[5] It was found that concern was often with the nature of the impairment rather than the total functional disablement, and decisions appeared to be influenced by several arbitrary factors. Nagi points out that since decisions of this sort are usually dichotomous, whereas capacities and limitations must form a continuum, any point at which the dichotomy is established must be arbitrary, and moreover only temporary, depending on technological and on policy factors.

Another field where both the clients and the services offered might be expected to be reasonably specific is that of vocational assistance and rehabilitation. However, the definition of the individual eligible to be placed on the disabled persons (employment) register contains many words which are open to different interpretations: he must be 'substantially' handicapped, prevented from obtaining work 'suited' to his qualifications, and have a 'reasonable' chance of being employed. Once accepted for the Register, the disabled person is eligible for very specific services—admission to retraining units, help with obtaining employment—but definitions as 'disabled under the act' are likely to depend on local employment conditions and the availability of retraining units. If conditions are unfavourable, the lightly handicapped can be excluded at one extreme, and the severely disabled defined as unemployable at the other.

If to be eligible for vocational help means official definition as disabled, it is not of course an unmixed blessing, as the clients know better than the rehabilitators. It has been shown very clearly that the register does not include either all the disabled who are at work, nor all the unemployed disabled who wish to find work. Whether or not registering affects a man's work chances unfavourably depends to some extent on the nature of the disability, but studies have shown that many workers certainly believe that they will be devalued.

Another British register which officially labels the disabled is that kept by local authorities. The most accurate section of these registers is that which enumerates the blind, for this has always been a statutory duty of local authorities, the voluntary societies for the blind are active and efficient, and statutory definitions of blindness exist. Yet even in this case it is obvious that the register is not complete, and even here it appears that vocational considerations influence the definition of the disability. The National Assistance Act defines 'blind' for the purposes of registration as 'unable to perform any work for which sight is essential' and this is interpreted as meaning not the blind person's usual work, but any work. In fact, the actual disablement, particularly of the partially-sighted, depends on a complex of factors difficult to take account of in legal and clinical definitions: not only on how much residual sight there is, but what sort of sight, what other disabilities may be present, and what the training and talents of the individual are. These conflicts have practical implications in the placement of partially-sighted people in blind workshops. Those managing the workshops complain that they may have difficulty in getting the younger partially-sighted—those who are attractive as employees— officially registered.

With regard to other disabled people—known as the 'general classes'— the keeping of comprehensive registers by local authorities was not compulsory before 1970. It was obvious that those which were kept were very selective; the variation between authorities, for instance, was great, ranging from 0·8 per 1,000 population in Chester to 10·7 in Kingston-upon-Hull.[6] In 1971 a national survey of the *Handicapped and Impaired in Great Britain*[7] was undertaken, and it was found that of those defined as handicapped (a number representing over 1,000,000 in the total population), only 5% were on local authority registers.

That so many disabled people should be officially unknown, and probably unhelped, was naturally a cause for social concern. Yet the requirement of the 1970 Act that those described without precise definition as the 'chronically sick and disabled' should be officially registered presented local authorities with many dilemmas. On the one hand, the trend in social welfare is towards a loosening of definitions, to avoid the inequities that arise, as has been shown, from rigid and out-of-date official categorizations; on the other, in a context of limited resources, definitions which are loose may mean that decisions have to be equally arbitrary in practice. Thus informal, organizationally-created defining processes become more and more important.

MEDICAL DEFINITIONS

The first defining agents of physical impairment are of course the medical profession. Like the agents of social welfare, they too have a generalized mandate: they must do their best within their resources to cure illness and provide physical rehabilitation services, but what is practicable and 'best' is necessarily left to clinical judgement; they are not bound to provide any given treatment in any individual case. The result in this case is that a categorization of patients by those specialized clinical definitions which best suit the organization's own structure has arisen. In the hospital, it is a convention that patients should be labelled as either 'medical' or 'surgical' and if as is often suggested medical consultants are more conscious than surgeons of the needs of the 'whole patient', then the likelihood of a patient's being referred to a medical social worker for help will be greater if he is treated in a medical ward. (On the other hand, several studies of rehabilitation centres have found that the orthopaedically disabled are disproportionately represented, compared with the medically disabled. In this vocationally-oriented setting, the clinical categorization has a different result.) In the hospital setting, categorization may even depend arbitrarily on the attitudes and training of individual consultants, whose use of rehabilitation services is known to vary widely. Total rehabilitation needs frequently cut across clinical categories, and are ill-served by the tradition that patients 'belong' to one practitioner. In the absence of specialists in rehabilitation (of whom there are very few) there is no one to press the claims of rehabilitation services upon regional hospital boards. Again, the location and administration of occupational and physical therapy departments is dictated by the organization's own structure, catering better for the needs of the in-patient than the out-patient.

In addition, and perhaps more importantly, there is an unavoidable incompatibility between the clinical and administrative defining systems. Administrative definitions ('sick', 'disabled', 'industrially injured', 'handicapped', 'unemployed', 'entitled to invalidity pension' and so on) are necessarily dichotomous, rigid, tied to arbitrary time-scales, and designed for large groups of people. Where a man is totally blind, or paraplegic, or has lost a limb, exact clinical definitions are relatively easy to make: few of those who are in fact disabled are, however, so easy to label. In less easy cases it is obvious that medical practitioners will dislike firm, permanent labels, and will wish to avoid situations where they are forced into definite prognoses. As Mechanic[8] has pointed out, doctors practise within a context of uncertainty. Yet the administrative structure, necessarily using the medical profession as defining experts, forces the doctor to sign certificates, pronounce as 'permanently unfit for his usual work', adjudicate on precise degree of motor incapacity. The administrative structure imposes its own time-table (e.g. six months is the Department of Employment's dividing-line between short and long-term incapacity) and develops conventions by which the actions of doctors are given arbitrary meanings (e.g. a man who is waiting for final review is not yet recovered). Medical personnel have, also, in Roth's[9] terms, to develop time-tables to structure the patient's career in the way which best fits their own organization ('We will review the case in three months'), and these time-tables, though less arbitrary that the administrative ones, may equally bear little relation to the patient's situation as he sees it, or may be misinterpreted by him.

Especially during the earlier stages of a serious disease process, there is reluctance to discuss alternative diagnoses and prognoses. Again, treatment may continue (in the case of serious injury, for instance) for a considerable time before pronouncement can be made on its ultimate degree of success in restoring function.

William Pegler was a young man whose legs had been badly broken and lacerated in a factory accident. He knew that there would be some permanent impairment, but he had not (nearly a year later) been formally defined as disabled because treatment was still continuing and it was not possible to give a final prognosis. Meanwhile, administratively, he was still 'sick'; there could be no registration as a disabled person or award of compensation, and no discussion had taken place with his employer about his future. At first he was happy in the role of 'convalescent' and pleased with his progress towards mobility. Between six and twelve months after the accident, however, as progress seemed to him to slow down, he became more and more discouraged and bitter. Because he had been over-optimistic about his recovery, he had not allowed for a long-term adjustment to his income, and he began to get into debt. He lost touch with his workmates and became less and less interested in his working future. With two small children in a poor and overcrowded flat, he admitted that he had become bad-tempered and violent, and his relationship with his wife became full of stress. His wife took a part-time job, but had to give it up because she was unhappy about his care of the children. A middle-class employee in Mr Pegler's situation might have been able to develop a new working role for himself gradually, but this man had no room to manoeuvre; he complained of the strain of being unable to see into the future, and began to fear, as succeeding assessment boards produced inconclusive results, that no one cared very much whether or not he ever returned to work. Eventually, it might well be that he would be offered some rehabilitative services, but by then it might be too late. (These examples, which are included simply as illustrations of some actual case histories, are taken from the author's current research, in which the careers of approximately 250 people who have had a serious or disabling illness or accident are being followed for one year.)

This is an example of a case where it seemed that the prognosis was genuinely uncertain. In other cases, the medical profession may be deliberately manipulating information for therapeutic purposes, and where (as in the British system) 'health' and 'welfare' areas of rehabilitation are administratively separated, there may well be barriers between them raised by the principle of 'medical confidentiality'.

Mrs Vera Cameron had been under intermittent treatment and investigation for some two years, and it was thought that she had a progressive disease with, eventually, a poor prognosis. She was a rather nervous young woman of twenty-seven, with children of five and three and a new baby, and it had been thought wise to conceal from her the probable diagnosis. She was greatly in need of practical and social help, for her disabling symptoms were making her family life very difficult. Her husband, and even Mrs Cameron herself to some extent, regarded the problem as largely psycho-neurotic, for she bore the stigma of an attempted suicide. This young family had, in fact, been known to the social workers of the local authority in connection with a minor law-infringement problem at a time of previous crisis, but they had no way of knowing the present situation, for they had no access to her medical history. The medical social workers in the hospital, who had, did not know that she had any problems at home; when in the hospital she was always so desperate to be discharged that she would have said anything that she thought might hasten this. The only possible agent of referral was the health visitor, but part of the complex problem was Mrs Cameron's intense possessiveness over her young baby, which made her relationship with the health visitor difficult. The pathway to help was blocked at every turn.

Agencies in the disability and rehabilitation field tend to categorize by clinical condition. Since functional definitions of handicap are difficult to make, it is easier to fall back upon a medical label. But again, this presents problems of incompatibility between medical and administrative systems, especially if communication between them is poor. A very large proportion of disabled people have multiple or ill-defined conditions, and the name of the disease may not describe the disabling condition, or the more serious or 'primary' diagnosis may not be the one which actually handicaps the patient in his daily life:

Mrs Macintosh, a widow in her early fifties, had no family and lived alone in one room on basic welfare benefits. She had been attending a diabetic clinic—though erratically—for some ten years, and medical agencies knew of her needs; since her hospitalization for a heart attack a district nurse and a home help, arranged by the hospital social worker, had been coming in daily. She was, in other words, known and cared for as a diabetic. It was only after talking to her for some time that one realized she was almost totally blind. She was not registered as a blind or partially-sighted person and was not known to the community social workers. She had no knowledge of the financial and practical advantages of registration. She had become blind gradually, over a number of years, and had narrowed her life by successive stages until it was restricted to the compass of a few steps from her fireside. Her greatest regret was a broken record-player which she said she could not afford to have mended.

INFORMAL DEFINITIONS

If the formal labels which are available for disabled and handicapped people are, as has been shown, anomalous, difficult to apply equitably, currently in a state of change, and to some extent incompatible with the medical categorizations on which they must depend, then it becomes more important to consider the informal defining processes which agencies apply to their clients.

Agencies necessarily have stereotypes of 'their' clients, and the nature of these stereotypes will depend not only on the agency's formal goals, and on the generality or specificity of its mandate, but also on its history, setting and market for resources. Voluntary agencies, for instance, depending for resources on public generosity, may be fettered in meeting actual current needs by the traditional definition of the proper client for charity. Scott,[10] in his study of agencies for the blind in the United States, found that there was an excess of services for children, employable adults, and the totally blind, whereas these were minorities compared to the partially-blind, the elderly and the multiply-handicapped. Fund-raising campaigns were necessarily projected in terms of stereotypes concerning youth, work and hope.

In the rehabilitation field (as in others) there are valued clients and unvalued ones, and the agency defines its own market for clients according to the resources available. Medical social workers, for instance, will readily admit that though their market is largely defined for them by medical personnel, by exerting some persuasive effort they could easily enlarge the number of potiential clients by two-fold or more. But their workload is already adjusted to just the amount (or probably a little more) that they find practicable. Any agency in the rehabilitation field could expand its universe of clients, but if the expansion is not controlled within administrative limits the system will collapse. In the long run, of course, new systems would have to be erected—the number of medical social workers would have to be doubled—but no practical worker can be expected to sacrifice present clients, and allow his own organization to be destroyed, in order to demonstrate that some other organization might be an improvement.

How agencies will define their market depends on their perception of their goals.

Clinical opinion about Mr William Lawson was that he was only slightly disabled, and he had been passed by assessment boards as fit for all but heavy work, but his own definition was that he was seriously disabled and quite unfit for work. Since his wife deserted him, three years ago, he had cared single-handed for four children, and financial problems were inevitable: as a result, he was in regular contact with both employment and welfare agencies. The actions of the Department of Employment suggested that they thought him a man in need of vocational rehabilitation, and possibly work-shy. He had, in fact, been offered retraining and refused it, in part because it would have meant his children going into residential care and in part because—probably quite realistically—he thought that employment in the suggested new occupation of clerk was hardly likely to provide a higher income than social security. The definition of social workers, on the other hand, was that he was a client who had struggled against adversity and for whom they had great sympathy: to them, the central feature of the situation was the motherless children. This conflict of definitions presented some problems. He was given as much financial aid as possible, but it was associated with a great deal of inspection and medical examination. Since Mr Lawson was much too immersed in day-to-day problems to plan for the future, fill in forms, keep appointments, or remember dates, he was perpetually on the edge of financial crisis.

The manner of defining the possible universe of clients will depend in part on whether the organization's formal goals are specific and measurable or diffuse and intangible. If the goals are tangible and specialized, then clients who are marginal are likely to be excluded. The extreme example of this is in the field of financial benefits: Nagi found that some applicants were not allowed benefits because their condition was not considered sufficiently serious, and yet were subsequently rejected by vocational rehabilitation agencies as being too severely disabled. In other rehabilitation fields, the client and the agency may disagree about the goals of the process; in particular, the agency may see the goal as very specific—learning to compensate for a particular handicap—while the client has some much more general goal of 'returning to normal' in view. Alternatively, the client may expect some specific practical service, while the agency defines its function in wider terms.

Mr and Mrs Wilson described how their disabled son had been sent to an industrial rehabilitation unit some years before, when he was in his early twenties. The local employment situation had not been easy at the time. and they had seen this as a great opportunity, the opening of a new life for the young man. They had expected him to learn some marketable skill, and were bitterly disappointed when (according to them) he had 'spent all his time doing silly tests—he could have done those here—and mending fish-boxes—there's plenty of those here, too. What's the training in that?'

Age is obviously a critical factor in the definition processes of most agencies. For any given degree of disablement, definition as eligible for rehabilitation is likely to change gradually from middle-age onwards. With the emphasis on employability which is, as has been shown, historically a feature of rehabilitation structures, this is inevitable: resources will not be spent on the retraining of men nearing sixty.

The sex of the disabled person is obviously also relevant. Because of the 'insurance' orientation of the welfare system, entitlement to services depends in many contexts on the National Insurance position of the patient: women not in the labour market have no administrative existence. In some ways this is an advantage to them, for they are less exposed to the redefining pressures of the system and better able to create their own role within their own time-table. On the other hand, formal rehabilitative help may depend upon being formally defined. The future of employed people who become disabled is usually (and eventually) given some consideration because they are in receipt of welfare benefits, but 'household duties' are not officially a job. Services to help the disabled housewife are available, but they have to be sought: they are not offered automatically or universally. Where an employed married woman is concerned, she is more likely to be expected to retire to her 'proper place' in the home than to be offered vocational rehabilitation.

These are variables of the disabled individual: variables of the disability state also affect the definitions applied by agencies. Disablements which commonly affect the economically active in the prime of life—crippling accidents, and (increasingly) diseases of the heart, for instance—receive much rehabilitation attention. Diseases which commonly affect the aged—arthritis, rheumatism, bronchitis—receive much less, even though the actual individual concerned may be young. It may also be suggested that, for those diseases which show a variation in incidence by social class, the diseases of affluence (e.g. heart diseases) are better catered for than the diseases of poverty (e.g. bronchitis). In part this may be because they are more likely to be fashionable specialisms, with research resources, special hospitals or units and consultant manpower devoted to them. Comparatively few resources are applied to the problem of the very common, and disabling, 'lower back pain' of the manual worker.

The visibility of the disability is another relevant variable. Society's guilt about its feelings of aversion towards the most visibly handicapped has always been one of the factors influencing the provision of help. These most visible disabilities are also, in fact, relatively uncommon: it is easier to structure services for a clearly-defined, relatively small group (the blind, paraplegics) than for a very large and ill-defined group (arthritics, bronchitics).

On the other hand, the most visible disabilities are also the most stigmatized, and the disabled themselves may resist the label, if they can. It has been suggested (notably by Freidson[11]) that since 'disabled' as an agency's category includes only those who have been so identified, it may be profitable to apply the concept of deviance to physical handicap. Certainly, disablements which are immediately visible (disfigurements, dwarfism) or are felt as threatening to the taken-for-granted world of inter-action (epilepsy, mental illness, spastics) are labelled, stigmatized, and possibly segregated, and sufferers may develop a wide range of concealing or managing techniques, as Davis[12] and Goffman[13] have shown. The imputed cause of a handicap as the sufferer's own responsibility may also affect his definition as deviant, as in the case of alcoholism. The application of concepts developed in connection with other forms of social deviance to disability in general is not, however, quite straightforward. Not all handicaps are stigmatized (including some which might equally be imputed to be the patient's own 'fault'), and the effects of labelling as disabled are not necessarily or wholly negative. Indeed, a man may be more stigmatized for deviant behaviour because he has *not* found a legitimizing label.

Mr Knight, who had been diagnosed as suffering from multiple sclerosis three years before, was a young man with two small children. He was increasingly handicapped by his symptoms, but did not know the name of his disease; he defined himself not as disabled, but as intermittently ill of different (though perhaps connected) things. He spent a great deal of time worrying about what seemed to him to be the unpredictable nature of his illnesses, and felt strongly that the neighbours considered him 'odd'. He spoke bitterly of the old body who put it about the 'scheme' that his ungainly walk was due to drink. What defence could he offer? Only 'I can't help it. I don't quite know why.' His general practitioner had mentioned 'nerves'; therefore, he had at the back of his mind some idea that his condition might be his own 'fault'. He did not see himself as entitled to any particular benefits, and had not sought the help of any welfare agency, though he was only intermittently employed at a very low wage and the family were in desperate financial straits. Then the day came when a consultant told him the name of his disease. His redefinition of his role was immediate and striking. He no longer felt himself to be isolated, a medical curiosity; there were many others like him. While he wished to go on working, he no longer saw his 'duty' to earn a wage in quite the same way. A difficult interview with his general practitioner ended with the suggestion that he might apply for a disabled person's car. He voluntarily approached a welfare agency for advice. He had previously seen himself as simply 'inadequate'; now he began to present himself to others as 'unfortunate', a member of a group to whom some assistance was perhaps owed by society.

The normal setting in which the disabling disease is treated, which is usually related to the time-pattern of its onset, would also seem to be crucial. In the case of a sudden accident, the pathway from operating theatre, to physiotherapist and prosthesis, to vocational training and the provision of aids to mobility and daily life, is straightforward. Where a slow and gradual deterioration is concerned, on the other hand, the pathway back and forward between general practitioner, out-patient clinics, different consultants, the Department of Employment and the Department of Health and Social Security is complicated, and there is less chance of any one person saying, at one definite point, 'It is my responsibility to define the client as eligible for rehabilitation services.'

Mr George Watt's chronic 'stomach trouble' had begun during Army service many years before. For reasons which seemed good to him at the time, he had not sought a discharge on health grounds, and he recognized that there might have been problems about proving that service had actually caused his illness. He had an excellent record as an NCO and on discharge had no difficulty in getting a supervisor's job. A long period of intermittent absence through sickness lost him this position, and he became a bus driver. Back trouble, difficult to diagnose, was now added to his gastric condition; he acquired an orthopaedic corset and lost his public service vehicle licence. Eventually he underwent a partial gastrectomy, after which he became an attendant at a garage. His back pain did not improve, and he was passed, without success, from orthopaedic to neurological specialists. At the time when he was last interviewed, he had been unemployed for seven months and spoke very bitterly of being 'thrown on the scrapheap'. He applied for many sedentary jobs, but who, he said, was going to give a responsible 'office' job to an ex-garage attendant? He felt that he had slipped downhill very gradually, and had not at any point been offered a helping hand. He was in arrears with his rent and threatened with eviction.

THE REHABILITATION PATHWAY

How do agencies find their clients? They may seek them out, as the voluntary agency does, or as the medical social worker may do if she circulates the hospital ward. In this case, the agency must have a pre-conceived image of its clientele, whether specific (all those in this city who suffer from disseminated sclerosis) or generalized (patients whose particular circumstances make it likely that they will need help). The client may seek out the agency, for instance, the disablement resettlement officer or the local authority social work department: here, the client has already defined himself and probably seeks from what he considers to be the appropriate place some very specific service, a new job, help with rehousing, an aid to mobility. He may well, in fact, find himself engaged in negotiations about the definition of his condition, but this was not his expectation.

Usually, however, the client is referred from some other agency, carrying with him their definition of his condition and his needs. There is, in the British system, so complex a network of possible pathways through rehabilitation services that the process by which a client finds himself in one sub-system rather than another may appear to be wholly arbitrary. Obviously, the points of transfer represent crucial positions for the client. The way in which he was defined as he entered will be important in deciding what direction he is sent in.

Because of the aura of authority which is attached in society to medical specialists and to medical certificates, this is probably the most effective sort of ticket to carry the client across inter-agency boundaries. Certainly, given two clients with the same degree of disability, it would seem, for instance, that the disablement resettlement officer is likely to define the one who comes, well certificated, straight from hospital, slightly differently from the one who is referred from the 'able-bodied' section of the 'labour exchange' after long-term receipt of sickness benefit. Nagi noted that in one of his sets of cases a referral from the Social Security Administration was an important cause of negative stereotyping.

Also, the sub-systems of agencies each have different languages, and different criteria for assessing disability; at the point of handover, translation difficulties may arise. The definitions of medical personnel are necessarily in clinical terms, and there is evidence that vocational rehabilitators have some difficulty in interpreting them in employment terms.

Tossed as the client may be between one sort of agency and another, it must not be assumed that the processes of definition are wholly passive; the patient himself is also involved. He may be considered disabled on clinical criteria and accept the definition: he may or may not define himself as in need of rehabilitation services, however. On the other hand, he may not be medically considered disabled, yet may be so affected emotionally and socially, by his injury or disease, that he himself insists on adopting a disabled role. In this case, especially in industrially-injured cases, there will be a tendency for those charged with helping him to regard him as 'difficult' rather than disabled. He is as much in need of rehabilitation services as if he *were* disabled, but perhaps of a different sort; he is likely to find it more difficult to obtain services, and to gain less benefit from them when he does. The ideal client for all rehabilitation services is cooperative, motivated to using his residual capacities to the full, has acknowledged his disability and had it legitimated. This man is fighting for legitimation.

Again, the patient may be medically defined as disabled but refuse to accept the label at the 'correct' time, the time of leaving medical care. Two labels are in fact involved: a generalized one of 'disabled' and a specific one which names his disability. He may be willing to accept the specific label—e.g. 'stomach ulcer'—if he sees no stigma attached to it, but not the generalized one. It is equally possible that he may be willing to be defined as handicapped, if this seems to offer some practical benefit, but will resist the specific label—e.g. 'epileptic'—if he knows that society stigmatizes it.

The type of analysis which has been suggested has several important implications, not only for practical social welfare but also for the socio-logical examination of processes in the medical field. It suggests, firstly, that a simple static model of 'disability' requires considerable refinement. What is the role of the disabled? It is generally agreed that Parsons's con-ceptualization of the sick role is hardly applicable to disablement or long-term chronic illness. It has been suggested that two distinct roles may be distinguished and Gordon,[14] for instance, has demonstrated that at least two were perceived by his subjects: stabilized illness or disability, and a temporary state of sickness progressing to either recovery or death. On the other hand, it seems probable that, in fact, an intricate pattern of 'disabled' roles exists in any given culture. The extent of this repertoire (e.g. disabled, handicapped, impaired, chronically ill, invalid, intermittently ill, crippled), the pattern of expectations and sanctions characterizing it, and the variables affecting role-adoption have been little studied. Obviously, the whole career of the disabled person is relevant, his work and family history as he becomes impaired, and his previous experience of health and sickness; not only his position at one point in time when a rehabilitation process is being applied to him. Disability is rarely static, and the individual's role is continually redefined and renegotiated.

The simple model of rehabilitation has tended to assume a linear pattern:

Physical ⟶ Functional ⟶ Rehabilitation ⟶ Outcome of
impairment ⟶ disability ⟶ process ⟶ process

and the emphasis has been on the variables which may determine the last
stage of the process—the 'success' or 'failure' of rehabilitation services.

In fact, since the number of people to whom rehabilitation services are
applied is (in Britain) a very small fraction of all those who are physically
impaired, it is obvious that the pathway must be more complex:

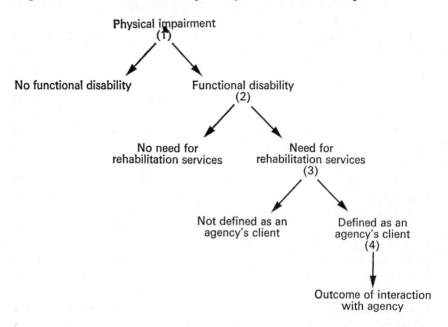

This paper has emphasized the variables at stage 3—the characteristics of
the impairment itself, of the individual, and of the agency, which may
affect how he comes to be defined—because this important stage has been
comparatively neglected, but each stage deserves equal attention. At stage
1, the dimensions of 'disability' require clearer analysis, and at stage 2
it can be suggested that the interaction of the nature of the disability with
the individual's family structure, history, and social environment (particularly working environment) may be a more profitable area of study
than the 'personality' variables to which some attention has been given
in the past.

A second implication of the approach which has been adopted is that
in this field the structure of welfare cannot be considered in isolation,
taking the system of medical care as 'given'. The situation of chronic,

or fluctuating, or permanent, physical impairment is one where the world of medicine and the world of welfare meet, and the interaction between them is of particular importance. Together they provide the constraining environment within which the individual negotiates his identity and his place in society, influencing not only what happens to him at one moment of crisis, but the whole pattern into which his life is set.

REFERENCES

1. J. K. Myers, 'Consequences and Prognoses of Disability', in M. B. Sussman (ed.), *Sociology and Rehabilitation*, American Sociological Association (1965).
2. E.g. T. Ferguson and A. N. McPhail, *Hospital and Community* (1954); M. McKenzie *et al., Further Studies in Hospital and Community*, for Nuffield Provincial Hospitals Trust (London 1962).
3. P. Townsend, *The Disabled in Society*, Greater London Association for the Disabled (London 1967).
4. Sally Sainsbury, *Registered as Disabled*, The Social Administration Research Trust, Occasional Papers on Social Administration, no. 35 (London 1970).
5. S. Z. Nagi, *Disability and Rehabilitation: Legal, Clinical and Self Concepts and Measurements*, Ohio State University Press (1969).
6. P. Townsend (1967), *op. cit.*
7. Amelia I. Harris and J. R. Buckle, *Handicapped and Impaired in Great Britain*, HMSO (London 1971).
8. D. Mechanic, *Medical Sociology*, Ch. 5, The Free Press (Glencoe 1968).
9. J. A. Roth, *Timetables*, Bobbs-Merrill (New York 1963).
10. R. A. Scott, 'The Selection of Clients by Social Welfare Agencies: The Case of the Blind', *Social Problems*, 14, 1966.
11. E. Freidson, 'Disability as Social Deviance', in M. B. Sussman (ed.), *Sociology and Rehabilitation*, American Sociological Association (1965).
12. F. Davis., 'Deviance Disavowal: The Management of Strained Interaction by the Visibly Handicapped', in H. S. Becker, *The Other Side*, The Free Press (Glencoe 1964).
13. E. Goffman, *Stigma: Notes on the Management of Spoiled Identity*, Spectrum Books (1963).
14. G. Gordon, *Role Theory and Illness*, College and University Press (Newhaven 1966).

13 | *Therapeutic behaviour, hospital culture and communication*

E. CASSEE

The way the hospital staff behave towards their patients has an important part to play in the healing process. Successful 'therapeutic behaviour' is facilitated when an open two-way communication process takes place: the staff must keep the patient informed about the nature of his illness and treatment, but also encourage him to express his fears and anxieties. An empirical investigation of nurses' behaviour showed that they failed to encourage patients to share their anxieties and emotions. If the nurse is to perform satisfactorily this element of her therapeutic role, she will be encouraged to do this if she is a member of a group where communication is open and within which she can express her own feelings and anxieties, which will in turn enable her to cope with closer emotional contact with her patients.

INTRODUCTION

During recent years more and more attention has been given to the social and psychological factors influencing the origin of diseases. The fact that there seems to be relatively little interest in the study of the influence of these factors on the healing process is striking. Research studies in this area are not only necessary in order to increase the effectiveness of care and cure, but they are also important for a better insight into the aetiology of diseases, since factors promoting or impeding recovery may well be identical to those causing illness.

It is, therefore, encouraging to find that there are some publications in which research into the effect of the behaviour of doctors and nurses on the cure and wellbeing of patients have been discussed. These studies demonstrate that the recovery of the patient to some extent depends on the way people behave towards him. In an experimental research study, Johnson[1] found that the time which surgical patients had to spend in hospital decreased if such patients were given suitable information and if they were encouraged to express their anxieties with regard to the coming operation. Pride[2] conducted an experimental study of the effect on the patient of the behaviour of nurses towards him. She examined the extent to which a patient's psychological stress is influenced by more intensive

224

communication. According to Janis,[3] stress can have a negative influence on the healing process. Pride measured the amount of stress by means of a physiological indicator: the potassium content in the urine. In this way she related the behaviour of the nursing staff to the somatic reactions of the patient. This methodologically refined experiment revealed that a more intensive communication with the patient leads to a reduction of psychological stress. The results of other experiments, e.g. by Elms and Leonard, Skipper and Leonard, Hendriksen, Tyron and Leonard, and Moss and Meyer[4] also pointed to a relation between the behaviour of nurses and the somatic reactions of patients. In these experiments blood pressure, heart rate, effectiveness of clysmata, and post-operative vomiting were used as indicators. Some authors also use the factor 'pain' as a criterion.

The results of all these investigations point to the existence of a relationship between the patient's wellbeing and recovery and the behaviour of the doctors and nurses caring for him. Further research will be necessary to establish the precise nature of these relationships, but the investigations already mentioned indicate that behaviour that is conducive to the healing process—'therapeutic behaviour'—has some special characteristics. Apparently, the patient's most positive reactions are obtained in a situation aiming at an *open two-way communication between therapist* (either physician or nurse) *and patient*. This open communication consists of at least two elements. In the first place, it includes informing the patient about the nature and seriousness of his illness, the treatment procedures to be followed, and the general rules prevailing in the hospital. The fact that this information must be compatible with the needs of the patient proved to be the main problem, as Dumas, Anderson and Leonard[5] have emphasized. It is necessary to know what is worrying the patient. Consequently, the second element in communication with the patient is to encourage him to express his anxieties, thus enabling him to take part in the decision-making concerning his treatment.

In this paper a report is given of an investigation into the prevalence and background of therapeutic behaviour in Dutch general hospitals. The investigation was carried out among a number of registered nurses who were attending a staff course.

METHOD

A questionnaire was given to 124 non-supervising registered nurses from approximately 100 different hospitals who attended a staff course. The questionnaire contained scales measuring the behaviour of the nursing staff towards the patient, the communication between nurse and doctor, and between nurses themselves. The results of this investigation are not likely to differ greatly from the average situation in Dutch hospital wards.

PREVALENCE OF THERAPEUTIC BEHAVIOUR

Does therapeutic behaviour form part of the work of a registered nurse in the Netherlands? In other words, may a patient expect to be provided with information about his illness and the things that are going to happen to him, and will he get the opportunity to express his anxieties concerning his illness? Table 1 gives gives some information about this question.

Table 1

To what degree do the nurses in your nursing unit pay attention to the following items? (In percentages, N=124)

	always / often	sometimes	seldom / never
1. Tell the patient what will happen to him, if he has to have an operation or has to undergo a certain examination	92	7	1
2. Explain to the patient why a certain examination or type of treatment is necessary	88	10	2
3. Explain to the patient why he gets a special diet or why his diet has been changed	86	12	2
4. Advise the patient on his problems and difficulties	73	26	1
5. Explain to the patient why he gets certain medicaments	59	33	8
6. Discuss the patient's anxieties with him	47	39	14
7. Discuss the patient's illness with him	25	41	34
8. Ask the patient what he thinks about a certain (prescribed) treatment	15	35	50

From this table it can be concluded that apparently only one aspect of therapeutic behaviour has been built into the nurses' role: providing information about nursing procedures. Most respondents stated that this is indeed common practice in the section in which they worked. The two other aspects appeared to be less self-evident. Whether the patient receives medical information from the nurse, or whether the patient is given the impression that he can discuss his emotions and stresses is not predictable. In less than 50% of the cases is the patient given the opportunity to talk about his anxieties with regard to his illness, and only 15% of the nurses stated that in their nursing unit the patient was commonly asked for his opinion. This outcome is also important for a correct interpretation of the statement that in most cases nursing information is indeed given, for how do we know that the information provided is the information the patient wants to know? The previously mentioned investigation by Dumas,

Anderson and Leonard[5] indicates that the information given is not always in line with the needs of the patient. According to these authors, doctors and nurses are inclined to provide only the information which they, from their professional point of view, consider to be important. It may well be, however, that the patient has a different opinion about what is or is not important.

The conclusion can be drawn, therefore, that in many cases there is no such thing as therapeutic behaviour since two-way communication, an essential part of it, is missing. Usually, however, there is one-way communication meaning that although the nurse provides the patient with some information the reverse process does not occur. This implies that the patient will suppress his emotions and anxieties and that this may impede his recovery; in addition he may not always receive the information he needs. The only possible conclusion left, therefore, is that the nurse may not be making a maximal behavioural contribution to the patient's recovery.

Why is it that this behavioural side of the nurse's role has scarcely been developed? This question needs to be answered, since in discussions nurses generally mention, and even emphasize, the importance of the above-mentioned aspects of therapeutic behaviour. Thus, here, too, ideology and practice do not always agree.

The reactions of those attending a training course for staff nurses gave us a clue with regard to a possible explanation of the findings in Table 1: 'Many nurses avoid this form of contact with the patient, since they do not know how to handle his reaction.' The interesting thing here is that their motivation for withholding information is *not* 'it is better for the patient because he cannot cope with it,' but 'it is better for the nurse because she does not know how to handle it.' From an emotional point of view, therapeutic behaviour is risky for both nurses and doctors, because it requires a more intimate and personal approach to the patient. Such an approach can be a source of uncertainty and embarrassment, for it may trigger off feelings which are difficult to control.

The scarcity of therapeutic behaviour on nursing units can be seen as a consequence of hospital culture which minimizes personal contact with the patient so as to safeguard the nurse against embarrassment. In this context Isabel Menzies[6] calls the hospital culture a 'defence mechanism'. The following is mainly based on her theories.

Nurses are in permanent contact with people who are ill or wounded and they are continuously confronted with suffering and death. In addition, their work is often filthy and repugnant. Too close a contact with patients often leads to tensions as nursing people nowadays may involve a continuous source of emotional stress and embarrassment. During the second half of this century, suffering and death have become increasingly transferred from our homes to specialized institutions, so that during our child-hood we are hardly ever confronted with these phenomena. Consequently, a sudden confrontation in a hospital causes emotional problems; neverthe-less, a nurse has to do her work with equanimity and a cheerful expression. That this is possible, can partly be ascribed to another process. For parallel to social development, in nursing as well as in care and cure in general, a culture has developed which aims at reducing tension and embarrassment by keeping personal contact with patients to a minimum. A great many aspects of the social structure in the nursing unit and in the rules and values regulating the task and work behaviour of nurses serve as 'uncon-scious' defence mechanisms against the risk of being overwhelmed by emotions. These rules and values make personal contact with the patient virtually impossible. Isabel Menzies gives examples of the working of such rules as defence mechanisms. These include:

(i) *The splitting-up of the nurse-patient relation by an extreme task division.* This means that the nurse does not have much contact with the patient. She is only allowed to wash him, or to feed him or prepare him for treatment. This procedure prevents her from coming into close contact with the totality of a certain patient and his illness, which makes her more or less immune to the emotions such a relationship might cause.

(ii) *The 'depersonalization' of patients and nurses.* Individual differences between patients and nurses and between nurses themselves are denied and reduced to a minimum in the hospital culture. Thus, nurses often talk about patients in impersonal terms, e.g. 'that woman with that stomach on unit 7a'. Moreover there is the idea that for a nurse all patients are alike and consequently it does not matter whom she nurses. The uniform adds to a further depersonalization of nurses. This depersonalization also pre-vents the development of a full 'person to person' relationship between nurse and patient.

(iii) *The frequent denial of and detachment from emotional stress caused by relations with patients.* The usual hospital policy is to prevent the development of personal relations with the patients (personal contacts with patients are, in some hospitals, forbidden); in addition, the general reaction to emotional outbursts of 'student' nurses is such that further emotions are repressed. The 'come, come' therapy ('come on girl,' 'pull yourself together,' 'we have all gone through it,' 'there is always a first time') is often applied.

(iv) *The almost 'ritual' task performance.* This reduces the stress derived from having to take (possibly far-reaching) decisions. In the hospital culture there is no need for personal decisions: 'Here we always do things that way.'

These and other aspects of the nursing culture, the way the work is done and the way people behave in the nursing unit, facilitate the avoidance of personal contacts with patients, so reducing emotional stress and embarrassment. It goes without saying that therapeutic behaviour, which encourages the patient to talk about his anxieties by creating a suitable atmosphere, will not grow easily in such a hospital culture. In the present situation, this type of behaviour evokes more emotions than the nurse might be able to handle. It is, therefore, not surprising that this side of the nursing role has, until now, been underdeveloped: the risks are too high. The hospital culture has, unintentionally and unconsciously, led to negative consequences for the patient, because the patient also 'learns' to repress his emotions. Inside as well as outside the hospital we have the ideal picture of the 'firm' patient: the patient who does not cry, pulls himself together and tries to make the best of it. Many patients, therefore, try to behave according to this criterion and not to be 'childish'—possibly at the cost of their own wellbeing.

Therapeutic behaviour may, from an emotional point of view, be considered risky behaviour, and this may be the reason why it is not yet part of the nurse's role. However, Table 1 shows us that in some nursing units therapeutic behaviour is more common than in others. How can these differences be explained? Risky behaviour has been the subject of social and psychological research during the last few years,[7] and although these studies have been concerned with different kinds of problems, some of the results are nevertheless interesting in this context. Thus, nearly all these investigations reveal that people individually take fewer risks than when they form part of a group. This phenomenon—the 'risk-shift'—may be of importance here, since it might provide a framework in which the degree of therapeutic behaviour on the nursing unit can be related to differences in group structure and hospital culture.

Although the results of the above-mentioned studies show slight differences, they agree on the factors which seem to facilitate risk-taking in groups. These include the degree to which risk-taking is a group norm, the degree to which discussion and exchange of information between group members is possible, and the degree to which the group members support the individual and share responsibility. With respect to the first factor, the conclusion must be that risk-taking as a group norm does not apply in this case. In the hospital the avoidance of risks is the norm. Instead of being taught to take more risks, nurses are instructed to take as few as possible. One way to stimulate therapeutic behaviour might be the discussion of this phenomenon. It will thus be possible to define an acceptable norm for taking emotional risks. The two other factors have in common the fact that they are related to the communication structure of the group. The more open this structure is, in terms of information and emotion, the more chance there will be of therapeutic behaviour being shown towards the patient. The exchange of information makes people less uncertain about what others think and do; emotional support in times of anxiety and stress makes one feel that one belongs to a group.

It will be clear by now that in the present hospital culture the stimulation of therapeutic behaviour in a nursing unit will cause much stress and strain. To deal with this problem, special attention will have to be given to the quality of interpersonal relations within the nursing unit. In other words, therapeutic behaviour will become possible as soon as communication within the nursing section is improved. This hypothesis can be formulated on the strength of the studies mentioned. However since these investigations were not directly related to the situation in a nursing unit it seems important to test this hypothesis. To this end we need in addition to the index of therapeutic behaviour (which can be constructed by counting the items of Table 1) an index representing the communication climate of the nursing unit. Thus a set of thirty-five questions (see Appendix p. 233) was formulated relating to the nature of communication between nurse and head nurse, nurse and doctor, nurse and student-nurse, nurse and nurse. By counting the answers we obtained an index for the openness of the communication climate of the nursing unit. In Graph 1, the relation between the openness of communication and the prevalence of therapeutic behaviour is shown.

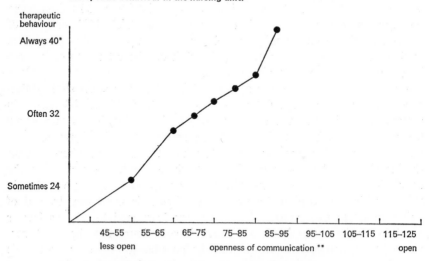

Graph 1
Relation between the openness of communication and the prevalence of therapeutic behaviour in the nursing unit.

* the therapeutic behaviour score theoretically ranges from 8 to 40 points.

** the openness of communication score theoretically ranges from 27 to 135 points.

Graph 1 illustrates how the prevalence of therapeutic behaviour increases with the openness of the communication climate, thus confirming our hypothesis ($\pi = 0.49$). We have already seen that the hospital culture in some respects functions as a defence mechanism against the strong emotional risks that result from contact with the patient. In this situation, stimulation of therapeutic behaviour is a dubious affair, since one has to break through this defence mechanism, possibly causing anxiety among people working on the nursing unit. Therefore changes in the behaviour of nurses and doctors are only possible if a solution to this problem can be found. Our findings warrant the conclusion that the introduction of therapeutic behaviour may be effected in the following way. The relations between staff within the nursing unit may be influenced in such a way as to create a feeling of security, indispensable as a basis for communication with the patient. Thus, the need for a defence mechanism becomes less urgent; one can fall back on the other members of the unit with one's emotional stress and uncertainty. It consequently becomes possible to establish more emotional contacts with the patient, as one does not need to repress one's own emotions.

Nursing management which aims at the promotion of therapeutic behaviour has primarily to deal with the 'communicative integration' within the nursing unit. The term 'communicative integration' refers to the exchange of information as well as openness in emotional matters. The particular importance of the last point is shown by a further analysis of the relationship between therapeutic behaviour and the communication climate.

Communication with patients

By means of a factor analysis we tried to find the underlying factors determining the degree of therapeutic behaviour and mutual communication between nurses, and the following dimensions could be distinguished.

(i) *Explanation of nursing matters.* This includes the following behavioural items: explaining to the patient the reasons for a certain examination or type of treatment; telling the patient what will happen to him if he has to have an operation or examination; telling the patient why he has to have a special diet or why his diet has been changed.

(ii) *'Medical' Information.* This includes the following behavioural items: giving the patient the pharmacological reasons for particular prescriptions; discussing the nature of the patient's illness with him.

(iii) *Emotionally open communication.* This was represented by the following items: supporting the patient in his problems and difficulties; talking to the patient about his anxieties concerning his illness; asking the patient's opinion about certain prescribed treatments.

Communication between nurses

The types of communication between the nurses could be differentiated in the following ways:

(i) *Formal open communication.* This includes the following behaviour or situations: the extent to which the nurses like each other; the extent to which the transfer of services works smoothly; the extent to which the mutual reporting is carried out in an informal manner; the extent to which there is friction between the nurses.

(ii) *Emotional open communication.* This includes the following behaviour or situations: the extent to which there is free discussion of the way the nursing unit is functioning; the extent to which the nurses consult each other about how to handle a certain patient; the extent to which the nurses discuss mutual difficulties.

The difference between formal open communication and emotional open communication is rather subtle. In formal open communication the contact seems to remain more or less superficial, while in emotional open communication deeper relationships are possible. Table 2 shows the result of bringing together the various aspects of therapeutic behaviour in relation to both forms of communication.

Table 2

Relationship between aspects of therapeutic behaviour and communication between nurses, in correlation coefficients (N=124)

Aspects of therapeutic behaviour	Communication between nurses	
	formal open communication	*emotional open communication*
Nursing explanation	0·26*	0·28*
Medical explanation	0·21*	0·23*
Socio-emotional communication	0·17	0·41*

* These correlation-coefficients are statistically significant.

From Table 2 it can be concluded that formal open communication relates to the giving of explanation in nursing and medical matters, but not to an open socio-emotional communication with the patient. The table shows that this communication with the patient appears only in those cases where the mutual communication between the nurses is emotionally open too. This is not surprising because the stress and embarrassment which may result from a more emotional contact with the patient can only be handled by nurses and doctors if their mutual communication encourages discussion of these emotions.

SUMMARY

Therapeutic behaviour is behaviour which aims at the provision of information for the patient, and which makes it possible for him to talk about his emotions. This type of behaviour is seldom found in the nursing units of Dutch general hospitals, since modern hospital culture rejects this kind of emotional contact. On the strength of social-psychological research into risk-taking it can be concluded that therapeutic behaviour may be promoted if communication within the nursing unit is made more open.

This hypothesis was confirmed in our investigation. A positive correlation was found between the openness of communication and the prevalence of therapeutic behaviour. Emotional openness between the members of the ward appeared to be especially important. Improvement of the quality of care should therefore start with the improvement of mutual communication between staff.

APPENDIX

Communication within the unit was measured on the basis of the following questions:

(i) *Relationship between nurse and head nurse.* How often do you discuss with your direct supervisor (always—often—sometimes—seldom—never):

    (a) ways of improving relations with other units
    (b) ways of improving relations within your own unit
    (c) ways of improving the standard of nursing care
    (d) ways of improving the management of nurses
    (e) ways of increasing the work satisfaction of nurses in the unit
    (f) ways of improving nursing training
    (g) your own personal problems

(ii) *Relationship between nurse and doctor.* How often or seldom will the doctor(s) working in your nursing unit:

    (a) have daily contact with the head nurse
    (b) make a daily visit to his (their) patients
    (c) ask the nurse(s) during his (their) ward visits questions about his (their) patients
    (d) have a cup of coffee or tea with the staff
    (e) discuss patients with the whole staff
    (f) listen to nurses' reports about the patients
    (g) instruct the staff on how to treat the patients
    (h) discuss the effects of medicines with the nurses
    (i) clearly support the nurses in conflicts with the patients
    (j) discuss the operation of the nursing unit with the whole staff

(iii) *Relationship between nurse and student nurse.* Please indicate how often or seldom the nurses in your nursing unit:

    (a) ask a student's opinion about ways of approaching the patient
    (b) explain to the students why a patient has to receive a particular type of treatment
    (c) explain to the students the background of a particular illness
    (d) ask a student about her study progress
    (e) ask a student's opinion about the nursing treatment of a patient
    (f) explain to the students why certain things on the unit have to be done
    (g) explain to the students why a patient receives certain medicines
    (h) encourage the students to talk to the patients

(iv) *Relationships between the nurses.* Please indicate how often or seldom:

    (a) the staff have coffee or tea together

  (b) a new nurse will receive clear information from the others about how to treat the patients

  (c) the mutual reporting is carried out in a formal manner

  (d) there are difficulties

  (e) there are free discussions on the way things are going within the nursing unit

  (f) the nurses consult each other about how to handle a certain patient

  (g) mutual difficulties are discussed with each other

  (h) all nurses are good colleagues

  (i) the transfer of duties works smoothly

  (j) a new nurse will be introduced to the patients by one of the older ones

Correlations between the various communicative relations are shown in the following table.

Table 3

Correlation between communication patterns* (N = 124)

	HN-N	D-N	N-N	N-SN
Communication head nurse/nurse (HN-N)	—	0·27	0·33	0·30
Communication doctor/nurse (D-N)		—	0·41	0·54
Mutual communication among nurses (N-N)			—	0·56
Communication nurse/student nurse (N-SN)				—

* All correlation coefficients are statistically significant.

REFERENCES

1. J. E. Johnson, 'The Influence of Purposeful Nurse/Patient Interaction on the Post-Operative Court', *American Nursing Association*, 1966, pp. 16-22.

2. L. F. Pride, 'An Adrenal Stress Index as a Criterion Measure for Nursing', *Nursing Research*, 17, 1968, pp. 292-303.

3. I. L. Janis, *Psychological Stress*, John Wiley (New York 1968).

4. R. Elms and R. C. Leonard, 'Effects of Nursing Approaches During Admission', *Nursing Research*, 15, 1966, pp. 39-47; J. K. Skipper and R. C. Leonard, 'Children, Stress and Hospitalization: A Field Experiment', *Journal of Health and Social Behavior*, 9, 1968 (no. 4), pp. 275-87; J. A. S. Hendriksen, 'Nurse Attendance Versus Use of Analgesic Medicine in the First Stage of Labor', *Nursing Research*, 15, 1966, p. 88 (Master's study, Loma Linda University, California); P. A. Tyron and R. C. Leonard, 'A Clinical Test of Patient-Centered Nursing', *Journal of Health and Human Behavior*, 7, 1966, 183-93; F. E. Moss and B. Meyer, 'The Effects of Nursing Interaction Upon Pain Relief in Patients', *Nursing Research*, 15, 1966 (no. 4), pp. 303-6.

5. R. G. Dumas, B. J. Anderson and R. D. Leonard, 'The Importance of the Expressive Function in Preoperative Preparation', *American Journal of Nursing*, 63, reprinted in J. K. Skipper and R. C. Leonard (eds), *Social Interaction and Patient Care*, J. B. Lippincott (Philadalphia 1965), pp. 16-27.

6. Isabel Menzies, 'A Case Study in the Functioning of Social Systems as a Defence Against Anxiety: A Report on a Study of Nursing Service of a General Hospital', *Human Relations*, 13, pp. 95-121.

7. N. Kegan and M. S. Wallach, 'Risk-Taking as a Function of the Situation, the Person and the Group', in *New Directions in Phycology 3*, Holt, Rinehart & Winston (New York 1967); R. Brown, *Social Psychology*, The Free Press (New York 1965); A. I. Teger and D. G. Pruitt, 'Components of Group Risk-Taking', *Journal of Experimental and Social Psychology*, 3, pp. 189-205; J. Rabow *et al.*, 'The Role of Social Norms and Leadership in Risk-taking', *Sociometry*, 29, pp. 16-27.

14 | *The inmate world*

E. GOFFMAN

A total institution may be defined as a place of residence and work where a large number of individuals, cut off from wider society for an appreciable period of time, lead an enclosed, formally administered round of life. Prisons serve as a clear example, but similarities may be found in institutions whose members have broken no laws. This analysis deals with total institutions in general and mental hospitals in particular. The main focus here is on the world of the inmate, not the world of the staff, and the impact of the total institution on inmates' identities and self-images.

It is characteristic of inmates that they come to the institution with a 'presenting culture' (to modify a psychiatric phrase) derived from a 'home world'—a way of life and a round of activities taken for granted until the point of admission to the institution. (There is reason, then, to exclude orphanages and foundling homes from the list of total institutions, except in so far as the orphan comes to be socialized into the outside world by some process of cultural osmosis, even while this world is being systematically denied him.) Whatever the stability of the recruit's personal organization, it was part of a wider framework lodged in his civil environment—a round of experience that confirmed a tolerable conception of self, and allowed for a set of defensive manoeuvres, exercised at his own discretion, for coping with conflicts, discreditings, and failures.

Now it appears that total institutions do not substitute their own unique culture for something already formed; we deal with something more restricted than acculturation or assimilation. If cultural change does occur, it has to do, perhaps, with the removal of certain behaviour opportunities and the failure to keep pace with recent social changes on the outside. Thus if the inmate's stay is long, what has been called 'disculturation'[1] may occur—that is, an 'untraining' which renders him temporarily incapable of managing certain features of daily life on the outside if and when he gets back to it.

The full meaning for the inmate of being 'in' or 'on the outside' does not exist apart from the special meaning to him of 'getting out' or 'getting on the outside'. In this sense, total institutions do not really look for cultural victory. They create and sustain a particular kind of tension between the home world and the institutional world and use this persistent tension as strategic leverage in the management of men.

The recruit, then, comes into the establishment with a conception of himself made possible by certain stable social arrangements in his home world. Upon entrance, he is immediately stripped of the support provided by these arrangements. In the accurate language of some of our oldest total institutions, he begins a series of abasements, degradations, humiliations, and profanations of self. His self is systematically, if often unintentionally, mortified. He begins some radical shifts in his *moral career*, a career composed of the progressive changes that occur in the beliefs that he has concerning himself and significant others.

The processes by which a person's self is mortified are fairly standard in total institutions;[2] analysis of these processes can help us to see the arrangements that ordinary establishments must guarantee if members are to preserve their civilian selves.

The barrier that total institutions place between the inmate and the wider world marks the first curtailment of self. In civil life, the sequential scheduling of the individual's roles, both in the life cycle and in the repeated daily round, ensures that no one role he plays will block his performance and ties in another. In total institutions, in contrast, membership automatically disrupts role scheduling, since the inmate's separation from the wider world lasts around the clock and may continue for years. Role dispossession therefore occurs. In many total institutions, the privilege of visiting away from the establishment or having visitors come to the establishment is completely withheld at first, ensuring a deep initial break with past roles and an appreciation of role dispossession. A report on cadet life in a military academy provides an illustration.

> This clean break with the past must be achieved in a relatively short period. For two months, therefore, the swab is not allowed to leave the base or to engage in social intercourse with non-cadets. This complete isolation helps to produce a unified group of swabs, rather than a heterogeneous collection of persons of high and low status. Uniforms are issued on the first day, and discussions of wealth and family background are taboo. Although the pay of the cadet is very low, he is not permitted to receive money from home. The role of cadet must supersede other roles the individual has been accustomed to play. There are few clues left which will reveal social status in the outside world.[3]

I might add that when entrance is voluntary, the recruit has already partially withdrawn from his home world: what is cleanly severed by the institution is something that had already started to decay.

Although some roles can be re-established by the inmate if and when he returns to the world, it is plain that other losses are irrevocable and may be painfully experienced as such. It may not be possible to make up, at a later phase of the life cycle, the time not now spent in educational or job advancement, in courting, or in socializing one's children. A legal aspect of this permanent dispossession is found in the concept of 'civil death': prison inmates may face not only a temporary loss of the rights to will money and write cheques, to contest divorce or adoption proceedings and to vote, but may have some of these rights permanently abrogated.[4]

The inmate, then, finds that certain roles are lost to him by virtue of the barrier that separates him from the outside world. The process of entrance typically brings other kinds of loss and mortification as well. We very generally find what are called admission procedures, such as taking a life history, photographing, weighing, fingerprinting, number-assigning, searching, signing away of personal possessions, undressing, bathing, disinfecting, haircutting, issuing institutional clothing and instruction as to rules, and assigning to quarters.[5] Admission procedures might better be called 'trimming' or 'programming' because in thus being squared away the new arrival allows himself to become shaped and coded into the kind of object that can be fed into the administrative machinery of the establishment, to be worked on smoothly by routine operations. Many of these procedures depend upon attributes such as weight or fingerprints which the individual possesses merely because he is a member of the largest and most abstract of social categories, that of the human being. Action taken on the basis of such attributes necessarily ignores most of his previous basis of self-identification.

Because a total institution deals with so many aspects of its inmates' lives, with the consequent complex squaring away at admission, there is a special need to obtain initial cooperativeness from the recruit. Staff often feel that a recruit's readiness to be appropriately deferential in his initial face-to-face encounters with them is a sign that he will pliantly take the role of the routinely pliant inmate. The occasion on which staff members first tell the inmate of his deference obligations may be structured to challenge the inmate to balk or to hold his peace forever. Thus these initial moments of socialization may involve an 'obedience test' and even a will-breaking contest: an inmate who shows defiance receives immediate visible punishment, which increases until he openly 'cries uncle' and humbles himself.

Admission procedures and obedience tests may be elaborated into a form of initiation that has been called 'the welcome', where staff or inmates, or both, go out of their way to give the recruit a clear notion of his plight.[6] As part of this rite of passage he may be called by a term, such as 'fish' or 'swab', which tells him that he is merely an inmate, and what is more that he has a special low status even in this low group.

The admission procedure may be characterized as a leaving off and a taking on, with the midpoint marked by physical nakedness. Leaving off, of course, entails a dispossession of property, important here because persons invest self-feelings in their possessions. Perhaps the most significant of these possessions is not physical at all, that is, one's full name; whatever one is thereafter called, loss of one's name can be a great curtailment of the self.[7]

Once the inmate is stripped of his possessions, at least some replacements must be made by the establishment, but these take the form of standard issue, uniform in character and uniformly distributed. These substitute possessions are clearly marked as really belonging to the institution and in some cases are recalled at regular intervals to be as it were disinfected of identifications. With objects that can be used up, for example pencils, the inmate may be required to return the remnants before obtaining a re-issue.[8] Failure to provide inmates with individual lockers, and periodic searches and confiscations of accumulated personal property[9] reinforce property dispossession. Religious orders have appreciated the implications for self of such separation from belongings. Inmates may be required to change their cells once a year so as not to become attached to them.

One set of the individual's possessions has a special relation to self. The individual ordinarily expects to exert some control over the guise in which he appears before others. For this he needs cosmetic and clothing supplies, tools for applying, arranging and repairing them, and an accessible, secure place to store these supplies and tools—in short, the individual will need an 'identity kit' for the management of his personal front. He will also need access to services offered by barbers and clothiers.

On admission to a total institution, however, the individual is likely to be stripped of his usual appearance and of the equipment and services by which he maintains it, thus suffering a personal defacement. Clothing, combs, needle and thread, cosmetics, towels, soap, shaving sets, bathing facilities—all these may be taken away or denied him, although some may be kept in accessible storage, to be returned if and when he leaves. In the words of Saint Benedict's Holy Rule:

Then forthwith he shall, there in the oratory, be divested of his own garments with which he is clothed and be clad in those of the monastery. Those garments of which he is divested shall be placed in the wardrobe, there to be kept, so that if, perchance, he should ever be persuaded by the devil to leave the monastery (which God forbid), he may be stripped of the monastic habit and cast forth.[10]

As suggested, the institutional issue provided as a substitute for what has been taken away is typically of a 'coarse' variety, ill-suited, often old, and the same for large categories of inmates. The impact of this substitution is described in a report on imprisoned prostitutes.

First, there is the shower officer who forces them to undress, takes their own clothes away, sees to it that they take showers and get their prison clothes—

one pair of black oxfords with cuban heels, two pairs of much-mended ankle socks, three cotton dresses, two cotton slips, two pairs of panties, and a couple of bras. Practically all the bras are flat and useless. No corsets or girdles are issued.

There is not a sadder sight than some of the obese prisoners who, if nothing else, have been managing to keep themselves looking decent on the outside, confronted by the first sight of themselves in prison issue.[11]

In addition to personal defacement that comes from being stripped of one's identity kit, there is personal disfigurement that comes from such direct and permanent mutilations of the body as brands or loss of limbs. Although this mortification of the self by way of the body is found in few total institutions, still, loss of a sense of personal safety is common and provides a basis for anxieties about disfigurement. Beatings, surgery or shock therapy—whatever the intent of staff in providing these services for some inmates—may lead many inmates to feel that they are in an environment that does not guarantee their physical integrity.

At admission, then, loss of identity equipment can prevent the individual from presenting his usual image of himself to others. After admission, the image of himself he presents is attacked in another way. Given the expressive idiom of a particular civil society, certain movements, postures and stances will convey lowly images of the individual and be avoided as demeaning. Any regulation, command or task that forces the individual to adopt these movements or postures may thus mortify the self. In total institutions such physical indignities abound. In mental hospitals, for example, patients may be forced to eat all food with a spoon.[12] In military prisons inmates may be required to stand at attention whenever an officer enters the compound.[13] In religious institutions there are such classic gestures of penitence as the kissing of feet[14] and the posture required of an erring monk—that he must 'lie prostrate at the door of the oratory in silence; and thus, with his face to the ground and his body prone, let him cast himself at the feet of all as they go forth from the oratory'.[15] In some penal institutions, we find the humiliation of bending over to receive a birching.[16]

Just as the individual can be required to hold his body in a humiliating pose, so he may have to provide humiliating verbal responses. An important instance of this is the forced deference pattern of total institutions; inmates are often required to punctuate their social intercourse with staff by verbal acts of deference, such as saying 'sir'. Another instance is the necessity to beg, importune or humbly ask for little things such as a light for a cigarette, a drink of water or permission to use the telephone.

Corresponding to the indignities of speech and action required of the inmate are the indignities of treatment others accord him. The standard examples here are *verbal or gestural profanations*: staff or fellow inmates call the individual obscene names, curse him, point out his negative attributes, tease him or talk about him or his fellow inmates as if he were not present.   .

Whatever the form or the source of these various indignities, the individual has to engage in activity whose symbolic implications are incompatible with his conception of self. A more diffuse example of this kind of mortification occurs when the individual is required to undertake a daily round of life that he considers alien to him—to take on a disidentifying role. In prisons, denial of heterosexual opportunities can induce fear of losing one's masculinity.[17] In military establishments, the patently useless make-work forced on fatigue details can make men feel their time and effort are worthless.[18] In religious institutions there are special arrangements to ensure that all inmates take a turn performing the more menial aspects of the servant role.[19] An extreme is the concentration-camp practice requiring prisoners to administer whippings to other prisoners.[20]

There is another form of mortification in total institutions: beginning with admission a kind of contaminative exposure occurs. On the outside, the individual can hold objects of self-feeling—such as his body, his immediate actions, his thoughts and some of his possessions—clear of contact with alien and contaminating things. But in total institutions these territories of the self are violated; the boundary that the individual places between his being and the environment is invaded and the embodiments of self are profaned.

There is, first, a violation of one's informational preserve regarding self. During admission, facts about the inmate's social statuses and past behaviour—especially discreditable facts—are collected and recorded in a dossier available to staff. Later, in so far as the establishment officially expects to alter the self-regulating inner tendencies of the inmate, there may be group or individual confession—psychiatric, political, military or religious, according to the type of institution. On these occasions the inmate has to expose facts and feelings about self to new kinds of audiences. The most spectacular examples of such exposure come to us from Communist confession camps and from the *culpa* sessions that form part of the routine of Catholic religious institutions.[21] The dynamics of the process have been explicitly considered by those engaged in so-called milieu therapy.

New audiences not only learn discreditable facts about oneself that are ordinarily concealed but are also in a position to perceive some of these facts directly. Thus prisoners and mental patients cannot prevent their visitors from seeing them in humiliating circumstances. (Wider communities in Western society, of course, have employed this technique too, in the form of public floggings and public hangings, the pillory and stocks. Functionally correlated with the public emphasis on mortifications in total institutions is the commonly found strict ruling that staff is not to be humiliated by staff in the presence of inmates.) Another example is the shoulder-patch of ethnic identification worn by concentration camp inmates.[22] Medical and security examinations often expose the inmate physically, sometimes to persons of both sexes. Collective sleeping arrangements cause a similar exposure, as do doorless toilets.[23] An extreme here, perhaps, is the situation of the mental patient who is stripped naked for what is felt to be his own protection and placed in a constantly-lit seclusion room, into whose judas-window any person passing on the ward can peer. In general, of course, the inmate is never fully alone; he is always within sight and often within earshot of someone, if only his fellow-inmates.[24] Prison cages with bars for walls fully realize such exposure.

Perhaps the most obvious type of contaminative exposure is the directly physical kind—the besmearing and defiling of the body or of other objects closely identified with the self. Sometimes this involves a breakdown of the usual environmental arrangements for insulating oneself from one's own source of contamination, as in having to empty one's own slops[25] or having to subject one's evacuation to regimentation.

I have suggested that the inmate undergoes mortification of the self by contaminative exposure of a physical kind, but this must be amplified: when the agency of contamination is another human being, then the inmate is in addition contaminated by forced interpersonal contact and, in consequence, a forced social relationship. (Similarly, when the inmate loses control over who observes him in his predicament, or who knows about his past, he is being contaminated by a forced relationship to these people— for it is through such perception and knowledge that relations are expressed.)

The model for interpersonal contamination in our society is presumably rape; although sexual molestation certainly occurs in total institutions, there are many other less dramatic examples. Upon admission, one's on-person possessions are pawed and fingered by an official as he itemizes and prepares them for storage. The inmate himself may be frisked and searched to the extent—often reported in the literature—of a rectal examination.[26] Later in his stay he may be required to undergo searchings of his person and of his sleeping-quarters, either routinely or when trouble arises. In all these cases it is the searcher as well as the search that penetrates the private reserve of the individual and violates the territories of his self. Even routine inspections can have this effect, as Lawrence suggests.

> In the old days men had weekly to strip off boots and socks, and expose their feet for an officer's inspection. An ex-boy'd kick you in the mouth, as you bent down to look. So with the bath-rolls, a certificate from your NCO that you'd had a bath during the week. One bath! And with the kit inspections, and room inspections, and equipment inspections, all excuses for the dogmatists among the officers to blunder, and for the nosy-parkers to make

beasts of themselves. Oh, you require the gentlest touch to interfere with a poor man's person, and not give offence.[27]

Further, the practice of mixing age, ethnic, and racial groups in prisons and mental hospitals can lead an inmate to feel he is being contaminated by contact with undesirable fellow-inmates. A prisoner describing his admission to prison provides an example.

> Another warder came up with a pair of handcuffs and coupled me to the little Jew, who moaned softly to himself in Yiddish.[28]

> Suddenly, the awful thought occurred to me that I might have to share a cell with the little Jew and I was seized with panic. The thought obsessed me to the exclusion of all else.[29]

One routine instance of this contaminative contact is the naming system of inmates. Staff and fellow-inmates automatically assume the right to employ an intimate form of address or a truncated formal one: for a middle-class person, at least, this denies the right to hold himself off from others through a formal style of address.[30] When the individual has to eat food he considers alien and polluted, this contamination sometimes derives from other persons' connection with the food.

A more thoroughgoing version of this type of contaminative exposure occurs in institutionally-arranged confessions. When a significant other must be denounced, and especially when this other is physically present, confession of the relationship to outsiders can mean an intense exposure and contamination of self.

A parallel example can be found in highly professionalized mental hospitals devoted to intensive milieu therapy, where patient-pairs conducting an affair may be obliged to discuss their relationship during group meetings.

In total institutions, exposure of one's relationships can occur in even more drastic forms, for there may be occasions when an individual must witness a physical assault upon someone to whom he has ties, and suffer the permanent mortification of having taken no action. Thus we learn of a mental hospital:

> This knowledge [of shock therapy] is based on the fact that some of the patients in Ward 30 have assisted the shock team in the administration of therapy to patients, holding them down, and helping to strap them in bed, or watching them after they have quieted. The administration of shock on the ward is often carried out in full sight of a group of interested onlookers. The patient's convulsions often resemble those of an accident victim in death agony and are accompanied by choking gasps and at times by a foaming overflow of saliva from the mouth. The patient slowly recovers without memory of the occurrence, but he has served the others as a frightful spectacle of what may be done to them.[31]

The extreme of this kind of *experiential mortification* is found of course in the concentration camp literature. 'A Jew from Breslau named Silbermann had to stand by idly as SS Sergeant Hoppe brutally tortured his brother to death. Silbermann went mad at the sight, and late at night he precipitated a panic with his frantic cries that the barracks was on fire.'[32]

In concluding this description of the processes of mortification, three general issues must be raised.

First, total institutions disrupt or defile precisely those actions that in civil society seem to have the special role of attesting to the actor and to those in his presence that he has some command over his world—that he is a person with 'adult' self-determination, autonomy and freedom of action. A failure to retain this kind of adult executive competency, or at least the symbols of it, can produce in the inmate the terror of feeling radically demoted in the age-grading system.[33]

A margin of self-selected expressive behaviour—whether of antagonism, affection, or unconcern—is one symbol of self-determination. This evidence of one's autonomy is weakened by such specific obligations as having to write one letter home a week, or having to refrain from expressing sullenness. It is further weakened when this margin of behaviour is used as evidence concerning the state of one's psychiatric, religious or political conscience.

There are certain bodily comforts significant to the individual that tend to be lost upon entrance into a total institution—for example, a soft bed[34] or quietness at night.[35] Loss of this set of comforts is apt to reflect a loss of self-determination too, for the individual tends to ensure these comforts the moment he has resources to expend. (This is one source of mortification that civilians practice on themselves during camping vacations, perhaps on the assumption that a new sense of self can be obtained by voluntarily foregoing some of one's previous self-impregnated comforts.)

Loss of self-determination seems to have been ceremonialized in concentration camps; thus we have atrocity tales of prisoners being forced to roll in the mud,[36] stand on their heads in the snow, work at ludicrously useless tasks, swear at themselves[37] or in the case of Jewish prisoners, sing anti-Semitic songs.[38] A milder version is found in mental hospitals where attendants have been observed forcing a patient who wanted a cigarette to say 'pretty please', or to jump for it. In all such cases the inmate is made to display a giving up of his will. Less ceremonialized, but just as extreme, is the embarrassment to one's autonomy that comes from being locked in a ward, placed in a tight wet-pack, or tied up in a camisole, and thereby denied the liberty of making small adjustive movements.

Another clear-cut expression of personal inefficacy in total institutions has to do with inmates' use of speech. One implication of using words to

convey decisions about action is that the recipient of an order is seen
as capable of receiving a message and acting under his own power to complete the suggestion or command. Executing the act himself, he can sustain
some vestige of the notion that he is self-determining. Responding to the
question in his own words, he can sustain the notion that he is somebody
to be considered, however slightly. And since it is only words that pass
between himself and the others, he succeeds in retaining at least physical
distance from them, however unpalatable the command or statement.

The inmate in a total institution can find himself denied this kind of
protective distance and self-action. Especially in mental hospitals and
political training prisons, the statements he makes may be discounted as
mere symptoms, and the non-verbal aspects of his reply attended to.[39]
Often he is considered to be of insufficient ritual weight to be given even
minor greetings, let alone listened to.[40] Or the inmate may find that a kind
of rhetorical use of language occurs: questions such as 'have you washed
yet?' or 'have you got both socks on?' may be accompanied by a simultaneous searching action by staff which physically discloses the facts,
making their verbal questions superfluous. And instead of being told to
move in a particular direction at a particular rate, he may find himself
pushed along by the guard, or pulled (in the case of overalled mental
patients) or frog-marched. And finally the inmate may find that a dual
language exists, with the disciplinary facts of his life given a translated
ideal-phrasing by staff that mocks the normal use of language.

The second general consideration is the rationale that is employed for
assaults upon the self. This issue tends to place total institutions and their
inmates into three different groupings.

In religious institutions, the implications environmental arrangements
have for self are explicitly recognized.

> That is the meaning of the contemplative life, and the sense of all the
> apparently meaningless little rules and observances and fasts and obediences
> and penances and humiliations and labours that go to make up the routine
> of existence in a contemplative monastery: they all serve to remind us of
> what we are and Who God is—that we may get sick of the sight of ourselves
> and turn to Him: and in the end, we will find Him in ourselves, in our own
> purified natures which have become the mirror of His tremendous Goodness
> and of His endless love. . . .[41]

The inmates, as well as the staff, actively seek out these curtailments of
the self, so that mortification is complemented by self-mortification,
restrictions by renunciations, beatings by self-flagellations, inquisition by
confession. Because religious establishments are explicitly concerned with
the processes of mortification, they have a special value for sociological
study.

In concentration camps and to a lesser extent prisons, some mortifications seem to be arranged solely or mainly for their mortifying power, as when a prisoner is urinated on, but here the inmate does not embrace and facilitate his own destruction of self.

In many of the remaining total institutions, moritfications are officially rationalized on other grounds, such as sanitation (in connection with latrine duty), responsibility for life (in connection with forced feeding), combat capacity (in connection with Army rules for personal appearance), 'security' (in connection with restrictive prison regulations).

In total institutions of all three varieties, however, the various rationales for mortifying the self are very often merely rationalizations, generated by efforts to manage the daily activity of a large number of persons in a small space with a small expenditure of resources. Further, curtailments of the self occur in all three, even in the case where the inmate is willing and the management has ideal concerns for his wellbeing.

REFERENCES

1. A term employed by Robert Sommer, 'Patients Who Grow Old in a Mental Hospital', *Geriatrics*, 14, 1959, pp. 586-7. The term 'desocialization', sometimes used in this context, would seem to be too strong, implying loss of fundamental capacities to communicate and cooperate.

2. An example of the description of these processes may be found in: Gresham M. Sykes, *The Society of Captives*, Princeton University Press (Princeton 1958), pp. 63-83.

3. Sanford M. Dornbusch, 'The Military Academy as an Assimilating Institution', *Social Forces*, 33, 1955, p. 317. For an example of initial visiting restrictions in a mental hospital, see: D. McI. Johnson and N. Dodds (eds), *The Plea for the Silent*, Christopher Johnson (London 1957), p. 16. Compare the rule against having visitors which has often bound domestic servants to their total institution. See: J. Jean Hecht, *The Domestic Servant Class in Eighteenth-century England*, Routledge & Kegan Paul (London 1956), pp. 127-8.

4. A useful review in the case of American prisons may be found in: Paul W. Tappan, 'The Legal Rights of Prisoners', *The Annals of the American Academy of Political and Social Science*, 293, May 1954, pp. 99-111.

5. See, for example: J. Kerkhoff, *How Thin the Veil: a Newspaperman's Story of his Own Mental Crackup and Recovery*, Greenberg (New York 1952), p. 110; Elie A. Cohen, *Human Behaviour in the Concentration Camp*, Jonathan Cape (London 1954), p. 120; Eugen Kogon, *The Theory and Practice of Hell*, Berkeley (New York 1950), pp. 63-8.

6. For a version of this process in concentration camps, see: Cohen, *Concentration Camp*, 1954, *op. cit.*, p. 120; Kogon, *Hell*, 1950, *op. cit.*, pp. 64-5. For a fictionalized treatment of the reception in a girls' reformatory, see: Sara Norris, *The Wayward Ones*, Signet Books (New York 1952), pp. 31-4. A prison version, less explicit, is found in George Dendrickson and Frederick Thomas, *The Truth About Dartmoor*, Gollancz (London 1954), pp. 42-57.

7. For example, Thomas Merton, *The Seven Storey Mountain*, Harcourt, Brace (New York 1948), pp. 290-1; Cohen, *Concentration Camp*, 1954, *op. cit.*, pp. 146-7.

8. Dendrickson and Thomas, *Dartmoor*, 1954, *op. cit.*, p. 85; also, *The Holy Rule of St Benedict*, chapter 55.

9. Kogon, *Hell*, 1950, *op. cit.*, p. 69.

10. *The Holy Rule of St Benedict*, chapter 58.

11. John M. Murtagh and Sara Harris, *Cast the First Stone*, Pocket Books (New York 1958), pp. 239-40. On mental hospitals, see, for example: Kerkoff, *How Thin the Veil*, 1952, *op. cit.*, p. 10. Mary Jane Ward, in *The Snake Pit*, New American Library (New York 1955), p. 60, makes the reasonable suggestion that men in our society suffer less defacement in total institutions than do women.

12. Johnson and Dodds, *Plea for the Silent*, 1957, *op. cit.*, p. 15; for a prison version, see: Alfred Hassler, *Diary of a Self-Made Convict*, Regnery (Chicago 1954), p. 31.

13. L. D. Hankoff, 'Interaction Patterns Among Military Prison Personnel', *US Armed Forces Medical Journal*, 10, 1959, p. 1419.

14. Kathryn Hulme, *The Nun's Story*, Muller (London 1957), p. 52.

15. *The Holy Rule of St Benedict*, chapter 44.

16. Dendrickson and Thomas, *Dartmoor*, 1954, *op. cit.*, p. 76.

17. Sykes, *Captives*, 1959, *op. cit.*, pp. 70-2.

18. For example, T. E. Lawrence, *The Mint*, Jonathan Cape (London 1955), pp. 34-5.

19. *The Holy Rule of St Benedict*, chapter 35.

20. Kogon, *Hell*, 1950, *op. cit.*, p. 102.

21. Hulme, *Nun's Story*, 1957, *op cit.*, pp. 48-51.

22. Kogon, *Hell*, 1950, *op. cit.*, pp. 41-2.

23. Brendan Behan, *Borstal Boy*, Hutchinson (London 1958), p. 23.

24. For example, Kogon, *Hell*, 1950, *op. cit.*, p. 128; Hassler, *Self-Made Convict*, 1954, *op cit.*, p. 16. For the situation in a religious institution, see: Hulme, *Nun's Story*, 1957, *op. cit.*, p. 48. She also describes a lack of aural privacy: thin cotton hangings are used as the only door closing off the individual sleeping cells (p. 20).

25. Anthony Heckstall-Smith, *Eighteen Months*, Allan Wingate (London 1954), p. 21; Dendrickson and Thomas, *Dartmoor*, 1954, *op. cit.*, p. 53.

26. For example, Murtagh and Harris, *Cast the First Stone*, 1958, *op. cit.*, p. 240; Lowell Naeve, *A Field of Broken Stones*, Glen Gardner, Libertarian Press (1950), p. 17; Kogon, *Hell*, 1950, *op. cit.*, p. 67; Holley Cantine and Dachine Rainer (eds), *Prison Etiquette*, Retort Press (Bearsville, NY, 1950), p. 46.

27. Lawrence, *The Mint*, 1955, *op cit.*, p. 196.

28. Heckstall-Smith, *Eighteen Months*, 1954, *op. cit.*, p. 14.

29. Heckstall-Smith, *Eighteen Months*, 1954, *op. cit.*, p. 17.

30. For example, see Hassler, *Self-made Convict*, 1954, *op. cit.*, p. 104.

31. Ivan Belknap, *Human Problems of a State Mental Hospital*, McGraw Hill (New York 1956), p. 194.

32. Kogon, *Hell*, 1950, *op. cit.*, p. 160.

33. Cf. Sykes, *Captives*, 1959, *op. cit.*, pp. 73-6, 'The Deprivation of Autonomy'.

34. Hulme, *Nun's Story*, 1957, *op. cit.*, p. 18. George Orwell, 'Such, Such Were the Joys', *Partisan Review*, 19, 1952, p. 521.

35. Hassler, *Self-made Convict*, 1954, *op. cit.*, p. 78; Johnson and Dodds, *Plea for the Silent*, 1957, *op. cit.*, p. 17.

36. Kogon, *Hell*, 1950, *op. cit.*, p. 66.

37. Kogon, *Hell*, 1950, *op. cit.*, p. 61.

38. Kogon, *Hell*, 1950, *op. cit.*, p. 78.

39. See: A. Stanton and M. Schwartz, *The Mental Hospital*, Basic Books (New York 1954), pp. 200, 203, 205-6.

40. For an example of this non-person treatment, see: Johnson and Dodds, *Plea for the Silent*, 1957, *op. cit.*, p. 122.

41. Merton, *Seven Storey Mountain*, 1948, *op. cit.*, p. 372.

15 | *Patterns of dying*
A. STRAUSS & B. GLASER

Death now seldom takes place at home but most often in hospital
or some other institutional setting; the care of the dying is
thus the responsibility of hospital staff. The medical and technical
aspects of care are usually efficiently and effectively performed,
but the socio-psychological factors in the situation are less
understood. This chapter focuses on the interplay of these factors,
elaborating the range of dying trajectories that exist and the
alternative responses that can be expected from hospital staff,
the patient and the family. Particular attention is paid to the
problematic nature of the dying process and the way in which
the social organization surrounding the patient is influenced by
this.

Probably less than one-third of all deaths in the United States now take
place outside of a hospital or other institutional setting. Changing health
practices and medical technology seem destined to bring about still further
institutionalization of dying. That people elect to die in such institutions—
or that their families make such choices for them—means that outsiders
to the family have been delegated responsibility for taking care of the
dying during their last days or hours. This delegation of responsibility,
whether partial or total, is of immense importance for everyone concerned:
for patients, families and the hospital staffs.

The last take their responsibilities with the utmost seriousness in accordance with the directives of professional practice and the dictates of conscience. But close scrutiny of terminal care suggests that only the more
strictly medical or technical aspects are professionalized. The training of
physicians and nurses equips them principally for the technical aspects
of dealing with illness. The psychological aspects of dealing with the dying
and their families are virtually absent from training.[1] Hence, although
physicians and nurses are highly skilled at handling the bodies of terminal
patients, their behaviour towards them otherwise is more or less outside
the province of professional standards. Much, if not most, non-technical
conduct towards and in the presence of dying patients and their families is
profoundly influenced by commonsense assumptions, essentially untouched
by professional considerations or by current knowledge from the
behavioural sciences.

It is significant that while technical aspects of terminal care are planned,
carried out explicitly, reported in writing or orally and reviewed either by

responsible superiors or by colleagues, in contrast most other actions of personnel towards and around dying patients are non-accountable.[2] Personnel do and say many things that only incidentally or accidentally reach the ears and eyes of other personnel. The psychological and social aspects of terminal care may be good, but are carried out on the basis of private initiative and judgement rather than as part of accountable decision-making.

INSTITUTIONAL DIFFERENCES

The research results incorporated in this chapter underscore how strikingly different are the modes and courses of dying on different types of wards in hospitals. The organizational efforts at each locale differ, in consequence, as the staff copes with the patterns of dying characteristic of their particular ward. Although staffs are well aware both of the dying patterns and the organizational patterns, they take very little cognizance in their planning and review of related matters that are not strictly 'nursing' or 'medical'. Traditionally only these latter matters are accountable, and only these are emphasized in schools of medicine and nursing.

All except very small hospitals are sharply differentiated internally among types of wards or medical services. On some wards there is little dying (obstetrics), but even on intensive care wards or cancer wards not all patients are expected to die or do so. Each type of service tends to have a characteristic incidence of death and tempo of dying. On many emergency services, for example, death is frequent and patients tend to die quickly. The staff, therefore, is geared to perform urgent, critical functions. Modes of dying also affect interaction between patient and staff, as well as the organization of the staff's work. For instance, on many intensive care wards, some patients are expected to die quickly if they are to die at all; others need close attention for several days because death is a touch and go matter; still others are not likely to die but do need temporary round-the-clock nursing. Most who die here are heavily drugged or past consciousness. Nurses or physicians do not need to converse with these patients. This is in contrast to what is typical of medical wards, where some patients are likely to die lingering deaths, fully conscious at least in the earlier phases of dying, and ready or eager to talk with the staff.

PATTERNS OF DEATH

The course of dying—or 'dying trajectory'[3]—of each patient has at least two outstanding properties. First, it takes place over time: it has duration. Specific dying trajectories can vary greatly in duration. Second, a trajectory has shape: it can be graphed. It plunges straight down; it moves slowly but steadily downwards; it vacillates slowly, moving slowly up and down before diving downwards radically; it moves slowly down at first, then hits a long plateau, then plunges abruptly to death. Dying trajectories themselves are perceived, rather than the actual courses of dying. This distinction is readily evident in the type that involves a short, unexpected reprieve from death. On the other hand, in a lingering death, bystanders may expect faster dying than actually occurs.

Since dying patients are defined in terms of when and how they will die, various patterns are commonly recognized by the hospital personnel and if possible terminal care is organized accordingly. For instance there is the abrupt surprise trajectory, as a patient who is expected to recover suddenly begins to die. Fast action is needed, and often a ward is not organized for this particular type of emergency. For an expected lingering death, however, with great pain expected at the end, the staff is likely to organize drug-giving with that end in mind.

Ordinarily there are certain events—let us term them 'critical junctures' —that appear and are directly handled by the organization of hospital work. These occur in either full or truncated form: (i) The patient is defined as dying. (ii) Staff and family then make preparations for his death, as he may do himself if he knows he is dying. (iii) At some point, there seems to be 'nothing more to do' to prevent death. (iv) The final descent may take weeks, or days, or merely hours, ending in (v) the 'last hours', (vi) the death watch and (vii) the death itself. There may be announcements that the patient is dying (by physician to staff, by staff to family members, by kinsmen to each other, much less often to the patient himself) or that he is entering or leaving a phase. Death itself must be legally pronounced and then publicly announced.

When these critical junctures occur as expected, on schedule, then all participants—sometimes including the patient—are prepared for them. For instance, the nurses are ready for a death watch if they can anticipate when the end will come. When, however, critical junctures occur unexpectedly, staff members and family alike are somewhat unprepared. For instance, a patient expected to die quite soon may vacillate sufficiently often for the patient to cause stress among kinsmen and hospital staff. Whenever he fades, the nurses may call the family, for, as one nurse said, 'if you do not call the family and the patient dies, that's wrong'. The family members arrive for their last look at the dying man, but he lingers. They finally leave, saying, 'please call us again'. Such a cycle affects changes in the activities and moods of the various participants— including the physician.

STAFF'S SENTIMENTAL MOOD

When the staff can predict the course of the patient's dying, its work with other patients as well as with him is made easier. Critical junctures can be planned so that manpower will not be withdrawn suddenly from scheduled tasks with other patients. Miscalculations in forecasting can play havoc with the organization of work and affect even the probabilities of his dying right then and there. When such crises occur, the staff attempts to regain control over the disrupted organization of work as quickly as possible. Since a revised notion of the patient's condition may necessitate new procedures of additional time spent at his bedside, considerable reordering of work, even changes in the division of labour, may be involved.

A disruption of the ward's organization of work is paralleled by a shattering of its characteristic 'sentimental mood' or order.[4] For instance, in an intensive care unit where cardiac patients die frequently, the mood is relatively unaffected by one more speedy expected death; but if a hopeless patient lingers on and on, or if his wife, perhaps, refuses to accept his dying and causes 'scenes', then both mood and work itself are profoundly affected.

Another important variable that affects what goes on during the course of dying is the intersecting of experiences people have had with illnesses or with hospitals. Thus, chronic patients, having lived with their symptoms, often are experienced in reading them, sometimes more so than some staff members (especially when the latter have had little experience with the specific disease). A heart patient who had been strapped into a certain position before being X-rayed once told a nurses' aide that she had better move him quickly into another position, lest his lungs fill up with fluid. She refused. To her horror, he soon began to pass out, and only by dint of quick action did the staff save him. By contrast, when a staff understands that its patients may know much about the specific symptoms of their fatal illnesses—and even about the courses of their illnesses—terminal care is unmarked by such incidents. Renee Fox's study of a chronic hospital provides many examples.[5] Patients may complain about their care, reviewing it against the background of stays at other hospitals. Personal careers may also greatly affect responses. For example, a dying patient who happens to be a nurse is likely to be upsetting to the attending nurses and even to others on the ward. A female patient who reminds a nurse of her own mother can be disturbing.

QUICK DYING

Before turning to 'slow dying', let us look at quick trajectories. Modern American hospitals—at least the more progressive ones—are, above all, set up to handle the latter. On the intensive care units, emergency wards, operating rooms and medical wards, medical technology and highly trained staff are concentrated, on constant call and in a relatively constant state of readiness to meet the challenge of saving ('heroically') if it makes sense to do so a patient who is dying quickly. As defined by staff, this may mean within minutes, hours or a few days.

Three general quick types are as follows. In the 'expected quick death', it is clear to the staff that the patient will almost certainly die in a few hours or, at most, a day or two. The case of 'unexpected quick dying, but expected to die' differs in that the staff are certain that the patient is dying, but do not anticipate the early turn for the worst. In a case of 'unexpected quick dying, not expected to die', a patient who has been expected to recover suddenly starts to die quickly, completely surprising staff, family, and other persons involved. In general, unexpected and expected quick deaths have differential impact on the staff and family. The former types are much more disturbing, since the basis of medical work and ward sentiment towards the patient is changed abruptly and drastically.

Even the expected quick trajectory has a fair degree of complex behavioural accompaniments. Consider only the family/staff interaction. Expected quick death usually or often means there are family members in the nearby waiting-room or hallway waiting for news. In the beginning, a nurse or doctor may tell them 'everything is going to be all right', but 'they know it's not and you know it's not'. But time moves fast, and family members must have some explanation to prepare them for the worst. As the patient worsens, the family is briefed by the doctor or a resident; they receive a preannouncement of impending death. This carries a tacit agreement, sometimes made explicit, that the staff will keep the family posted as often as possible on the patient's condition; and so some family members feel no need to ask questions while waiting. Others may want to ask questions as the time plods on, but may be afraid. Others simply ask whenever they see any staff member. A frequent answer until the patient has died is, 'he is still not out of danger' or 'he's still with us'.

The proximity of the family to the dying patient raises the possibility of the staff's having to manage scenes (such as public and loud crying) and also, since a quick death is expected, having to manage the family's desire to be present at the death or to take a last look at him before or after death. In some cases, the last look or witnessing of death is allowed and turns out to be no problem to the staff. In other cases, family members faint and must be revived. Some are given a corner of privacy, so that they may cry and gain control of themselves.

The presence of the family at the bedside during death must be carefully handled by staff since a scene or tantrum is very disrupting to the sentimental order of the ward—including the reactions of other patients. Moreover, there is a danger that a relative might upset bedside equipment or the dying patient. Staff members may also feel embarrassed and helpless in this situation because there is, they feel, nothing to say—unless they are simply to tell the family it is hopeless.

When an obviously soon-to-die patient arrives on a ward and when there is no time to try anything to save him, the usual manoeuvre is to put him in a room by himself. When there is time, yet clearly no chance of saving the patient, the staff watches, waits and gives comfort care until death. They time their efforts according to his downhill progression, all the while remaining unusually alert for a cue that would indicate the possibility of redefining his outlook to 'has chance'. Should this critical juncture occur, they stand ready with skills, and hopefully equipment, to try to save the patient. Staff members frequently refer to the frustration and helplessness they feel while they wait, holding their power in abeyance for a change in the patient that would give them a chance to act.

UNEXPECTED DYING

On the other hand, simply because a patient has been given no chance and shows no sign of a change in condition, the staff does not *ipso facto* do nothing. If there is time, the effort may nevertheless be made to save or perhaps only to prolong his life, even in the face of little chance of success. Hence, when there is time, they may create a chance where there was none, and organize their last-ditch heroics accordingly, sometimes successfully. Last-ditch heroics may be encouraged by several factors. One is that the patient is of such high social value that his loss must be averted at all costs, if possible.[6] A medically interesting patient may also stimulate last-ditch heroics. When there is time for the family or even the patient to participate in a decision of last resort, especially in surgery, the choice often hinges upon the relative likelihood that if saved the patient will be able to live a normal life. Neither the family nor the patient typically wishes to reverse the outcome if they recognize that it will unquestionably result in prolonged ordeal or pain.

In contrast to expected quick deaths, the unexpected have surprise as a main feature and surprise may vary from relatively little to complete. It makes a considerable difference whether the surprise comes as an emergency or as a crisis. An emergency situation almost always implies that the facilities for mobilization of life-saving action are at hand and that action can be initiated at a moment's notice. In the crisis situation adequate preparation is often lacking so that the need to act immediately more or less immobilizes the staff. In the emergency situation they tend to recover quickly from surprise, mobilize immediately, and promptly achieve a solid feeling about what is happening. In the crisis situation the relative disarray of work and sentiment requires a much longer period of resolution before the organization of work and the sentimental order are both solidly re-established.

When a patient is expected to die, but not quickly, the staff attempts to anticipate timing as specifically as possible. They then develop sentiments according to the stages of the trajectory. On medical wards, when an unexpected quick death begins in a lingering patient, expected stages may be entirely left out of the dying. For example the family, as yet unprepared, must be found and told their relative is almost dead, an often shattering task for the nurse or doctor as well as for the family. Staff work and sentiments lose their customary tempo and continuity. Sudden procedural shifts may be required. Facilities must be obtained quickly and the right physician found, or the patient must be moved to the intensive care unit. Or if he remains, extra nursing staff may have to be found to help with other patients until the crisis can be turned to an emergency.

Having become personally involved with the patient and his family, the nurses may suffer some shock at the dying. They may expect the lingering patient to be alive each day as they arrive on the ward. For the time being they forget he is dying. On the other hand, the unexpected quick trajectory may be well received on the medical ward. If a patient has been lingering in pain, has been degenerating, has been comatose for months, is draining his family of all their money, has clearly reached the point of 'nothing more to do', with nothing much to make his last weeks and days socially meaningful or even comfortable, the staff may wish that he die or be allowed to die.

Wards with a greater frequency of deaths tend to temper staff for the surprises as well as for the expected. A surprise can be warded off: 'we generally lose them anyway.' Protection against surprise is sustained by other facets. The dying patient would have lasted only a few days anyway, so the temporal loss is not great. The unexpected quick dying may be welcome relief from bearing even a few more days of an ordeal painful to all. The quicker death also maintains the ward personnel's motivation to rescue patients, by relieving them of a 'no chance' patient sooner than expected and opening a bed for a patient who can be saved. The intense work and intense focus on medical aspects of saving also provide buffers. Staff have less time to dwell on the surprise and the sad fact of imminent death. Rather they must concentrate on mobilizing for the emergency and preventing crisis. Part of this intensity in medical care involvement is induced by closer collaboration with the physician than on wards where slower dying is more typical.

SLOW DYING

Among the more complex types of dying trajectories are those that are quite properly thought of as 'slow'—whether the time of death is certain or uncertain, and whether the patient dies sooner or earlier than expected. One main property of lingering death is its potential unpredictability, with regard to both the biological and human aspects of dying. To be sure, many a patient slowly declines, or lingers on plateaux between several declines or abrupt deteriorations, without unexpected important events occurring. But in a decline of any considerable duration, a number of special events are probable. Anyone can begin to make a special story of the dying. Despite the death, the story may have happy endings for its main characters. Or it may be a very sad story indeed.

The slow decline, then, is fraught with both hazard and opportunity. On the hazard side, the dying may take too long, the bodily deterioration may be unexpectedly painful or unpleasant, the patient may discover he is dying when he is not supposed to know and so on. On the other hand, slow decline may allow a man time to make his will, round off unfinished business and family affairs and even permit him to patch up differences with his spouse or other members of the family. Slow dying also furnishes the setting for courageous or tranquil endings, and a participation that buoys the staff. All these consequences are less likely to occur with swift or sudden dying.

Slow dying, then, is likely to be accompanied by an evolving story, stretching over weeks or months; or perhaps stories, since staff members do not always agree with each other's versions. If dramatic enough, patients' stories are long remembered by people who participated in them. Even trajectories that are fairly uneventful right down to the last phases can produce memorable stories. An interesting feature of the continuing story is that people who have never seen or been involved in the care of a patient sometimes react to it. Dying patients may become personages not only for personnel who care for them, but also for those who work elsewhere in the hospital. Thus one patient whom we observed set such difficult problems for the nursing and medical staff, involving the management of her pain, that she provoked persistent discussion extending during periods of crisis far beyond the ward. Personnel were discussing her story on other floors, in the hospital's restaurant and even in the classrooms of the associated school of nursing.

EFFECTS OF PATIENT ON STAFF

Strangers may react to a dying patient's story, but the reactions of those in prolonged, direct contact with him are necessarily more complex. They cannot simply react to the story or to the person lying in the bed. When the patient groans, requests something, complains or grows angry at them, their answering actions are not towards isolated behaviours but towards elements of a continuing story. A reverse logic implies that a patient's reactions to staff members can be directed towards altering or sustaining the story that they have constructed about him; indeed a patient may, from his first days at the hospital, deliberately attempt to shape the staff's collective story. Patients who die quickly can produce dying stories, but patients with slow trajectories are much more likely to have stories that are consequential for their nursing and medical care. One important consequence of any patient's story—one we dare not overlook—is its influence on the efforts made in his behalf, and thereby (whether we wish to admit this or not) on whether his life will be shortened or prolonged and to what purpose.

Unless a person dies abruptly, with virtually no warning, the dying trajectory includes a stage of 'last days' and perhaps even 'last weeks'. The hospital staff usually finds itself engaged in a complex juggling of tasks, people and relationships. Its juggling consists, first, of organizing a number of potentially shifting treatment and care tasks. As a patient becomes visibly sicker and weaker, the staff typically stop certain activities and simultaneously initiate new ones. The comfort care activities may become very detailed and may now require considerable nursing skill; the medical care necessary to keep him alive may remain quite complex, although different from earlier medical care.

THE FAMILY'S CONCERN

Meanwhile, the staff must also juggle people and relationships whose existence can cause great disruption to the ward's work and sentimental order. If the patient is visible to other patients, their reactions to his last weeks and days must be taken into account, particularly in so far as they may see his dying as a rehearsal of their own. And both the family and the patient present problems of management.

With families, problems tend to centre around four issues: (i) the family needs to be prepared for the forthcoming death; (ii) they may need to be persuaded to delegate responsibility for the dying person to the hospital; (iii) they may require coaching in proper modes of behaviour while at the hospital; and (iv) they may need to be helped in their grieving, either for their own sake or for the sake of preventing disruption of ward activity. The nature of these central problems suggests that the personnel may be considerably engaged in working with the family during the patient's last days. Such problems do not arise if there is no family or no one close enough to visit the hospital. In American geriatric hospitals, for example, family-handling problems are minimal.

If a family is to be prepared for a patient's death, it first must be fore-warned. Lingering trajectories allow the physician great latitude in timing his notice to the family. Indeed, he does not know exactly when the patient will die and may not be able to predict whether there will be temporary reprieves, plateaux and even reversals. His first tidings may be long delayed; they may consist initially of cues to stimulate a gradually growing awareness; these may be repeated. Ineffective pacing of forewarnings—or insufficient trust by the family—may result in their shopping around for a 'better' doctor, one with a 'cure', even though cure is really not the issue. Usually, the physician first communicates with the 'strongest' family member, who then has the responsibility of disclosure to the other relatives.

During the last days, family members may ply the staff with queries about how long the patient has to live and whether he will die peacefully. Those queries must be handled. If they are not, scenes are likely to erupt on the ward.

Some families can accept the forthcoming death of a relative, but others need help in coming to terms with the event. The staff then offers rationali-zations or supports those of the kinsmen: 'yes, it will be a blessing if he goes soon,' 'yes, he is lucky that he has no pain at all.' If the last days stretch into weeks, the staff can sustain the relatives' acceptance by dis-playing equanimity and by giving undiminished comfort care to the patient. They can give reassurances that he will die peacefully. They can correct unfounded expectations about how he will die. When reprieves occur, staff can signify quietly that death is still on the way without encouraging false hopes. If need be, the nurses can put pressure on the physician to 'explain again' to a relative who will not face the facts.

Relatives' acceptance of a forthcoming death may relate to whether they already partly have overcome their grief. Virtually everybody may be fairly well 'grieved out' if the end comes slowly, especially if the patient's social value is relatively low (for instance, if he is a very old person). If at all possible, a tactful staff allows close kinsmen plenty of time with the dying person, especially during the last days, so that they can quietly live through their grief. Sometimes personnel do not recognize grieving as such—it has many individual and cultural variants. But by and large they do understand that a wife must be with a dying husband, children with a dying parent, that separation would be more painful than partici-pation in the dying. Some hospitals have convenient rooms where relatives may wait when they cannot stay at the bedside.

When it seems advisable that the dying person should remain ignorant of his forthcoming death, family members must not display their grief before the patient. Staff members may have to warn kinsmen about this danger or take steps to prevent its occurrence. Since grieving may begin the instant that close kinsmen are forewarned of death, the staff may immediately begin giving support.

GRIEF WORKERS

Nursing personnel often find their role as sympathetic listener or comforter a major one during the final days. They are especially moved when they see the patient's death as a grave social loss, or when they associate it with their own personal past, or sometimes when a family member has behaved admirably. Social workers may tend especially, with self-consciousness, to become 'grief workers', attempting with professional deliberateness to 'work through' the grief of relatives; this is perhaps most noticeable on pediatric wards. Priests, chaplains, and nuns also engage in such activities; indeed they may be called on by a desperate nursing staff afraid of the disastrous effects of death and unable themselves to help the relative. Psychiatrists may also be called in to work with family members.

The staff's problem of getting suitable behaviour from the family members is linked closely with whether the family is adequately prepared for the death and does its grieving on schedule. A wife may cause upsetting scenes, for instance, if she is not prepared for her husband's death when it finally draws near. A relative who grieves too early and too openly may disturb the patient; even if the latter is quite aware of his forthcoming death, he may not be sufficiently resigned to it.

The staff may also have to coach relatives in appropriate bedside behaviour. If family members visit in too great numbers, a rule may be laid down that only close kin may visit 'from now on'—especially as death becomes imminent. A family that is too noisy may need to be reprimanded; the staff may forbid access to the ward to all but the closest kin. In rooms with several patients, visitors may be especially careful not to disturb nearby patients with chattering or sobbing. When a patient has a private room, kin still may need to be taught not to 'get in the way'. Often a nurse will ask someone to leave the bedside or the room when she suspects that a nursing or medical procedure may disturb the onlooker. Visitors may also harass the staff by making what the latter considers unjustified, over-anxious or just plain fussy demands. Various tactics are used to make the offending person behave properly. What is considered inappropriate depends not only on the patient himself, but also on how attached the personnel have become to the patient, how well they have come to know the family member, or the nature of the patient's evolving story. The staff, however, may call on other family members to restrain the over-demanding person or one who offends in other ways.

JURISDICTIONAL DISPUTES

The staff's final problem is that the kinsmen may not willingly delegate the patient's care during his last hours. Such unwillingness may vary in seriousness. At its most extreme, the patient simply is withdrawn from the hospital, usually against professional advice. (This is much more prevalent in countries like Malaya or Greece, where the hospital is less accepted as a place to die than in the United States.) Sometimes an American family takes a patient home during his last days because it believes it can provide adequate care there; the family may discover its error and return him to the hospital.

Even families who know very well that their dying kinsman should remain in professional hands may try to interfere with the staff, suggesting or demanding that certain things be done differently. The staff require and develop counter tactics to cope with this behaviour. More generally, however, hospitals allow close kin to carry out routine comfort care while the nurses and physicians give the more difficult or professionalized care. As life draws to a close, sometimes the staff tactfully allows a mother or wife to take over the comfort care almost totally if this is possible.

Neither the severity of problems that a family will present to the hospital staff nor the degree of success the staff will have in managing a family during the last weeks and days are entirely predictable. (The reverse of the question is the problems the family will have with the staff.) Among the structural conditions that militate against the relative tranquillity and success of the interaction are the number of visiting relatives, the distance from which they have come, the experience they have had with hospital customs and rules, the amount of trust they have in the professionals, and the amount or kind of ward space.

LEAVETAKINGS

At the last weeks become days, and the days become hours, a critical juncture arises. It comes when close relatives say final farewells to the dying patient or—if he is not aware—when they take their last looks at him alive. Told that he has not long to live or warned by their own senses, they take leave. These leavetakings are likely to be awesome ceremonies, even when the dying man is comatose, has been socially dead for some time or is elderly. Each day's separation implies the possibility that *this* may be the last time visitors will see the patient alive. When family members travel considerable distances to visit at the hospital, they may be able to come only on weekends or at several day intervals. They must make each farewell not knowing whether they will 'ever see him again'. The anguish may be shared by some staff members. Where 'final' leavetakings

are frequent and anguished, the disruption of scheduled work and sentimental order is sometimes devastating to the staff.

As for the patient himself: he is much more likely than his family to
be the centre of the staff's attention, unless he is comatose, scarcely sentient,
or so ill as hardly to be reacting as a person. Under these latter conditions,
the staff's juggling of its work around him need only be minimal. When
last days stretch out interminably on wards organized for faster turnover
of patients, or when mode of dying is so extraordinarily unpleasant as to
disturb staff members, the personnel face major problems.

If the dying person is sentient but unaware of his impending death, then
the staff's problems may be associated with keeping him unaware, or at
least keeping his suspicions sufficiently damped down. If his pain is great,
he can be 'snowed' with drugs during his final days.

If he has become aware that he is dying, he must come to terms with
dying. If he has had many months to face his mortality, he has probably
entered or re-entered the hospital better prepared than if his period of
awareness has been short or sudden. If he is not elderly and has not already
come to terms with the inevitability of death, a quick decline is likely
to precipitate crises of awareness for the sentient patient and his family.

Even in slow dying, the breakthrough of awareness during last days
can be traumatic. The staff sometimes has little control over the structural
conditions that determine the impact. For instance, a patient may know
he has an extremely serious illness, but not regard it as fatal. Then he
suddenly is told, intentionally or not. We observed, for example, the first
days of a teenager who had learned of his imminent death from a friend
who had learned of it from another friend, whose parents in turn had
received the information from the patient's parents. The blinding news,
combined with a deep sense of his parents' betrayal, resulted as the staff
members put it in the boy's almost complete 'withdrawal' and 'apathy'.
Consequently, the staff could not be of much help.

TRANSACTIONS WITH DEATH

The patient may come to terms with his own mortality if his awareness
and understanding develop sufficiently early so that he can confront his
dying. Coming to terms involves two separate processes. The first consists
of facing the annihilation of self, of visualizing a world without one's self.
The second process consists of facing up to dying as a physical and perhaps
mental disintegration. Some people are fearful of dying in great pain, or
with extreme bodily disfiguration, or with loss of speech or of 'just lying
there like a vegetable'. Others think hardly at all about these aspects of
dying, but tremble at the prospect of the disappearance of self. Moreover,
some patients who have come to terms with the idea of death may only

later focus on dying, especially when they are surprised, dismayed or otherwise affected by bodily changes. On the other hand someone who lives with his dying long enough may become assured that he will 'pass' peacefully enough, and only then fully face the death issue.

Most frequently perhaps, patients come to terms by themselves or with the help of close kin. Nurses, however, may be drawn into the processes. The patient typically initiates the 'death talk'; the nurse tends to listen, to assent, to be sympathetic, to reassure. The nurse may even cry with a patient. Occasionally, a patient repeatedly invites nurses into conversations about death or dying, but they decline his invitations. Their refusals tend to initiate a drama of mutual pretence: neither party subsequently indicates recognition of the forthcoming death, although both know about it.

Other parties, too, sometimes play significant roles in such processes. In one such situation, an elderly patient was rescued from the isolation of mutual pretence by a hospital chaplain who directly participated in his coming to terms; eventually the chaplain also persuaded the wife, and to some extent the nurses, to enter into the continuing conversation. Patients sometimes rely on members of the clergy to move their spouses to faster acceptance of the inevitable and thus ease their own acceptance.

A HARD THING TO TALK ABOUT

On the whole, American nurses and staff physicians seem to find it difficult to carry on conversations about death or dying with patients.[7] Only if a patient has already come to terms with death, or if staff can honestly assure him he will die 'easily', if he is elderly, do they find it relatively easy to talk about such topics with him. Unless a patient shows considerable composure about his dying, nurses and physicians lose their composure, except when they are specially trained or specially suited by temperament or have some unusual empathy with a patient because of a similarity of personal history. When the patient's conversation during the last days is only obliquely about death and dying—consisting for instance of reminiscences of the past—and is not unpleasant or unduly repetitious, he has a better chance of inducing others, including the nurses, to participate in his closing of his life. Clergymen also are expected to play major roles in this phasing out of patients. Psychiatrists sometimes perform analogous functions during the phasing out of more secular-minded patients.[8]

The closing-off of various aspects of everyday business is important. These include material and personal matters, like the drawing up of wills and the settling of quarrels. Physicians may allow a businessman to close his affairs, though the patient may have to insist on his right to do so. The physician may permit distraught families to urge reluctant patients to draw up, alter or sign wills. A lawyer is sometimes brought in by the family or physician to help persuade the patient. A chaplain or priest sometimes considers that his professional duties include bridging relationships between the dying person and an alienated spouse or offspring.

Sometimes the patient accepts his forthcoming death even before the staff. Moreover, the patient's 'social willing' may shock his family or the staff precisely because he has imaginatively reached his life's end before they have. One patient, for instance, relied on the intervention of his sister (who happened to be a nurse) to will his library to a neighbouring college; his wife would never discuss the matter with him. A more extreme instance of social willing, which shocked a hospital's personnel, was when a patient during his last days insisted on signing his own autopsy papers.

DYING VERSUS WORK SCHEDULE

Still another great barrier may block even the best-intentioned staff from providing adequate help to a patient when he faces his demise: the immense difference between the staff's and the patient's conceptions of time. The staff operates on 'work time'. Their tasks are guided by schedules usually related to many patients, both dying and recovering. But a dying patient's personal sense of time often undergoes striking changes once he becomes aware of his impending death. The future is foreshortened, cut out, or abstracted to 'after I am gone'. The personal past is likely to be reviewed and reconceptualized.[9] The present takes on various kinds of personal meanings. Things previously taken for granted may now be savoured as unique but unfortunately transitory. Occasional reprieves, recognized as only reprieves, evoke temporally significant reactions running from 'Oh, God! take me, I was prepared and now will not be prepared' to gratefulness for unexpected time.

The important point is not so much the variability of temporal reconstructions as the difficulty outsiders have in grasping these personal reconstructions (sometimes they are completely unable to). One cannot know about them unless privy to the dying person's thoughts. He may keep them to himself, especially in a situation of mutual pretence. He may not be able to express them clearly, especially when he becomes less sentient. A busy staff may have little time to listen or to invite revealing talk, particularly if patients are competing for attention. In many American hospitals nursing aides spend more time in patients' rooms than the nurses do, even during last days. When aides manage to grasp a patient's temporal re-ordering of his life, they may be unable to pass along this knowledge to the nurses, or not feel free to do so or assume that the information is unimportant. And they are not ordinarily accountable for reporting such information.

When the patient's personal time and the staff's work time are highly disparate, considerable strain may be engendered. Nor is the source of the trouble necessarily evident to either. Sometimes, of course, the staff does sense something of a patient's reconceptualizations, without necessarily realizing their deep import, and may somewhat adjust its own work time to his requirements.

ALONE WITH ONE'S DEATH

A staff's failure in understanding a patient's attempts at achieving psychological closure in his life contributes to another process: the patient's increasing isolation, whether or not he perceives it. He may of course understand very well that staff members are not interested in his awesome problem, or cannot grasp its nature even if they wish to. If he has tried to communicate with the staff, he may despair of their understanding. Or he may prefer to communicate with his family or his minister, although he may actually be unable to 'reach' them either.[10]

It is not only the communications problem that produces isolation, however. In all the countries we have observed, we found strong tendencies to isolate a dying patient during his last days in the hospital. Isolation techniques—perhaps 'insulation' is a better term—have their source in various structural conditions. For instance, if everyone agrees a patient should be kept unaware, then attempts to buffer him from knowledge immediately set in motion a train of insulating mechanisms. The isolating process is also called into play if the patient accepts or invites mutual pretence about his dying. The insulating mechanisms are blunted, however, if the patient is openly aware; even then, staff may avoid death talk or even the patient's room or bedside. The patient who will not accept his fate or is dying in a socially unacceptable way also arouses avoidance— sometimes by his family as well as the staff.

During a patient's last days, the staff lightens its work and increases the probability of giving good comfort care by moving him closer to the nursing station. Of course, he may be grateful for the added security of being near the staff, but the move may frighten him despite explanations. The move not only forewarns the aware patient, but it also isolates him from satisfying friendships he has made with other patients. Because of unpleasant odours or perhaps uncontrollable groans and sobbing, he may even be moved into a separate room. At the last, the staff tends to put him either into a single room or with a comatose patient. If the room-mate is not comatose, he may complain about the dying patient's behaviour, and this would stimulate the staff to move one or the other. Of course, when patients are moved to an intensive care ward, they are quite isolated from people other than the staff, including their families.

All these conditions contribute to the isolation of dying patients. Although a patient may welcome being alone, or alone with kinsmen, he may also fight against his insulation. He may plead successfully to be left with friends and acquaintances, and the staff will wait until he is no longer sentient before moving him. A patient who is already in a single room may devise tactics to get personnel into his room and to increase the time they spend with him, by making urgent demands and complaints or by making himself appealing. The limits of demand tactics are suggested by what happened to one woman who customarily fixed her listeners by the repeated tale of her life. This tactic drove them into non-response while they took care of her creature comforts.

A patient can gain more attention from the personnel if he can charm them. The better they like him, the more contact they are likely to give him anyway, unless his dying distresses them so much that they cannot bear to be around him. In slow trajectories, a staff member may pull away from a patient not just to minimize contact with him, but to minimize her own emotions and reactions. She is attempting to lessen the chances of his biography having a lasting impact on her own. On the whole then, under these kinds of structural conditions, it is much easier for patients to gain relative privacy from staff intrusions than to get attention. To the extent that patients fail in either aim, they lose the contest over the shaping of their own passing.

MANIPULATION OF TRAJECTORY

There are two especially critical junctures with immense potential for disturbing either the patient or the staff. The first occurs when someone decides to prolong the patient's life, although others believe he should be allowed to die quickly. The second juncture occurs when someone decides to hasten a patient's death, although others believe this intervention should not be made. These decisions sometimes involve the patient's participation —especially the decision to shorten his life.

His role in the decision not to prolong his dying, or perhaps even to hasten it, is not limited to negotiating with the physician. Patients directly shorten their lives by various actions—by not eating, by fatally exposing themselves to cold air at open windows or more overtly still by suicide. Patients who are being kept alive through intravenous feeding or machinery are less likely near the end to kill themselves by pulling out the tubes or by asking that the machine be turned off; but we have known a successful instance of each action.

Decisions to prolong or shorten life, however, usually are made by the close kin or by physicians, rather than by the patients themselves. Physicians know what patients and families often do not; life can be extended or shortened for at least a few hours or days and sometimes longer by various

medical tactics. Several factors bear upon the physician's decision. The
nature of the illness is one determinant. During the last days of certain
patients—for instance, geriatric cases—physicians customarily make no
great attempts to stretch out the dying. In general hospitals, physicians are
more likely to keep life going as long as they judge it sensible to do so:
institutional pressures constantly remind them that this is their professional
task. Indeed, if a patient unsuccessfully attempts to end his life, physicians
are very likely to take steps to prevent renewed attempts.

NURSE VERSUS DOCTOR

Nurses in all countries seem to be caught in a bind over prolonging or
hastening the dying process. By and large, they tend to resist prolongation.
They do not always agree with the physician that a patient's life should be
prolonged. 'What is the sense of it?' they ask among themselves, sometimes
even asking the responsible physician. Nurses may show their disagreement
openly and may exert direct pressure on physicians. When they do not
attempt to influence his decision, they may harbour disturbing doubts about
the paradoxical power of modern medicine; it can extend life for good
reason or for none at all.

Family members sometimes may have a major share in shaping this
last phase of the dying. Occasionally there may be a conflict between the
physician and the family over the family's desire to shorten the ordeal.
Or, if the patient is dying at home, the family may rush him to the hospital
in order to give him a few more days or weeks. They may ask the doctor
to bring in a consultant or shop around for another doctor, although usually
he cannot prolong the patient's life. Although kinsmen may request the
doctor not to prolong the dying, he in turn may force on them a direct
decision as to whether to shorten life. Rather than precipitate a direct
confrontation with the moral decision, he may gently ask whether there
is 'any more we should do', and the relative, sadly or gratefully or with some
other emotion, probably signals 'no'. Perhaps more often, close relatives
either leave the decision up to the doctor, or are unaware that he and the
staff explicitly exercise control over shortening or lengthening life.

WHO WILL PLAY GOD?

The essential issue in these last days is who shall have what kinds and
degrees of influence in shaping the end of the patient's life. That issue
involves not merely how the patient shall die, but also how he shall live
while dying. A dying person can hold almost complete control over how
he lives his last days by not entering a hospital, or can regain it by leaving
the hospital.[11] Yet his trajectory may depart radically from his expectations
of it, requiring new decisions. Opinions of doctors and nurses also may

need to be modified or even reversed during prelude to death.

Above all, to shape the trajectory during the last days requires juggling tasks, people, and relationships. It also requires juggling time: time for tasks, time for people, time for talk. Most subtle of all, everyone is juggling the time chance still allows; control over aspects of dying may be manageable for a time, but not for ever. These various contingencies are immensely unstable: For the staff, the patient can be kept unaware just so long. His family can be kept under control just so long; the strain of waiting or of continual farewells mounts. The staff itself can stand for just so long a patient acting unacceptably in the face of death. During the last days, every major person in the dying drama operates within a context of multiple contingencies.

DISPOSING OF THE FAMILY

Consideration of the patient ends with his death. But the hospital's work is not yet finished. It must dispose of the body; it must wind up its relationship with the family; it must write a conclusion to the patient's story. Hospitals are well organized for disposing of the body (a process we shall not discuss here), but they vary in the procedures for disposing of the family and have little or no organization for ending the patient's story—the staff does this latter task on its own, as any particular story seems to require. It is generally felt that the sooner the hospital achieves these dispositions the better, so pressure is put on the staff to expedite them.

'Disposing of' the family involves the announcing of death; it also may involve allowing the kinsmen a last look at their dead relative. Both situations involve problems of management and may, under various conditions, have untoward consequences either for staff or for family. There may be difficulties in ushering the family off the ward. The family members still must settle details of the death with the hospital.

DISPOSING OF THE EVENT

After the body and family are gone from the ward, there remains only the staff's disposition of the patient's story among themselves. This disposition is a social-psychological process that brings the story of the patient's dying and death to a close in their minds. The degree to which it is necessary varies. At one extreme are the stories of patients whose trajectories and deaths are typical and expected. These stories are routine and never really bothersome; since they were accurate before death, there is no need to develop post-mortem stories. When these patients are gone, they tend simply to be forgotten.

But several kinds of patients have a strong or unusual story in death; it is difficult to forget. Some have an inaccurate pre-death story; some, none at all. The post-mortem story explains what happened and is part of the staff's bringing the case to a close, in effect erasing it from the sentimental order of the ward. Characteristics of the patient himself and of the family also help generate a post-mortem story about the patient (e.g. he was a wonderful person while facing death, or a mother would not visit the dying son). The two principal factors in bringing the story to a close are the autopsy findings and the staff's dicussion among themselves and with the relatives. Staff members may also have to come to terms with the patient's story through personal grieving and introspection. Sometimes all three ways are combined.

The post-mortem story is mainly developed within the ward until it is forgotten. Sometimes the manner of death is so momentous, however, especially with surprisingly quick trajectories, that the story breaks through the boundaries of the ward itself. If the patient has been on several wards, news may travel in shock waves throughout the hospital. In the surprise suicide or operating-table death, the story may become further formalized by a coroner's inquest, and perhaps then be picked up by the newspapers and spread through the community. These cases, of course, are statistically rare.

Perhaps the most positive story is the 'perfect image of death' that nurses and doctors sometimes give family members who have missed the death scene and a last look. They tell such a story even when the death was unpleasant. These stories are told because it is, first of all, difficult to tell an uncomfortable story to a relative. Also, such a story might cause the family to create a scene. More important, perhaps, the staff often feels that the relative has been denied rightful participation in the death, so a vacuum remains to be filled. They fill it with the eulogy of a death occurring in comfort and peace. The family members leave the hospital with a good feeling. Such an outcome makes the nurses feel better too.

A SET OF RECOMMENDATIONS

We shall end with four recommendations based on our text:

(i) *Training and giving terminal care should be amplified and deepened in schools of medicine and nursing.* The changes need to be fairly extensive. Experimentation will be necessary before faculties can be satisfied that they have provided adequate training in the aspects of terminal care—psychological, social and organizational—now relatively neglected. How and when to teach these matters—these are questions. The most extensive initial educational turmoil is likely to come from faculty members' own attitudes towards dying and death—not only their personal anxieties and

aversions to talking openly about dying in any except contemporary technical terms, but also their deep-seated professional attitudes that social,
psychological and organizational matters are irrelevant or minor in the
cure of illness and the care of patients. In short, the educational reform
that we advocate goes beyond merely humanizing the curriculum a little
more.

(ii) *Explicit planning and review should be given to the psychological,
social and organizational aspects of terminal care.* The corrective reform
called for is again rather radical. Hospitals need to make their personnel
accountable for many social and psychological actions that currently are
left to personal discretion and only incidentally are reported upward—or
downward or sideways. Personnel need to understand the characteristic
trajectories of dying that occur on their specific wards, not merely as medical
but also as organizational and social phenomena. All wards need to develop
mechanisms for insuring a wider awareness of degrees of agreement and
disagreement about what is to be done to, for, and around dying patients.
Each ward needs mechanisms for discovering its patterned disagreements
and for mitigating their destructive impact on the care of patients. It also
needs to understand its patterned agreements, for these can also be destructive to medical and nursing care.

(iii) *There should be explicit planning for phases of the dying trajectory
that occur before and after residence at the hospital.* Most planning for
phases of dying outside the hospital is strictly medical, or deals with
financial aspects of the patient's life or with his geographic mobility. But
the illness careers of dying patients take them in and out of hospitals, and
adequate terminal care often cannot be given unless the connections between
hospital and outside world are explicitly rationalized. Planning also must
be done around clinic visits for ambulatory patients whose visits represent
phases of dying trajectories currently regarded either as purely medical
matters or as psychologically unconnected with death.

(iv) *Medical and nursing personnel should encourage public discussion
of issues that transcend professional responsibilities for terminal care.* Two
problems that we believe need public as well as professional debate are
the withholding of addicting drugs until 'near the end' and the 'senseless
prolonging' of life. About the first issue: although there is some disagreement among staff about this matter, particularly about the pacing of such
drugs, personnel generally seem to share the usual public horror of
addiction. But this view is not accepted by all Americans, nor would they
all be inclined to favour the withholding of addicting drugs from dying
patients if this practice were more widely known. More important, perhaps,
is the second issue of prolonging life, since modern technology makes it
increasingly probable, beyond where patients are capable of appreciating
the extra moments, days or months. Families as well as staff members may

suffer. Debates are frequent within the hospital about particular cases of prolonging life. Yet each physician and occasionally each nurse must make decisions about particular patients' lives, basing the decision on a sense of professional responsibility combined perhaps with standards of public conscience and sensibility. Although the physician and nurse can decide for particular patients, they cannot decide the wider issue. That must be debated, we suggest, by the general public. With some certainty, one can predict that this issue will be increasingly discussed openly as medical technology becomes increasingly efficient.

REFERENCES

1. Jeanne C. Quint, *Nurse and the Dying Patient*, Macmillan (New York 1967); Howard Becker *et al.*, *Boys in White*, University of Chicago Press (Chicago, 1961).
2. Anselm Strauss, Barney Glaser and Jeanne Quint, 'The Non-accountability of Terminal Care Hospitals', *Journal of the American Hospital Association*, 38, January, pp. 73-87.
3. Barney Glaser and Anselm Strauss, *Time for Dying*, Aldine (Chicago 1968), p. 1.
4. Barney Glaser and Anselm Strauss, *Awareness of Dying*, Aldine (Chicago 1965).
5. Renee Fox, *Experiment Perilous*, Free Press (New York 1959).
6. Barney Glaser and Anselm Strauss, 'The Social Loss of Dying Patients', *American Journal of Nursing*, 64, June, 119-21.
7. Jeanne C. Quint, *Nurse and the Dying Patient*, Macmillan (New York 1967).
8. *See* E. K. Ross, 'The Dying Patient's Point of View', Chapter 8 in O. G. Brim et al. (eds) *The Dying Patient*, Russell Sage (New York 1970).
9. Bernice Kavinovsky, *Voyage and Return: an Experience with Cancer*, Norton (New York 1966).
10. Jeanne C. Quint, 'The Impact of Mastectomy', *American Journal of Nursing*, 63, November, pp. 88-97.
11. Lael Wertenbaker, *Death of a Man*, Random House (New York 1957).

IV | The sociology of the doctor/patient relationship

16 Conflict and conflict resolution in doctor/patient interactions

M. J. BLOOR & G. W. HOROBIN

The belief that the doctor/patient relationship is fundamentally reciprocal is questioned. Closer scrutiny of the relationship shows that it contains elements likely to generate conflict. The source of the conflict lies in two basic assumptions held by doctors as to how their patients should behave. They believe patients should use their own judgement as to when it is appropriate to seek medical advice; however, patients are later expected to defer to the doctor's judgement when undergoing medical treatment. These conflicting expectations held by the doctor place the patient in a 'double-bind' situation. This example serves as a caution against accepting too readily the assumption that the professional/client relationship is necessarily reciprocal and unproblematic.

Despite Eliot Freidson's statement elsewhere in this volume[1] that '... the separate worlds of experience and reference of the layman and the professional worker are always in potential conflict with each other,' relatively little attention has been paid in the sociology of medicine to the possibility of conflict between doctor and patient. More often than not, a functionalist stance is taken in which the roles of professional and client are seen as being articulated in a fundamentally reciprocal relationship and any conflict which occurs is held to stem from inadequate role performance. This view is explicit in the writings of Talcott Parsons on the sick role[2] and occurs more implicitly in the work of subsequent writers such as Wilson[3] who have built on Parsons's work. In recent years medical sociologists have devoted considerable attention to the examination of the extent to which Parsons's prescriptions for patient behaviour—the sick role—correspond to empirical reality. Our purpose here is rather different: we intend to focus attention on this alleged reciprocity of doctor and patient roles. We shall argue that doctors' expectations of patient behaviour are incipiently contradictory; that is, the patient is placed in a situation which can be likened to a 'double-bind'. This contradiction between expectations renders the reciprocity of doctor/patient behaviour problematic, and conflict may be generated. Further we hope to show that these contradictory expectations are implicit in Parsons's analysis so that the reciprocity he postulates between doctors and patients is spurious. We would hope that the viewing of

271

reciprocity between doctors and patients as problematic and as something which may need to be 'worked at' by both parties if overt conflict or at least covert dissatisfaction is not to occur, will increase our understanding of the behaviour of doctor and patients.

THE PARSONIAN MODEL

Parsons views illness as a socially legitimized state which exempts the sick individual from the roles and tasks for which he has been socialized. The role of the sick person ('the sick role') consists of two rights and two obligations:

> Incapacity defined as illness is interpreted as a legitimate basis for the exemption of the sick individual, to varying degrees, in varying ways and for varying periods according to the nature of the illness, from his normal role and task obligations.[4]

> This incapacity is interpreted as beyond his powers to overcome by the process of decision-making alone, in this sense he cannot be 'held responsible' for the incapacity. Some kind of therapeutic process, spontaneous or aided, is conceived to be necessary to recovery.[5]

> To be ill is thus to be in a partially and conditionally legitimated state. The essential condition of its legitimation, however, is the recognition by the sick person that to be ill is undesirable, that he therefore has an obligation to try to 'get well' and to cooperate with others to this end.[6]

> So far as spontaneous forces, the *vis medicatrix naturae*, cannot be expected to operate adequately and quickly, the sick person and those with responsibility for his welfare, above all, members of his family, have an obligation to seek competent help and to cooperate with competent agencies in their attempt to help him to get well; in our society, of course, principally medical agencies.[7]

Parsons views the doctor's role as essentially the obverse of the sick role. The doctor must apply his technical knowledge to the task of healing the patients as efficiently as possible. The emphasis on efficiency in Parsons's conception is an inevitable concomitant of his belief in the 'functionality' of the medical system for the wider social system. In the interests of efficiency the doctor's role is an 'achieved' role rather than an 'ascribed' role, and the doctor is obliged to be 'collectivity-orientated' and 'universalistic' in the use of his skills; in the interest of efficiency the sick person must allow the doctor the right to be 'affectively neutral' and 'functionally specific'.[8]

Parsons's general objective is to describe the structure of social systems. The basic type, the paradigm, of social systems is the stable interaction of two actors. Such two-person systems can be and are stabilized on the basis of the shared values and expectations of the participants. Similarly and by extension, he argues, complex systems can achieve stability over time by the sharing of basic values. Such values are internalized through the socialization process, and give legitimacy and predictability to social actions which are institutionalized as social roles. Institutions, complexes of roles, are both complex patterns of standardized social action and expressions of shared cultural values. Further, institutions have functional significance for the maintenance over time of the system.

It is clear that any behaviour which clashes with or negates the shared values of the system is potentially disruptive for that system, the more so if such behaviour tends to recur. Illness, by interfering with and distorting 'normal social role and task performance', is seen as one such form of disruptive deviance. To cope with deviant behaviour, social systems develop mechanisms of social control acting to prevent its occurrence or, failing that, to prevent its spread. Thus sanctions against preventable disruption are developed and institutionalized in the law, and 'collectivities of role-performing actors' are recruited to administer the law. When the behaviour cannot be prevented, however, as in the case of illness, it must be controlled by assigning approved roles to the deviants and by recruiting individuals to reciprocal roles aimed at helping the deviant to revert to his normal tasks and roles.

Parsons's thesis, then, is that illness and therapy can be seen as aspects of the social equilibrium of society. He is only peripherally concerned with what he sees as the biological processes of the organism and their technical manipulation in treatment. 'It is with this motivated aspect of illness, whether its symptoms be organic or behavioural, that we are concerned. Our fundamental thesis will be that illness to this degree must be considered to be an integral part of what may be called the "motivational economy" of the social system and that, correspondingly, the therapeutic process must also be treated as part of that same motivational balance.'[9]

Parsons's belief in the 'functionality' of the medical system for the wider social system, and indeed, his interest in the therapeutic process largely as an illustration of his theory of social systems, would appear to be root of many medical sociologists' dissatisfaction with the sick role concept. While numerous studies have documented *variations* in the role conceptions and role performances of sick person and therapist,[10] Parsons's interests demand a macroscopic theoretical perspective and a mode of analysis which cannot throw light on these variations and is not designed to.[11] Parsons's concern is not to specify what empirical reality *is*, but merely to *selectively* describe it in a conceptually unambiguous manner. In this task, Parsons's tool is the 'ideal type'. Parsons himself has commented on the nature of ideal type analysis in his discussion of the work of Max Weber. The ideal type is '... an ideal construction of a typical course of action, or form of relationship which is applicable to the analysis of an indefinable plurality of concrete cases, and which formulates in pure logically consistent form certain elements that are relevant to the understanding of the several concrete situations'.[12]

Ideal types have two main characteristics, 'abstract generality and ... the ideal-typical exaggeration of empirical reality.'[13] Thus an ideal type need not be isomorphic with the empirical reality it describes; it selects certain aspects of the phenomenon under study as important while others are ignored. (If Parsons *were* concerned with explicating the *range* of behaviour observable in the doctor/patient relationship, he would have to abandon his unimodal definition of social role [i.e. his assigning of only one set of rights and obligations to a given social position]. Many authors in recent years have taken the view that, at least in complex western societies, a number of different sets of norms may be associated with a given social position. However, if a 'multimodal' definition of doctor and patient roles is adopted, the reciprocity of those roles immediately becomes problematic.)

One further problem of Parsons's formulation should be mentioned here. The insistence on the functionality of the medical care sub-system for the wider social system leads Parsons to make no conceptual distinction between a sick role and a patient role. Since it is necessary to return the sick to 'normal functioning' as speedily as possible, then functionally impaired people should become doctors' patients.

Sick role and patient role can, of course, be distinguished conceptually if, as seems almost axiomatic, not all sick people are patients and not all patients are sick. Thus a person may claim a sick role without seeking treatment while in other cases treatment may proceed without the person claiming exemption from normal roles and tasks. A number of factors may determine whether the sick role follows or precedes the patient role or whether one or other is not taken. One obviously relevant factor is the 'objective' illness condition. Thus, for example, a stigmatized but not incapacitating condition such as a venereal disease may bring a person to treatment, to the patient role, while he may prefer not to claim a sick role. On the other hand, brief predictable incapacitating illness such as influenza may involve taking a limited sick role but foregoing a patient role. Other possible combinations of illness, sick role and patient role are possible so that for example the woman enjoying an uncomplicated pregnancy is allotted a patient role without either being ill or claiming a sick role. A good deal of the argument which has developed about, for instance, Parsons's insistence on the obligation to seek competent help as an element in the sick role, could have been avoided if this elementary distinction had been made.

TYPIFICATION AND THE SICK ROLE

Alfred Schutz has termed sociological concepts 'constructs of the second degree';[14] he argues that they represent a refinement and reification of those 'first degree' typifications by which actors perceive and structure their social world. Parsons's ideal-typical notion of the sick role is thus a 'construct of the second-degree' developed from 'common-sense typifications' of patients.

Analysis of the behavioural prescriptions associated with the sick role shows that it is a permissive role in so far as the various obligations and expectations of the sick person permit the doctor to apply his technical expertise in healing the sick with the maximum efficiency. As we pointed out above, Parsons's concern with the necessity of rapidly returning the sick person to 'normal functioning' is clear. Thus, the 'common-sense typification' of the sick person that Parsons has refined in his sick role concept is that of the person who lets the doctor heal him with the most speed; the ideal patient is the cooperative patient.

This in turn suggests that Parsons's sick role concept is based on doctors' typifications of the ideal patient, since in our society only doctors are held to be competent to specify how the sick may best cooperate in the minimization of illness. In other words, the sick role represents what Parsons thinks doctors believe their patients *should* act like.

Thus the harmoniousness of Parsons's conceptualization of the doctor/patient relationship is achieved tautologically. The complementarity of doctor and patient roles is inevitable if the role of patient represents the role of doctors' ideal patients; the behaviour of such a patient will naturally be the complement of the doctor's efforts on his behalf.

TYPIFICATION AND DOCTORS

We now wish to take our argument a stage further and show that some of the expectations doctors have of patients place the latter in a 'double-bind' situation such that incipient conflict may be structurally generated in the situation of medical practice. (A number of authors have attempted to show that schizophrenic behaviour may stem from, or be exacerbated by, the subjection of persons to contradictory expectations. These authors have used the term 'double-bind' to describe this situation of contradiction. It is not, of course, our view that doctors induce schizophrenia in their patients: we use the term 'double-bind', not in the technical sense in which it is used in the mental illness literature, but in its 'everyday' sense.)

The concern of British doctors about the proportion of 'trivial' conditions presented to them is well documented. When Ann Cartwright and associates[15] asked a sample of GPs what they found most frustrating about their work, 'unnecessary consultations for trival conditions' came top of the list; fully one third of the doctors responding had this as their most important grievance. The problem was often associated with 'unnecessary' night calls, e.g. 'unnecessary late calls and unnecessary night visits and the hundreds of neurotics who take advantage of free treatment'; 'lack of intelligent use of the GP service by patients'. Twenty-six per cent of the doctors felt that more than 50% of their consultations were trivial, unnecessary, or inappropriate. Forty-eight per cent of Mechanic's[16] sample of British GPs reported 'having too many patients who present trivial or inappropriate complaints' as a serious problem. At a more anecdotal level, the same impression is given by Ferris.[17] Advertisements have gone out on TV asking people to refrain from calling out doctors to deal with cases at night which they, the patients, think can wait till the morning surgery.

Our impression of these data is that despite the maxim 'the art of general practice is to distinguish between minor ailments and the early symptoms of illness', many doctors feel that patients should, but a 'minority' often fail to, assess their own condition as to its seriousness and as to the appropriateness of medical treatment as a therapeutic agent, before deciding whether or not to present themselves to their GP.

A further source of dissatisfaction of British GPs with their work is the alleged decline in the deference patients accord to their doctors: '... respect for the doctor has gone completely in this area'; '... one feels one doesn't get the respect one ought to'.[18]

This lack of deference is clearly related to the patients' diagnostic and prognostic assertiveness—'She always 'as a red medicine and it's that what she needs now.' Fifty-six per cent of Ann Cartwright's GPs felt that 'patients nowadays tend to demand their rights rather than ask for help and advice'.[19]

It would seem then that doctors tend to typify the ideal patient as someone who is able to assess symptomatology with sufficient expertise to know *which* conditions he should present, and *when* he should present them to the GP, but at the same time one who, having assessed his condition, will defer to the doctor's assessment on presentation.

This situation can be clarified by the employment of the conceptual framework that Schutz developed in his analysis of the social distribution of knowledge.[20] Schutz constructs three ideal types: 'the expert', 'the man in the street', and the 'well-informed citizen'.

The expert's knowledge is restricted to a limited field but therein it is clear and distinct. His opinions are based upon warranted assertions; his judgements are not mere guesswork or loose suppositions.[21]

The man on the street has a working knowledge of many fields. His is a knowledge of recipes indicating how to bring forth in typical situations typical results by typical means. The recipes indicate procedures which can be trusted even though they are not clearly understood. By following the prescription as if it were a ritual, the desired result can be attained without questioning why the single procedural steps have to be taken and taken exactly in the sequence prescribed. This knowledge in all its vagueness is still sufficiently precise for the practical purpose at hand.[22]

... The well-informed citizen ... stands between the ideal type of the expert and that of the man on the street. On the one hand, he neither is, nor aims at being, possessed of expert knowledge; on the other, he does not acquiesce in the fundamental vagueness of mere recipe knowledge.... To be well-informed means to him to arrive at reasonably founded opinions....[23]

The doctor (the expert), then, expects his prospective clients to be 'well-informed citizens' in so far as the decision to seek medical aid is concerned; indeed much health education work is directed towards the end of increasing the population's knowledge of health matters to enable them to arrive at reasonably founded decisions in this sphere. However this role prescription for the 'proto-patient' contrasts with an opposite role prescription for patient behaviour, where the patient is expected to defer to the opinion of the doctor. It is this situation which constitutes our 'double-bind': the sick person is expected to analyse his condition in terms—is it serious or non-serious, does it require medical treatment or some other alleviative action, etc.—which imply diagnostic and prognostic evaluation, but on presentation to the doctor the sick person is expected to 'forget' his own prior assessment of the condition and defer to the doctor's; the sick person is first encouraged to participate in and then excluded from the therapeutic process. As Schutz[24] puts it, 'the expert ... knows very well that only a fellow expert will understand all the technicalities and implications of a problem in his field, and he will never accept a layman or dilettante as a competent judge of his performances.' This would seem to imply that the more well-informed the citizen, the greater the potentiality of conflict. It is axiomatic that the sick doctor is a bad patient, and Ann Cartwright's finding that middle-class respondents are rather more critical of their doctors than working-class respondents[25] might be at least partially explicable in these terms. It seems then that the doctor's prescriptions for his client's behaviour are such that there is an inherent propensity to conflict and frustration: if the client complies with the doctor's expectation that he leave the diagnosis and prognosis of the disorder entirely in his hands, he is liable to present the doctor with a high proportion of trivial conditions; if the client complies with the doctor's expectation that he assess his own condition he is less likely to exhibit a deferential manner, more likely to attempt to impose his own diagnosis and prognosis on the doctor, and more likely to be critical of the doctor's evaluation.

CONFLICTING ROLE PRESCRIPTIONS IN THE SICK ROLE

We have already tried to show how doctor's typifications of ideal patient behaviour may, of themselves, exercise a disruptive influence on the doctor/ patient relationship in so far as they incorporate conflicting role prescriptions for the patient. It has also been our purpose to show that Parsons's sick-role concept represents what Parsons thinks doctors believe their patients should act like.

Therefore we would expect these conflicting role prescriptions to be implicit in the sick role. A close inspection of the prescriptions of the sick role indicate that this is so.

In his two main statements of the sick role concept Parsons stresses the relativity of the 'obligation to seek technically competent help'. In *The Social System* the obligation is dependent 'on the severity of the condition';[26] in *Social Structure and Personality* the obligation is dependent on the extent to which spontaneous recovery can be expected.[27] Clearly then, the sick person must reach some assessment of his condition before making the decision to seek medical aid; the sick person must act as a well-informed citizen.

At the same time the sick person is expected to 'cooperate' with the doctor in the healing process. What does this cooperation entail? Parsons is quite clear that it is not an equal partnership, a mutual search for the true diagnosis and most efficacious treatment regime—'... the sick person is not, of course, competent to help himself ... he does not "know" what needs to be done or how to do it.'[28] 'Cooperation', then, consists of obeying the doctor's instructions; the patient must defer to the doctor's superior knowledge.

Given that some kind of prior diagnosis is necessary, we may ask how the ill person—the proto-patient—goes about the task. Clearly the lay referral system[29] is extremely important in this respect, though it must not be assumed that all ill people seek advice from others before consulting a physician. Certainly there is a strong probability that married couples will tend to discuss with each other their symptoms and feelings unless the assumed condition is either strongly stigmatized or transgresses sexual taboos. Suchman's[30] study in Washington Heights showed that three-quarters of respondents discussed their symptoms with others before seeking care. Thus the process of symptom interpretation in the proto-patient phase may involve no lay consultants or many, depending on the general nature of the condition, the availability of lay consultants, their presumed competence, and relevance, and possibly such orientating contingencies as age, education, social class, etc. We may hypothesize, however, that the proto-patient who has negotiated a diagnosis with his lay consultants is likely to present to his doctor a relatively well developed set of requests or 'offers'. Such a patient is likely, one might suppose, to be less compliant in his interaction with the doctor than is the patient whose proto-patient career has been foreshortened. In the former case, the potentiality for conflict in the doctor/patient relationship may be increased.

This hypothesis as it stands is too crude, however, and needs further modification. In the first place we have assumed that the proto-patient phase culminates in the establishment of an acceptable diagnosis. Clearly there is no guarantee that this will occur. It may well be that confusing and even conflicting advice will be given so that the ill person goes to his doctor without a ready-made diagnosis. In such a case, the doctor— the expert—is not placed in a situation of competition with the lay consultants—the well-informed citizens—for the allegiance of the patient, and the patient is more likely to be compliant.

Secondly, even if a firm diagnosis is negotiated during the proto-patient stage, this need not lead to conflict with the doctor. Indeed, if the diagnoses of patient, lay consultants and doctor more or less coincide, so that the doctor is seen to be providing confirmation and reinforcement, a mutually satisfactory exchange may occur.

Thirdly, the patient is, in most cases, not entering into interaction with his doctor for the first time. Presumably each illness episode and each patient career become organized into some kind of meta-career, with both doctor and patient socializing each other into a set of expectations of the other's role. We shall return to this point later, but here it should be noted that these expectations will help to shape both the form and the content of the exchange.

THE RESOLUTION OF CONFLICT

We have argued that, in part, frustrations voiced by medical practitioners concerning their patients can be traced to two points of origin. Firstly, there is the failure of doctors to appreciate that in encouraging patients to assess their disorder before deciding to call on their doctor, they are encouraging patients to arrive at an assessment of their condition which may contrast with the doctor's conclusions. In the second place, frustration arises from their failure to appreciate that in asking their patients to defer to their trained expertise, i.e. to accept that a physician is the only person capable of arriving at trustworthy clinical judgements, doctors may be discouraging patients from assessing their condition prior to presentation. No doubt the difficulties of the patient in this situation are exacerbated by the lack of consensus within the medical profession concerning what constitutes appropriate grounds for seeking a consultation. For example, while some doctors attempt to treat 'anxiety states' and other psychiatric disorders, others may dismiss patients with such complaints as 'neurotics' or 'malingerers'.[31]

Throughout our argument so far we have been careful to refer to the 'incipiency' or 'potentiality' of conflict between doctor and patient. It is not our view that overt conflict is endemic in doctors' consulting rooms; there is little doubt that many consultations proceed harmoniously with no apparent discontent felt by either party. If this is so, we need to consider some of the reasons why conflict may be absent.

One such reason may lie in the content of the interaction itself. A number of theorists concerned with interaction situations have stressed the potential instability of face to face interaction: the possibility of 'exposure', loss of 'face', acrimony, is rarely absent.[32] Given this instability, doctors and patients may employ interaction strategies, what Goffman[33] has called 'techniques of impression management', both to stabilize the interaction and to help them achieve their own ends (a specific medication, certification, etc.). The use of these techniques by both doctors and patients may be for the purpose of consciously manipulating the other party but they may also be employed because their use is part of the learned 'ceremonial order' of things. In such a manner conflict is avoided: thus, the patient may employ a deferential demeanour when faced with the doctor, despite having drawn his own conclusions about the nature of his complaint, simply because he feels such behaviour is fit and proper.[34] Alternatively, the patient may simply be cowed by the superior power of the doctor in such situations, or the patient may decide to steer clear of a potential conflict on the grounds that such conflicts are distressing and undesirable.

In addition, as the doctor/patient relationship is commonly a *series* of interaction situations, harmony may emerge over time as each encounter brings doctor and patient closer to an understanding.

Clearly though, reasons for the absence of acrimony, frustration, etc., need not be sought purely in the content of the doctor/patient encounter: often conflict may be absent from a particular encounter as a result of atypical expectations entertained by doctors and patients. We would not want to argue that the expectations that doctors, in our analysis, have of patients are universal and invariant. These expectations will vary according to the influence of a number of factors, one of which is clearly the nature of the medical care system in which the consultation takes place. One might expect the doctor to accommodate to the expectations of his patients more readily in a fee for service care system—the customer in such a system is more likely to be 'right'. Koos remarked that the major attractiveness of Dr Z, one of the 'Regionville' doctors, for many of his clients appeared to be 'his willingness to fit both diagnosis and treatment to the expectations of his patients'.[35] The nature of the medical care system will also have an influence on the nature and extent of impression-management techniques employed by doctor and patient; we should especially note that a highly bureaucratized system may tightly constrain both doctors and patients in their consulting room behaviour.

Not only the nature of the medical care system, but the 'location' of the consultation within a medical care system, can influence the expectations entertained by patients and doctors. Thus, Freidson has described how doctors who have access to professional colleagues as referents (e.g. hospital doctors, GPs in a group practice, etc.) may manifest a different orientation to patients as compared to their 'isolated' colleagues. An analogous situation is said to exist in the American Forestry Service where isolated rangers may be 'captured' by the local population and so may relax their control over forest administration in favour of local interests.[36] Again, this factor can influence the employment of impression-management techniques.

More specifically, the nature of the training given to doctors, both formally in the medical school and informally in the most formative years of medical practice, varies tremendously, and for this reason alone we should expect variations in doctors' expectations of patients (and in impression-management techniques employed by doctors).

One final and most important variable influencing both the nature of the expectations entertained by both parties and their actual interacting behaviour is the nature of the disorder as conceptualized by the two inter-actants. Patients with complaints that are difficult to diagnose accurately and which do not respond quickly or obviously to medical treatment are likely to have different expectations and behave in a different manner from patients suffering from great pain and discomfort in acute illness, or from patients routinely seeking repeat prescriptions or certification for sickness benefit. Indeed, one might go so far as to question whether most patients have any clearcut expectations of the doctor's role and their own patient role at all divorced from specific illness contexts. Rather one might argue that expectations occur among patients in relation to specific illness problems—chronic incapacitating illness, non-incapacitating short-term illness, etc.

Despite mutual socialization and the use of the dramaturgical props of impression-management, accommodation does not always occur and the relationship may be terminated by the patient changing his doctor, or in extreme cases, by the doctor requesting the patient so to transfer. However, we should not regard the resolution of conflict as an end in itself, remembering that accommodation may occur at the price of ineffectual therapeutic intervention.

CONCLUSION

While considerable effort has been expended on attempts to discover to what extent Parsons's prescriptions for the sick role have any empirical validity (efforts which, in our view, have been somewhat misdirected since they failed to appreciate the ideal-typical status of the concept), Parsons's assumption that the doctor/patient relationship is a reciprocal relationship has not hitherto been subject to scrutiny. Our assessment is that Parsons has merely draped doctors' assumptions about how patients should behave in a sociological cloak. For this reason alone the assumption of reciprocity should be suspect, but Parsons has incorporated into his analysis without amendment two assumptions made by doctors about how patients should behave which are potentially conflicting and which may place patients in a double-bind, so that it is difficult to fulfil both prescriptions. It seems then that we would be quite unjustified in assuming reciprocity between doctors and patients.

The contradiction in expectations, the double-bind, that we have discussed is of course common to all professional-client relationships, not just to that of doctors and patients (although the contradiction is perhaps clearest in the medical sphere, in Britain at least, because of the absence of fees except in the small private sector): the client is encouraged to seek professional aid in the solution of his problem but may not, once he has sought professional aid, participate in the definition of the problem or the formulation of a solution. Since the client, in making his decision about whether to seek professional aid, has already arrived at some definition of his problem at least, and since, in the case of illness, considerable effort and expense has been expended in helping the client to arrive more knowledgeably at his definition, the possibility of professional/client conflict is very real.

There is a need, then, to view reciprocity of professional and client behaviour as problematic and to focus our attention on the factors in these encounters and their inter-relationships which militate against or work in favour of reciprocity. Arguably, it is only through such a focus and the concomitant development of an encounter-based model of professional/client behaviour that our understanding of such relationships will be increased.

REFERENCES

1. E. Freidson, 'Dilemmas in the doctor-patient relationship', p. 285 in this volume.
2. See especially: T. Parsons, *The Social System*, Routledge and Kegan Paul (London 1951); T. Parsons, *Social Structure and Personality*, Free Press of Glencoe (New York 1964).

3. R. N. Wilson, 'Patient/practitioner Relationships', in H. E. Freeman, S. Levine and L. Reeder (eds), *Handbook of Medical Sociology*, Prentice-Hall (Englewood Cliffs, NJ, 1963), pp. 273-319.

4. Parsons, *Social Structure*, 1964, *op. cit.*, p. 274.

5. Parsons, *Social Structure*, 1964, *op. cit.*, p. 274.

6. Parsons, *Social Structure*, 1964, *op. cit.*, pp. 274-5.

7. Parsons, *Social Structure*, 1964, *op. cit.*, p. 275.

8. Parsons, *Social System*, 1951, *op. cit.*, pp. 434-5.

9. T. Parsons, 'Illness and the Role of the Physician: a Sociological Perspective', *American Journal of Orthopsychiatry*, 21, 1951, p. 452.

10. See for example: E. L. Koos, *The Health of Regionville*, Hafner (New York 1954); G. G. Kassebaum and B. O. Baumann, 'Dimension of the Sick Role in Chronic Illness', *Journal of Health and Human Behaviour*, 6, 1965, pp. 16-27.

11. Various suggestions have been made for the emendation of Parsons's sick-role formulation to facilitate the study of variations in the performance. See, for example: A. Twaddle, 'Health Decisions and Sick Role Variations: an Exploration', *Journal of Health and Social Behaviour*, 10, 1969, pp. 105-15. However, in none of these amended versions is reciprocity of doctor and patient behaviour given any attention.

12. T. Parsons, *The Structure of Social Action*, Free Press of Glencoe (New York 1949), p. 606.

13. T. Parsons, *Social Action*, 1949, *op. cit.*, p. 605.

14. A. Schutz, 'Concept and Theory Formation in the Social Sciences', *Collected Papers*, vol. 1, M. Natranson (ed.), Martinus Nijhoff (The Hague 1967), pp. 48-66.

15. A. Cartwright, *Patients and their Doctors: a Study of General Practice*, Routledge & Kegan Paul (London 1967).

16. D. Mechanic, 'General Practice in England and Wales', unpublished.

17. P. Ferris, *The Doctors*, Gollancz (London 1965).

18. Cartwright, *Patients and their Doctors*, 1967, *op. cit.*, p. 56.

19. Cartwright, *Patients and their Doctors*, 1967, *op. cit.*, p. 56.

20. A. Schutz, 'The Well-informed Citizen, an Essay on the Social Distribution of Knowledge', *Collected Papers*, vol. 2, A. Broderson (ed.), Martinus Nijhoff (The Hague 1964).

21. Schutz, 'Well-informed Citizen', 1964, *op. cit.*, p. 122.

22. Schutz, 'Well-informed Citizen', 1964, *op. cit.*, p. 122.

23. Schutz, 'Well-informed Citizen', 1964, *op. cit.*, p. 122.

24. Schutz, 'Well-informed Citizen', 1964, *op cit.*, p. 123.

25. Cartwright, *Patients and their Doctors*, 1967, *op. cit.*, pp. 208-9.

26. Parsons, *Social System*, 1951, *op. cit.*, p. 437.

27. Parsons, *Social Structure*, 1964, *op. cit.*, p. 275.

28. Parsons, *Social System*, 1951, *op. cit.*, p. 441.

29. E. Freidson, *Patients' Views of Medical Practice*, Russell Sage (New York 1961).

30. E. A. Suchman, 'Stages of Illness and Medical Care', *Journal of Health and Human Behaviour*, 6, 1965, pp. 114-28.

31. One intriguing response from the more psychiatrically oriented members of the profession to the problem of the patients who present for 'trivial' reasons has been to argue that such patients have an underlying, unverbalized psychiatric problem which is the 'real' reason for presentation and which the doctor should encourage the patient to divulge (see, for example, J. D. Frank, 'The Uncooperative Patient—a Therapeutic Challenge', *Medical Annals of the District of Columbia*, vol. 17, 1949, pp. 668-72). If our analysis of the 'double-bind' is correct, of course, such a gambit from doctors will merely serve to confuse many patients.

32. See, for example, the discussion by Joan Emerson, 'Behaviour in Private Places: Sustaining Definitions of Reality in Gynaecological Examinations', in H. P. Dreitzel (ed.), *Recent Sociology Number 2*, Collier Macmillan (New York 1971), pp. 74-97.

33. E. Goffman, *The Presentation of Self in Everyday Life*, Anchor (New York, 1959).

34. The 'inconsistency' in such behaviour need not, of course, be manifest to the patient: social action is normally based not on wide-ranging, coherent ideologies but on situation-specific clusters of ideas, and the presence of objectively logical constraints on the simultaneous endorsement of two such clusters of ideas need not be subjectively felt by the actor. See: P. E. Converse, 'The nature of belief systems in mass publics', in D. Apter (ed.), *Ideology and Discontent*, Free Press (New York 1964).

35. E. L. Koos, *Regionville*, 1954, *op. cit.*, p. 58.

36. H. Kaufman, *The Forest Ranger, a Study in Administrative Behaviour*, John Hopkins (Baltimore 1963).

17 | *Dilemmas in the doctor/patient relationship*

E. FREIDSON

This chapter argues that certain conflicts may be endemic in the role relationship between physician and patient due to differences in perspectives and uncertainties inherent in the routine application of knowledge to human affairs. Conflict occurs especially when the patient, on the basis of his own lay perspective, tries in some way to control what the physician does to him. It is more likely to occur when the patient defines his illness as potentially critical than when he sees it as minor and ordinary. Ways in which conflict can be forestalled are suggested, but the problematic nature of the outcome is emphasized.

Struggle between patient and doctor seems to have gone on throughout recorded history.* Almost 2500 years ago, the Hippocratic corpus presented doctors' complaints about the non-professional criteria that people use to select their physicians,[1] criticism of patients for insisting on 'out of the way and doubtful remedies'[2] or on over-conventional remedies like 'barley water, wine and hydromel'[3] and for disobeying the doctor's orders.[4] The physicians who have left us historical documents largely treat the patient as an obstacle, a problem of 'management'. From their point of view the patient is very troublesome, full of anxiety, doubt and fear, insisting upon using his own scanty knowledge to evaluate the practitioner.

The patients who have left us documents often treat the physician as a potential danger to which one must respond cautiously and whom one must always be ready to evade. Patients have circulated stories about the occasions on which they successfully cured themselves, or continued to live for a long time in defiance of medical prognoses. This sort of literature may be represented by the Roman 'epigram about a doctor Marcus who touched a statue of Zeus, and although Zeus was made of stone he nevertheless died'[5] and by this mild little story from Benvenuto Cellini.

I put myself once more under doctors' orders, and attended to their directions, but grew always worse. When fever fell upon me, I resolved on having recourse

* Reprinted, with some revision, from *Patients' Views of Medical Practice* (New York: Russell Sage Foundation, 1961), by permission of the author and publisher. Copyright 1961 by the Russell Sage Foundation.

285

again to the wood: but the doctors forbade it, saying that if I took it with the fever on me, I should not have a week to live. However, I made my mind up to disobey their orders, observed the same diet as I had formerly adopted, and after drinking the decoction four days, was wholly rid of fever.... And after fifty days my health was re-established.[6]

The struggle between physician and patient has continued into modern times. The cases recorded in Paul's volume,[7] in the work of Saunders,[8] Clark,[9] and Koos[10] and in my own study[11] have indicated that on important occasions patients do not necessarily do what they are told by physicians. They persist in diagnosing and dosing themselves and in assigning heavy weight to lay advice and their own personal dispositions. It is difficult to get them to cooperate wholly with health programmes which, professionals believe, are for their own good.[12]

That the problem continues today is somewhat paradoxical, for it seems unquestionable that the medical practitioner has reached an all-time peak of prestige and authority in the eyes of the public as a whole. The physician of today is an essentially new kind of professional whose scientific body of knowledge and occupational freedom are quite recent acquisitions. His knowledge is far more precise and effective than it has ever been in the past, since for the first time in history it could be said that from ' "about the year 1910 or 1912 ... [in the United States] a random patient with a random disease consulting a doctor chosen at random stood better than a fifty-fifty chance of benefiting from the encounter".'[13] The physician has obtained unrivalled power to control his own practice and the affairs that impinge upon it and the patient now has severely limited access to drugs for self-treatment and to non-medical practitioners for alternative treatment. But the ancient problem continues.

THE CLASH OF PERSPECTIVES

It is my thesis that the separate worlds of experience and reference of the layman and the professional worker are always in potential conflict with each other.[14] This seems to be inherent in the very situation of professional practice. The practitioner, looking from his professional vantage point, preserves his detachment by seeing the patient as a case to which he applies the general rules and categories learned during his protracted professional training. The client, being personally involved in what happens, feels obliged to try to judge and control what is happening to him. Since he does not have the same perspective as the practitioner, he must judge what is being done to him from other than a professional point of view. While both professional worker and client are theoretically in accord with the end of their relationship—solving the client's problems—the means by which this solution is to be accomplished and the definitions of the problem itself are sources of potential difference.

The very nature of professional practice seems to stimulate the patient on occasion to be especially wary and questioning. Professional knowledge is never complete, and so diagnosis, made with the greatest of care and the best of contemporary skill, may turn out to be inappropriate for any particular case. These mistakes may occur in two basic ways.[15]

First of all, it is obvious that in every age, including our own, there are likely to be worthless diagnostic categories and associated treatments —sometimes merely harmless without contributing anything to cure, sometimes downright dangerous. As Shryock put it for an earlier time, 'No one will ever know just what impact heroic practice [heavy bleeding and dosing with calomel] had on American vital statistics: therapy was never listed among the causes of death.'[16] In addition, in every age, including our own, there are likely to be diseases unrecognized by contemporary diagnostic categories—as typhoid and typhus were not distinguished before 1820, as gonorrhoea and syphilis were once confused, and as mental diseases are no doubt being confused today. Thus, the best, most well-intentioned contemporary knowledge may on occasion be misdirected or false and some of the patient's complaints wrongly ignored.

Second, however, is a considerably more complex source of error that flows not from knowledge so much as from the enterprise of applying knowledge to everyday life. In so far as knowledge consists in general and objective diagnostic categories by which the physician sorts the concrete signs and complaints confronting him, it follows that work assumes a routine character. This is the routine of classifying the flow of reality into a limited number of categories so that the individual items of that flow become reduced to mere instances of a class, each individual instance being considered the same as every other in its class.

The routine of practice not only makes varied elements of experience equivalent—it also makes them *ordinary*. This seems to be the case particularly in general medical practice. In general medical practice, while the range of complaints may indeed be unusually wide, the number of complaints falling within a rather narrow range seems to be overwhelming. In our day, for example, complaints that are categorized as upper respiratory infections are exceedingly common. Like malaria in the nineteenth century, they are so common that they are considered ordinary. And in so far as they are considered ordinary it is not legitimate for the patient to make a great fuss about the suffering they involve. His subjectively real pain is given little attention or sympathy because it is too ordinary to worry about. His likely response to this may be gauged by reading Dr Raffel's account of the reception of his complaint of acute sinusitis.[17]

What also happens is that more of reality than proves to be appropriate tends to be subsumed under the ordinary and commonly used categories. This again seems to be in the very nature of professional practice—if *most* patients have upper respiratory infections when they complain of sneezing, sounds in the head, a running nose and fatigue, then it is probable that it is an upper respiratory infection that is involved when *one* particular person makes the complaint. It may indeed be an allergy, or even approaching deafness[18] but it is not probable—that is to say, it has not commonly been the case in the past. The physician cannot do otherwise than make such assumptions, but by the statistical nature of the case he cannot do otherwise than to be sometimes wrong.

THE PATIENT'S PROBLEM

These problems of diagnosis are not only problems for the doctor but also problems for the patient. All the patient knows is what he feels and what he has heard. He feels terrible, his doctor tells him that there's nothing to worry about, and a friend tells him about someone who felt the same way and dropped dead as he was leaving the consulting room with a clean bill of health. The problem for the patient is: when are subjective sensations so reliable that one should insist on special attention, and when can one reasonably allow them to be waved away as tangential, ordinary and unimportant; when is the doctor mistaken? The answer to these questions is never definite for any individual case, and indeed cannot be resolved decisively except by subsequent events. All of us know of events that have contradicted the judgement of the physician, and of course many others that have contradicted the patient.

(In discussing one of the mammoth but well-intentioned and probably competent 'professional' mistakes of the past, St Theresa calls the practitioner's routine and easygoing attitude a temptation by the devil of the client: '[A spiritual director must not be] of the kind that teaches us to be like toads, content if our souls show themselves just capable of catching small lizards.... I believe the devil is very successful in preventing those who practise prayer from advancing further by giving them false notions of humility. He persuades us that it is pride that gives us such great aims, and that makes us wish to imitate the saints and desire martyrdom.'[19]

Most of the sensible priests who have devoted themselves to soothing underemployed women who fear for their souls have been lost to history. St Theresa, however, has left them a monument in her ungrateful remarks about one of their harried colleagues, for they all ran the same risk of assuming that they were confronted by a hysterical lady rather than by a future saint. She, like the cancerophobic patient who actually turned out to have a sensational tumour, is the symbolic case that stiffens the backbones of those who wish to imitate the saints in spite of being told they are quite holy or healthy enough.)

The situation of consultation thus proves to involve ambiguities which provide grounds for doubt by the patient. Furthermore, those ambiguities are objective. Most reasonable people will agree that the doctor is sometimes wrong, whether by virtue of overlooking the signs that convert an ordinary-appearing case into a special case or by virtue of the deficiencies of the knowledge of his time. He is less often wrong now than he was a hundred years ago, but frequency is not really the problem for the individual. Even if failure occurs once in ten thousand cases, the question for the patient is whether or not it is he who is to be that one case, a question that no one can answer in advance. If the evidence of his senses and the evidence of his knowledge and that of his intimate consultants are contradicted by the physician, the patient may feel it prudent to seek another physician or simply to evade the prescriptions he has already obtained.

THE ROLE OF CONFIDENCE

If it is true that the very practice of medicine, through the process of diagnosis, is permeated with objective uncertainty of which the patient may become aware, it is at least as important to understand why patients do cooperate with doctors as to understand why they do not. One reason seems to be the ignorance of the patient—he may not be aware of or be sensitive to the contingencies of practice. Another reason seems to be the kind of situation with which the patient is confronted—whether it is a crisis situation that motivates him to be sensitive to uncertainties, or a routine situation that blunts his sensitivity and attention. There is still another possible reason, however, which, if true, is more strategic than the patient's ignorance or the variable context of consultation. I refer to the special status of the professional in society that (unlike the businessman with his motto, *caveat emptor*) supposedly entitles him to *a priori* trust and confidence.[20]

The usual conception of confidence seems to be shallow and parochial. It is indeed true that under ordinary circumstances one goes to a doctor assuming that the doctor knows his business and that his judgement may be trusted, but it is no less true of the ordinary use of other services. It is a mistake to assume that the title 'profession' confers a kind of expert authority on the practitioner which is greatly different from the authority of any fairly esoteric craftsman. Simmel pointed out some time ago that 'our modern life is based to a much larger extent than is usually realized upon the faith in the honesty of the other. . . . We base our gravest decisions on a complex system of conceptions, most of which presuppose the confidence that we will not be betrayed.'[21] Under normal circumstances we have confidence in a mechanic's ability to grease our car properly just as we have confidence in a physician's ability to prescribe the right drug for us and a pharmacist's ability to fill the prescription accurately. In the same fashion we have confidence in a variety of other service workers— appliance repairmen, bank clerks, carpenters, fitting-room tailors, and so on. Faith in the honest application of specialized ability by a consultant seems to be connected not only with the use of those who are called professionals, but also with the use of any kind of consultant whose work is fairly esoteric. Such confidence must exist if life is to function smoothly, routinely.

However, there seems to be a generic distinction in the way the definition of the situation of consultation varies. On the one hand, there is an unthinking and fundamentally superficial sort of confidence that is automatically attached to any routine consultation. It is manifested in un-critical cooperation with the consultant. This sort of confidence sustains the doctor/patient relationship in about the same way it sustains any consultant/client relationship. It appears to waver when the client's expectations are not fulfilled by the consultant and when the problem of consultation comes to be seen as critical (that is, non-routine) to the patient. Questions arise when the consultant does not act as he is expected to, when the diagnosis seems implausible, when the prescription seems intolerable and unnecessary, and when 'cure' is slow or imperceptible. They become pressing when the problem of consultation assumes what seem to be serious proportions. Under such circumstances what is needed to sustain the relationship is at least a different quantity if not a different quality of confidence.

It may be that it is this latter sort of confidence which is in the minds of those who make a special connection between professions and client confidence. Certainly it is true that three of the old, established professions deal with some of the most anxiety-laden topics of existence —the body, the soul and human relations and property. Plumbing, internal combustion engines and clothing are not likely to occasion as much anxiety. In this sense doctors, clergymen and lawyers are more likely to require for their practice a special kind of confidence than are plumbers, mechanics and fitting-room tailors. But, we may observe, it is precisely this special sort of confidence that is problematic for professions in general and medi-cine in particular; it is precisely this sort of confidence that does *not* flow automatically from professional status. Routine confidence is automatic, but grants no special advantage to the professions. Confidence in crises, however, is demanded but not necessarily obtained by consultants with professional standing.

THE ROLE OF CULTURE

One of the things that breaks routine and thereby suspends routine confidence is an occasion in which the patient's expectations are not met. Instead of prescribing what seems to the patient to be a good sensible remedy like barley water, wine and hydromel, or penicillin, the physician suggests that the patient go on a dietary regimen or simply take aspirin. Obviously, on such an occasion as this, we have in essence a clash of culture or education. The patient's culture leads him to expect what the doctor's culture does not suggest.

Cultural differences between patient and doctor have received a great deal of attention. The tenor of contemporary writings suggests that much patient/doctor conflict can be eliminated by reducing the differences between the two.

Some—particularly those writing about fairly exotic patients who cannot be expected to become 'educated' quickly[22]—suggest that the physician should be able to get patients in to see him and to reduce conflict during consultation by adjusting himself to the patient's expectations. If, for example, his prospective patients interpret the professional attitude of detachment and impersonality to be hostile, the doctor should be prepared to behave in a less 'professional' and more sociable way.[23] On the whole, the recent movement to bring social science into American medical schools seems to share this perspective: by teaching the prospective physician more about 'the patient as a person', it is presumed that when he starts to practise he will be better equipped to understand, tolerate and adjust himself to those expectations of the patient that contradict his own.

But how far can we expect the physician to adjust himself to the patient's lay (and sometimes bizarre) expectations without ceasing to practise modern medicine? There is of course a great practical difference between automatic and rigid compliance to a set of scholastic propositions and a more flexible kind of behaviour, and certainly professionals would agree that the latter is likely to produce the 'better' practitioner. But flexibility must remain within limits or it becomes 'irresponsible'. The physician can listen closely to the patient and adjust to him only so far. If his adjustment is too great, the physician must deny the heritage of special knowledge that marks him off as a professional—in effect, he ceases to be a professional. Thus, we may say that some conflict in the physician/patient relationship may indeed be forestalled by educating physicians to be somewhat more understanding and flexible with patients, but that there is a line beyond which the physician cannot go and remain a physician. Some patients' expectations cannot be met.

It might be suggested that at the point where the physician must stop adjusting, the patient must begin. After the physician has accommodated himself to the patient as far as he can, the patient should make all further accommodation if conflict is to be forestalled without destroying medical authority. With the proper 'health education' it is believed that the patient will understand and believe in enough of modern medicine to be able to approach his illness from the same perspective as the physician. Thus, *patients* are to be changed so as to conform to the expectations of the doctor. (Talcott Parsons in fact seems to define the role of the patient by reference to the expectations of the physician, for what he describes is not at all typical of what empirical studies show to be the expectations of patients and their lay consultants.)[24]

The relation of health education to the reduction of conflict is, however, by no means clear. As one way of assessing it we might contrast the consequences of two extremes. First, we may ask, what sort of conflict exists when the patient has no 'health education' at all—that is to say, no culturally determined expectations of the doctor. Situations like this are often found in veterinary and paediatric medicine—at least when the parent or owner of the patient does not take a surrogate sick role. Patients in both cases lack any health education. As such, they lack any of the knowledge that would lead them, when ill, to seek a physician. Unassisted, they are likely either to seek a familiar sympathetic person or, like the lion in the fable, lie helpless somewhere waiting for the chance and professionally unqualified kindness of an Androcles. If they should happen to strike upon a treatment situation, they prove incapable of indicating by any but the crudest and largely involuntary means—like a swollen paw and roars of distress—what it is that is wrong with them. Nor can they themselves be counted upon to follow or even to submit to the treatment prescribed; indeed, it often happens that they must be physically restrained to be treated.

It is patent that there are shortcomings in working with patients with no health education at all, but are there any virtues? One is that while the patient may be incapable of illuminating his complaint by reason of his lack of education, he is also incapable of obscuring it by irrelevancies and misinformation, or compounding it by imaginative anticipation. Another is that he has no expectations about treatment, so that once the consultant establishes control there is no contradiction of his authority. Another is that simply by reason of the fact that the patient cannot cooperate it is permissible to use physical restraint, a very convenient device for practice that cannot be used on people who theoretically can but will not cooperate. And finally, apocryphal but worth citing nonetheless, the ignorant client, once won over, may, like Androcles' lion, show undying gratitude and devotion to his healer. If this is true, it is no mean virtue.

However, the virtues of the completely ignorant patient may seem small in the face of the shortcomings. After all, patients who are educated in health affairs will have the knowledge to allow them to recognize symptoms so as to come in to see the doctor in time, to give a useful history, and to cooperate intelligently with treatment. Surely people with the most health education will be more cooperative and will not struggle with the doctor.

It does not seem to be so simple. The physician is the one with the greatest possible health education, but there are good grounds for believing that he is not a very cooperative patient at all. The physician is reputed to be given to a great deal of self-diagnosis and treatment. This follows in part from his advanced health education, which makes him feel competent to diagnose himself 'scientifically', and in part, like his susceptibility to drug addiction, from his privileged access to the medication that his self-diagnosis calls for. And when, after the long delay caused by self-diagnosis and treatment, the physician does seek the aid of another, he is reputed to be an argumentative and uncooperative patient incapable of repressing his own opinions in favour of those of his consultant. (The bad reputation of the doctor as patient is not limited to the United States. From the Soviet Union, Pondoev observes, 'If we ask any doctor he will agree with any other than the most difficult patient is a sick doctor. No other patient interferes so much with the doctor in his work as does the ailing doctor.... Nothing is more difficult than to convince the sick doctor that he is mistaken in his own diagnosis.')[25] This too seems to follow from his very health education, for it gives him a 'scientific' position in which to stand and counter that of his consultant, and it gives him a clear insight into the uncertainties of practice such that he may feel strongly justified in holding to his own opinion.

This view of physicians as patients is supported only by the plausibility of what is essentially gossip. It is made substantially more credible, however, when we look at the behaviour of well-educated middle-class patients. Fairly well versed in modern medicine, they can on occasion cooperate beautifully with the physician, but on occasion they are also quite active in evaluating the physician on the basis of their own knowledge and shopping around for diagnoses or prescriptions consonant with their knowledge. They are more confident and cooperative on a routine basis, perhaps, but they are also more confident of their own ability to judge the physician and dispose themselves accordingly.

Whether health education resolves or encourages conflict in the doctor/ patient relationship, then, seems to depend upon the situation. Where the well-educated, acculturated patient's expectations are being met (and they are more likely to be met by a physician than are those of worse-educated patients), his cooperation can be full and intelligent by virtue of the correspondence between his conceptions and those of the doctor. But by the nature of the case, so much of diagnosis and particularly treatment being a matter of opinion even within the profession itself, the patient's expectations will on

occasion be violated: here his education is more likely to encourage conflict than to resolve it, for it allows the conflict to be justified by the same
authoritative norms as those of the physician himself. A worse-educated
patient may be far more manageable.

THE ROLE OF LATENT STATUS

Thus far, the only clear way by which professional authority seems able
to sustain itself consistently appears to lie in an at least partial compromise
of the *content* of that authority—by taking patients' expectations into
account and adjusting practice to them. At the point of adjustment to the
patient beyond which professional authority must be sacrificed, however,
an additional non-medical element may work to control the patient without
compromise. In political affairs we would call it power; in professional
affairs we lack an adequate term but might call it ability to intimidate.
(I find myself severely handicapped by this terminological problem. The
physician has no administrative authority or power such as is attached
to an office in an organization. The 'authority' of his expert status is, as
we have seen, problematic. But if he is, say, upper-middle-class, and his
patient lower-class, he has leverage over his patient that does not rest on
authority or expertness as such and that exists in spite of the fact that the
patient is paying him for his service. To my knowledge there is no analyti-
cally appropriate term for this type of influence.) This mode of resolving
conflict flows not from the expert status of the physician but from the
relation of his status in the community to that of his patient.

   In the consulting room the physician may be said to have the manifest
status of expert consultant and the latent status[26] of his prestige in the
lay community. His latent status has no necessary relationship to his
technical qualification to be an expert, but obviously impinges upon his
relation to his patients. Indeed, latent status seems crucial for sustaining
the force of manifest or professional status, for while many occupations
possess expert knowledge, few have been able to control the terms of their
work. The established professions, however, have obtained both the political
power requisite for controlling the socio-legal framework of practice, and
the social prestige for controlling the client in consultation. Both the power
of the profession and the prestige of the practitioner are quite separate
from the 'authority' inherent in technical expertness. They seem to be
critical conditions for reducing doctor/patient conflict *without* compro-
mising expert knowledge. However, even when professional power and
technical expertness are high, the relative prestige of the practitioner varies.
It is not a constant. It has varied through history; within any particular
society it varies from one practitioner to another; within any particular
practice it can vary from one patient to another. What are the consequences

of variation in relative latent status for the doctor/patient relationship?

When the physician has had a *lower* standing than his patient 'more on a footing with the servants',[27] he is likely to have to be either complaisant or nimble or both to preserve the relationship. This necessity is clearest in instances in which social standing was accompanied by absolute power and in which the severest result could ensue from failure. For example:

> Astragasilde, Queen of France, on her death bed had begged her husband, Gontrano, to throw her doctor out the window immediately after her death, which was done with the greatest punctuality.... In the fifteenth century, John XXII burned an unsuccessful physician at Florence and, on this Pope's death, his friends flayed the surgeon who had failed to keep him alive.[28]

Under such circumstances the difficulties of practice according to strictly professional standards must be very great indeed—beyond fear of severe punishment for failure, considerable frustration could be caused by the way a patient of relatively high standing could effectively refuse to cooperate, as the difficulties of Dr Henry Atkins, physician to Charles, Duke of Albany indicated.[29]

Even today is seems plausible to think that physicians of eminent and powerful men have a trying practice and that their behaviour in the presence of superordinate patients will differ considerably from their behaviour in the presence of 'charity' patients in a hospital out-patient clinic.[30]

> [upper-class] patients and their families make more demands on psychiatrists than other patients.... These patients and their families usually view the physician as middle class. In such relationships the psychiatrist is not in a position to exert social power; he is lucky if he is able to rely on professional techniques successfully. All too often he has to carry out complicated manoeuvres *vis à vis* a critical, demanding, sometimes informed and sometimes very uninformed 'VIP'. Some VIPs push the physician into the role of lackey or comforter, and some psychiatrists fall into such a role.[31]

Obviously, where the relative latent status of the physician is below that of the patient, he is not in a very good position to obtain cooperation. Overt or covert conflict seems likely to ensue.

On the other side we have a situation in which the physician has considerably higher standing than his patient. The most extreme example illustrating this is found in the case of James IV, King of Scotland, who practised on his subjects. Here, while the physician's behaviour might be qualified by his sense of paternalistic or professional responsibility, we should expect that his standing is sufficiently intimidating to the patient so that, while the patient is in his hands, he will be in a position to impose the full weight of his professional knowledge. However, in response to his lack of control over his own fate, the patient seems to be inclined to adopt the defence of evasiveness. He may avoid coming in to see the physician in the first place—King James, as a matter of fact, paid his patients a fee to get them into his consulting room—or he may play dumb, listen politely while in the consulting room and, once outside, ignore the physician's advice. Evasive techniques seem to be very common in instances where the physician is in a position to intimidate his patients. As Simmons has observed: 'the deference doctors receive as upper-status persons can easily be mistaken for voluntary respect and confidence. This error could prevent perception of substantial resentments and resistances of patients.'[32]

CONCLUSION

This paper has argued that objective differences in perspective between physician and patient and uncertainties inherent in the routine application of knowledge to human affairs make for incipient conflict between patient and physician. Conflict occurs especially when the patient, on the basis of his own lay perspective, tries in some way to control what the physician does to him. It is more likely to occur when the patient defines his illness as potentially critical than when he sees it as minor and ordinary.

There seem to be three ways by which conflict may be forestalled, but each is problematic. The doctor may accommodate to the demands of the patient, but if he should do so extensively he ceases to be the doctor. The patient may be educated in health affairs so as to be more in agreement with the doctor, but education also equips him to be more self-confident and self-assertive in evaluating the doctor's work and seeking to control it. Finally, the physician may attain such relatively high social standing as to gain an extra-professional source of leverage for controlling the patient, but the patient tends to answer by only superficial cooperation and covert evasiveness.

In the light of these dilemmas it might be asked how it is that medical practice can even persist, let alone grow as much as it has over the past fifty years. Pain and desire for its relief are the basic motives of the patient, and they are not diminished by any of the elements of contradiction in the doctor/patient relationship. The prospective patient will not stop seeking help, but the way these dilemmas are managed will figure in what he seeks help for, when he seeks help, the way in which he seeks help, whom he seeks help from, and how he will behave in consultation. How some of the dilemmas are managed, of course, also involves the physician—his willingness and ability to accommodate to the patient, and the presence of situations in which he must accommodate if he is to keep his practice. They are reflected in the way he tries to deal with the patient. Thus, the doctor/patient relationship is not a constant as Parsons seems to imply[33] but obviously a variable. As I have tried to show elsewhere,[34] systematic differences in the doctor/patient relationship such as Szasz and Hollander discuss[35] may be seen to flow from historical and situational variability in the strength and content of struggling lay and professional systems.

REFERENCES

1. W. H. S. Jones (trans.), *Hippocrates*, Heinemann (London 1943), volume II, pp. 67, 281, 311.
2. Jones, *Hippocrates*, 1943, *op. cit.*, volume I, p. 317.
3. Jones, *Hippocrates*, 1943, *op. cit.*, volume II, p. 67.
4. Jones, *Hippocrates*, 1943, *op. cit.*, volume II, pp. 201, 297.
5. G. S. Pondoev, *Notes of a Soviet Doctor*, Consultants Bureau (New York 1959), p. 87.
6. Benvenuto Cellini, *The Autobiography of Benvenuto Cellini*, John A. Symonds (trans.), Modern Library (New York, n.d.), p. 128.
7. Benjamin D. Paul and Walter B. Miller (eds.), *Health, Culture and Community*, Russell Sage Foundation (New York 1955).
8. Lyle W. Saunders, *Cultural Differences and Medical Care*, Russell Sage Foundation (New York 1954).
9. Margaret Clark, *Health in the Mexican-American Community*, University of California Press (Berkeley, Calif., 1959).
10. Earl Lomon Koos, *The Health of Regionville*, Columbia University Press (New York 1954).
11. Eliot Friedson, *Patients' Views of Medical Practice*, Russell Sage Foundation (New York 1961).
12. E.g.: Sidney Cobb, Stanley King and Edith Chen, 'Differences Between Respondents and Non-Respondents in a Morbidity Survey Involving Clinical Examination', *Journal of Chronic Diseases*, 6, August 1957, pp. 95-108.
13. Alan Gregg, *Challenges to Contemporary Medicine*, Columbia University Press (New York 1956), p. 13.
14. Cf.: Howard S. Becker, 'Some Contingencies of the Professional Dance Musician's Career', *Human Organization*, 12, Spring 1953, pp. 22-6; Robert K. Merton, 'The Role-Set: Problems in Sociological Theory', *British Journal of Sociology*, 8 June 1957, pp. 106-20.
15. Everett C. Hughes, *Men and Their Work*, The Free Press (Glencoe, Ill., 1958), pp. 88-101.
16. Richard H. Shryock, *Medicine and Society in America*, New York University Press (New York 1960), p. 111.
17. M. Pinner and B. F. Miller (eds.), *When Doctors are Patients*, W. W. Norton (New York 1952), pp. 236-41.
18. Pinner and Miller (eds), *When Doctors Are Patients*, 1952, *op. cit.*, pp. 62-72.
19. J. M. Cohen (trans.), *The Life of Saint Theresa*, Penguin Books (Baltimore, Md., 1957) p. 89.
20. Edward Gross, *Work and Society*, Thomas B. Crowell New York 1958), p. 78.
21. Kurt H. Wolff (ed. and trans.), *The Sociology of Georg Simmel*, The Free Press (Glencoe, Ill., 1950), p. 313.
22. Margaret Mead, *Cultural Patterns and Technical Change*, International Documents Service (UNESCO), Columbia University Press (New York 1955).
23. Clark, *Mexican-American Community*, 1959, *op. cit.*, p. 215.
24. Talcott Parsons, *The Social System*, The Free Press (Glencoe, Ill., 1951).
25. Pondoev, *Soviet Doctor*, 1959, *op. cit.*, pp. 104-5.

26. Alvin W. Gouldner, 'Cosmopolitans and Locals: Toward an Analysis of Latent Social Roles—I', *Administrative Science Quarterly*, 2, December 1957, pp. 281-6.

27. George Eliot, *Middlemarch: A Study of Provincial Life*, A. L. Burt (New York, n.d.), p. 91.

28. David Riesman, *The Story of Medicine in the Middle Ages*, Paul B. Hoeber (New York 1935), p. 365.

29. J. J. Keevil, 'The Illness of Charles, Duke of Albany (Charles I), from 1600 to 1612. An Historical Case of Rickets', *Journal of the History of Medicine and Allied Sciences*, 9, October 1954, pp. 410-14.

30. E. S. Turner, *Call the Doctor*, St Martin's Press (New York 1959), p. 211.

31. August B. Hollingshead and Frederick C. Redlich, *Social Class and Mental Illness*, John Wiley (New York 1958), p. 353.

32. Ozzie G. Simmons, 'Social Status and Public Health', *Social Science Research Council Pamphlets*, no. 13, 1958.

33. Parsons, *Social System*, 1951, *op. cit.*

34. Eliot Friedson, 'Client Control and Medical Practice', *American Journal of Sociology*, 65, January 1960, pp. 374-82.

35. Thomas S. Szasz and Marc H. Hollander, 'A Contribution to the Philosophy of Medicine', *AMA Archives of Internal Medicine*, 97, 1956, pp. 585-92.

18 | *Difference between patients' and doctors' interpretations of some common medical terms*

C. M. BOYLE

Multiple-choice questionnaires completed by a sample of out-patients were compared with those completed by their doctors, to evaluate differences between their interpretation of some commonly used medical terms. There were significant differences between the 'majority doctors' definition' of medical terms and the number of patients agreeing with the definitions in all cases except the term 'a good appetite'. It is suggested that unless the patient is cross-examined, recording of symptoms—particularly in computer studies—may be unreliable.

INTRODUCTION

Computers are being increasingly introduced into clinical medicine with a view to making diagnostic procedures more objective. This necessitates a close scrutiny of current medical vocabulary and the interpretation put on common medical terms by patients and doctors.

This paper presents the results of a multiple-choice questionary survey designed to evaluate differences between doctors and patients on two issues: (i) interpretation of some commonly used medical terms, and (ii) knowledge of gross anatomy of some important organs.

METHOD

Two multiple-choice questionnaires, including such commonly used terms as 'arthritis', 'heartburn', 'palpitation', 'the heart', 'the stomach', and 'the kidneys', were designed for the survey. The full contents of these questionnaires are given in Tables 1 to 12 and Figures 1 to 8. To detect any 'systematic' guessing tendencies the questionnaires were printed with the terms, illustrations, and multiple-choice alternatives in the reverse order. Questions were all of the force-choice type, the patients being instructed to guess if they did not know an answer. This method was felt to approximate more faithfully to the doctor/patient interview situation.

The clinical material included patients aged seventeen or over who were attending for the first time at medical, surgical, dermatological, otorhino-

299

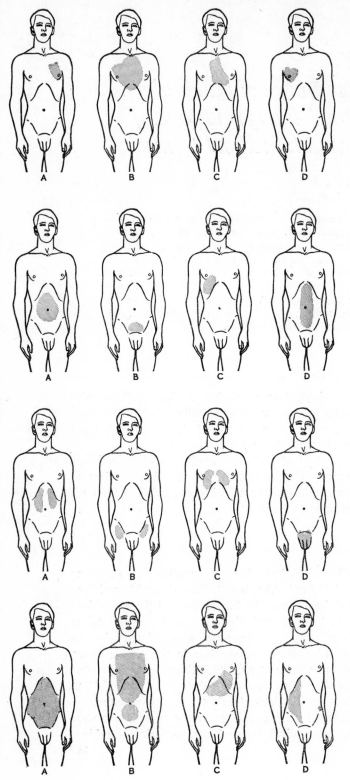

Fig. 1   Distribution of positions of the heart. **A**, 47 patients (41·2%), 2 doctors (5·7%). **B**, 17 patients (14·9%), χ^2 5·07; D.F. 1; P < 0·025 (females > males), no doctors. **C**, 48 patients (42·1%), 33 doctors (94·3%) χ^2 25·3; D.F. 1; P < 0·0005 (doctors > patients). **D**, 2 patients (1·8%), no doctors.

Fig. 2   Distribution of positions of the bladder. **A**, 27 patients (24·1%), no doctors. **B**, 67 patients (59·8%), 35 doctors (100%) χ^2 18·44; D.F. 1; P < 0·0005 (doctors > patients). **C**, 9 patients (8·0%), no doctors. **D**, 9 patients (8·0%), no doctors.

Fig. 3   Distribution of positions of the kidneys. **A**, 52 patients (46·0%), 35 doctors (100%) χ^2 29·05; D.F. 1; P < 0·0005 (doctors > patients). **B**, 55 patients (48·7%), no doctors. **C**, 2 patients (1·8%), no doctors. **D**, 4 patients (3·5%), no doctors.

Fig. 4   Distribution of positions of the stomach. **A**, 67 patients (58·8%), no doctors. **B**, 22 patients (19·3%), no doctors. **C**, 23 patients (20·2%), 35 doctors (100%) χ^2 43·21; D.F. 1; P < 0·0005 (doctors > patients). **D**. 2 patients (1·8%), no doctors.

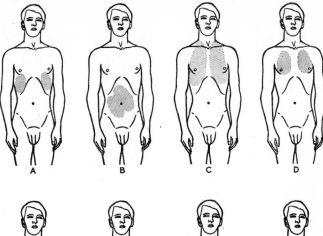

Fig. 5 Distribution of positions of the lungs. **A,** 36 patients (33·3%), no doctors. **B,** 2 patients (1·9%), no doctors. **C,** 55 patients (50·9%), 35 doctors (100%) χ^2 25·24; D.F. 1; $P < 0.0005$ (doctors > patients). **D,** 15 patients (13·9%), no doctors.

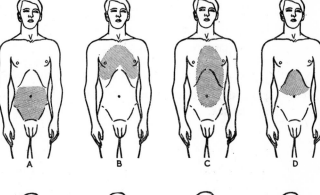

Fig. 6 Distribution of positions of the intestines. **A,** 83 patients (76·9%), 35 doctors (100%) χ^2 8·3; D.F. 1; $P < 0.005$ (doctors > patients). **B,** 1 patient (0·9%), no doctors. **C,** 13 patients (12·0%), no doctors. **D,** 11 patients (10·2%), no doctors.

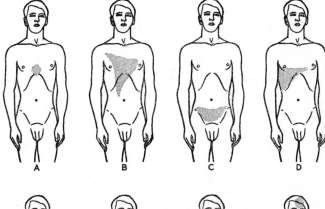

Fig. 7 Distribution of positions of the liver. **A,** no patients, no doctors. **B,** 6 patients (6·1%), no doctors. **C,** 45 patients (45·5%), no doctors. **D,** 48 patients (48·5%), 35 doctors (100%), χ^2 25·53; D.F. 1; $P < 0.0005$ (doctors > patients).

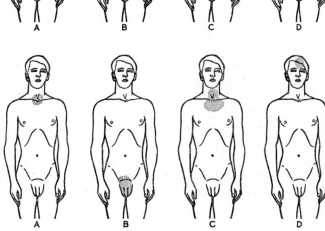

Fig. 8 Distribution of positions of the thyroid gland. **A,** 72 patients (69·9%), 35 doctors (100%) χ^2 11·91; D.F. 1; $P < 0.001$ (doctors > patients). **B,** 3 patients (2·9%), no doctors. **C,** 25 patients (24·3%), no doctors. **D,** 3 patients (2·9%), no doctors.

laryngological or antenatal out-patient clinics at the Southern General Hospital. This is a teaching hospital serving the urban area of the south-west of Glasgow and the rural districts of Argyll and the Inner Isles. At the admission desk the patients were given a questionnaire and asked to complete it while waiting to see the doctor and to return it before leaving. Patients inadvertently taking their questionnaire home were sent a stamped addressed envelope in which to return them.

A control group of doctors' replies was also obtained. Of the forty-two physicians and surgeons on the staff of the general medical and surgical units thirty-five cooperated in the survey. This group comprised house officers (28·6%), senior house officers/registrars (34·3%), senior registrars/SHMOs/medical assistants (5·7%), and consultants (31·4%).

Non-parametric tests of significance appropriate to sample size (χ^2 test with Yates's continuity correction or Fisher's Exact Test) were performed for each term and illustration to detect differences in interpretation between patients and doctors or differences in interpretation among patients due to age or sex.

RESULTS

A total of 234 questionnaires were completed satisfactorily by patients from a possible 257—a response rate of 91·1%. Reasons for failure were: inadequate understanding of instructions (3·9%), failure to return questionnaire after taking it home (2·3%), unwillingness to cooperate (1·2%), no spectacles (0·8%), no time (0·4%), and severity of illness (0·4%).

The average age of the men was 45·4 years, and that of the women forty-one years, and the male:female ratio was about 2:3. The patients were distributed by age as follows: seventeen to twenty-nine years, 30·7%; thirty to forty-four years, 25·2%; forty-five to fifty-nine years, 25·2%, and sixty and over, 18·9%. The lower social classes predominated as judged by the Registrar General's classification: class 1, 1·4%; class 2, 8·2%; class 3, 39·0%; class 4, 22·6%; and class 5, 28·8%.

The results of patients' and doctors' answers to the multiple-choice questions are shown in Tables 1 to 12 and Figures 1 to 8. No tendency to 'systematic' guessing was found from analysis of the reversed-order questionnaires.

The doctors were unanimous in their choice of definition for seven of the twelve terms—'arthritis', 'heartburn', 'jaundice', 'palpitation', 'bronchitis', 'piles', and 'flatulence'. They reached a level of agreement of over 90% for 'least starchy food', 'a medicine', and 'a good appetite'. 'Constipation' was defined as 'not opening one's bowels every day' by 11·4%, and 'diarrhoea' as 'passing a lot of bowel motions in a short time' by 31·4%. The very low level of agreement in this case may have been due to a poor wording of alternative definitions. Apart from the 5·7% of doctors who chose the small 'heart' placed well to the left, they were unanimous in their choice of anatomical site for all organs.

The patients did not reach complete agreement of definition for any term. By comparison with the 'majority doctors' definition', between 80 and 90% of patients answered 'a good appetite', 'arthritis', 'heartburn', and 'bronchitis' correctly. About three-quarters correctly defined 'jaundice', 'least starchy food', and 'piles', while only 50 to 60% agreed with the majority of doctors for 'constipation' and 'palpitation'. The lowest responses for correct definition of terms were for 'a medicine' (43·2%), 'flatulence' (42·9%), and 'diarrhoea' (37·0%). Patients displayed a considerable lack of knowledge of simple anatomy, the best understood terms being 'intestines' (76·9%) and 'thyroid gland' (69·9%), and the poorest 'heart' (42·1%) and 'stomach' (20·2%).

Table 1

Distribution of Definitions of 'Arthritis'

Definitions	Patients* n=113	Doctors n=35
A disease due to muscle strain or a 'pulled muscle'	5 (4·4%)	—
Any disease causing a painful back	1 (0·9%)	—
Any disease with sore arms or legs	9 (8·0%)	—
Lumbago	1 (0·9%)	—
Any disease causing a painful joint or painful joints†	97 (85·8%)	35 (100%)

* Six patients did not answer this question.
† P=0·01015 (Fisher's Exact Test; doctors>patients).

Table 2

Distribution of Definitions of 'Heartburn'

Definitions	Patients* n=112	Doctors n=35
Passage of wind through the mouth	9 (8·0%)	—
Excess saliva	5 (4·5%)	—
A burning sensation behind the breastbone†	95‡(84·8%)	35 (100%)
A dull ache in the stomach	1 (0·9%)	—
A feeling of the heart thumping inside the chest	2 (1·8%)	—

* Seven patients did not answer this question.
† P=0·007157 (Fisher's Exact Test; doctors>patients).
‡ χ^2=4·16; D.F. 1; P<0·05 (females>males).

Table 3

Distribution of Definitions of 'Least Starchy Food'

Definitions	Patients* n=107	Doctors n=35
Fish and chips	2 (1·9%)	—
Bacon and eggs†	80 (74·8%)	34 (97·1%)
Jam tart and custard	13 (12·1%)	—
Bread-and-butter pudding	1 (0·9%)	—
Mince and potatoes	11 (10·3%)	1 (2·9%)

* Twelve patients did not answer this question.
† $\chi^2 = 6·99$; D.F. 1; $P < 0·01$ (doctors>patients).

Table 4

Distribution of Definitions of 'Jaundice'

Definitions	Patients* n=111	Doctors n=35
Generally sick and unwell—with yellow vomit	11 (9·9%)	—
Pale skin and anaemia (bloodlessness)	1 (0·9%)	—
Generally unwell, whether yellow skin or not	6 (5·4%)	—
Yellow skin and eyes†	85 (76·6%)	35 (100%)
Headache, furred yellowish tongue, and 'run down' feeling	8 (7·2%)	—

* Eight patients did not answer this question.
† $\chi^2 = 8·44$; D.F. 1; $P < 0·005$ (doctors>patients).

Table 5

Distribution of Definitions of 'A Medicine'

Definitions	Patients* n=111	Doctors n=35
Any drug to open the bowels	1 (0·9%)	—
Any substance used to treat disease†	48 (43·2%)	32 (91·4%)
Any tablets except simple things like aspirin, Askit powders, etc.	6 (5·4%)	—
Anything prescribed by a doctor	47 (42·3%)	3 (8·6%)
A tablet or liquid to relieve constipation	9 (8·1%)	—

* Eight patients did not answer this question.
† $\chi^2 = 23·03$; D.F. 1; $P < 0·0005$ (doctors>patients).

Table 6

Distribution of Definitions of 'Diarrhoea'

Definitions	Patients* n=108	Doctors n=35
Passing loose bowel motions†	40 (37·0%)	24 (68·6%)
Opening one's bowels more than once a day	4 (3·7%)	—
Passing a lot of bowel motions in a short time	59 (54·6%)	11 (31·4%)
Straining to pass bowel motions	4 (3·7%)	—
Passing a lot of wind by the back passage	1 (0·9%)	—

* Eleven patients did not answer this question.
† $\chi^2=9\cdot32$; D.F. 1; P<0·005 (doctors>patients).

Table 7

Distribution of Definitions of 'Palpitation'

Definitions	Patients* n=103	Doctors n=35
A feeling of breathlessness—especially when excited	27 (26·2%)	—
A feeling of fright and panic	15 (14·6%)	—
A dull ache over the heart	—	—
A pain in the chest, usually over the heart	7 (6·8%)	—
A feeling of the heart thumping inside the chest†	54 (52·4%)	35 (100%)

* Twelve patients did not answer this question.
† $\chi^2=23\cdot78$; D.F. 1; P<0·0005 (doctors>patients).

Table 8

Distribution of Definitions of 'Constipation'

Definitions	Patients* n=107	Doctors n=35
Passing a lot of wind by the back passage	6 (5·6%)	—
Passing loose bowel motions	—	—
Passing dark-coloured motions	1 (0·9%)	—
Difficulty in opening one's bowels†	64 (59·8%)	31 (88·6%)
Not opening one's bowels every day	36 (33·6%)	4 (11·4%)

*Eight patients did not answer this question.
† $\chi^2=8\cdot59$; D.F. 1; P<0·005 (doctors>patients).

Table 9

Distribution of Definitions of 'Bronchitis'

Definitions	Patients* n=106	Doctors n=35
Any disease causing a bad cough	3 (2·8%)	—
Wheezing, cough, and spit; usually worse in winter†	85 (80·2%)	35 (100%)
Severe influenza	3 (2·8%)	—
Breathlessness	9 (8·5%)	—
Any chest complaint	6 (5·7%)	—

* Nine patients did not answer this question.
† $\chi^2 = 6·66$; D.F. 1; $P < 0·01$ (doctors>patients).

Table 10

Distribution of Definitions of 'A Good Appetite'

Definitions	Patients* n=108	Doctors n=35
When you are not constipated after a big meal	1 (0·9%)	—
A strong need for food because you feel your stomach is empty	6 (5·6%)	2 (5·7%)
When you do not get indigestion after a big meal	1 (0·9%)	—
When you enjoy your food and look forward to eating it†	95 (88·0%)	33 (94·3%)
When you eat your food and are not sick after it	5 (4·6%)	—

* Seven patients did not answer this question.
† $P = 0·1044$ (Fisher's Exact Test; doctors>patients—not significant).

Table 11

Distribution of Definitions of 'Piles'

Definitions	Patients* n=102	Doctors n=35
Any disease of back passage, whether painful or not	1 (1·0%)	—
Any disease of back passage, but usually painful	3 (2·9%)	—
Enlarged blood vessels at the back passage†	75‡(73·5%)	35 (100%)
Any pain at the back passage	6 (5·9%)	—
Any bleeding at the back passage	17 (16·7%)	—

* Thirteen patients did not answer this question.
† $\chi^2 = 9·92$; D.F. 1; $P < 0·005$ (doctors>patients).
‡ $\chi^2 = 4·74$; D.F. 1; $P < 0·05$ (males>females).

Table 12

Distribution of Definitions of 'Flatulence'

Definitions	Patients* n=105	Doctors n=35
Passage of wind through the mouth or back passage†	45 (42·9%)	35 (100%)
Passage of loose bowel movements	2 (1·9%)	—
A sort of chest pain	10 (9·5%)	—
An acid taste in the mouth—especially after eating food	31 (29·5%)	—
Stomach ache—usually after eating food	17‡(16·2%)	—

* Ten patients did not answer this question.
† $\chi^2=32\cdot7$; D.F. 1; $P<0\cdot0005$ (doctors>patients).
‡ $\chi^2=6\cdot05$; D.F. 1; $P<0\cdot025$ (females>males).

The difference between the 'majority doctors' definition' and the number of patients agreeing with that definition was significant for all terms and illustrations except the term 'a good appetite' ($P=0\cdot1$). In only a few cases were there significant differences between male and female patients. Thus more females chose the correct definition of 'heartburn' ($P<0\cdot05$), and more males the correct meaning of 'piles' ($P<0\cdot05$). More females than males thought that 'flatulence' meant 'stomach ache—usually after eating food' ($P<0\cdot025$) and that the 'heart' occupied almost the entire thorax ($P<0\cdot025$). Age alone did not appear to affect ability to define terms correctly.

DISCUSSION

In the rapidly advancing field of medical computer technology, with the ultimate aim of 'diagnosis by computer', it is mandatory to have either a vocabulary of totally unambiguous medical terms or a knowledge of the syntactic, semantic or pragmatic limitations of our existing medical terminology. It would seem that the latter alternative is more practicable, and questionary surveys of the present type might well have a part to play in defining these limitations.

Romano[1] was the first to consider this subject when he asked fifty patients to define sixty medical terms and abbreviations often used in bedside conferences. Many of these terms, however, were highly technical and no detailed analysis was presented. Others[2] have conducted statistical studies of patients' understanding of medical terms and diseases, but many of these tended to concentrate more on patients' knowledge of the aetiology, treatment and prognosis of certain diseases than on their ability to agree with the majority of doctors over the more basic issue of definition. Samora and his colleagues[3] concluded that 92·8% of their group of patients had an 'adequate' knowledge of the word 'constipated', and Riley[4] found that 57% of his sample correctly identified seven or more of twelve foods containing sugar or starch. In another series[5] 94·9% of out-patients had 'exact knowledge' of the meaning of 'a drug or remedy' and 79·8% had 'exact knowledge' of the term 'diarrhoea'. In Ley and Spelman's 1967 study[6] 96·5% chose the correct multiple-choice definition of 'arthritis' and 86·1% correctly identified one of the early symptoms of 'chronic bronchitis' as 'a persistent cough during winter'.

In the present survey significant differences were found between patients' and doctors' interpretation of all terms and illustrations except the term 'a good appetite'. Perhaps some form of 'reliability factor' will have to be constructed for each medical term in common usage before any significance can be attached to it. In addition, the educational level of the patient must be considered, as relationships between vocabulary performance and educational attainment have been reported.[7] In his small study of neuropsychiatric patients, however, Redlich[8] found the correlation between knowledge of terms and IQ to be poor.

For the clinician the results probably do no more than formalize and lend statistical verification to his impression that clinical interrogation often reveals large areas of misunderstanding between conventional medical opinion and the vagaries of the lay mind. This misunderstanding, however, must be identified and evaluated scientifically if techniques such as self-completion medical questionnaires or patient-activated computer programmes are to play a reliable part in clinical medicine.

REFERENCES

1. J. Romano, *Journal of the American Medical Association*, 117, 1941, p. 64.
2. F. C. Redlich, *Yale Journal of Biology and Medicine*, 17, 1945, p. 427; L. Pratt, A. Seligmann and G. Reader, *American Journal of Public Health*, 47, 1957, p. 1277; A. W. Seligmann, N. E. McGrath and L. Pratt, *Journal of Chronic Diseases*, 6, 1957, p. 497; J. Samora, L. Saunders and R. F. Larson, *Journal of Health and Human Behaviour*, 2, 1961, p. 83; C. S. Riley, *Medical Care*, 4, 1966, p. 34; P. Ley and M. S. Spelman, *Communicating with the Patient*, Staples Press (London 1967); A. O. Plaja, L. M. Cohen and J. Samora, *Milbank Memorial Fund Quarterly*, 46, 1968, p. 161.
3. Samora *et al.*, *J. Health and Human Behaviour*, 1961, *op. cit.*
4. Riley, *Medical Care*, 1966, *op. cit.*
5. Plaja *et al.*, *Milbank Memorial Fund Quarterly*, 1968, *op. cit.*
6. Ley and Spelman, *Communicating*, 1967, *op. cit.*
7. Seligman *et al.*, *J. Chronic Diseases*, 1957, *op. cit.*; Samora *et al.*, *J. Health and Human Behaviour*, 1961, *op. cit.*
8. Redlich, *Yale J. of Biology and Medicine*, 1945, *op. cit.*

Contributors, sources and acknowledgements

ERNEST BECKER, Professor of Sociology and Anthropology, Simon Fraser University, Burnaby, Canada.
'Socialization, Command of Performance and Mental Illness', from *American Journal of Sociology*, 67, 1962.

MILDRED BLAXTER, Research Fellow in Sociology, University of Aberdeen.
'"Disability" and Rehabilitation: Some Questions of Definition.' Previously unpublished.

M. J. BLOOR and G. W. HOROBIN, Medical Research Council Medical Sociology Unit, University of Aberdeen.
'Conflict and Conflict Resolution in Doctor/Patient Relationships' was presented in an earlier version at the Second International Conference on Social Science and Medicine, Aberdeen, Scotland, September 1970. The authors are grateful to Alan Davis and Philip Strong for their critical comments on earlier drafts.

CHARLES MURRAY BOYLE, Clinical Methods Research Group, Gardiner Institute, Glasgow.
'Difference Between Patients' and Doctors' Interpretation of Some Common Medical Terms', from the *British Medical Journal*, 2 May 1970.
   The author takes pleasure in thanking Dr J. F. Adams and Dr J. T. Ireland for their unfailing cooperation and constructive criticism. Professor Bernard Lennox, Dr Christopher Evans (National Physical Laboratory), Dr Sheila K. Ross and Dr Victor Hawthorne made helpful suggestions regarding the questionnaires, the cost of which was met by a grant from the Board of Management for Glasgow South-Western Hospitals. Illustrations were prepared by the department of medical photography and illustrations, Southern General Hospital, for the questionnaires, and by Mr Gabriel Donald of the Western Infirmary for the article.
   The survey would not have been possible without the cooperation of Dr R. G. H. Cunningham, medical superintendent of the Southern General Hospital, sister and staff of the out-patient department, and the physicians and surgeons who kindly agreed to participate.

EWOUT TH. CASSEE, Senior Research Fellow, Netherlands Institute for Preventive Medicine, Leiden.
'Therapeutic Behaviour, Hospital Culture and Communication' was prepared for the Second International Conference on Social Science and Medicine, Aberdeen, Scotland, 2-9 September 1970.

FRED DAVIS, Professor of Sociology, Graduate Sociology Program and School of Nursing, University of California, San Francisco.
'Professional Socialization as Subjective Experience: The Process of Doctrinal Conversion Among Student Nurses', from *Institutions and the Person*.
   The writing of this paper was aided by a grant from the US Public Health Service, No. NU 00024. The author wishes to thank Howard S. Becker, Virginia

309

Olesen and Elvi Whittaker for their helpful comments on an earlier draft. He owes an extraordinary debt to Anselm L. Strauss, who patiently devoted long hours to helping him formulate the basic scheme of the paper. Through assistance of a USPHS Travel Grant (Ch-00261) a slightly different version of the paper was read at the Sixth World Congress of Sociology, Evian, France, September 1966.

RENÉE C. FOX, Professor and Chairman, Department of Sociology, Professor of Medicine and Psychiatry, University of Pennsylvania, Philadelphia.
'Training for Uncertainty', from R. K. Merton *et al.* (eds), *The Student Physician*, Oxford University Press (London 1957).

ELIOT FREIDSON, Professor of Sociology, New York University.
'Dilemmas in the Doctor/Patient Relationships' from A. M. Rose (ed.), *Human Behaviour and Social Processes*, Routledge & Kegan Paul (London 1962), reprinted (with some revisions) from *Patients' Views of Medical Practice*, Russell Sage Foundation (New York) by permission of the author and publisher.

D. G. GILL, previously attached to the Medical Research Council Medical Sociology Unit, University of Aberdeen. At present at the School of Medicine, University of Missouri, Columbia.
'The British National Health Service: Professional Determinants of Administrative Structure', from the *International Journal of Health Services*, 1 (no. 4), 1971.

The author wishes to thank his colleague Mr G. W. Horobin, assistant director, Medical Sociology Unit, for his comments on an earlier draft of this paper. His appreciation also goes to John McKinlay, formerly of this Unit, with whom the basic conception of this paper was originally discussed.

ERVING GOFFMAN, Benjamin Franklin Professor of Anthropology and Sociology, University of Pennsylvania, Philadelphia.
'The Inmate World', in this volume, reprinted from pp. 22-31, 33-9 and 44-7 of Donald R. Cressey (ed.), *The Prison*, Holt, Rinehart & Winston (New York 1961), as 'On the Characteristics of Total Institutions: the Inmate World'.

JULIAN TUDOR HART, attached to the Epidemiology and Medical Care Unit, Medical Research Council's Clinical Research Centre, Harrow. Works at Glyncorrewg Health Centre, Glamorgan, Wales.
'The Inverse Care Law', from *The Lancet*, 27 February 1971.

The author is grateful to Professor W. R. S. Doll, FRS, for advice and criticism; to Miss M. Hammond, librarian of the Royal College of General Practitioners; and to the clerks of the Glamorgan and Monmouthshire Executive Councils for the National Health Service for data on recruitment of general practitioners in their areas.

MARGOT JEFFERYS, Professor of Medical Sociology, Bedford College, University of London.
'The Doctors' Dilemma—a Sociological Viewpoint', from *Social and Economic Administration*, 4, 1970.

DAVID MECHANIC, John Bascom Professor of Sociology and Director, Centre for Medical Sociology and Health Services Research, University of Wisconsin, Madison.

NANCY MILIO, Adjunct Professor, Seminar on Issues in International and US Health Care, Boston University, School of Nursing.
'Values, Social Class and Community Health Services', from *Nursing Research*, 16 (no. 1), Winter 1967.

ARNOLD M. ROSE, University of Minnesota.
'A Socio-psychological Theory of Neurosis', from A. M. Rose (ed.), *Human Behaviour and Social Processes*, Routledge and Kegan Paul (London 1962).

A condensed form of this paper was presented at the Fourth World Congress of Sociology, Stresa, Italy, August 1959, and appears in the *Proceedings* of that Congress, International Sociological Association (Louvain 1960).

ANSELM L. STRAUSS and BARNEY G. GLASER.
'Patterns of Dying', from B. Rimo (ed.), *The Dying Patient*, reprinted with some modifications from the various chapters of our *Time for Dying*, Aldine Publishing (Chicago 1968).

The authors are much indebted to their associate Jeanne C. Quint.

IRVING KENNETH ZOLA, Professor and Chairman, Department of Sociology Brandeis University, Waltham, Massachussetts.
'Culture and Symptoms—an Analysis of Patients' Presenting Complaints', from the *American Sociological Review*, 31, 1966.

The data collection for this study was supported by the Departments of Psychiatry and Medicine of the Massachusetts General Hospital. The final writing and analysis was supported by the National Institute of General Medical Sciences, grant No. 11367. For their many substantive and editorial criticisms the author wishes to thank Margot Adams-Webber, Dr Bernard Bergen, Anne Goldberg, Mariene Hindley, Dr Philip E. Slater and Dr Mark Spivak. The greatest debt however is to Dr John D. Stoeckle and Leonora K. Zola who together read and criticized more drafts of this paper than the author cares to remember.

'Medicine as an Institution of Social Control' presented at the Medical Sociology Conference of the British Sociological Association at Weston-Super-Mare in November 1971.

This paper was written while the author was a consultant in residence at the Netherlands Institute for Preventive Medicine, Leiden. For their general encouragement and the opportunity to pursue this topic he will always be grateful. His special thanks for their extensive editorial and substantive comments go to Egon Bittner, Mara Sanadi, Alwyn Smith and Bruce Wheaton.

Index